CW01558414

MORE DISPUTES AND DIFFERENCES

Books by Derek Roebuck
Published by HOLO Books: The Arbitration Press

A Miscellany of Disputes 2000
Ancient Greek Arbitration 2001
The Charitable Arbitrator 2002
Early English Arbitration 2008
Disputes and Differences 2010
Mediation and Arbitration in the Middle Ages 2013
The Golden Age of Arbitration 2015
Arbitration and Mediation in Seventeenth-Century England 2017

with Bruno de Loynes de Fumichon
Roman Arbitration 2004

With Susanna Hoe
Women in Disputes 2018

With Francis Calvert Boorman and Rhiannon Markless
English Arbitration and Mediation in the Long Eighteenth Century 2019

Neil Kaplan and Robert Morgan (eds)
Lawyer, Scholar, Teacher and Activist
A Liber Amicorum in Honour of Derek Roebuck 2021

MORE DISPUTES
AND DIFFERENCES

ESSAYS ON THE HISTORY
OF ARBITRATION AND ITS
CONTINUING RELEVANCE

Derek Roebuck

Edited by Susanna Hoe

For Dave
with many thanks
as always
Susanna
26/9/22

HOLO BOOKS
THE ARBITRATION PRESS
OXFORD
2022

First published 2022 by
HOLO Books: The Arbitration Press
Clarendon House
52 Cornmarket
Oxford OX1 3HJ

email: holobooks@yahoo.co.uk
www.holobooks.co.uk
and www.centralbooks.com

British Library Cataloguing in Publication Data
A catalogue record for this book is available from the British Library

ISBN 978-1-9196318-3-7

Produced and typeset for HOLO Books: The Arbitration Press by
Stanford DTP Services, Northampton, England
Printed and bound by CPI Group (UK) Ltd

For Neil Kaplan who introduced Derek to the concept of arbitration history and supported him thereafter

And for Francis Calvert Boorman and Rhiannon Markless who contributed to Derek's last volumes, and now continue his work

SUBSCRIBERS

We owe a special debt of gratitude to those who have sponsored this book by agreeing to be subscribers. Their support, not only financial, has lightened the burden of publication.

Vasily Anurov
John Baker
Francis Boorman
Stewart Boyd
Christian Burset
Rosy Calvert
Clyde Croft
Susan Faircloth
Octavio Ferraz
Bruno de Loynes de Fumichon
Hew Dundas
Neil and Mary Gold
Arthur Harverd
Mary Hiscock
Charles Jarrosson
Neil Kaplan
Toby Landau

Catharine Macmillan
Rhiannon Markless
Robert Markless
Alexander Muranov
Karyl Nairn
David Neuberger
James Oldham
Bernard Rix
Stephen Sedley
David Seipp
Audley Sheppard
Joe Smouha
Edna Sussman
Royale Thompson
Marcio Vasconellas
Brian White
Jules Winterton

CONTENTS

PART TWO: PAST, PRESENT AND FUTURE

PART THREE: LANGUAGE, RESEARCH AND COMPARISON

PREFACE

This is not the book that Derek planned to publish. He left one paragraph of an intended Introduction which reads:

> This collection of twenty-two papers is unlike that published in 2010 as *Disputes and Differences*.[1] That reproduced articles in the form in which they had been published, but the papers here, though based on published articles, are all newly worked. I hope they will tell coherent stories about some aspects of the history of arbitration, not only in England.

As far as I can ascertain, Derek only had the strength and eyesight to start working on Chapter 2, Cleopatra in Egypt. I have been left, therefore, with having to publish what was originally written. Because Derek was going to re-write, he used the word 'essays'. I have kept that description, particularly in the book's subtitle where he also used it;[2] it's a good shorthand for the original chapters, lectures, articles etc., and an attractive word.

A second decision with which I was faced was that Derek left two tables of contents, yet he seems to have been working on the earlier, not the later of them. I have, therefore, gone with the earlier one. That seems to be in the order in which the essays were published or delivered. But, given that he wanted to 'tell coherent stories about some aspects of the history of arbitration', I have put them into a historical chronology,[3] at least in Part One, 'The Past'. Part Two, 'Past, Present and Future', is as that subtitle suggests. Part Three, 'Language, Research and Comparisons', encompasses some of Derek's particular interests. I should add, however, that many of the history essays also nod to the future. There are now 25 essays or chapters: I have added three I thought should be there. The date of publication does not necessarily indicate Derek's progression of thinking over time: it may have depended on what he was working on then, or what he had read as editor of *Arbitration* or read or heard elsewhere.

---

1. Derek Roebuck *Disputes and Differences: Comparisons in Law, Language and History* Oxford, HOLO Books: The Arbitration Press, 2010 [*Disputes and Differences*]
2. I have added to his *Essays on the History of Arbitration 'and its Continuing Relevance'*.
3. The date of publication (or, indeed, delivery of a lecture), and publication details appear above each chapter.

Two chapters here appeared in the *Liber Amicorum* published in Derek's honour in 2021.[4] I have decided to include them as they are integral to the historical flow, and as Derek wanted. He obviously could not have foreseen their *Liber Amicorum* use, and I could not say no when I was asked if they could be included in that. I could not even be sure that I was up to the job of preparing this book for publication: it looked daunting, apart from the subject matter. I have had to rummage through files saved from an earlier computer, often with titles with a trigger for Derek, not necessarily for me, and several memory sticks, to find each piece so that I had a digital copy on which to work and then to send to be copy edited. It was something that I would have helped Derek with anyway, given the condition of his health. But often there was more than one version; I had to find the latest update. Sometimes Derek had already put a printed out draft in a 'More Disputes and Differences' ring binder; others I found by foraging in a myriad other paper files indicating that was the one to be published; sometimes I had the relevant journal against which to check versions.

This might be the appropriate place to suggest what qualifications I have for the task, beyond being a bereft widow and writer of women's history. From when we met in 1979, particularly after we left London for Papua New Guinea and Hong Kong, we both read each other's drafts and commented upon them. Derek was better than I at accepting suggested corrections; as the cleverer of us, he was always generous enough to value mine. When it came to his arbitration histories, this is particularly relevant to my current task: he used to say that if I didn't understand something he had written, no one would, and he would change it appropriately, often according to my suggestion. Nor did he reject suggested additions.

Then in about 2017, Derek suggested we write together a book about women and their place in the history of mediation and arbitration. Although this took me away from what I had been researching for a while,[5] I could hardly refuse, and we set to. I'm happy to say that working together on *Women in Disputes*[6] went remarkably smoothly. Though it was not the first of our joint publications,[7] this time we were equal partners.

---

4. Neil Kaplan and Robert Morgan eds *Lawyer, Scholar, Teacher and Activist: A Liber Amicorum in Honour of Derek Roebuck* Oxford, HOLO Books: The Arbitration Press 2021 [*Liber Amicorum*]

5. As I draft this preface, *Sardinia: Women, History, Books and Places* is to be published on 17 March 2022 Oxford HOLO Books: The Women's History Press.

6. Susanna Hoe and Derek Roebuck, *Women in Disputes: A History of European Women in Mediation and Arbitration* Oxford, HOLO Books, 2018. The book was able to include the place in dispute resolution of Eleonora d'Arborea, a much revered *giudicessa* in medieval Sardinia.

7. Susanna Hoe and Derek Roebuck, *The Taking of Hong Kong: Charles and Clara Elliot in China Waters* London, Curzon Press, 1999 (hb) Hong Kong, Hong Kong University

I have made only one 'improvement' to Derek's text, cutting in half an inordinately long sentence. Such sentences are more my style than his; I'm surprised he was allowed to get away with it at the time. I have, however, added to footnotes; for example, where he mentions a book in embryo, I have noted when it was published. My additions are those in square brackets ending 'SH', so as not to be confused with those in which Derek added an explanation within a quotation. All chapters that have previously been published elsewhere are reprinted by kind permission of the publishers and I give the relevant details at the top of the chapter. Sometimes at the end of a chapter I have added what I have called a 'tailpiece', a sort of *mise en scène*. Translations are Derek's unless he noted another source. If he had been able to complete the book, even in its present form, he might well have cut out repetitions occurring in more than one chapter. I have not attempted that, and I don't think there is a problem: the use again is relevant to the particular point he was making. Not only that, not every reader will read the book straight through: some may dip in and out, others only read a chapter that is of interest to them.

I'm sorry for any index shortcomings: Derek would have made connections not apparent to me. In compiling it, I have been alerted to how many questions he asked sprinkled throughout each piece of writing; I have, therefore, included the entry 'questions' in the index. They are sometimes rhetorical, but often Derek expects the reader to give serious thought to them.

Derek left no Introduction, apart from the paragraph I quote at the beginning of this Preface, and no Conclusion. For the former, I have borrowed from his chapter in a book published in honour of Neil Kaplan Derek's explanation of how he came to be prompted to put the words Arbitration and History together.[8] As for the Conclusion, any attempt to emulate what Derek might have written was out. I have, therefore, reverted to my own field, and highlighted how he has, in these 25 chapters given space to women; as a good feminist, he rarely needed to be prompted!

Press, 2009 (pb). For this, Derek unearthed in Hong Kong's record office a hitherto unknown proposal by Elliot for the arbitration of disputes between foreign traders in China waters. Derek's findings were published as 'Captain Charles Elliot RN, Arbitrator: Dispute Resolution in China Waters 1834-1836' in *Arbitration International* 1998 89-116, and re-published in the *Liber Amicorum* 97-131.

8. The concept of the history of law was by no means alien to Derek: he had published two editions of *The Background of the Common Law* (Port Moresby, University of Papua New Guinea Press, 1983; Hong Kong, Oxford University Press, 1990), a slim volume still used by students and, indeed, others.

As I read these essays for the last time before they go for text editing, I am struck anew by how startlingly erudite Derek was; I'm pretty sure it's not because I'm *parti pris*.

Susanna Hoe
Oxford
August 2022

ACKNOWLEDGEMENTS

Derek would probably have thanked more people than I can fathom. Those to whom the book is dedicated, Neil Kaplan, Francis Calvert Boorman and Rhiannon Markless, are thanked by that; and they have continued to support me in this endeavour.

I know that Derek was, for example, in touch with the BBC journalist Sarah Rainsford when he first used her piece about the Turkish butcher mediator – to ask about its use and to thank her for it, not only for its use. I'm sorry to anyone I have inadvertently left out. My biggest regret is not to have been able to find the correspondence with the scholar who, some years ago, sent Derek the cartoon that has become the cover. If by chance he should see this volume with its use of his thoughtful present, I hope that he will get in touch – susanna@holobooks.co.uk – so that I can thank him properly.

One of the most demanding tasks of preparing Derek's book for publication has been gaining permission to use articles, chapters and lectures that were first used elsewhere. Although, not surprisingly, given the number of chapters here, it has taken a while, I have to thank those who responded quickly, and even those whose systems demanded more time and effort. I thank them particularly because not one has charged for the use. The details of original use, and the permission to re-use, appear above each piece.

Without exception, when Derek gave the lecture that has become a chapter, travelling to places such as Bath, Caserta and Frankfurt, the hospitality was generous. Thanks in retrospect, from me personally, and on Derek's behalf. In the same way, I thank the Chartered Institute of Arbitrators (CIArb). It has given permission for the reprinting here of seven articles that originally appeared in its journal, *Arbitration*, of which Derek was editor for 10 years. (The archive of the CIArb journal (1915-2021) is now available via Kluwer Law online, Kluwer Arbitration and the member portal on the CIArb website.) I also express my appreciation for CIArb's creation of the annual Roebuck Lecture. Derek's inaugural lecture appears here.

Thanks, too, to the Institute of Advanced Legal Studies (IALS) of which Derek was, for many years, a Senior Associate Research Fellow, a scholarly home which he very much appreciated. Often they hosted launches of Derek's histories of arbitration and, as I write, I have been invited to attend the unveiling of the plaque in the Conference Room which honours both Derek and Johnny Veeder whom Derek so admired. I can remember quite clearly an occasion in the Council Chamber – 'Derek Roebuck in Conversation with Johnny Veeder' – which launched Derek's volume on the seventeenth century. A lecture that Derek gave at the IALS on another occasion is included here.

I can never tire of thanking the 'team' who produce HOLO Books' volumes, those of both The Arbitration Press and The Women's History Press. They have both done so for many years – Susan Faircloth who has with such patience, kindness, generosity and competence done much more than text edit, and Dave Stanford who makes sure that our volumes arrive from the printers as we would all wish. He also helps me with sometimes easy things for him, difficult for me, so promptly and with such good grace.

And, finally, I thank Derek: working on completing this volume for him has not only reminded me of his extraordinary erudition, perseverance and unremitting hard work, which he made look easy, but it has also been a great solace.

INTRODUCTION

Susanna Hoe

How did Derek come to write his several volumes of the history of arbitration and mediation? Why did he need a prompt to do so? And how did it come about? It was not as if legal history was alien to him. He had not only published two editions of *The Background of the Common Law*, but also drawn on it and, indeed, the history of other countries and jurisdictions in books and articles on comparison, another of his varied interests.[1] To some the answer to those questions is well known. It is for those who don't know that it is told here. To do so I have shaved off the first part of a chapter Derek wrote for a book in honour of Neil Kaplan.[2] What follows is in Derek's own words. From them you can see why Neil is the primary dedicatee of this book and, it should be said, his support in every way has continued beyond Derek's death, including his editing (with Robert Morgan) of the *Liber Amicorum* in honour of Derek.[3]

I speak as an old[er] friend with a special debt.[4] Neil has always been a strong supporter of legal education in Hong Kong. Twenty years and more ago I relied on him for insights and knowhow and sometimes influence, when I was trying to set up a new law school. We wanted to offer the first postgraduate degree in arbitration. That required the collaboration of the Chartered Institute of Arbitrators, which Neil secured. I knew nothing of arbitration then. Thirty years of practice as a solicitor and of teaching law had left me ignorant of any form of dispute settlement other than negotiation and litigation.

1. With Mary Hiscock – see Chapter 25 below – and others he published 10 volumes on Credit and Security in different Asian jurisdictions and Australia.
2. 'Neil Kaplan – Patron of Learning' in Chiann Bao and Felix Lautenschlager eds *Arbitrators' Insights: Essays in Honour of Neil Kaplan* chapter 18 pp317-325 London, Sweet & Maxwell, 2012. The rest of that chapter appears below as Chapter 6, 'The Medieval Idea of Arbitration' (Derek's sub-title).
3. Neil Kaplan and Robert Morgan eds *Lawyer, Scholar, Teacher and Activist. A* Liber Amicorum *in Honour of Derek Roebuck* (Oxford: HOLO Books: The Arbitration Press, 2021).
4. Derek had mentioned Neil's influence on younger colleagues.

Neil led me through the learning process. We became friends. I watched as he created that massive pioneering work: *Hong Kong and China Arbitration*. One day, with the guileless look that should have its own amber light, he said he thought it would be enhanced by a preliminary chapter on the history of arbitration. 'You're a legal historian', he said, 'Write it for me'. What could I do? I swear it was the first time that the words 'arbitration' and 'history' had been in my head together. I procrastinated. 'When do you want it for?' 'June', he said. It was already February. 'Not a chance', I said, 'You know what I've got on my plate'. Fortunately my tongue ran on: 'I couldn't possibly manage anything before November'. 'You're on' was his instant reply.[5] You can learn a lot about negotiation from Neil.

The result is that for almost the last twenty years I have concentrated my research on the history of alternative dispute resolution in its various forms. Most recently I have just finished *Mediation and Arbitration in the Middle Ages: England 1154 to 1558*.[6] I offer to Neil, with thanks and affection, a summary of what I have found.[7]

5. The chapter in question, 'A Short History of Arbitration' (1994), is included in the *Liber Amicorum*. How Derek researched and wrote it, without his own and other libraries in Oxford and London, I will never know. It should be noted, though, that the library of Victor Tunkel, for many years Secretary of the Selden Society, had, thanks to Derek, been bought by City University, Hong Kong for its Law School of which Derek was Dean. In spite of all his later volumes, the chapter still holds its own.
6. It was published in 2013, one of 11 books that Derek published on the subject. He had originally thought all could be contained in one volume!
7. What Derek offered is Chapter 6 below.

PART ONE

THE PAST

1. THE PREHISTORY OF DISPUTE RESOLUTION IN ENGLAND

Derek Roebuck

My understanding and experience of British prehistory lead me to the view that the Ancient Britons were a resourceful bunch. Their insular society worked well: they seem to have kept their feuding to manageable proportions.

Frances Pryor Britain BC p438[1]

1. INTRODUCTION

I am convinced that the present practice of mediation and arbitration cannot be understood without a knowledge of how it has come to be what it is now. Discussions of what should happen in the future, for example the arguments about whether mediation should be controlled by the state, or whether the same third party can act as both mediator and arbitrator, seem dangerously ill-informed when mediation is assumed to be an ancient Chinese or a late twentieth century American invention.

There are those who believe that recognisable processes of formal arbitration in England began with the birth of the common law or even with what they unhelpfully call the first Arbitration Act 1697.[2] Yet even a cursory glance at the ways in which earlier societies dealt with disputes – long before there were courts, or judges, or lawyers, or even written law – not only shows that they have always used mediation and arbitration. There is early evidence of assemblies where they met to deal with a wide range of business, including disputes between individuals and groups. There is no evidence, and no reason to believe, that they behaved

1. This article has been sparked off and informed by his two recent, comprehensive, accessible and lively books: Francis Pryor *Britain BC: Life in Britain and Ireland Before the Romans* London, Harper Perennial 2004 and *Britain AD: A Quest for Arthur, England and the Anglo-Saxons* London, Harper Collins 2004. No one who has not read them can rely on their old general knowledge of England's early history, however much they may want to argue with his conclusions.
2. For example 'the very inefficiency of the Courts had inspired, by 1680, the first experiments in arbitration ever held outside the trade guilds', DR Coquillette *The Civilian Writers of Doctors' Commons, London* Berlin, Duncker and Humblot 1988 139.

irrationally. Mediation no doubt led to settlements and arbitration to awards, which in early society the group would normally enforce. When the sources become richer, they reveal techniques and procedures which may possibly lead to better practice today.

My work on the early history of mediation and arbitration has already produced volumes on Ancient Greece and Rome.[3] Now I am working on early English arbitration and have found that there is no justifiable starting point later than prehistory.[4] But can anything at all be known about what happened before history, that is written sources, began? I believe so. Because the different parts of the British Isles have different histories, and practically because I cannot read Celtic languages, all my present work is restricted to England: not Ireland, nor Scotland, nor Wales.

For more than 700,000 years there have been humans in what is now England. They have been living in communities, cooperating in hunting, making and possibly trading in tools, and carefully burying their dead for half a million years.[5] They have probably been talking to one another since no later than 250,000BC.[6] Perhaps some of them were our hominid ancestors, like us in many basic ways, social as well as genetic. We know nothing of how they resolved the disputes they must have had. The recent discovery of a jawbone suggests that *homo sapiens*, our own kind, has lived here for more than 37,000 years.[7] New finds keep pushing these dates back but that seems to be the earliest realistic starting point for a study of dispute resolution in England.

Until about eight thousand years ago, England was part of the land mass of north-western Europe. Then the strip by which travellers could walk to and from the peninsula was finally inundated and the islands

3. Derek Roebuck *Ancient Greek Arbitration* Oxford, HOLO Books 2000; Derek Roebuck and Bruno de Loynes de Fumichon *Roman Arbitration* Oxford, HOLO Books 2004; '"Best to Reconcile": Mediation and Arbitration in the Ancient Greek World' (2000) 66 *Arbitration* 275-287.

4. I hope to publish *Early English Arbitration* next year. It may go up to the twelfth century. This article is based on the present draft of Chapter 2, Chapter 1 being concerned with such technicalities as definition and language. Chapters 3 on Roman Britannia and 4 to 8 on the Anglo-Saxon periods up to Cnut are done. I followed a digression and produced a lecture 'Customary Law before the Conquest', delivered at the Institute of Advanced Legal Studies on 27 February 2006 but not yet published, which covers much of the same ground as this article and includes some of the same text. [*Early English Arbitration* was published in 2008 – SH.]

5. SA Parfitt and 17 others 'The Earliest Record of Human Activity in Northern Europe' (2005) 483 *Nature* 1008-12.

6. Based on studies of the development of the human throat, tongue and ears, eg *New Scientist* 22 June 2004, but a much earlier date, c500,000BC is suggested by Sverker Johansson *Origins of Language: Constraints on Hypotheses* Amsterdam, Benjamins 2005.

7. Tom Higham, Oxford Radiocarbon Accelerator Unit, *BBC News* 27 April 2005.

took their separate form. Now we think of England, Ireland, Scotland and Wales, but those nation-states are comparatively very recent.

The written record starts only two thousand years ago and most of it is unreliable. Not all historians are as scholarly as Tacitus, in one passage at least, where he writes:[8] 'However, who the people were who first lived in Britain, whether indigenous or immigrants, is not sufficiently proved, as usual among foreigners.'

Long before the Roman occupation, however, there is the better evidence of archaeology, which, though it says nothing directly about how disputes were resolved, tells us much about what was going on in the evolving communities.[9] Thanks to archaeological scholarship, we know much more than Tacitus could. It may take imagination to produce pictures from the faint hints which lie scattered in the astonishing scholarship of the archaeological reports, but they should not be ignored.

Archaeological evidence does not usually provide what we are looking for directly; as Jacquetta Hawkes wrote:[10] 'The evidence for historical events during those centuries is tenuous and as easily broken as a cobweb. Archaeology catches so much of general life, so little of particular events.' For example, though there is no direct evidence for how they resolved disputes, there is ample evidence of highly developed societies at a much earlier date than we are used to believing. Their social and technological development makes it inconceivable that the people, who four thousand years ago devised Stonehenge or over three thousand years ago used the exquisite gold cups found at Rillaton in Cornwall or recently in Woodnesborough in Kent (both now in the British Museum), had not worked out a system for coping with at least some of their differences in a peaceful way, with replicable routines and the expectations of fairness they arouse.

2. SOCIETY

Ancient Greek Arbitration and *Roman Arbitration* were about dispute resolution in societies dominated by cities, civilised at least in that sense. Athens was a city and Greece a land of city-states. Rome, too, was a city and the centre of a great empire with many cities. England was not a land of cities. Nor did it begin to have effective central government or comprehensive administration until a thousand years ago. Even when it was one or more Roman colonies, the colonial government did not

8. RM Ogilvie and IA Richmond eds *Tacitus: Agricola* Oxford, Clarendon P 1967 11 p99; the best new translation is AR Birley tr *Tacitus: Agricola and Germany* Oxford, Oxford UP 1999.
9. Neil Faulkner *Decline and Fall of Roman Britain* Stroud, Tempus 2004 pp259-62.
10. Jacquetta Hawkes *Dawn of the Gods* New York, Random House 1968 p66.

control the whole of the country. Greece and Rome made much use of writing and produced fine literature. England had none at all before the Romans came.

Throughout the Palaeolithic or Old Stone Age, roughly 500,000BC to 8000BC, there is evidence that the population grew, if slowly, and larger groups formed. There appears to have been enough room for all. For the first 36,000 years or so of habitation by *homo sapiens*, until about 750BC, England was lightly populated, with many communities little larger than an extended family. Larger groupings were based on extended kin. There is plenty of evidence that they gathered together for social purposes. The larger social group, whether called kin or clan or tribe, provided insurance against some of the risks of life, including the ill-effects of disputes, which arise naturally in every society. If families do not attend such gatherings, they live in backwardness, says Homer of the Cyclopes in a precocious flash of anthropological insight: 'they have no assemblies where counsel is taken nor customary laws.'[11] Pryor suggests that even in the Mesolithic, from say 8000 to 5000BC, when the population grew more rapidly: 'people didn't live in such close proximity that disputes and rivalry for scarce resources could give rise to social competition.'[12] I wonder. That can only be true for competition between groups; there must have been normal competition as well as cooperation within the group of the extended family, at least.

Up to this time, Stone Age people had fed themselves by gathering food in the wild or by hunting. Now they gradually added farming, which allowed them to cluster more densely but required the exchange of stock for breeding, if not the trading of surplus:[13]

> Farming is a vastly more efficient means of producing food calories than hunting or gathering. It allows many more people to live in the landscape, and that in turn means that communities have to live alongside each other. So they must find ways of settling disputes....

The first hunter-gatherer-farmers were still nomadic too, to some degree, but eventually, probably after c3000BC, they foraged abroad less often and came to settle on a piece of land they called their own. Not

11. *Odyssey* 9.112; *Ancient Greek Arbitration* p70.
12. Pryor *Britain BC* p104.
13. Pryor *Britain BC* p111. It used to be accepted that farming was introduced by an 'invading wave' from abroad but archaeological scholarship (particularly the results of mitochondrial DNA tests) has cast doubt on that. Indeed, modern archaeological research finds little evidence of 'invading waves' at any time, though this, as so many matters, is hotly disputed. For the controversy about the Anglo-Saxon invasions see now Don Henson *The Origins of the Anglo-Saxons* Hockwold-cum-Wilton, Anglo-Saxon Books 2006.

in individual ownership, of course, but a part of the clan, inalienable, belonging as much to all its members, dead and living and still to be born, in the temporary stewardship of those alive who represented the clan for the time being. That is hard enough for us to comprehend but it is even harder to realise that there was land ownership before there were linear boundaries. Most of us now can only think of boundaries as lines drawn round plots. It was possible for earlier communities to grade the authority they had over land according to its nearness to their ancestral sites, often the burial places of ancestors. Boundaries were then circumferences from central ancestral burial places, so that the community (clan members alive or dead) might have exclusive rights to occupy land near the nodal points, but diminishing rights of use the further away they went, perhaps to grow things and keep animals nearby, to hunt and gather further away, where they might share those rights with other groups. That is still the way land ownership is thought of in some communal societies in the islands in the north of Papua New Guinea today. There is no direct evidence that it was ever so in England but:[14]

> One clue may be provided by a series of large Bronze Age burial mounds, often with multiple circular ditches surrounding them, which appear to be evenly spaced at roughly half-kilometre intervals along the southern part of this landscape. It's as if some time around 2500BC people decided that the fertile pastures of the southern Welland Valley had to be parcelled up in an equitable fashion, and enlisted the help of their dead ancestors to ensure that the arrangement was not abused.

My suggestion that prehistoric societies may have had more sophisticated concepts of space and boundaries and 'ownership' played no part in that insight of Pryor. Is the evidence, from England in the Bronze Age and Papua New Guinea today, all the more convincing for being quite unconnected? Which is more elaborate, the linear boundary or the measurement from nodes? This provides an insight into the nature of customary law which should never be ignored. The development of our legal system as, dare I say it, of our popular theology, has been a process of simplification, not elaboration, until modern times.[15]

3. TRADE

There cannot be trade without disputes. There is evidence of trade even in the Old Stone Age, including half-finished flint tools and Baltic amber in

14. Francis Pryor *Britain AD* pp79-82 and 226: 'barrow burial is about territoriality'.
15. See eg Peter Lawrence *The Garia: An Ethnography of a Traditional Cosmic System in Papua New Guinea* Melbourne, Melbourne UP 1984.

the form of beads. Regular patterns of reiterated trade would be unlikely
if disputes could only be resolved by violence when the parties could
not settle them for themselves. The definition of 'trade' at that time is
debatable but not during the period covered by this article, the following
eight millennia. For our purposes it does not matter whether goods have
become commodities or are exchanged within a market economy. There
was widespread distribution all over England of stone axes in the New
Stone Age.[16] Some could be used to chop down trees but others would
have shattered and must have been prized by their recipients for their
appearance. They were exchanged for something, goods or services or
privileges. Though we do not know what those were, they must have
been of value to those who received them. Neither side need have put
much value in what they gave in return. The anthropologists who have
studied the Kula ring and other forms of reciprocity have shown how
such systems may work.[17]

There was cross-Channel trade for 3000 years before the Romans
interfered with it. The main exports were slaves, corn and raw materials.
The discovery on the seabed off Dover of a cargo of 352 bronze
implements, exported from France, is only one bit of evidence for
cross-Channel trade about 1500BC, perhaps two centuries before the
first wheel discovered in England was made.[18] There is some evidence
that the Veneti of Brittany had their own permanent trading-posts in
England about then.[19] Recent finds from wrecks off Salcombe in Devon
and Dover in Kent, dating from c1200-1000BC, show cross-Channel
trade flourished between south-west England and Brittany until Caesar's
attacks on Brittany in 57BC, after which most trade switched to Kent and
the Thames estuary, except for wines, figs, glass and other luxuries to
supply the requirements of the sophisticated pre-Roman Iron Age British.

There is archaeological support for the stories preserved by Pliny
and Herodotus of exports of tin from Cornwall c600BC. Strabo, writing
cAD20, said the Phoenicians took care to monopolise the trade and kept
the route a secret, until Publius Crassus, governor of Hispania Ulterior,
managed the voyage to Cornwall (c95BC) and saw how tin was mined
and found the people peaceable.[20] The Phoenician merchants knew not
only the sea-routes; they used their knowledge of the markets to sell tin

16. *Britain BC* pp150-151.
17. Bronislaw Malinowski, *Argonauts of the Western Pacific* London, Routledge and
Kegan Paul 1922, essential reading for an understanding of England in the Stone Age.
18. *Britain BC* pp297, 300.
19. Barry Cunliffe 'Britain, the Veneti and Beyond' (1982) 1 *Oxford Journal of Archaeology*
39-68.
20. Strabo *Geographica* 3,5,10-11; TW Potter and Catherine Johns *Roman Britain* London,
British Museum, new edn 2002 pp14-15.

throughout the Mediterranean. Nothing is known of how they settled their disputes with their suppliers in England, though there is no reason to suppose they forwent the techniques and procedures they were used to elsewhere. It is possible to speculate that they had regular meetings of some kind, with rules for mediation and arbitration, especially if you can accept that the root of all the 'arbit-' words, in all languages, is to be found in Phoenician traders' pidgin.[21] The wrecks off Salcombe in Devon and Langdon Bay in Kent show that scrap metal was being traded across the Channel by the Middle Bronze Age (c1200-1100BC).[22] If there is trade in scrap metal, can you imagine there being no disputes which required some systematic process for their resolution?

4. CUSTOM AND LAW[23]

Wherever humans are found, at whatever time in history, they are social animals. If circumstances force them to be alone, they seek to rejoin the group when they can. It may well be that a permanent grouping is necessary for the survival of human young. The smallest group, the family, is in communal societies (as I prefer to call pre-state societies) not just a mother, father and their children. These extended families have relations with other neighbouring groups and wider kin with whom they congregate at certain times for agreed purposes, which can include the resolution of inter-kin disputes. This seems to be a universal phenomenon.

Any group of humans living together as a community needs common rules to govern the behaviour of the individuals within it. Even within a group seeking to function as a family there must be some system, however rudimentary and implicit. The rules of a kin group have more effective sanctions than those of a state. Life in such communal societies has been observed in recent times by anthropologists. It is fair to accept, if great care is taken, that some fundamental characteristics of modern communal societies are similar to those in earlier societies which archaeology shows had similar ways of life.

Communal life is public. There is little privacy and opportunities for eccentricity are limited. There is little chance of conduct deemed antisocial passing unnoticed or being attributed to the wrong person. Moreover, the sanctions are often immediate and applied until they work,

---

21. *Roman Arbitration* p19.
22. Potter and Johns *Roman Britain* p13.
23. Much of what follows is taken from my *Background of the Common Law* Hong Kong, Oxford UP 2nd edn 1990, Chapter Two, 'Communal Societies and Customary Law'. See now Adam Kuper *The Reinvention of Primitive Society: Transformations of a Myth* London, Routledge 2005.

that is until the culprits give up their antisocial behaviour and admit their faults, or have their capacity to misbehave removed.

The rules are, of course, unwritten, but they are better known in their entirety than the laws are to citizens of states. The greatest technological advance in the law is the use of writing, which reduces individual and communal memory as it provides the techniques of recording and reminding, provided the rules can be expressed simply enough. But an even more basic difference is economic. Economic relations are far more complex in more modern societies and much of the complexity of their laws is the result. On the other hand, a great deal of the complexity of communal law stems from the group's concern to control much more of what would now be considered the private lives of its members. For example, communal groups have comparatively few members so that selection of spouses from within them is limited. The health of the group requires a wider definition of incest. In our society, anonymous adoption has made possible the unwitting marriage of siblings, which would be unthinkable in a communal society. All the members of any communal group know the rules of their customary law in detail and expect hard punishment for their breach and the facts are not likely to be in dispute. Everywhere in modern communal societies there are legal rules of a complexity, sophistication and abundance that modern legal scholars find hard to comprehend. There is no reason to doubt that the rules of customary law were just as complex in prehistoric England.

It is also fair to assume that the customary laws of the various groups shared certain characteristics. Modern law has categories, used for the purposes of exposition and application: public and private; civil and criminal; property and obligations. Customary law does not, all law being one, consecrated by long use, general acceptance and the group's religion, superstitions, magic, whatever we choose to call what they believed. Customary law cannot be openly questioned by anyone on the grounds of utility or fairness. It is an essential attribute of the group. Yet it is always assumed, for that very reason, that to find it you must look for whatever rules produce a result in the best interests of the group (or those with power within it). Expediency is all, whatever formula is needed to produce it. That does not mean that there are no legal principles; just that, after the decision-makers have clarified them and applied them to the problem, you can be sure that there is no danger of the heavens falling.

The group ideology assumes that customary law is unchanging and unchangeable and is now what it has been since time began, yet it constantly responds to new stimuli, particularly technological innovation. It has probably been doing so for ever, with no consciousness of progress, let alone discussion of reform. It is changed to meet the needs of those with power. They are the ones who in the assemblies declare what the customary law is, and those who in applying it fix the details of its rules not just for that dispute but in the memories of everybody for the future.

5. ASSEMBLIES AND DISPUTE RESOLUTION

From about 4000BC the Stone Age inhabitants of England started to build a variety of spectacular communal edifices, which we now call monuments. Any of them may have relevance to dispute resolution. To take causewayed enclosures first, found all over southern England.[24] Most of them were probably not dwellings, as first thought, nor tombs, but many were provided with a front courtyard admirably suited for assemblies 'for the transaction of the necessary business of tribal life.'[25] A common feature is a line of posts, often of impressive size.[26] Beasts could have been tied to them, though they are usually bigger than necessary for that purpose. It is common to find animal bones there, with evidence of some eaten there and others slaughtered to be eaten elsewhere.[27] They could also mark the places where the elders stood or sat in the assembly, like the polished stones in the *Iliad*, discussed below.[28]

There may well have been what historians, anthropologists and archaeologists all call 'ritual' elements, as there is in most things we do publicly now, from umpires walking out together to start a cricket match to many aspects of the most modern arbitral hearing, with electronic chess clocks now unconsciously but exactly replicating the water-clocks of their forebears in Ancient Greece. In prehistoric times we can call it ritual or magic if we like. I prefer to think of it as early science, particularly when it is a part of technology, such as the mines at Great Orme in north Wales, 'thought to have yielded a rather extraordinary 175 to 238 tons' of

24. *Britain BC* pp162-173.
25. Isobel Smith *Windmill Hill and Avebury: Excavations by Alexander Keiller 1925-1939* Oxford, Oxford UP 1965 p19. This is not the place to speculate about their religious uses.
26. There is a splendid drawing in *Britain BC* p203, figure 36.
27. Once an animal was killed, it had to be eaten within a few days. Surplus fresh meat could not be stored. When herds outgrew the food to feed them or the labour to tend them, there had to be a feast. When labour greatly exceeded the need for it, did communities join in building monuments? Richard Bradley *The Social Foundations of Prehistoric Britain: Themes and Variations in the Archaeology of Power* London, Longmans 1984 is a scholarly treatment of these and allied problems, especially at pp64 and 166.
28. There are also striking similarities in overall shape and interior disposition of space between the reconstructions of the long barrow at West Kennet, *Britain BC* p201 figure 35, and of the tomb at Apesokari in Crete, Nanno Marinatos *Minoan Religion: Ritual, Image and Symbol* Columbia, U of South Carolina P 1944 p12 figure 14 and p19 figure 19. Both have a space in front of the entrance suitable for public gatherings. Marinatos writes (p14, her italics): 'Cult implements and offerings were found *outside* the tombs, thus suggesting periodic visitation... by *sizable groups of people*.... The area outside the tombs is spacious, capable of serving communal gatherings.'

copper in the Bronze Age.[29] Better to stick with what we can be confident about: the processes in the assemblies were clearly accompanied by solemn acts which were customary and replicated and intended to have some consequence.

The assemblies could well have been seasonal, which would have avoided the need to give notice, but they could also have been called whenever necessary. The location of causewayed enclosures beside rivers may be significant if they were used for dispute resolution. The river was often not just a border between the territories of different kin groups; it was a safer way of getting there than crossing alien land.

Another kind of Stone Age edifice is the barrow. It may, like the long barrow at West Kennet near Avebury, greet you with impressive stones standing at the entrance. When barrows were filled with earth, that seems to have signified some kind of completion, some sealing-off, including – who knows?– perhaps the settlement of a dispute. The artefacts buried in a round barrow at Lockington, south of Derby, may have been intended to recognise such a settlement, around 2100-1900BC. They include two decorated gold armlets, not a pair, and a long copper dagger made in Brittany and found in its scabbard. It is usually assumed that these were intended to accompany some dead man to another world.

I suggest a simpler explanation, which – though of course still the merest speculation – accounts for the armlets not being a pair, as one would expect if they were to be worn in the next world, where no doubt fashion would matter. The parties to a dispute brought it before some kind of tribunal in a public traditional assembly, which we can assume existed at that time. A settlement was mediated or arbitrated. After 'ritual' preparation (nearly as awe-inspiring as a visit to a solicitor's office, followed by a conference with a QC in an inn of court) the award was 'sealed' and its terms remembered by solemn repetition accompanied by 'ritual' depositing of the tokens of settlement, exchanged armlets and the customary sheathing and burying of the hatchet, or rather an expensive imported dagger. We might be well advised to remove the word 'ritual' in this paragraph and replace it with 'rational'.

Assemblies in the Bronze Age were clearly more than religious ceremonies. Farmers needed to meet to exchange livestock to renew the bloodline, even if they do not have to sell their surplus stock. There is evidence of conspicuous consumption at feasts. Is there any evidence that disputes were settled there? Pryor asks the question:[30] 'Why had many

---

29. *Britain BC* pp264-275. It is scarcely possible that in 5km of passages, some 70m deep, and some so tiny that only children could have worked them, mining could have been carried out without disputes arising.
30. *Britain BC* pp275-276.

of the Bronze Age implements dredged from the River Thames ... been partially melted down?' His answer is that they were 'votive offerings':

> Now I think I'm beginning to understand what might have been in people's minds as they partially melted down their spearheads, then dropped them into the river – doubtless with a spectacular hissing explosion of steam. It would be hard to imagine a stronger symbolic statement.

Symbolic of what if not of the ending of hostilities, of settlement of a dispute? Is any other explanation more likely? In his later work, *Britain AD*, Pryor writes:[31] 'In most cases, those offerings reflect rank, status or the avoidance of conflict .... conflict that has been avoided through some symbolic act.' Avoided or resolved?

The most compelling object of all, however, is also perhaps the most beautiful. It was made of polished flint about 3200BC and, though found not in England but in Ireland at Knowth in County Meath, is of direct relevance.[32] It is usually called a 'macehead'. That term seems as misleading as it is anachronistic, if mace has its common modern meaning of a staff symbolising authority, usually royal. Just looking at it, though, is enough to proclaim its association with public speaking. It is a stylised human head, only about 80mm tall and 60mm wide, not much bigger than a knob on a walking stick, of polished brown and white flint, with a great gaping mouth. It has a slot which shows it was meant to be fitted on to the top of a staff. Do we know anything about such 'speaking-staffs' in other times and places? We do indeed! Homer's *Iliad* and *Odyssey* are full of descriptions of assemblies. The fullest account of an arbitration is in the description of the assembly portrayed on the shield of Achilles.[33]

> Men were crowded together in an assembly. A dispute had been stirred up there, and two men were disputing about the reconciliation-payment for a man who had been killed. One was pleading 'all to be yielded', pointing it out to the citizens, but the other refused to accept anything. Both men had put it to a knowing-one to reach an end. And men, supporters of each side, were cheering on both of them, so marshals

31. *Britain AD* p217.
32. I know Knowth is in Ireland and this article is restricted to England but this specimen is irresistible. Maceheads both of antler and stone have been found in England, Bradley *Social Foundations* pp46, 48-9, 55. A few of sandstone and of quartzite are described and illustrated in WF Rankine 'Stone Maceheads with Mesolithic Associations from South-Eastern England' (1949) 15 *Proceedings of the Prehistoric Society* 70-76.
33. *Iliad* 18.497-508. The references to other passages in the *Iliad* and *Odyssey* and in later literature are in *Ancient Greek Arbitration*, where the speaking-staff is more fully discussed.

were restraining the crowd. The elders sat on polished stones in a sacred circle and one after another took the speaking-staff (*skēptron*) of the shouting marshals in their hand and adjudicated.

The elders are given seats on polished stones in the sacred circle.[34] Each elder takes the speaking-staff from one of the marshals, whose function is to keep the crowd in order, and speaks out in turn. No speaking-staff has so far been found by archaeologists in Greece, to my knowledge, but it would not be surprising if the imagery were similar. It does not signify royal power or the equivalent of the Roman *imperium*, as the lictors' *festuca* did.[35] The wide-open mouth has double significance. First, it proclaims the authority of the president of the assembly to conduct proceedings. He or his marshal calls for order and he decides who shall speak. Similar formality survives even now in the body language of a French meeting, when the *président* decides to *donner la parole*, rather like a modern conductor without a baton. Secondly, it shows that only one person may speak at a time and that is the one holding the staff. That is a convention which all must honour at the risk of being shunned as a lout. That is the dramatic point of the earlier passage in the *Iliad*, when Achilles, the celebrity superstar athlete, behaves so petulantly, turning on his commander-in-chief Agamemnon, who has taken his slave girl:[36]

> You drunk with the face of a dog and the heart of a doe, you never have the guts to fight ... you just take the booty of anyone who stands up to you .... You listen to me – I swear a great oath by this staff which the Greeks hold in their hands when they turn over their judgments in their minds – they who (for Zeus) guard customary law, *themis*,– I swear you this great oath – you'll be sorry!

And he does the unthinkable – he throws the staff down. I'm sure no Irish speaker would have treated the beautiful Lowth 'macehead' with such disrespect. But is it too far-fetched to see the many 'maceheads' found in England being used similarly as speaking-staffs in English assemblies? No other more convincing explanation has been offered for their use.

6. WHAT THE ROMANS FOUND

By the Iron Age, there were large tribes, some led by chiefs who would be kings, both peoples and rulers known by name from later sources.

---

34. Until recently they still did sit on polished stones in a half circle in Rarotonga in the Cook Islands to deliberate in the assembly. I have taken photographs of the stones.
35. Gaius *Institutes* 4.16.
36. *Iliad* 1.224-45. [Derek did his own translations from Greek and Latin. Sometimes it's more obvious! – SH.]

Pryor suggests that there were places on their borders where they met in assemblies, before Roman occupation curtailed a trend towards conglomeration in larger kingdoms.[37] He finds 'little trace of feuds', by which he means violent vendettas rather than the regular kin-based systems for the resolution of disputes in Anglo-Saxon times. This was a land of socially highly developed and economically prosperous communities.[38]

> From a technological point of view, the native inhabitants of Britain had been fashioning iron tools and weapons for some seven hundred years. They grew most of the common crops that we see in the modern countryside, and they had possessed sophisticated wheeled vehicles for well over a thousand years. Their clothes were made from brightly dyed woven cloth, and their artists and craftsmen were capable of producing works of art that could hold their own alongside the finest creations offered by the ancient world.

That is not what the Roman sources say. What mattered to Tacitus was that the Britons were ready to fight. They had not yet been unmanned by Roman ways, as Tacitus said they were to become as a matter of colonial policy and as the Gauls already had. But in many ways they resembled the Gauls, to whom Tacitus said they were related:[39]

> Those nearest to the Gauls are like them, either because of the continuing strength of their common origin or because the two countries run close together from opposite directions, so that the weather gives them their physical appearance. But taking everything into account it is likely that the Gauls invaded the neighbouring island. You can detect their religion there, and their superstitious persuasions. The language is quite similar.

Could the customary law and practices of dispute resolution, too, have been similar? Julius Caesar tells a likely story about how the Celts in Gaul settled their disputes:[40]

> [The druids] are the ones who lay down the law for almost all disputes, public and private, and whether something is considered a crime, and whether there has been a killing, and if there is a dispute about

37. Bradley *Social Foundations* p167.
38. *Britain BC* pp405-406, 409, 431.
39. Tacitus *Agricola* 11.
40. Caesar *Gallic War* 6.13-14.

inheritance or boundaries they settle it. They lay down remedies and penalties. If any individual or group does not abide by their decision, they ban them from sacrifices; for them this is the gravest punishment. Those that they ban are held to be impious and accursed and everyone keeps clear of them, cutting them and refusing to talk to them, lest they suffer some harm from contact with them. If they try to exert their rights they will not be given them and they are granted no honour.

Caesar says that the community relied on the druids to lay down the law, which of course was customary law then. He also stresses that they had no written laws but the druids kept them in their memory.[41] Though there is no reason to rely on this as evidence even of how the Gauls resolved their disputes, their British kin had similar druids, and it is likely that they too had a hand in resolving disputes. Though the Romans had no objection to communities resolving their own disputes by customary law, they did not find druids an acceptable alternative authority. Tacitus says that the Romans massacred the last of them on Anglesey, on the pretext that their human sacrifices were abhorrent.[42] Druids or no, those well developed British communities had systems for resolving disputes which continued after the Romans set up their colonial government with its own laws for some people in some parts of England. And there is evidence that those systems continued to function long after the Romans had gone.

7. WHAT CAN WE KNOW?

What can we learn from all these scraps of evidence and the application of disciplined imagination to them? There are some fundamental things which we can with confidence say we know. Before there are any surviving written sources, the archaeological evidence shows that communities in what is now England met in assemblies. So much is clear from the barrows and roundhouses and standing stones and most strikingly from the 'maceheads'. We may infer replicated procedures, and probably rules, for the resolution of disputes from the relics of trade. There must have been customary law of some kind because there always is, even in what we know of the Stone Age elsewhere, and always at the stage of development which societies in England had reached by the Iron Age. We know nothing of its content.

We may speculate that dispute resolution followed the procedures we may observe in contemporary or recent communities with similar

---

41. There were 'law-speakers' who remembered customary law and others who remembered royal decrees in Anglo-Saxon times, GP Krapp and E van Kirk Dobbie eds *The Exeter Book* New York, Columbia UP 1936, 'The Gifts of Men' lines 41-43 and 72-73.
42. Tacitus *Annals* 14.30.

technological, economic and social cultures. Disputes within the family were dealt with privately, as they usually are now. Families were more extended then and so the need for resort to neutrals arose only when the dispute was between two larger groups or individuals from those groups. Then arbitration became a formal matter. As far as we know, it always took place in an assembly, though not necessarily one called for that purpose. Assemblies may well have had more general functions. Not surprisingly, there is no evidence of private ad hoc dispute settlement.

There is no evidence, and no reason to believe, that the deliberations of the assemblies was formalistic, ritualistic, or in any way less rational than ours. It is hardly likely that they would have been bound by modern formalistic rules of evidence. They would no doubt include rather more of what was known or reputed to be the parties' characters and reputations. Perhaps also, at some stages, their place in society. They may have relied on oaths, as we still pretend we do in litigation, though not in mediation and arbitration. From evidence of later periods – which, of course, it is folly to rely on, or to ignore – it seems likely that the aim of the assembly was usually settlement. Mediation would be tried first (and throughout) and adjudication was a last resort and even then likely to concentrate on what was expedient, even if there was talk about rights. Enforcement would depend on social pressures, backed up by communal force where that was available. If all this failed, no doubt there was the kind of tribal warfare which still goes on in the Highlands of Papua New Guinea. That, too, might well be formal rather than full-blooded. And, in some cases, negotiation probably continued after the award, as sometimes it does today.

8. CONCLUSION

This article does not try to draw conclusions for use in present practice or in proposals for reform. That is for others to do. Its only ambition is to provide those who make decisions about the future of dispute resolution with sufficient knowledge of how and when it all started, in England at least, so that whatever programmes they decide on for the future will not be based on false prehistorical premises.

[TAILPIECE – SH
Derek mentions Papua New Guinea in passing. It is worth adding here that we lived there, and Derek taught law at the University, for five years – years and experiences which were pivotal to his writing of this chapter and many other insights throughout his subsequent thought and writing. The Kula ring in the Trobriand Island, so written about by Malinowsky, still functions; indeed, we bought half a shell necklace that was part of it.

Our stay in Papua New Guinea allowed travel to other Pacific Islands, such as Vanuatu where Derek taught twice face to face for two weeks, after distance teaching police students. He mentions the semi-circle of stones in the Cook Islands. I remember how he stopped and did a double take at the obviousness of one of the functions of the elders who sat on them. When Derek mentions the so-called 'macehead' found in Knowth, in County Meath, Ireland, he is speaking from having gazed at it in the National Museum of Ireland, Dublin. It can also be seen online. I'm pretty sure we visited the archaeological site where it was found. Being able to link it to the shield of Achilles was one of those moments that fire up the brain, and the imagination.]

2. CLEOPATRA COMPROMISED: ARBITRATION IN EGYPT IN THE FIRST CENTURY BC[1]

Derek Roebuck

Today is Valentine's Day, so we must all think of love. When Cleopatra spoke to her lovers, what language did they use? She was renowned for her linguistic skills. Plutarch wrote a century after her death:[2]

> Her beauty it is said was not astonishing nor inimitable; but it derived a force from her wit, and her fascinating manner, which was absolutely irresistible. Her voice was delightfully melodious, and had the same variety of modulation as an instrument of many strings. She spoke most languages, and there were but few of the foreign ambassadors whom she answered by an interpreter. She gave audience herself to the Ethiopians, the Troglodites, the Hebrews, Arabs, Syrians, Medes, and Parthians. Nor were these all the languages she understood, though the *kings* of Egypt, her predecessors, could hardly ever attain to the Egyptian.

However widely she ranged, there was no problem. All her lovers spoke Greek. It was her mother tongue and, if not theirs, they had learned it at school.

In the same way that I am now speaking English, if we were transported to Cleopatra's Alexandria I would be speaking to you in Greek. It was not only the language of the administration and of education and the majority of the volumes in the great library there, throughout the civilised world as it was then defined it was the language of polite discourse. Julius Caesar's last words to his friend would have been '*kai su*?' not '*et tu, Brute*?' Anthony's, as he died in Cleopatra's arms, are unlikely to have been the pompous artificialities Plutarch relates but whatever they said to one another was in Greek.

1. An address at the Opening Ceremony of the First Frankfurt Investment Arbitration Moot Court, February 14, 2008.
2. John and William Langhorne tr *Plutarch's Lives* London, Tegg 1878 'Antony' p640.

So, if we are to understand how disputes were resolved in the first century BC in Egypt, we can answer with confidence what I believe should always be the historian's first question: what language did they use? That will give us the first answers to our questions about dispute resolution then.

Cleopatra VII lived from 69 to 30BC. She was the last of the Greek dynasty founded by Alexander the Great's general Ptolemy in 323BC. She became queen at 17 with her younger brother Ptolemy XII, whom she had married as a young girl. Marriage of royal siblings was one of the few non-Greek customs of the Ptolemies.[3] Otherwise they remained Greeks. Not surprisingly, they dealt with disputes in a Greek way. Even when Egypt became a Roman province in 31BC, the Roman ways and Roman law took a long time to influence and never did determine the practice of dispute resolution. Cleopatra knew nothing of the Roman *compromissum*, the standard form of submission to arbitration in Rome in her day. She was never compromised in that way, though it was said that Julius Caesar arbitrated between her and her rival Ptolemy for the throne. If he did, I'm sure he was no more swayed by improper motives than Paris was by the thought of Helen of Troy.

From Alexandria the Ptolemies ruled Egypt and their neighbouring dominions. Their power depended on agriculture, heavily taxed and controlled by a hierarchical military bureaucracy, in which Greeks predominated. Outside Alexandria and the two other large Greek towns Naucratis and Ptolemais, which had their own city laws, the whole country was divided into districts, each *nomos* under its governor, the *stratēgos*. Within each district were many villages, each governed by an administrative officer, the *epistatēs*, an official well known in Athens and other parts of Greece. In the three big cities the Greeks kept up their traditional social groups, the demes. In the countryside they formed foundations to build and run gymnasia, men's clubs which excluded

3. Cleopatra and Ptolemy were probably blood brother and sister. It is sometimes suggested that sibling marriage in Egypt then was only between royal children but Roman census returns (after this time, of course) suggest otherwise. I find it hard to believe that sibling marriage was as common as it appears among ordinary families in Egypt and suspect a form of adoption of a suitable young man into a family without a male heir, who would then marry a daughter of the family. Sabine R Huebner 'Brother-Sister Marriage in Roman Egypt: a Curiosity of Humankind or a Widespread Family Strategy?' (2007) 97 *Journal of Roman Studies* 21-50 has the latest information and arguments. 'Adoption' has many different forms and meanings, which have caused problems when an English Common Law definition has been applied in criminal prosecutions in British colonies. The problem has been avoided by robust and sensitive courts in Papua New Guinea: Derek Roebuck 'Law and Language: The Ethics of Ignorance' in Charmian Thirlwall and P.J. Hughes eds *The Ethics of Development: Language, Communication and Power* Port Moresby, University of Papua New Guinea P. 1989 pp24-41, 29-30.

Egyptians, where they could carry on their Greek traditions of education, sport and culture. The colonial apartheid was not strict. There was plenty of intermarriage. But there was no doubt who were the colonial masters.

In the first century BC the legal system[4] dealt with this dichotomy by a decree of 118BC of Ptolemy VII plus Cleopatra his wife (who was also his step-daughter) plus Cleopatra his sister (who was also his former wife).[5] Actions between Greek and Greek went to the Greek judges. Between Egyptian and Egyptian they were heard by 'people's judges'. Otherwise the language in which the parties created their documents was taken to signify their choice of venue and law. All official documents were in Greek.

Both private and public arbitration were common. Both started with attempts to bring about a settlement. A fragment of papyrus from the middle of our period, dated 60BC, shows how private arbitration worked. It contains a complaint against a creditor who was refusing to accept the terms of an award which fixed periodical payments and created a charge on the debtor's flax crop. It reads:[6]

During the lifetime of my father .... he entered into a contract for the loan of money, which we established before the arbitrators whose names are set out below, with me promising to pay 100 *artabas* which he had all the use of. [I have repaid] 70½ *artabas*, which leaves 29½ *artabas* outstanding under the settlement.

Now he is trying to strip me of the flax I have sown. I believe that, if it is clear that this has been agreed in writing with the village authorities, he should not be allowed to seize any of the crops sown by me nor do anything by force until the new harvest, with me then paying 22½ of the 29½ *artabas*....

4. Raphael Taubenschlag *The Law of Greco-Roman Egypt in the Light of the Papyri 332BC-640AD* 2nd edn, Warsaw, Pánstwowe Widawnictwo Naukowe 1955 pp481-494; Zaki Aly 'The Judicial System at Work in Ptolemaic Egyptian Law-Courts' (1945) *Bulletin de la Société Royale d'Archéologie d'Alexandrie* 3-31; Derek Roebuck *Ancient Greek Arbitration* Oxford HOLO Books 2001, Chapter 14.

5. 'They have also decreed as follows in respect of litigation between Egyptians and Greeks, whether by Greeks against Egyptians, or by Egyptians against Greeks .... Egyptians who have entered into contracts in Greek with Greeks shall bring and defend actions before the Greek judges (*chrêmatistai*). But even Greeks, if they enter into contracts in Egyptian with Egyptians, shall all have their actions heard by the people's judges (*laokritai*) according to the laws of the countryside. Actions between Egyptians and other Egyptians shall not be heard by the Greek judges but shall be decided by the people's judges in accordance with the laws of the countryside.' Loeb *Papyri* II pp58-75 no 210, at p72; *P Teb I* no 5; Jósef Modrzejewski 'Chrématistes et Laocrites' *Symposion 1974* pp375-96; PW Pestman *The New Papyrological Primer* 2nd edn Leiden, Brill p87 no9.

6. *BGU 8* p93 no 1818.

These are the arbitrators: Xenon, son of Ammon, Ap..., T... [the other names are lost]

The three arbitrators are called *koinoi*, which means that they are friends of *both* sides. That was the understanding not only among the Greeks but in England until what I call modern times. You chose your arbitrators not because they had nothing in their heads or hearts relating to the dispute but because they were trusted as friends by both sides and knew plenty about them and the facts in dispute.

There are many other papyri from earlier and later times, which show a full range of subject matter submitted to private arbitration. The earliest is an arbitration clause in a marriage contract from 310BC:[7]

If Demetria is discovered to have done wrong ... Heraclides shall prove whatever he accuses Demetria of before three men whom they shall both approve .... Heraclides shall not be allowed to ... do wrong to Demetria. If ... Demetria proves that before three men, whom they both shall choose, Heraclides shall pay back the dowry .... Enforcement shall be exactly the same as it would be if Demetria had ... won a judgment according to law against Heraclides personally and all his property on land and at sea.

Just like today's Hollywood Cleopatras. True love expressed in a pre-nup! Other documents include submissions to arbitration of an existing dispute,[8] fragments of awards, and a whole series of documents in a construction dispute.[9] All are private and ad hoc.

The Greek tradition of resolving disputes by *public* arbitration was also routine in Ptolemaic Egypt. More than a hundred documents reveal the systematic use of government-ordered mediation by Diophanes, the *stratēgos* of the Arsinoite district between 222 and 218BC.[10] They were found in the cartonnage of mummies, presumably having been sold by his office to embalmers as waste paper. They cover the widest range of subject matter and provide evidence of the procedure by which disputes were resolved in Egypt by petitions to the king delivered to the office of

7. *P Elef* 1 pp18-22; Loeb *Papyri* I pp3-5 no1.
8. *BGU* 6 no1465.
9. Derek Roebuck '"Best to Reconcile": Mediation and Arbitration in the Ancient Greek World' (2000) 66 *Arbitration* 275-87; *Ancient Greek Arbitration* p310 and pp313-17.
10. *P Ent* has a full introduction and commentary and references to the scholarly literature that these papyri had by then engendered, including in particular Paul Collomp *Recherches sur la Chancellerie et la Diplomatique des Lagides* London, Oxford UP 1926 pp167-176; also Raphael Taubenschlag *Opera Minora* Warsaw, Pánstwowe Widawnictwo Naukowe 2 vols 1959 II pp575-636 and Napthali Lewis *Greeks in Ptolemaic Egypt* Oxford, Clarendon P 1986 pp56-58; Martí Duran I Mateu '*Diaita i Dialusis*: Arbitratge i Conciliació a la Grècia Antigua' U of Barcelona doctoral thesis 1999 pp1364-1488.

the *stratēgos*.[11] There the originals were filed by clerks who made a copy which the petitioner took to the *epistatēs* of the defendant's district with this formula scribbled on the bottom:[12]

'To [name of the *epistatēs*]. Best to reconcile them. If you cannot, send [them] back for us to examine. [date].'

On the back was written a note, stating the names of the parties and describing as briefly as possible the substance of the complaint.

In the most serious criminal cases, the *epistatēs* was expressly told to refer the matter to the *stratēgos* without attempting to mediate. At the other extreme, in small debts and other straightforward matters, a variation instructs the *epistatēs* to arbitrate himself if his mediation fails and then enforce his award.[13] Otherwise, the hundred examples show that the *epistatēs* was instructed to mediate if he could over a wide range of subject matter. If he succeeded, the settlement was recorded on the petition, which the petitioner took back to the office of the *stratēgos* to be registered and, if necessary, enforced. If the mediation failed, the office of the *stratēgos* disposed of the matter according to regular routines of litigation.

How successful were the efforts of the *epistatēs* to bring about an agreed settlement? Though his mandate might appear to provide simple alternatives, to mediate successfully, or arbitrate, or refer the matter on, he had all the official standing he needed to supplement his powers of persuasion. It would have been a determined litigant who was prepared to face the cost and trouble of a journey to the *stratēgos* in Crocodilopolis, to say nothing of the displeasure of the *epistatēs*, a middle-ranking officer with police powers, whose own performance may well have been judged in part by his ability to resolve disputes occurring within his administrative responsibility. Once he had heard the parties and received

11. *P Ent* pxxxvi; nos 21 from 28 January 222BC, 41 from 26/27 February 221, 17 from 13 January 218, 9 from 11 May 218; others whose dates are not legible may also relate to those dates, Lewis *Greeks in Ptolemaic Egypt* p56.

12. *P Ent* pxlviii: 'mutilées, tachées, effacées, déteintes, elles se présentent souvent, au premier abord, commes de vagues mouchetures noirâtres.'

13. *P Ent* pp106-107 no 42. 'To Ptolemy basileus greetings from Apollonius of .... I am wronged by Dositheus, of the same town. He borrowed some hoes from me and four bronze drachmas and, despite my repeated requests, he has not returned them to me, but is trying to drag the matter out. So I beg you, basileus, if it pleases you, to instruct Diophanes the *stratēgos* to write to Agathocles the *epistatēs* to force Dositheus to give me back what he owes me. Thus, thanks to you, saviour of all, I shall have obtained justice. Farewell.

To Agathocles. Examine the matter and do what is necessary for him to obtain justice. Year 1, 28 Gorpiaius – 12 Tybi.'

any testimony, any competent *epistatēs* would be able to come to his own conclusions on the facts and law. Not many of those with disputes, whether petitioners or defendants, would be strong enough to refuse to submit to whatever settlement the *epistatēs* finally suggested.

Even if the *epistatēs* were unsuccessful and one of the parties insisted on the matter being returned to the jurisdiction of the *stratēgos*, the hearing before the *epistatēs* was not in vain. Even if the endorsement instructed him just to send the matter back, he had to make a report. That would include the statements of the parties and any evidence that they produced. The *epistatēs* took sworn evidence from the parties and sent it under seal to the *stratēgos*.[14] The *stratēgos* would not normally hear the testimony again or even admit new evidence.

No doubt there were often difficulties in enforcing the orders of superior officers, whether awards or judgments. But a party against whom an award was made, or who had agreed to a mediated settlement, could not have escaped enforcement for ever. The system appears to have worked well enough.

Cleopatra provided her subjects with a wide range of courts but no one had to submit their disputes to them. On the contrary, all were encouraged to avail themselves of private arbitration by the willingness of the authorities to lend their support to arbitration agreements and awards. Moreover, if they approached the authorities with their claims, hoping to commence litigation at once, they were referred to an official with instructions to mediate.

Almost any kind of dispute was arbitrable. Most of the surviving documents record disputes about farming and agricultural property. Others are evidence of commercial activities, fraud and simple debts. There are construction disputes and industrial conflicts between workers and management. But there are also matrimonial, succession, and family quarrels and what we would now classify as crimes – assaults, robbery, sheep and donkey stealing, insulting behaviour and wrongful imprisonment – and the difficulties which private citizens faced when they took on the collection of taxes.

Any free person could submit to arbitration. There was no prohibition against Egyptian women appearing themselves as parties to an arbitration, whether private or public, or, indeed, to litigation. Greek women, though, faced cultural barriers.

Arbitrators were male, often the superiors of both parties, but they could be anyone who was thought by the complainant to have the power to enforce attendance at the mediation sessions and the award

14. Lewis *Greeks in Ptolemaic Egypt* pp67-68 and 167 n9, citing and translating *P Turner* 16.

if arbitration became necessary. Though there are instances of two and three private arbitrators sitting together, in practice most of the evidence shows a single arbitrator hearing the dispute. Their names survive in some of the documents.

The arbitration could rest on an arbitration clause or a later agreement to submit. The evidence shows an almost casual practice of calling on a third party *ad hoc*. The parties could provide in their agreement that the award of arbitrators was to have the force of law, and in every jurisdiction, not just the one where the agreement was made. That does not mean it would have been effective, but it does mean that the parties thought it would.

Every conclusion must remain vulnerable, waiting to be refuted by the discovery of new evidence. But one conclusion is unlikely to be shaken: in Cleopatra's Egypt, mediation and arbitration, all part of one process, were regular and widespread.

Now, at last, we must turn to the Decree. How can we fit into this background Cleopatra's decree and its subscription, perhaps in her own hand '*ginesthoi*', 'So be it!'? It is an ordinance – God preserve us from anachronism but it looks so much like an early English writ! It grants exemption from taxes and other impositions to Publius Canidius, Mark Antony's general at the Battle of Actium:[15]

We have granted to Publius Canidius and his heirs the right to export 10,000 artabas of wheat per annum and to import 5,000 Coan amphoras of wine per annum free of all taxes and other impositions. We have also exempted in perpetuity all the land he owns in Egypt from taxes otherwise due in any way either to the state or to me and my children. We have also granted that all his tenants be exempt from personal liabilities and from taxes without anyone exacting anything from them, so that they do not even have to contribute to the occasional assessments in the *nomoi* or pay for the upkeep of soldiers or officers. We have also granted that his animals used for ploughing and sowing as well as beasts of burden and ships used for transporting wheat are likewise exempt from impositions and taxes and cannot be commandeered. Let this be written to those whom it may concern, so that they know it and act accordingly. So be it!

This was received by the officials to whom it was addressed in Alexandria on February 23, 33BC. Two years later, Antony and Cleopatra were defeated at Actium and killed themselves. Egypt passed into the control

15. Berlin P 25 239, on display at the Agyptisches Museum und Papyrussammlung, Berlin.

of Octavian and later became part of the empire. For many generations, though, legal practice and the resolution of disputes by mediation and arbitration went on as before. It was a long time after our period that those who wanted to practise law in Egypt learned and introduced Roman law into dispute resolution. Throughout the 1st century BC, the practice of law in Egypt was Greek, in its colonial Egyptian form.

So, arbitration of all kinds, private and public, was alive and well in Cleopatra's Greek Egypt. It was not Roman in any way. It was as refined as it needed to be and we should not assume that Roman practice or indeed our own would have been an improvement.

Plutarch, followed by Bernard Shaw, insists that Cleopatra was established on her throne by the arbitration of a Roman, but that was not the result of any compromise and Roman law played no part in her tragic end.

We shall never know what she said to Antony but there is some exciting recent evidence of her relationship with Julius Caesar, for the discovery of which I take full credit. It comes from an esoteric source whose authenticity is clearly proved (for graduates of the Dan Brown school of history) by Shakespeare's hidden reference to it in *Antony and Cleopatra* itself. At the end of Act I, Cleopatra threatens to thump her maid in the teeth for suggesting that she once thought as highly of Caesar as she now does of Antony. If she ever gave that impression, she says, it was the youthful folly of:

My salad days,
When I was green in judgment, cold in blood,
To say as I said then.

Now what else could that be but a hidden clue to my new source, of great relevance, like all I have said, to our moot. In *Salad Days*, the favourite musical of my youth, in Act II, in the night club, the manager sings:

Cleopatra,
Held the key to every heartre
And the secret of her artre
Was to keep her men at bay.
She used to tease 'er
Sugar daddy, Julius Caesar,
By not allowing him to squeeze 'er
More than once or twice a day.

Except that I'm sure she would have made an exception if there had been a Valentine's Day then.[16]

[TAILPIECE – SH
Derek ends this lecture given in Frankfurt, as his footnote details, quite
unusually, as you see. But it was more dramatic than it appears on the
written page: he sang it. He had a wonderful bass voice, and he did
particularly enjoy the cleverness of those words, but I have to admit that
the serious young mooters from all over the world, from several different
cultures, were a bit nonplussed.]

16. Which could not have happened before 1382, when Chaucer first mentioned it in his *Parlement of Foules*.

A lecture delivered on 10 December 2010 in Bath for the Bath Royal Literary and Scientific Institution. Not previously published.

3. WHAT LAW WAS THERE IN ROMAN BATH?

Derek Roebuck[1]

1. INTRODUCTION

Aquae Sulis: what a wealth of meaning can be won from just two words! 'Waters of Sul' we can translate them, a common Latin word and a British proper noun. Wanting a Latin name for what we now call Bath, the Romans noted the waters, then as now its most distinctive and positive characteristic, and they recognised a local deity, with whom Bath's British inhabitants identified the health-giving spring.

Like the Chinese, the Romans knew exactly what they wanted from their empire and were content if they got it. They were not interested in imposing their religion. Until well into the fourth century, when Christianity became exclusively the state religion, they didn't really have one in imposable condition and they quite enjoyed having foreign gods living alongside their own.

Their policy was not all that different towards the legal system. Roman law was an extraordinary, even unique technological and social advance. To live by it was a privilege. It was extended to non-Romans as a favour. So how would those who lived here in Aquae Sulis have gone about making a claim or defending it? There is no general history of Roman law in Britannia and, if there were, would it answer these questions? There are few primary sources. I will try to set them all out. But it will take more than scholarship to suggest some answers.

In my favourite book about Bath, *Roman Bath Discovered*, Barry Cunliffe tells us his feelings on Christmas Eve 1964, as he stood 14ft below the city level on the newly rediscovered bottom step of the temple:[2] 'a rare occasion for evocative, rambling thoughts about what it would have been like to stand on this spot 1600 years earlier, what sounds, what light, what movements.' A polymath like Cunliffe, one or other of whose books I always seem to find essential when I stray into

---

1. Senior associate research fellow, Institute of Advanced Legal Studies, University of London.
2. Barry Cunliffe *Roman Bath Discovered* Stroud, Tempus new edn 2000 (Cunliffe).

another discipline, has a right to let his imagination wander. The control which his vast knowledge allows him ensures that his conjectures are as good as most people's conclusions. Can a mere lawyer, who tries to write about the history of dispute resolution, have helpful fancies? Let's see.

2. THE METHOD AND THE MATERIAL

But first, what do we know? What can we depend on before our fancy takes flight? A few literary references, the general background and the odd bit of particular knowledge provided by archaeological discoveries, and inferences from what we know happened in other provinces, applied by analogy; together they allow us to paint a thin wash of background, with a few features, usually out of focus.

No cohesive contemporary account has survived of the society the Romans found anywhere in what is now Britain, let alone specific to Bath. Roman literature allows tiny, unconnected glimpses of the way the British lived. How the colonial elite here must have laughed when they read the wild stories in the contemporary popular media coming from Rome, like those of Caius Julius Solinus, with his naked savages feeding their babies with meat on the tips of their swords.[3] His and other Latin descriptions of the British way of life are untrustworthy, unless we can catch them unawares, when they tell us something dependable by chance, in texts prepared always for a purpose other than to preserve the facts.[4]

No one wrote in the indigenous languages but there must have been plenty of oral tradition. The colonials had many local acquaintances, if not friends, even relatives by marriage, from whom they could see how the British lived. Some British people had enough Latin and could read and write in that second language. The technology was readily available but no indigenous literature has survived. Archaeology provides substantial evidence of how people lived;[5] but the scraps of wood, pewter tablets and blocks of stone on which writing has survived make few relevant references to law or any disputes.

The best arguments come from that wicked source, *mutatis mutandis*. How reliably can we argue that the Roman colonial administration applied in Britannia much as it did in other provinces?[6] For our purposes,

3. Theodor Mommsen ed *C. Julii Solini Collectanea Rerum Memorabilium* Berlin 1895, 2nd edn 1958.
4. Compare for example the testimonies of Gildas and Bede, discussed by the archaeologist-historian Neil Faulkner in *Decline and Fall of Roman Britain* Stroud, Tempus, 2000 pp259-62.
5. Martin Millett *The Romanization of Britain: an Essay in Archaeological Interpretation* Cambridge, CUP 1990.
6. The argument is made more fully by Andrew Lintott *Imperium Romanum: Politics and Administration* London, Routledge 1993 and in Derek Roebuck and Bruno de Loynes de

I need to show first that, though law, custom and practice might differ in detail from province to province and between an Italian town and a British spa, the system which the Roman colonial administration applied was likely to have been similar.[7] While there is little direct evidence, I am confident that, if the imperial authorities had made special provision for Britain, that in itself would have been interesting enough for some mention of the legislation to have survived.

3. WHAT WE THINK WE KNOW OF HISTORY

It might be possible to attempt to tell the story of how the law developed over more than four centuries but the best I can hope for is a snapshot. I have to pick a moment. Like Barry Cunliffe, I have let my imagination loose on the early years of the fourth century. But that picture cannot be delineated unless the details have some historical background. What do we really know about it?

Julius Caesar invaded Britain in 55BC and again the following year but did not stay. We can take his word for it, though there is not a bit of archaeological evidence. By then there had been ready and regular travel and trade between Britain and the Roman provinces across the Channel for generations. Roman merchants had already settled in Britain. Cymbeline became king of most of southern Britain and had coins minted naming himself '*Cunobelinus Rex Brittonum*'. His kingdom fell apart when he died in AD42 and the emperor Claudius took the opportunity to invade the following year with 40,000 troops, an enormous army. A new Roman province was quickly settled, encompassing most of the southern half of Britain, geographically including whatever was here in Bath, where by AD100 there was a Roman temple.

Few of the new colonials had any roots in Rome itself or even in Italy. The others came from all parts of the empire. Most of the soldiers and settlers, men and women, could well have been from the nearest existing provinces in Gaul, of much the same stock and some speaking languages not totally dissimilar from the British, perhaps the Belgae in Bath and their namesakes in Northern France. In AD61 the Roman army crushed the uprising against Roman tyranny led by Boadicea. Thereafter the borders of Rome's British provinces stretched to what are now Scotland, Wales and Cornwall, with forts to keep other British at bay, and later Hadrian's Wall to keep out the Picts. But the Romans never imposed their

---

Fumichon *Roman Arbitration* Oxford, HOLO Books: The Arbitration Press 2004 (*Roman Arbitration*) pp8-10.
7. Joan Liversidge *Britain in the Roman Empire* New York, Praeger 1968, particularly Chapter 11.

administration over all within their borders. Unlike most other provinces, Britannia still had many unsettled areas.

Within those parts subject to ordinary Roman colonial rule, however, many of the British upper class adopted Roman ways and prospered. My favourite authority on all things to do with everyday Roman life, Lindsey Davis, creator of Marcus Didius Falco, puts these words into the mouth of a British playwright, Urbanus – she has a way with names – in Rome in the time of Vespasian:[8]

> The wild warriors on the fringes probably believe they will lose their souls if they wash in a bathhouse. Others accept the gifts of Empire. Since becoming Roman was inevitable, I grabbed it; my family had means, luckily. The poor are poor wherever they are born; the well-to-do, whoever they are, can choose their stamping ground. I was a lad who could have turned awkward in adolescence; instead I saw where the good life lay. I went hotfoot for civilisation, all the way south through Gaul. I learned Latin.

Urbanus sounds to me like the scion of a rajah's family in a novel by EM Forster. Like the British imperial administration, the Roman where it could co-opted local leaders, those with power over land and people, and strengthened their control so long as they performed the functions allotted them. From the Romans' point of view, the most important was to keep order, including the settlement of disputes. The provincial government with the governor at its head, assisted by his finance minister, the *procurator*, controlled the settled areas, with a small staff of civil servants, technically in military service, but they relied on those who were already used to power to ensure law and order.

4. THE IMPERIAL LEGAL SYSTEM

Bath never was, as far as we can tell, subject to Roman military occupation. It was not formally a municipality, like London, or a *colonia*, like Colchester, Gloucester, Lincoln or York. So, what legal system applied? Specifically, did the administration require Bath's inhabitants to transact their private business according to Roman law?

Roman law applied according to the status of the person. It had always applied to all Roman citizens, which included all retired army officers. Since AD212 the Edict of Caracalla had extended Roman citizenship to all free inhabitants of the empire. Only men, of course, were full citizens;

---

8. Lindsey Davis *Ode to a Banker* London, Arrow 2009.

not women, certainly not the many slaves. Roman law *applied* to them, but they did not have its privileges.[9]

The magistrates were likely to be appointed from the local landowning class or local chiefs, depending on the district, and to know the customary law as well as anyone. The governor, even though a foreigner, would take advice and apply the local law, if he thought it appropriate.

5. THE SOURCES FROM BRITTANIA

How do the bits and pieces of evidence from Britannia fit into that general background? There are few Roman records of cases from here. What few there are, though, show that they were dealt with uniformly with cases from elsewhere. When imperial authority made a decision, called a rescript, in a private dispute, it had the force of law not only for those parties but for everyone else. Not only the decision itself but the reason for it was authoritative.[10]

Justinian's *Digest* stated the law as at AD533, 200 years after our chosen time, but much of it was drawn from opinions of jurists in treatises published centuries earlier. Just a few arose from litigation in Britannia.[11]

On 20 November AD319, about the time of our snapshot, the emperor Constantine wrote to Pacatianus, *vicarius* (deputy governor) of the Britannias:[12]

Every *decurio* is bound to pay the portion for which he himself is liable ... but he is in no way liable for any other *decurio* or other magistrate's jurisdiction.

This shows that *decuriones*, elected local authorities in Britannia, were subject to the same obligations as their counterparts elsewhere and is some evidence for the more general conclusion that local government was organised in much the same way throughout the empire.

9. It is important not to jump to conclusions about the effect of Caracalla's Edict: Tony Honoré 'Roman Law AD200-400: From Cosmopolis to Rechtsstaat' in Simon Swain and Mark Edwards *Approaching Late Antiquity: The Transformation from Early to Late Empire* Oxford, Oxford UP 2003 pp109-132 (Honoré); *Roman Arbitration* p44.
10. The modern distinction between case law and legislation was not so sharply drawn until AD398, when a law provided that 'past and future rescripts, given when a judge has consulted the emperor on a point in the case before him, have effect only for the case about which the emperor was consulted'. Honoré p129.
11. I have been greatly and generally helped by the work of ME Jones 'The Legacy of Roman Law in Post-Roman Britain' (Jones) in RW Mathison ed *Law, Society and Authority in Late Antiquity* Oxford, Oxford UP 2001 particularly at pp52-56. He points out that there are other rescripts made by emperors while they were in Britannia but not specifically referring to Britannia.
12. *Codex Theodosianus* 11.7.2.

There are other authorities in the *Digest*, which show what the law was. Technical questions of the inheritance law might require the opinion of a leading lawyer. A passage in the *Digest* quotes the famous jurist Javolenus Priscus on a matter of inheritance which arose here as early as the second half of the first century:[13]

> Seius Saturninus, a chief pilot from the Britannic fleet, by will appointed Captain Valerius Maximus his heir on trust, requiring him to restore the inheritance to his son Seius Oceanus when he reached sixteen years. Seius Oceanus died before he reached that age. Now Malleus Seneca, who says he is Seius Oceanus's uncle, claims these goods by right of family relationship. But Captain Maximus claims them for his own, because he to whom he was instructed to restore them is dead .... My opinion was that ... the goods belong to whomever the other goods of Oceanus belonged.

Early in the second century, Neratius Priscus, a leading jurist in Rome, sent an opinion to his brother Marcellus, almost certainly at that time in authority in Britannia. He advised that, according to Roman law, a general bequest of the contents of a house would include clothes:[14]

> Especially as in this case, where the testator had excluded the silver and the books of account. Because, he says, anyone who excluded those things must have intended to include everything else that was in the house.

An inheritance might need the notional intervention of the emperor himself. About the end of the second century, a rescript of Septimius Severus and Caracalla instructed the governor of Britannia how to deal with a problem arising from the Roman practice of a father making a will for his under-age child:[15]

> It is Julian's opinion that he ought first to appoint an heir for himself and then for his son. If, however, he should make a will first for his son and then for himself, that will be invalid. This opinion was approved in a rescript of our emperor to Virius Lupus, governor of Britain.

There is even part of a will, in Roman form, which has survived from North Wales, at the very limit of Roman administration. The fragment of text translates as:[16]

13. *Digest* 36.1.48.
14. *Digest* 37.7.12.43; John Morris (Revd Sarah Macready) *Londinium: London in the Roman Empire* London, Phoenix 2005 p185.
15. *Digest* 28.6.2.4.
16. RSO Tomlin 'A Roman Will from North Wales' (2001) 150 *Archaeologia Cambrensis*

... before I die, I order that ... be my sole heir ... Let all others for me be disinherited ... on these terms only that as much as I shall give, have given, shall have ordered to be given ...

Then followed a provision requiring the heir (whose name is lost) to accept the estate within 100 days or lose the inheritance.

Conviction of a serious crime could deprive the criminal of testamentary capacity. He might try to preserve his will by committing suicide before the formal deprivation. That would not work. But suicide was not a crime and did not itself affect testamentary incapacity. The emperor Hadrian wrote to Pomponius Falco, probably the governor of Britain (no relation to Lindsey Davis's Marcus Didius Falco):[17]

But anyone who commits suicide because they are tired of life or cannot bear ill health or to make a point, like some philosophers do, their wills are valid. In a letter to Pomponius Falco, the divine Hadrian said that the same distinction applied to a soldier's will, so that if he preferred to die because he realised he had committed some military offence, his will was invalid. But if he was tired of life or in pain or grief, his will was valid.

What an insight that gives into the life of a Roman soldier in Britain!

In a letter which has survived from Hadrian's Wall about AD100,[18] well known but irresistible, Claudia Severa, wife of Commander Aelius Brocchus, wrote to her friend Sulpicia Lepidina, wife of Flavius Cerialis, Commander of Vindolanda, inviting her to her birthday party:[19]

Claudia Severa to her Lepidina, greetings! I send you a warm invitation, sister, to come on 10 September to celebrate my birthday. See that you come to us to make the day happier for me by your company if you come. Give my regards to your Cerialis. My Aelius and my little son send their regards too.

143-156, with a photograph, drawing, translation and commentary; Derek Roebuck *Early English Arbitration* Oxford, HOLO Books: The Arbitration Press, 2008 (*Early English Arbitration*) p41.

17. *Digest* 28.3.6.7.

18. AK Bowman *The Roman Writing Tablets from Vindolanda* London, British Museum 1983.

19. AK Bowman and JD Thomas 'New Texts from Vindolanda' (1987) 18 *Britannia* 137-40. The tablet is on display in the Roman Britain room at the British Museum, London and pictured in TW Potter and Catherine Johns *Roman Britain* London, British Museum, new edn 2002 p58.

What a wonderful stoke of luck that we can celebrate her birthday here tonight!

As usual that was dictated to and written by a secretary but the next sentence is a PS in Claudia's own hand:

> I look forward to seeing you, sister. Fare you well sister, my dearest soul, as I hope to fare well. Ciao!

That shows she was not only at home in Latin but able both to read and write it. It is the earliest surviving woman's handwriting, I believe.[20]

Not all women were so fortunate, as another case in the *Digest* shows:[21]

> A woman was sent to the salt mines for her crime. She was taken from there by foreign bandits and sold according to commercial law. She was redeemed and restored to her proper situation. Her price must be repaid to Cocceius Firmus out of public funds.

And a woman could be sold as a slave to a slave of a slave. Poor misnamed Fortunata was sold to Vegetius about AD100 in what is now Poultry in the City of London.[22] The document follows the standard Roman precedent, even though a slave could not legally own a slave.

More germane to our story, a fragment of a conveyance of land was found at Chew Stoke. I could not believe it when I checked and found that is not a dozen miles west of where we are now.[23] It is only a scrap but just a phrase shows it is based on a Roman law precedent:

> *Ita uti optimo maximoque iure esset* [name missing] *habere recte liceat.*
> The purchaser shall have the legal right to the use of the land to the best and furthest extent the law allows.

---

20. A letter of unknown date speaks of a debt: 'That hundred pounds of sinew from Marinus, I'll settle that. Since you wrote to me about this he has not mentioned it. I have written to you several times that I've bought about 1,000 pecks (*modii*) of grain, so I must have cash. If you don't send me some, at least 500 *denarii*, I am going to lose what I've given as deposit, around 300 *denarii*, and that will be an embarrassment'; AK Bowman, JD Thomas and JN Adams 'Two Letters from Vindolanda' (1990) 21 *Britannia* 33-54, 43-52; *Early English Arbitration* pp237-238.
21. *Digest* 49.15.6. This case's British origin is argued in E Birley *Roman Britain and the Roman Army* Kendal, Titus Wilson 1976 pp51-52, 87-103, Jones pp53-54.
22. RSO Tomlin '"The Girl in Question": a New Text from Roman London' (2003) 34 *Britannia* 41-51.
23. EG Turner 'A Roman Writing Tablet from Somerset' (1956) 46 *Journal of Roman Studies* 115-118, with photograph and transcription.

That meant, in our legal language, the vendor was transferring all his rights in the land, free from encumbrances. The coincidence of language is not accidental: the same words are discussed three times in Justinian's *Digest*.[24]

These scattered fragments show that all over Britannia from the early years of Roman occupation to its end, lawyers and clients were using standard Roman precedents, and specifically here in Bath, if the conveyance originated here.

And there were indigenous lawyers in Britannia, or at least trained advocates. Juvenal, as early as the second century AD, wrote of them:[25]

Fluent Gaul has taught the British advocates.

By that he meant that those who wished to plead in English litigation went to Gaul to the schools which famously taught rhetoric there. Tacitus said the Britons showed a greater aptitude. He says his father-in-law, Agricola, when Governor of Britannia:[26]

Educated the sons of the leading men in the liberal arts and thought more highly of the natural abilities of the Britons than the educated accomplishments of the Gauls.

If ever there was any doubt about the use of Roman models of arbitration in Britannia, it has been dispelled by the discovery of part of an award from the City of London. It is one page originally written in wax on wood, bearing the date 14 March AD114.[27] The skills and scholarship of Roger Tomlin have revealed that the unnamed arbitrator was a surveyor who fixed the boundaries of a wood in Kent in the technical way later described in the *Digest*.

There is just one other find which may throw light on dispute resolution. I am delighted to follow Barry Cunliffe's interpretation of the third-century curse tablet found here. He says it shows that 'another use of the divine power was adjudicating in disputes'. The text reads:[28]

24. 18.1.59, 21.2.75, 50.16.126.
25. Juvenal *Satires* XV 111: *Gallia causidicos docuit facunda Britannos*. The schools ranged from Marseilles in the south, where Tacitus says Agricola himself was educated, *Agricola* 4, to Toulouse, Bordeaux and Trèves; *Early English Arbitration* pp53-54.
26. Tacitus *Agricola* 21.
27. RSO Tomlin 'A Five-Acre Wood in Roman Kent' in Joanna Bird, Mark Hassall and Harvey Sheldon eds *Interpreting Roman London: Papers in Memory of Hugh Chapman* Oxford, Oxbow 1996 pp209-215; *Early English Arbitration* pp50-51.
28. Cunliffe p64: 'Uricalus, Docilosa uxor sua, Docilis filius suus et Docilina, Decentinus frater suus, Alogiosa, nomina eorum qui iuraverunt. Qui iuraverunt ad fontem deae Sulis pridie Idus Apriles quicumque illic periuraverit deae Suli facias illum sanguine suo illud

Uricalus, Docilosa his wife, Docilis his son and Docilina, Decentinus his brother, Aligiosa, the names of those who have sworn an oath. Those who have sworn an oath at the spring of the goddess Sul on 12 April, whichever of them has perjured themselves by doing so, make them satisfy the goddess Sul with their own blood.

I am not sure that Sul was being asked to adjudicate. I guess rather that the parties believed that swearing such an oath would deter all those named from going back on an agreed settlement arising from a mediation or arbitration. The creation of the tablet would fix the promise publicly in everyone's minds.

6. HOW IT MAY HAVE WORKED IN PRACTICE

If you will accept the factual background to be as I have suggested, I hope you will now allow me to attempt to describe how I believe a routine dispute might have been dealt with, by means of a fictional account of a difference between neighbours, Sextus the Roman and Morgan the Briton.[29] On what we know, or think we know, let your imagination loose with mine.

About AD340, Sextus Valerius Latinus retired with the rank of centurion after thirty years' service in the Sixth Legion, his last period served on Hadrian's Wall. He had gathered a nice nest-egg, one way or another. He had made two trips to Bath on rest and recreation leave and fancied retirement there, near enough to the baths to have somewhere to relax and have fun during the dark, cold winters he had just about got used to in his British posting. The community of old soldiers and the prosperous market town and tourist centre, with direct roads to Winchester and London would suit him. After all he was not a Roman, having been born in Gallia Belgica, what is now Northern France. He had only been to Rome twice and disliked its heat, noise and stress. He could never afford a decent house there or live as he had become accustomed. Moreover, he had married a wife, Severa, from quite near his birthplace. They shared the same mother tongue but at home they and their children spoke the vernacular soldiers' Latin. The family had known no other land than Britannia as their home.

So, when he was about to retire in his late forties, he decided he would build a villa as close to town as he could afford but in the heart of the countryside. There were already thirty or more of the kind he aspired to within twenty-five miles of the baths. He acquired some land, of a

satisfacere.'
29. Rereading Cunliffe I see how much I owe to Chapter 8 'The People of Roman Bath' for stimulating my imagination.

decent size, with room for a Roman-style, or rather Roman-colonial-style house, a vegetable garden and orchard. He thought he might try his hand at growing a vine or two, or perhaps using his influence and his pension to promote a local industry, like pewter bowls or curse tablets for tourists.

Sextus had bought the land from a local, Morgan. Morgan had signed his Latin name, Marius Valerius Oceanus, on a document drawn up in the form of a Roman conveyance, like the one from Chew Stoke, in which Morgan said he was the sole owner of the land and conveyed to Sextus all the same rights as he himself had.

Morgan and his extended family lived on adjoining land and the two families were good enough neighbours. His wife, who liked to use her Latin name Claudia, got on well with Severa and the children played together. The two wives usually conversed in vernacular Latin, which Claudia was trying to master, but they found that they could get along in their mother tongues, which were mutually comprehensible but with quite different pronunciations. The rude words were the same. Severa sometimes complained about the British children's nits but all went well until the first floods. Then the rainwater coursed through Morgan's land, which lay higher up, broke through the stone wall Sextus had built on the boundary and washed away his orchard and garden. Sextus suggested that Morgan should make a culvert to take future floods away and pay for the damage. Morgan said he was not at fault. If Sextus wanted to keep away the flood, a natural phenomenon, he should build his own defences.

Sextus's first thought was to resort to the imperial administration. What was it for if not to protect people like him? Aquae Sulis may not have had the formal status of a municipality but it was the centre of administration for a wide area, perhaps subordinate to Winchester. It had its own local councillors. He had access to the office of the Provincial Governor in Londinium, if needs be, and he knew someone who knew a lawyer in Winchester.

Marius Morgan was just as much a Roman citizen as Sextus Valerius, when it suited him. He knew he had the same rights as Sextus. Moreover, he was related to the councillors. His family had been there forever. They knew how to deal with difficult incomers.

Both knew their rights, or thought they did, but each wanted to make sure. So each took advice.

Sextus's lawyer, Gaius, explained to him that Morgan was not liable for water flowing from his land unless he had changed the natural use. He cited the authority of Ulpian, who wrote in the early years of the third century that there was no action if the water caused damage naturally.[30] Of course, if Sextus could show that Morgan had altered the flow of water,

---

30. Ulpian *Edict* 53 (*Digest* 39.3).

perhaps by digging a trench or building an obstruction, it would not be the water but the change of use that caused the damage and Sextus might have a case. He would first have to make a complaint to the two local councillors charged with responsibility for civil disputes, the *duoviri iuri dicundo*. He doubted whether the local military commandant would be interested but it might be worth a try. It would all cost money.

Morgan sought advice from an architect he knew. There were plenty of professional architects and surveyors working in Bath at this time.[31] Lucius had been trained as an apprentice in Londinium and had acquired some legal learning and liked to display it. He knew nothing of Ulpian but he consulted one of his textbooks and quoted first Frontinus, who wrote in the second century AD. He read out:[32]

> A dispute arises about the flow of rainwater. If accumulated rainwater cuts across a boundary and flows onto adjoining land, and a conflict arises, that is an ordinary legal matter. But if it is about the position of the boundary itself, that needs a surveyor and no legal dispute arises.

'Fine', interrupted Morgan, 'but we're not arguing about the boundary.' Lucius scrolled down a bit and found a passage in Agennius Urbicus, who wrote a commentary on Frontinus:[33]

> A dispute about keeping rainwater out ... arises in different ways in different regions ... in Italy or some other provinces it is no slight wrong if you send water onto another's land, nor in Africa if you stop it flowing.

'Yes', said Morgan, 'But we're not in Africa. What can you tell me that's relevant to here and now?' 'Did you say there was a party wall?' asked Lucius. 'Vitruvius, my first student textbook, has something to say on that. Did you know he worked for Julius Caesar?' 'Really?' said Morgan. Undeterred, Lucius found the passage and read:[34]

> So when arbitrators are appointed for party walls, they do not value them at the cost of building but they find the contracts for their construction and deduct one eightieth for each year's depreciation – payment is due on the balance – and they are thereby pronouncing

31. Cunliffe p99.
32. Brian Campbell *The Writings of the Roman Land Surveyors* London, Society for the Promotion of Roman Studies 2000 (Campbell) p9.
33. Campbell p21.
34. Vitruvius *On Architecture* 2.8.8.

an award that they cannot last for more than 80 years. But there is no deduction on brick walls so long as they are standing straight.

'Our wall was stone but never mind about party walls, what was that about arbitration?' said Morgan. 'That's an idea' Lucius agreed, 'why don't you try it out on Sextus?' 'Will it cost me a lot of money?' 'Probably not'. 'Can you arrange it?' 'I'll try', said Lucius.

Meanwhile Sextus had approached the local authority and been referred to the *duoviri*. He found them to be polite and ready to hear his case. He also discovered both were Morgan's uncles. So he decided to put his case to Gaius Severius Emeritus, the centurion in charge of the region, as he styled himself.[35] Emeritus had no jurisdiction over a civil matter such as this. He had plenty of experience, though, and no little wisdom. 'Get yourselves an arbitrator, soldier, and don't waste your money or your prospects of a tranquil life. It's just not worth it. I'll do it if you like.'

So when Lucius approached Sextus with an offer to go to arbitration, Sextus accepted and suggested Emeritus. Sextus did not want to offend the locals he would have to live with. Morgan knew that there would be trouble if he got across the imperial authorities. He was also shrewd. He knew Emeritus by reputation and guessed that he would be astute enough not to show bias in favour of a fellow centurion. A date was fixed.

Any free person, citizen or not, male or female, could make a binding arbitration agreement, called a *compromissum*, submitting most civil disputes to a single arbitrator, chosen by the parties. Both parties agreed to pay the same penalty each to the other if they failed to submit to and participate fully in the arbitration and to comply with the award. The authorities would enforce payment of the penalty against a party who defaulted.[36] But there was no need to make a *compromissum*, which would cost lawyers' fees. The parties could put themselves in the hands of someone they trusted, a good man, as the Romans called him. This *bonus vir* was not thought of as free of ties to either side or without knowledge of the background. On the contrary, he was chosen because he was the friend of both sides and knew what they were like and something of the circumstances.

So that is what Sextus and Morgan did. Their wives approved and their children were relieved. They had all been to the theatre a couple of weeks back to see a modernised production of a classical play about true love

---

35. Cunliffe p130.

36. When Agricola was governor of Britannia the authority on arbitration law, Javolenus Priscus, was his *legatus iuridicus*, acting not only as his legal adviser but his deputy in charge of the administration of justice. He is one of the earliest authorities represented in the *Digest*, which quotes him often, e.g. 4.8.39.1.

thwarted by a family feud and it had made an impression on two of the teenagers.

All the family turned up to the hearing, held in Emeritus's chamber. Sextus and Morgan told their stories in their own words, Morgan's Latin being no more than adequate but Sextus making no attempt at rhetoric, which he had always privately despised.

Emeritus asked them whether they had anything more to say. Then he asked whether anyone else had anything to add. No one said anything. So Emeritus gave his advice. He referred to Morgan by his Latin name, Marius, throughout.

I have nothing but goodwill towards you all. I know Marius and his family well as law-abiding and loyal citizens, whose qualities have been noted by the imperial authorities for generations. Sextus I know by reputation as a fine soldier and leader of men, who left the legion with the highest commendation and I have heard nothing against any of his family. I am therefore sad to see contention between the two families and will be happy if I can be of assistance in restoring harmony.

Two matters cause you concern, both arising from the unusually heavy rains some months ago. The first is the destruction by flood waters flowing from Marius's land of Sextus's gardens and other incidental damage. The second is how best to avoid similar damage in future.

Sextus has told me in detail of the damage to his gardens and orchard. Marius has not seriously questioned the extent. The newly-planted orchard was partially destroyed with the loss of 12 apple trees and six pears, most of the cherries and six experimental vines. All the vegetables were lost but they would probably not have survived the severe winter, even without the floods.

The floods broke down what you have both called the party-wall but the stone is still there. I had a look at the site. It is clear that there should be some kind of wall and culvert there to prevent similar damage when the next floods come. That needs expert advice, which could lead to an improved structure which would provide controlled irrigation to the advantage of both farms, even in normal circumstances.

My proposal, therefore is this: Marius, you and your family have farms all round Aquae Sulis. It would cost you little to find better saplings, from stronger local stock, than Sextus could buy on the open market. Find him 12 apples and 6 pears. May they flourish as a sign of the restored cooperation between your families.

Sextus, get the architect Lucius to work out how to handle the water. He seems to know a lot about rainwater. Each of you pay half of his fees – which will also be his fair reward for bringing you together in this arbitration, which costs you nothing and saves you much. The stones are there. If more are needed, they are at Sextus's expense but Marius, you must find enough labour to supplement Sextus's garden slaves and a supervisor to satisfy you both that the work is of the required standard. Refer to me any matter of uncertainty or difference between you.

Finally, within one month, at a time convenient to all, you will both invite my wife and me to a party – on the boundary if the weather is fine. Each of you, Sextus and Marius, shall provide two amphoras of good wine. I shall send you two fat lambs.

If you agree to this settlement there will be no need for me to swear an oath and proceed to a formal award. The settlement will be put in writing by my clerk and you both will sign it before witnesses. Each of you will have a copy and another will be kept in my office.

Morgan and Sextus agreed and all lived happily ever after. But they did not leave it at that. They had their written binding settlement. Sextus and Morgan vied to provide the better wine and they had a merry party. The two teenagers 'came to an understanding', shall we say. But the wives insisted on just a little ceremony, which fitted both their old traditions, Roman and Belgic. They paid half each for a little pewter tablet which read:

Sextus, Severa his wife, Titus and Aelius his sons and Marcia his daughter, and Marius, Claudia his wife, Decius his son and Helena and Maia his daughters, the names of those who have sworn an oath. Those who have sworn an oath at the spring of the goddess Sul on 10 April, whichever of them perjured themselves by doing so, make them satisfy the goddess Sul with their own blood.

What a pity that tablet is still to be found!

If nothing else, I hope this little flight of fancy, mixed with bits of other scholars' careful work, will put to rest Lindsey Davis's Falco's unforgivable insult to Bath:[37]

37. Lindsey Davis *The Silver Pigs* London, Arrow 2000 p139; but see now her *A Body in the Bath House* 2002 and *The Jupiter Myth* 2003 both London, Arrow Books for Falco's later experiences in Britannia.

At Aquae Sulis I spent five weeks.... Hot springs gushed out of the rock at a shrine where puzzled Celts still came to dedicate coinage to Sul ... There was that furtive atmosphere of commerce disguised as religion which always hangs around shrines .... Oh there were plans, but there always are plans .... I could not believe that anything could ever be made of this place.

But that was in the early AD70s. How wrong he has been proved to be!

First published in (2011) *Revista Română de Arbitraj* 29-39. Reproduced by kind permission of both the original publisher (the National Chamber of Commerce and Industry of Romania) and the current publisher of the journal (Wolters Kluwer).

4. THE LIFE AND DEATH OF THE *COMPROMISSUM*

Derek Roebuck[1]

ABSTRACT

It is often assumed and sometimes argued that Civil Law and practice have had little or no effect on the development of the Common Law, in particular the law of arbitration. To show that to be untrue, the use, development and decline of the *compromissum* in Roman law, in France and for centuries in England are described and compared, relying on primary sources.

1. INTRODUCTION

Whenever people have disputes which they cannot resolve themselves, they tend to look to a third party for help. Unless that third party can get them to agree, they need some form of adjudication, usually arbitration unless they live in a state which offers them litigation. Even if litigation is available, they may still prefer arbitration but only if the state will both enforce ... the agreement to cooperate in the arbitration and abide by the resulting award.

The histories of both civil law and common law illustrate how the problem of enforceability has dominated the relations between arbitration and the state legal systems which, until modern times, did not provide an adequate machinery for the enforcement of simple mutual promises. The courts would not enforce a contract to place a dispute before arbitrators, whether that dispute had already arisen or not, nor to do whatever was necessary for a satisfactory hearing, nor to comply with an award. Those who wanted to make a binding arbitration agreement needed to resort to something other than a simple contract. There is sufficient evidence from both civil and common law jurisdictions to show how lawyers helped

---

1. Senior Associate Research Fellow, Institute of Advanced Legal Studies, University of London; editor, *Arbitration*.

those who wished to have their dispute arbitrated. One method was the *compromissum*, a creature of Roman law and practice.

The purpose of this essay is to discover whether there is any connection or even contemporaneity between the development and decay of the *compromissum* in the civil law and common law. The evidence is positive and starts early.[2]

2. THE *COMPROMISSUM* IN CLASSICAL ROMAN LAW

For Roman law, a tablet from Herculaneum records an arbitration agreement from the first century AD. It was a *pactum* made by *stipulatio*:[3]

> In the dispute between L Cominius Primus and L Appuleius Proculus about the boundaries of the Numidian land of L Cominius Primus and the Stlasanician land of L Appuleius Proculus, as to which L Cominius Primus and L Appuleius Proculus each in turn in respect of this dispute it is to be written ... in respect of that dispute they have by stipulation and pact agreed as follows: that Ti. Crassius Firmus should be arbiter *ex compromisso* between L Cominius Primus and his heir and L Appuleius Proculus and his heir and should render his award or order his award to be rendered, openly in his presence and in the presence of each other, before the first day of February next, and may postpone that day when he renders his award or orders it to be rendered or orders it to be postponed, and if anything shall be done or fail to be done, against these agreements, 1,000 sesterces of good money shall be properly paid, fraud being absent from this matter and arbitration and to be so in the future.

That was a classical *compromissum*, a formal stipulation promising to submit the boundary dispute to a named arbitrator. It provided for either party to pay the same substantial penalty if it failed to cooperate in the arbitration or abide by the award.

'Roman law never recognised the principle of freedom of contract'.[4] Even as late as Justinian's time, the law did not enforce a simple agreement

2. Such evidence as there is allows the tentative assumption that the Roman colonial legal system applied *mutatis mutandis* in Britannia and that the *compromissum* was part of it, Derek Roebuck *Early English Arbitration* (Oxford: HOLO Books 2008) p31. But there is no evidence of any survival into Anglo-Saxon times.
3. Derek Roebuck and Bruno de Loynes de Fumichon *Roman Arbitration* (Oxford: HOLO Books, 2004) pp115-16 citing *Tabulae Herculanenses* 76. A similar penalty clause is preserved in *Tabulae Herculanenses* 81.
4. René David *L'Arbitrage dans le Commerce International* (Paris: Economica 1981) [David] p118.

to go to arbitration.[5] Nor could damages be claimed for failing to perform an award. But throughout the history of Roman law a mutual promise – *com-promissum* – could be made to do the job. Each party must have made the necessary solemn promise – *stipulatio* – to submit their dispute to a named arbitrator and cooperate in the arbitration and comply with the award, or pay a penalty which was the same for both sides if they failed. Roman law enforced the penalty not the arbitration agreement. The penalty fell due automatically unless a condition was fulfilled: that condition was performance of the arbitration agreement.

According to the Roman law classification of contracts, *compromissum* was a *pactum*, one of a category perhaps originally conceptualised as pacts which brought together in peace, *pax*, the victim and perpetrator of a wrong.[6] Its essential elements were: details of the dispute; names of the parties; the appointment of an arbitrator; an agreement between the arbitrator and the parties (and their heirs) to render an award by a fixed date; a penalty clause with the elements: 'A has stipulated 1,000 sesterces of good money. B has promised the same'.

It was that penalty clause which made the agreement enforceable. The court would enforce payment of the penalty if the agreement was broken by either party. It would not give damages for breach of contract. When any of the terms of the *compromissum* was broken and the state became involved, the *iudex* did not concern himself with the award but merely imposed the penalty which the parties themselves had stipulated. The penalty gave the parties a level of security they fixed for themselves, because they could choose whatever penalty they wanted and could agree upon. That level was usually high.

3. THE *COMPROMISSUM* IN LATER CIVIL LAW

That form of submission of a dispute to arbitration was taken up by the Christian church. It was a sin to break a promise made by oath. The Church sometimes threatened excommunication of those who broke their faith.[7] But an unpaid penalty was a debt. All the evidence seems to show that the *compromissum* was widely used and worked well in both lay and ecclesiastical courts.[8] It became standard in the civil law

---

5. But as sharp a mind as Pomponius thought it should be and the reforming emperor Justinian tried to introduce it by legislation.

6. It was contrasted with another form of negotiated settlement, *transactio*, which was not a pact but fell into the class of innominate contracts, whose validity required a *causa*, not quite the equivalent of consideration in the common law.

7. RH Helmholz *The Oxford History of the Laws of England I: The Canon Law and Ecclesiastical Jurisdiction from 597 to the 1640s* (Oxford: Oxford UP 2004) p165. Giulio Vismara *La Giuridizione Civile dei Vescovi (Secoli I-IX)* Milan: Giuffrè 1995.

8. Anne Lefebvre-Teillard 'L'Arbitrage en Droit Canonique' (2006) *Revue de l'Arbitrage* 5.

jurisdictions of Western Europe, where arbitration provided an answer to disputing parties 'despairing of knowing before which authority to bring their suits'.[9]

An Ordinance of François II (husband of Mary, Queen of Scots) of August 1560 was intended to support arbitration. It made arbitration obligatory for mercantile disputes, '*différends entre marchands pour fait de leur commerce*', and it put difficulties in the way of appeals against awards. It made their arbitration agreements binding without a penalty clause. But the general law was that a party could appeal against the award unless the *compromissum* included a *rato manente pacto* clause.

My favourite French authority provides a precedent from seventeenth-century France:[10]

COMPROMISE

The undersigned have come to an agreement as follows to terminate amicably the proceedings commenced or to be commenced between them concerning the execution of ....   & for that purpose
Mr   of   has named as arbitrator Mr   of   ; and
Mr   of   has named as arbitrator Mr   of   and for third arbitrator they have agreed on Mr   of   .

And the said parties will take instructions from their arbitrators to produce to them within   [days] each and every of their documents and will deposit for this purpose the sum of   to be forfeited in case of appeal to the one who acquiesces in the award; with every power that they give to the aforesaid arbitrators to judge and award; desiring that their award should be executed according to the provisions of the Ordinance ....

If you like, you can then deliver the compromise to a notary to be put in proper form .... You can add to or subtract from the compromise ... or the summons to arbitration ... whatever you consider appropriate according to the usage and the style of that part of the country where the parties are.

Furthermore, the shorter and simpler the compromise the better. It will often be more trouble to draft a compromise to suit the objections

9. Marc Bloch *Feudal Society* (Chicago: U of Chicago P 1961) p359; Yves Jeanclos 'La Pratique de l'Arbitrage du XIIe au XVe Siècle: Eléments d'Analyse' (1999) *Revue de l'Arbitrage* 417.
10. Derek Roebuck *The Charitable Arbitrator: How to Mediate and Arbitrate in Louis XIV's France* (Oxford: HOLO Books 2002) p231, facsimile of original text pp145-146.

of the parties, who so easily get excited, than to judge the substance
of the matter.

Though this appears to show that the penalty was merely and specifically
for breach of the agreement not to appeal against the award, that
cannot be assumed. The penalty still fell due for failure to cooperate in
the proceedings, or abide by the award, by resorting to litigation. The
ordonnances insisted on a party paying the penalty before resorting to
the courts.

An insight into the processes of change can be gained from a French
textbook of the middle of the 18th century:[11]

> Despite the penal clauses and stipulations inserted in agreements in
> default of performance, the judges, who consider them almost always
> as mere threats, usually either give the party some time to repair the
> default by speedy payment, or they fix the damages and interests
> according to the circumstances. One should also point out that the
> penalty for default in *compromis* and arbitrations has no place within
> the jurisdiction of the Parlement of Toulouse and one is never ordered
> to pay it, even when the sum has been deposited and put in the hands
> of third parties. That has been decided by many judgments ....[12] It
> is otherwise in Paris, Bordeaux and other places, where anyone who
> refuses to obey an arbitral award is subject to the penalty in default and
> must pay it before being able to appeal, according to the Ordinance
> of François II of August 1560, which has not been confirmed by the
> Parlement of Toulouse.

Claude Serres was a professor of French law in Montpellier who was
trying to reconcile the practice in the south of France with new legislation
and the practice in Paris.

What was just beginning to take its place was the *clause
compromissoire*, the arbitration agreement, which provided that *future*
disputes were to be arbitrated. That, of course, is what modern business
requires. The reservation of the *compromissum* for disputes that have
occurred and of the *clause compromissoire* for those in the future is
not logically necessary. There is no intrinsic difficulty in drafting a

---

11. Claude Serres *Les Institutions du Droit Français* (Paris: Cavelier 2nd edn 1760) p465.
This period is fully described in Jean Hilaire 'L'Arbitrage dans la Période Moderne (XVIe-
XVIIIe Siècle)' (2000) *Revue de l'Arbitrage* 187.
12. Here Serres lists his authorities. The provincial Parlements opposed arbitration because
it reduced their jurisdiction and with it their revenues. The same is said of the judges in
England but without justification, Derek Roebuck 'The Myth of Judicial Jealousy' (1994)
10 *Arbitration International* 395.

compromissum to deal with disputes which have not yet occurred, nor a *clause compromissoire* for existing ones. But that had so much become the practice that the distinction seemed natural. As the author of *The Charitable Arbitrator* warned, though, to get disputing parties to agree the terms of a *compromissum* could be harder than to get them to agree to a settlement of the dispute itself.

As with so many aspects of French life and law, it was the Revolution of 1789 which made a qualitative change. The idealists of the French Revolution favoured arbitration, which they linked with freedom of contract, with freedom generally and with their antipathy against the Parlements as part of the old regime.[13] The 1793 Constitution created public arbitrators, annually elected, to do the work of the civil courts of first instance. But within a few years there was reaction and the Civil Procedure Code 1806 discouraged arbitration by requiring the formality of an *exequatur* from the court before an award became enforceable. The English prejudice against 'ousting the jurisdiction of the courts' became in French '*une* éviction *des tribunaux, contraire à une saine conception de la justice*', 'a displacement of the courts, contrary to a healthy conception of justice'.[14]

The Cour de Cassation decided in 1843 that a simple *clause compromissoire* was invalid. It must name the arbitrators. That, it pronounced with scant regard for reason or experience, would stop thoughtless parties from foolishly placing their trust in arbitrators who were neither capable nor worthy. Soon the case law allowed such clauses in international trade and later in all commercial contracts but the invalidity in other matters was preserved in the Civil Code of 1972 Article 2061:

> *La clause compromissoire est nulle s'il n'est disposé autrement par la loi.*

An arbitration clause is invalid unless legislation provides otherwise.

It is not until 1981 and the new Civil Procedure Code that a clear change in policy can be seen.[15] The modern law is found in Book IV, Articles 1442 to 1486. Article 1442 defines a *clause promissoire* as 'an agreement by which the parties to a contract bind themselves to submit to arbitration disputes which may arise in relation to that contract'. Article 1433

---

13. J.-J. Clère 'L'Arbitrage Révolutionnaire: Apogée et Déclin d'une Institution (1790-1806)' (1981) *Revue de l'Arbitrage* 5; Carine Jallamion 'Arbitrage et Pouvoir Politique en France du XVIIe au XIXCe Siècle' (2005) *Revue de l'Arbitrage* 3.

14. David p128.

15. Jean Robert *L'Arbitrage: Droit Interne et Droit Internationale Privé* (Paris: Dalloz 6th edn 1993) Annexe 3.

requires it to be in writing, either in the main contract or another which refers to it.

Article 1447 defines *compromis* as 'an agreement by which the parties to an existing dispute submit it to the arbitration of one or more persons'.[16] It must be in writing. There is no mention of a penalty. The *compromis* seems in practice to have fallen now into desuetude. One survey supported the: 'unquestionable conclusion that arbitration by *compromis* was of very little importance in the whole scheme of dispute resolution and its tiny quantitative share ought to lead to an admission of failure of arbitration by *compromis*'.[17]

4. THE EARLY DEVELOPMENT OF THE *COMPROMISSUM* IN ENGLAND

Until well after the Norman Conquest litigation was handled in the courts of shire and hundred. There the whole community validated the decision, whether it was a judgment of the assembly or an award of arbitrators. In 1087, the Domesday Commissioners received a report which explained how that worked. In a dispute over the ownership of land in the shire court, Bishop Geoffrey wrote:[18]

This was established and sworn before me and before Urse de Abetot, Osbern son of Escrop, and the other barons of the king, the whole shire making the decision (*judicante*) and bearing witness.

With the birth of the common law at the end of the twelfth century the jurisdiction of the royal courts expanded but that jurisdiction was not claimed to be general. Indeed, the judges were careful to insist on its limits. They were not concerned with everyday transactions. Enforcement of them could be left where it had always been, [with] the relevant community, whether local or trade or church or guild. If you wanted your contract to be enforceable by the state, the royal courts would help you

16. David neatly describes the law and practice in other Western European jurisdictions pp129-148.

17. Bruno Oppetit *Théorie de l'Arbitrage* (Paris: PUF 1998) pp97-98. I have not yet been able to consult what may be the most recent and authoritative text: Eric Loquin *Compromis et Clause Compromissoire* (Paris: Fascicules Jurisclasseur de Procédure Civile: Arbitrage Fascicule 1020 2009). All that I know about the history of the *compromissum* in France has been explained to me by my friend Bruno de Loynes de Fumichon but he cannot be blamed for my remaining invincible ignorance. His yet unpublished paper *L'Arbitrage, Droit Naturel a Valeur Constitutionelle, Pendant la Décennie Révolutionnaire (1789-1799)* says it all so much better.

18. RC Van Caenegem *English Lawsuits from William I to Richard I* I (1990) 106 Selden Society no15D p39; Derek Roebuck *Early English Arbitration* (Oxford: Holo Books 2008) p207.

only if you made it in one of the acceptable forms. In this the English government acted exactly as the Roman had done.

By the fourteenth century the common law courts would enforce debts but would accept only one form of proof of a contract: a deed.[19] The common law did not concern itself with what was in the document, so long as it was written, sealed and delivered. [Either] the agreement was ...a 'covenant', as a contract by deed came to be called, or its enforcement was left to some other tribunal. That did not mean that the judges turned a blind eye to such agreements. They did not say they were invalid. They just refused to enforce them. That discrimination may now look like a technical quibble but then it was as natural as the urge of lawyers to get round it, particularly when they could find no other adequate means of enforcement or the validity of the contract came to be considered during the course of proceedings brought on some other ground, as arbitration agreements sometimes were, for example in an attempt to bar litigation.

There is plenty of evidence of arbitration from the early thirteenth century and of the recognition of awards by the courts. The word *compromittere* is regularly used[20] but there is no sign of a penalty.

It has often been asserted that the English common law grew quite independently of Roman law influences. Much is made of the different legal system in another part of the United Kingdom, Scotland. It is true that Scotland has always had its own law and that its common law took more from Roman law, directly and overtly, than English did. Its founding text is *Regiam Majestatem*, possibly compiled as early as 1230, which was largely based on the first great English text, commonly called *Glanvill*, written 1187-1189.[21]

A clue to a still prevalent misunderstanding may be found in an inadequate translation of the bit of *Regiam Majestatem* which deals with the effect of an arbitration. It is based not upon *Glanvill* but is an addition to the text taken from contemporary ecclesiastical law and practice.[22] The edition and translation is Lord Cooper's. He says in his introduction (p27):

> The excursus on Arbitration has a much better background ....Though in this case also the rules are formulated on the basis of Roman and

19. Derek Roebuck *The Background of the Common Law* (Hong Kong: Oxford UP 2nd edn 1990) pp93-98 explains shortly the development of the common law of contract.
20. E.g. CT Flower ed *Introduction to the Curia Regis Rolls* (1944) 62 Selden Society pp292, 417, 461-462.
21. Lord Cooper ed *Regiam Majestatem and Quoniam Attachiamenta* (1947) 11 Stair Society. GDG Hall ed *Tractatus de Legibus et Consuetudinibus Regni Angliae qui Glanvilla Vocatur* (London: Nelson 1965) [*Glanvill*] plx thinks little of Cooper's edition: 'there is no modern scholarly edition'.
22. Peter Stein 'The Source of the Romano-Canonical Part of Regiam Majestatem' (1969) 48 *Scot Hist Rev* 107.

Canonist texts, the treatment is more practical, and it is reasonable to assume that the writer knew from experience what he was talking about.

If that is right, the practice in Scotland then was to make use of the *compromissum* and the penalty was essential. The first ten chapters of Book II relate to arbitration. Chapter 8 is headed 'On the Effect of an Arbitral Award' and reads:

> The effect of arbitrations is that the awards of arbitrators should have force whether or not they are fair, so long as they have been seriously declared and are not against the laws and the arbiter is not guilty of fraud and the arbitration is validated by some penalty. If it is not validated by a penalty but by the agency of an oath or solemn promise, it is valid according to canon law but is not binding according to the laws of the realm.

Cooper translates the last clause: 'it will be valid by the canon law but not by the law of the realm'. That is not quite right. The Latin says clearly that the award is *valid* under canon law but is not *binding* by the laws of the land: '*secundum iura canonica valet sed secundum leges regni non tenet*'. That distinction is vital and illuminates all the subsequent development of the medieval law in England. It was not that the English common law courts refused to recognise the *validity* of arbitration agreements: they refused to enforce them – in the royal courts they did not *bind*.

5. ROYAL COURTS AND COVENANT

Glanvill did not deal directly with arbitration. He allowed actions for debt only if the evidence was in the required form:[23]

> When the debtor appears in court on the appointed day, if the creditor does not have either a gage or sureties or any proof other than the debtor's expression of good faith, that is not evidence in the king's court. Of course, any breach of, or offence against, good faith can found an action in a church court.

He makes it clear that the royal court would not allow an action in contract, even where a gage had been pledged:[24]

---

23. '*Verumptamen de fidei lesione vel transgressione inde agi poterit in curia christianitatis.*' I prefer to take both *lesione* and *transgressione* with *fidei*, compare GDG Hall *Glanvill* X 12, p126, who does not translate *vel transgressione* at all.
24. *Glanvill* X.8.

On this it should be noted that the king's court does not usually protect or warrant this kind of private agreement either about giving and receiving things as pledges or other similar agreements, whether made out of court or even in other courts than the king's court. Therefore, if they are not performed, the king's court will not interfere.

He confirms this clear disavowal of jurisdiction in concluding his chapter X 'On Pleas of the Debts of Lay Persons':[25]

So we deal briefly with the said contracts which arise from the consent of private persons because, as said before, the king's court does not usually protect private agreements, nor does the king's court interfere with even such contracts as may be deemed to be similar to private agreements.

Agreements to arbitrate arise from private agreement. *Glanvill* could hardly have made it clearer that the royal court wanted no truck with them. The parties must be taken to have deliberately chosen to keep them private.

Yet trade was growing. The ordinary routines of commerce must have been based on simple, private agreements without the formality of a deed. Trade uses executory contracts, those made by mutual promises of future conduct: 'I will pay if you deliver' in exchange for 'I will deliver if you will pay'. And the remedy which both buyer and seller wanted must have been a sum of money awarded as damages as soon as possible after that contract was broken, so that the disappointed party could find another buyer or seller. Although for centuries there had been other courts which enforced such contracts, some parties must have seen advantages in trying to get the royal court involved, once they were broken.

The settlement of a dispute, whether by agreement, mediated or otherwise, or by an award of an arbitrator, might be made enforceable by having the king's court make a concord. The fees the court could charge for its services might make such jurisdiction attractive. But how could an agreement to arbitrate a present or future dispute be made enforceable? How could the king's court be persuaded to help? The answer was to insist on the formalities of what came to be called a 'covenant'. If a contract were of sufficient importance to justify an agreement to arbitrate, it should not be too much trouble to write it down and add the parties' seals. At first these 'private agreements' might be enforced in the king's courts. In the earliest records of the work of the king's courts there are instances of actions on an agreement without more, *de placito*

25. *Glanvill* X.18.

conventionis, where *conventio* just meant 'agreement' and had not yet
acquired the technical meaning 'covenant'. The earliest Curia Regis
Rolls contain enough examples, though none of them mention arbitration
directly. From 1199:[26]

> Norfolk. A day has been given to the Abbot of Dirham and Roger
> Buch' on a plea of agreement (*conventionis*) ... and meanwhile they
> may have a licence to make a concord.

The need for a deed was not clear until the thirteenth century.[27] Thereafter,
agreements to arbitrate were enforced as covenants, if they complied
with the formal requirements for a contract under seal, sometimes called
a 'specialty'. In 1312, John Cooper and his wife Alice brought an action
about rights in land against Isabel Delgod. The Coopers' counsel pleaded
that a part of the dispute had been the subject of an arbitration. The report
does not make it clear whether it was the arbitration agreement or the
award which they wanted to put in evidence. Bereford CJ would not
allow an oath to be evidence of an arbitration. He demanded a deed:[28]

> Bereford CJ: What have you got about this arbitration?
>
> Denham: We're ready to prove it.
>
> Bereford: This is something which depends on a specialty, so no other
> proof is any good.

But in the following year, 1313, in a case from the Eyre of Kent, Staunton
J made it clear that, although a deed always had to be produced if the
claim (or defence) was based on a covenant, that was not required if it
was the award which was pleaded.[29] That need not be incorporated in
a deed. It could and would be proved by an averment, that is evidence
given on oath before a jury.

> Hamo of Beracre was summoned to answer the claim of Thomas Scott
> that he pay him back the thirty pounds he owes him .... Thomas says
> that he and the said Hamo, by a certain indented writing ... submitted
> themselves to the arbitration of William de Hegham, William de
> Nadyngtone, Eudo de Sligh and Ralph de Ensyng of all the disputes
> and demands arisen between them .... If either of them should refuse
> to carry out the award of those arbitrators ... he and his heirs were

---

26. CRR I 94 and also 357 from 1200 and II 35 and 80 from 1201 and 276 from 1203.
27. FW Maitland *Bracton's Note Book* (London: Clay 3 vols 1887) 1.186 in 1222?
28. *Cooper v Delgod* YBB 5 Ed II (1312), (1916) 33 *Selden Society* 175-80.
29. *Scot v Beracre* YBB 6 Ed II (1313), (1912) 27 *Selden Society* 23.

obliged by the same writing, on the testimony of the said arbitrators, to pay the said thirty pounds forthwith after the arbitration, and the other party would be free of all claims and demands .... On the basis of the said submission, the arbitrators arbitrated and awarded the said Thomas fifteen pounds for his actions and demands in full satisfaction of all his claims and pronounced their award .... Hamo refused to pay the fifteen pounds; therefore ... Thomas is now entitled to an action for the thirty pounds ... and offers a certain writing.

Hamo admitted the writing was his deed, *factum*, but denied that the arbitrators had pronounced the award as pleaded. He asked that this question of fact be decided by a jury, *ponit se super patriam*, and Thomas did the same.[30]

So there shall be a jury and the sheriff is ordered to make the arbitrators come. And later they made a concord.

That is the account preserved in Latin on the roll. The agreed settlement means that there was no judgment to record but there are two Year Book reports of the arguments of the five counsel. They are quite full, in Law French, with the interventions of two judges, and give a fresh picture of how such matters were dealt with.

This arbitration agreement, the earliest to be treated at length in the Year Books, was in the form of a Roman law *compromissum*. But would that cause problems with the law of usury? In the following excerpt, Malmerthorpe and Friskeney were the plaintiff's counsel, Stonore, Passeley and Westcote the defendant's; Staunton and Spigurnel JJ the judges:

Stonore: He asks for this debt on the basis of a submission that we made to an arbitration of four etc but he has nothing from this arbitration which would found a cause of action, and we ask for judgment.

Malmerthorpe: We have put before you a deed by which you submitted to the above arbitration and you have not denied at all that they arbitrated; and we ask for judgment.

Staunton J: You are not in a church court here where everything you plead must be in writing. [Another report has the judge say:[31] 'You are not in a church court where the award, *sentence*, must be in writing, but you are under the law of the land, in which it is enough to prove the award by oath, *suffit daverer larbitrement*.]

30. *Scot v Beracre* YBB 6 Ed II (1313), (1912) 27 *Selden Society* 24.
31. *Scot v Beracre* YBB 6 Ed II (1313), (1912) 27 *Selden Society* 27.

Stonore: He specified his cause of action on two things, the submission and the award. He has nothing to show of the award, neither a deed nor evidence from the testimony of the arbitrators that they made an award.

Malmerthorpe: We are not asking for the money which the arbitrators awarded, the fifteen pounds, but the thirty pounds which you are bound to pay if you do not abide by the award.

Passeley: The debt you are asking for is like a penalty ....

Friskeney: We are basing our claim on your own deed for evidence and not as a penalty for [non-payment of] a debt. This is not a case about usury.

Staunton J: Answer that!

Stonore: There would seem to be another reason why we do not have to reply to that. They say that the arbitrators awarded that he owed fifteen pounds ... but they cannot put in the award.

Spigurnel J: The deed itself acts instead of an acquittance of what you submitted to.

Stonore: Again they do not deserve an answer, because the deed which you have put before the court is evidence of nothing more than that we submitted to arbitration and agreed that, if either party refused to abide by the award, as evidenced by the arbitrators, etc. But the arbitrators have never provided or published such evidence, so we cannot have dissented from their award.

[The deed which evidenced this was read out]

Friskeney: Does he agree that there has been an award?

Spigurnel J: No he does not, because he says there is no evidence of any award being pronounced by the arbitrators, so how could they refuse to abide by it?

Westcote: If they made their award privately, that is like working out your judgment among yourselves, where even if you have decided everything of your judgment it is no judgment until it is delivered. And so it is here.

Malmerthorpe: They did arbitrate but would not listen but went off in defiance.

Stonore: No award was pronounced by the arbitrators.

And so issue was joined, that is the matter was adjourned for the facts to be decided by a jury. But the parties settled; an unsatisfactory conclusion in some ways but it proves the use of the *compromissum* in England in 1313.

6. DEVELOPMENT OF THE ENGLISH *COMPROMISSUM*

The Common Law courts continued to encourage the use of the English equivalent of *arbitrium ex compromisso* by enforcing penal bonds entered into mutually by parties to a dispute, promising to submit to arbitration and abide by the award.[32] The courts of Equity did the same. In *Spynell v Taillour* in 1484 three Lombard merchants brought a bill in Chancery to recover a debt on a bond.[33] The wording of the bill was faulty so the matter was transferred to King's Bench, where exception was again taken to defects and the case was heard by all the judges in the Exchequer Chamber. The debt arose from a joint and several penal bond to secure arbitration. The defendant, one of the obligees of the bond, said he need not pay because there was no arbitration. The plaintiffs gave evidence of an award ordering another of the obligees to pay by instalments. On this issue a jury of 'mixed tongue', twelve English and twelve foreign, was summoned. The record sets out the bond in full, with the names of the arbitrators (with the Duke of Gloucester as umpire), and also the award in full. The jury found that the award had been made as alleged. They also assessed the plaintiff's damages and costs.

The parties in the Court of Admiralty also often executed a penal bond.[34]

Though Equity later came to relieve those who had entered into penal bonds, it did not do so to allow them to escape from an arbitration agreement. Moreover, such relief was not the creation of Courts of Equity, which it predates by centuries. As early as 1308, Bereford J in *Umfraville v Lonstede*[35] refused to allow a claim for a penalty which was good according to the rules of common law because to do so would be inequitable:

'*Ceo n'est pas purement dette, mes une peyne, et veez par quele equite vous poez demander ceo peyne!*' 'This is not just a debt but a penalty, so look for what equity gives you the right to ask for this penalty!'

He drew back from giving judgment *against* the bond holder, though, contenting himself by telling his counsel that he would not grant him his rights at law even if he kept demanding them for seven years: 'because the judgment of the law should not be done like this'.

---

32. AWB Simpson 'The Penal Bond with Conditional Defeasance' (1966) 82 *Law Quarterly Review* 392-422; Edward Powell 'Arbitration and the Law in England in the Late Middle Ages' (1983) 33 *Transactions of the Royal Historical* Society 5th series 49, 54.
33. (1945) 64 Selden Society 96-101.
34. (1894) 6 Selden Society lxix.
35. (1904) 19 Selden Society 58-59.

The best treatment of the use of the penal bond is still AWB Simpson's. As well as an authoritative statement of the law and practice, it is a masterpiece of English prose, giving joy at every rereading. It deals lucidly and convincingly with the technicalities of pleading and justifies their demands:[36]

The common law made only slight concessions to paternalism .... It was easy enough to execute a bond, and impossible to do so without meaning to do so. Granted that businessmen wish to know where they are, and that the basis on which business is conducted is that bargains are there to be kept, the conditioned bond had obvious attractions. The widespread use of the conditioned bond, both in England and upon the Continent, is only explicable upon the ground that it provided, albeit at the cost of some individual hardship, what the commercial community wanted ....

A remarkable feature of the history of the common law of contract is the fact that although agreements under seal could be sued upon by writ of covenant for damages, in practice the action of covenant was very rarely used; instead people preferred to use the conditioned bond sanctioned by the action of debt .... A plaintiff who sued on a bond put the pleading onus on the defendant.

If the agreement were by *compromissum*, the party wishing to enforce it would merely sue in debt for the penalty. That would force the defendant to plead the existence of the condition – the agreement to go to arbitration and abide by the award – and performance of that condition.

7. A HYBRID JURISDICTION: THE *COMPROMISSUM* IN OXFORD

The University of Oxford had its own jurisdiction, part customary, ecclesiastical but confirmed by royal charter. Its records provide many examples of the use of the *compromissum*.[37] In 1439 the Master and Fellows of the Great Hall of the University of Oxford entered into a *compromissum* with David Clowdysley to stand by the award, decree and arbitration of four arbitrators, with a penalty of 100 shillings.[38] Thirty years later, when the same hall had become 'the Great Hall or University College', its Master and Fellows entered into a *compromissum* with

36. Simpson 411-412.
37. Henry Anstey *Munimenta Academica or Documents Illustrative of Academical Life and Studies at Oxford* (London: Longman 2 vols 1868) [Anstey] provides many examples in their original languages: usually Latin, occasionally French or Middle English
38. Anstey II pp518-519.

Robert Wright, to abide by the award of two Bachelors of Civil Law, penalty twenty pounds.

Though not all the records follow the *compromissum*'s standard form, they disclose that a regular procedure was available, descended from the *compromissum* of Roman law, with great flexibility and, indeed, opportunities for ingenuity.[39] Though the records of awards of the middle of the fifteenth century tend to be in the common, though not too rigid, form of *compromissa*, they allow for descriptions of individual initiatives by resourceful arbitrators.[40]

On 21 July 1452, Thomas Condale, servant of New College, and John Morys, tailor, chose Robert Mason as arbitrator and mediator and promised to abide by his award:[41]

> under a penalty of a hundred shillings, this penalty being stipulated by each of them on each's solemn promise to the other, in case anything of the decision or award of the arbitrator or mediator shall not be obeyed, that the one who does not obey the decision shall incur the penalty of the said stipulation, to be paid effectually to the party who obeys.

8. RULE OF COURT

Lawyers learned to make arbitration agreements binding by having them recognised by a court, which they called 'making them a rule of court'. The practice was for the parties to enrol the *compromissum* in one of the courts, usually the Court of Common Pleas or Nisi Prius, so that any breach would be a contempt, enforceable by an attachment by which the party not in default could have the other imprisoned. The parties had three ways to make their *compromissum* a rule of court. They could put a clause in their submission; they could make a separate memorandum in the presence of one or more witnesses; or, when already in court, they could submit the controversy itself to the foreman or members of the jury. The parties showed their consent by affidavit and the court granted counsel's motion as a matter of course. The award had the force of a judgment without more. A party breached the rule not only by failure to perform the award but also by any act or omission which hindered the arbitrators in making the award. Specifically, it was a breach of the rule to revoke the arbitrators' authority.

---

39. The English language record of the dispute between Thomas Draper and the vicar of St Peter's in the East, above, shows not only that the forms used in Latin were followed when English was preferred but that they were misunderstood. It provided that the penalty should be payable to whichever was the victim of a default – following the standard *compromissum* clause. But there was no question of the penalty being paid to Draper, the only one who could have defaulted. The injured party could only have been the vicar.
40. Anstey II 637-638.
41. See also Anstey II pp712-715.

But in the second half of the 17th century the courts began to question whether such attachments in default should be automatic. In 1670, no less a personage than Sir Matthew Hale, Chief Baron of the Exchequer 1660-71, sitting as an arbitrator, had made his award but it appeared that one party had already revoked the submission. The Court of King's Bench refused to accept that that was a contempt, despite the arbitration agreement having been made a rule of court. They said it was wrong to send men to prison without a hearing.

9. THE FIRST LEGISLATION AND THE DYING OF THE BOND

The Government was not prepared to see arbitration hampered in this way and produced what is called the first Arbitration Act 1697, though there had been legislation before which mentioned arbitration. The preamble proclaims its objects:[42]

> for promoting trade, and rendering the awards of arbitrators the more effectual in all cases, for the final determination of all controversies referred to them by merchants and traders, or others, concerning matters of account or trade, or other matters ....

If the parties made their arbitration agreement a rule of court under the Act, either party after the other's default could enter an affidavit and the court would automatically issue a rule that: 'the parties shall submit to and finally be concluded by the arbitration'. Only proof of fraud or corruption or other such misbehaviour by the arbitrator could be pleaded against enforcement.

But even where the parties made their arbitration agreement a rule of court and thereby enforceable by a court order leading to imprisonment for contempt of it, lawyers knew that it was always better to have a penal bond. That was because the obligation on a bond survived the death of the maker against the estate, while the court order could not be enforced against the dead.[43]

Equity came to relieve debtors of the burden of penal bonds and statute also intervened,[44] but still the *compromissum* with penalty was in common use. Consider this precedent from as late as 1799:[45]

---

42. 9 & 10 Wm and Mary c15; whether the year is stated as 1697 or 1698 depends on the choice of calendar.
43. Matthew Bacon *The Compleat Arbitrator* (Clark, NJ: Lawbook Exchange 2009) p34.
44. E.g. Statute of Fines (1696-1697) 4 & 5 Anne c3 (or 16) and (1705) 8 & 9 William III c11.
45. Stewart Kyd *A Treatise on the Law of Awards* (Clark, NJ: Lawbook Exchange, 2009) p398.

I, AB am held and firmly bound to EF in the sum of £500 of good and lawful money of Great Britain to be paid to EF or to his certain attorney, executors, administrators, or assigns, for which payment I bind myself, my heirs, executors and administrators. The condition of this obligation is that, if AB his heirs etc shall well and truly stand to the award of MN and PQ arbitrators made in writing on or before the – day of – then this obligation be void.

Is it likely that this should be so similar to its Roman and contemporary civil law counterparts unless those who drafted them were carrying on a *practice* which had begun in Rome and was known to them? It is not necessary to show an unbroken handing-down from one lawyer or scribe to another. It is not necessary to show that both drew on a common unbroken teaching tradition. If the same elements are in both, that is some evidence of relationship and possibly of influence, however etiolated. Lawyers drafting documents are much more likely to borrow than invent.

A modern agreement to refer the dispute after it has arisen has only these simple elements: 'By this agreement A and B agree to refer the disputes set out in the schedule to the arbitration of C.' There is no sign of a bond, a condition or a penalty; no mention of heirs or assigns; no good and lawful money; just no echoes at all. But such backward-looking agreements are rare. The modern arbitration agreement is made to deal with future disputes. As early as 1602 *Slade's Case*[46] had made new law. Mutual promises were recognised as sufficient to make a binding contract – an executory contract as it became known – where neither party had yet performed.[47] There was no longer any technical difficulty in enforcing such contracts. That is how the *compromissum* met its death in England. When pleading and procedure had developed to accommodate it, and commercial practice had created the demand, parties and practitioners were able and obliged to produce the modern arbitration agreement, which became standard not only for future disputes but for the tiny number in modern practice which deal with disputes which have already arisen.

10. CONCLUSION

This sketch of the problem is no more than a preliminary skirmish in my struggle to understand the development of the law and practice of

46. (1602) 4 Rep 91; 76 ER 1072. There is a short and simplified treatment in *Background* pp96-7.
47. JH Baker 'New Light on Slade's Case' (1971) 29 *Cambridge Law Journal* 51-67 and 213-36, reprinted in JH Baker *The Legal Profession and the Common Law: Historical Essays* (London: Hambledon P 1986) pp393-432. Also David Ibbetson 'Sixteenth-Century Contract Law: *Slade's Case* in Perspective' (1984) 4 *Oxford Journal of Legal Studies* 293-317.

arbitration in the history of the common law. It will have served its purpose if it causes uncertainty in those who confidently assume that English arbitration law and practice have learned nothing from the civil law and that the common law and civil law are alien and antithetical. But a full treatment of the extent of the influence of Roman law and practice in the development of their English counterparts awaits more research. I would be delighted if the faults in this essay were to provoke a response from readers who share a similar interest in any aspect of the history of dispute resolution in any of the many jurisdictions to which this journal travels.[48]

---

48. My address is roebuck@btinternet.com. [Because of Derek's death, this e-address no longer responds. But the next chapter (5) provides his further thoughts on *compromissum*, perhaps following his invitation here. Any future emails concerning any chapter should be directed to susanna@holobooks.co.uk. – SH]

5. THE ENGLISH *COMPROMISSUM*: WHAT CAN BE LEARNED FROM ITS HISTORY?

Derek Roebuck[1]

1. INTRODUCTION[2]

Last year in this journal I made some preliminary suggestions about the place of the Civil Law formula of the *compromissum* in the development of the law and practice of arbitration in the history of the Common Law.[3] It was hardly enough to dispel the common assumption of lawyers in both systems that English arbitration law and practice learned nothing from the Civil Law and that the Common Law and Civil Law are and always have been fundamentally alien and antithetical. My conviction that a proper understanding of their commonalities is of prime scholarly importance may not be enough to convince others that the effort required to solve the problems is justified. I hope this article will be more persuasive, particularly if it shows that those solutions have some relevance to contemporary practice.

That earlier article showed that the problem of enforceability dominated relations between arbitration and litigation. Courts in the Middle Ages would not enforce a contract to go to arbitration. Those who wanted to make a binding arbitration agreement had to resort to something other than a simple contract. Lawyers in both Civil Law and

---

1. Senior Associate Research Fellow, Institute of Advanced Legal Studies, University of London; editor emeritus, *Arbitration*.
2. This article is based in part on a lecture 'Arbitration, Mediation, Conciliation: Pitfalls of Prescription' delivered at the 2nd International Conference on Law, Language and Professional Practice, Caserta, May 2012 and on chapters of my *Mediation and Arbitration in Medieval England: 1154 to 1558* Oxford, HOLO Books due end 2012. [This was published in 2013 – SH.]
3. Derek Roebuck 'The Life and Death of the *Compromissum*' (2011) 1 *Revista Română de Arbitraj* 29-39. [This essay, 5, 'The English Compromissum', appears not to have been published. It was obviously intended for the same Romanian Arbitration Law Journal. Not only is it on Derek's draft table of contents as such – though, instead of page numbers he has typed '???', but in the paper draft it is in the file marked Romania with the other essays published there. The first paragraph starts, 'Last year in this journal I made some preliminary suggestions'. So, perhaps it was never sent; perhaps it was never received; perhaps his contact on the journal left; I can find no correspondence about it – SH.]

Common Law jurisdictions used the formula of the *compromissum*, inherited from Roman law and practice. This essay continues the enquiry into connections between the development of the *compromissum* in the Civil Law and Common Law, using what later sources tell us to address problems of our own time.[4]

2. ARBITER, ARBITRATOR SEU AMICABILIS COMPOSITOR

It all starts with Justinian's *Digest*:[5]

> The Lex Julia prohibits a *iudex* from accepting appointment as *arbiter* in a matter in which he is *iudex*.

The *iudex* was a person appointed by the praetor, by the Roman state, to try a case to a conclusion according to law. An *arbiter* was appointed by the parties and had discretions which a *iudex* did not. Both *iudex* and *arbiter* were private persons. They needed no legal qualifications. But it would be a contempt for a *iudex* to prefer his own opinion of what was just over the outcome prescribed by the law of the State.

That prohibition never applied in England. There a judge would commonly take a matter away to handle it privately as arbitrator, which included attempting mediation. In France the prohibition continued; but it was not always what the parties wanted, so French lawyers found a way round it. First in Bourgogne in AD1249 and then commonly in the fourteenth century the parties' lawyers would draft the *compromissum* so that the dispute was submitted to an *arbiter*, *arbitrator seu amicabilis compositor*.[6] Huguccio had pointed out at the end of the twelfth century that there was a difference between an *arbiter* and an *arbitrator*.[7]

> So he is not an *arbiter* but an *arbitrans* or *arbitrator* and it is not called an award, *arbitrium*, but a settlement, *arbitratus*, a kind of agreement.

That is the point to keep in mind. The result of the mediation process has never been a judgment imposed on the parties but is always the product of their own agreement. It follows logically that it cannot be appealed

---

4. Derek Roebuck and Bruno de Loynes de Fumichon *Roman Arbitration* (Oxford: HOLO Books, 2004) and Derek Roebuck *Early English Arbitration* (Oxford: HOLO Books 2008) provide evidence of earlier developments.
5. D.4.8.9.2.
6. The story is fully told by Anne Lefèbvre-Teillard '*Arbiter, Arbitrator seu Amicabilis Compositor*' (2008) *Revue de l'Arbitrage* pp369-387 [Lefèbvre-Teillard].
7. Lefèbvre-Teillard pp372-373.

against. The parties must abide by it because that is what they have declared to one another that they wanted.

Of course, the parties may want to leave open the possibilities of an appeal. If they say so, they can make that part of their agreement. It is just a matter of careful drafting. So lawyers invented the phrase *arbiter, arbitrator seu amicabilis compositor* and inserted it into the standard form of *compromissum*. Once there the conservatism of drafters ensured its retention.

They invented another phrase, too, *in alto et basso* in Latin and its equivalents in other languages, 'in high and low' in English, to indicate that first that they intended all forms of dispute resolution to be included. That comprehensiveness was of two kinds.[8] Ducange's great dictionary of medieval Latin is still the best and fullest treatment I can find. It suggests that the primary meaning is 'in whatever jurisdiction, from highest to lowest', *omnimodam jurisdictionem, omnimodam potestatem*; and then only by extension 'unconditional'. I believe that when notaries thought at all about the meaning of the words they were using – and according to where and when they were drafting – they incorporated by this formula the ideas of 'by whatever means of dispute resolution' and 'all disputes of whatever kind now existing between the parties'.

Jurists both civil and canon might argue that a submission must be one thing or the other: either to an arbitrator, *arbiter*, or to a mediator, *arbitrator vel amicabilis compositor*, but the parties were not concerned with such theoretical niceties. Their culture had always known the inclusive process whereby the 'arbitrators', call them what you will, had used every means they could to arrive at a settlement. 'Bottom up' custom prevailed over 'top down' law.

3. ARBITRATION IN ENGLAND IN THE MIDDLE AGES

Today a process has to be either mediation, where a third party is agreed on by the parties to try to bring them to a settlement, whose only force comes from their subsequent agreement; or arbitration, where the third party adjudicates and the parties are bound by their previous agreement to abide by the award. But, in the Middle Ages in England, there was one routine process which everybody then called arbitration, in which the

8. *Alto et basso* is a stock phrase in the medieval *compromissum* in France, Lefèbvre-Teillard p379 and still in mid-15th century England, Henry Anstey *Munimenta Academica, or Documents Illustrative of Academical Life and Studies at Oxford* London, Longmans, Green (Rolls Series) 1868 II [Anstey II] pp550-551 and 637-638. My edition of Ducange is *Glossarium Manuale ad Scriptores Mediae et Infimae Latinitatis ex Magnis Glossariis Caroli du Fresne, Domini du Cange, et Carpentarii etc* Halle, JJ Gebaver's Widow and Son, 1772 I, *sub* ALTUS.

parties asked third parties to help them resolve the dispute by whatever means they could.

Nowadays much is made of the need for mediators and arbitrators to be neutral and impartial. In the United States there are elaborate rules which discourage the appointment of those with previous acquaintance of either party.[9] There is nothing God-given about this. It was not always so. Many societies have preferred what the Greeks called a *koinē*, someone common to both parties, equally the friend of both, or, as in 1344 Pope Clement VI declared himself to be, when acting as mediator between Edward III of England and Philip VI of France: *persona privata et amicus communis*, acting 'in a private capacity and as a friend of both sides'.[10] In the Middle Ages in England it was usually clear by implication and often expressed that the third parties were chosen just because they were already 'friends to both sides'.

Most often, each side appointed two such 'friends'. The four then got together and discussed everything they thought was relevant, not only what we would now divide into matters of fact and law but also anything they knew about the background of the dispute, including the reputations of the parties generally and their families and what was being said in the community about the dispute. They argued and did deals, consulting their parties as appropriate. If they could come to an agreement, they submitted it to the parties. If the parties accepted it, well and good. If not, the 'arbitrators' might make an award.

If the arbitrators were equally divided, with the parties' agreement they would add a fifth arbitrator and try again to come to an agreed award or consent to the determination of the majority. Alternatively, the parties might, at the time of deadlock, or even perhaps by prior agreement when the dispute was first submitted to them, provide for the appointment of an umpire, a single decision-maker substituted for the arbitrators.

However agreement was achieved, the records commonly say that the parties then agreed on the award – with a kiss perhaps, or a feast – but, if one was not happy with the award, it depended on the power of the arbitrators to enforce it. Of course, people then knew the difference between the *concepts* of mediation and arbitration but the *process* they used did not keep them separate. That explains the even number of arbitrators and the potential need for an umpire.

As was said in a great land dispute between Burton Abbey and Thomas Okeover in 1418:[11] 'The arbitrators having the great desire and

9. The law is more practical in England, e.g. *A & Ors v B & Anor* [2011] EWHC 2345 (Comm).

10. Eugène Déprez 'La Conférence d'Avignon (1344)' in AG Little and FM Powicke eds *Essays in Medieval History Presented to Thomas Frederick Tout* Manchester 1925 p304.

11. Edward Powell 'Settlement of Disputes by Arbitration in Fifteenth-Century England'

goodwill, from the affection they have for the parties, to make a final accord between them.' To improve the chances of success, even when the rights were plainly all on one side, arbitrators would give something to the loser, to assuage ill-feeling and wounded pride, if nothing else. As in this case: the abbey got the lands, Okeover had to pay rent for them; but the abbey was to pay him five marks for a general release of any claims he might have. Not because there was evidence of any claims but because the abbey's concession to that token payment would increase the chances of a successful settlement. It was the restoration of peace that mattered.

4. THE SCOPE OF ARBITRATION

Arbitration in England long predates the Common Law. Its roots are deep in custom. It grew from below with little help from legislation or even much from case law until the end of the sixteenth century. In medieval England the word 'arbitration' was used for the whole range of dispute resolution outside litigation. Arbitration in this wider sense was the usual method of resolving disputes. The records show that litigation, even when it was used, rarely concluded a dispute.

Arbitration was readily available to all kinds of people. Kings submitted their differences to other kings or the pope. The records of the city of York show that a labourer, Aynour Johnson, was a party to an arbitration arranged by the municipal authorities in 1484, a few months before the end of the Wars of the Roses.[12] Foreign merchants brought their disputes to the Mayor of London's arbitration scheme, even when there was no English element. If one party was English and the other foreign, an arbitration was arranged with two English and two foreign arbitrators.[13] Before Henry II expelled the Jews from England in 1294, it was not uncommon for one Jewish and one Gentile arbitrator to sit together as a panel.[14]

The scope of arbitration had few limits. None of the Roman Law restrictions applied. Questions of ownership of land, of status – free or servile, criminal charges including murder and rape, were all resolved by arbitration without their arbitrability being questioned. Arbitrators even decided questions of church law. Treason and blasphemy seem to have been the only substantial exceptions.[15]

Mediation and arbitration were ordinarily used in medical negligence cases, with great sophistication compared with modern methods, and on

---

(1984) 2 *Law and History R* 21-43, pp29-30, citing Burton-on Trent Public Library D27.
12. *Medieval Arbitration* Chapter 1.
13. *Medieval Arbitration* Chapter 10.
14. *Medieval Arbitration* Chapter 13.
15. *Medieval Arbitration* Chapters 5, 6 and 7.

4 December 1439 the king's Council even thought it wise to submit to arbitration a scientific dispute about astronomy:[16]

> Richard Monke of London, chaplain to Thomas Gosse, mercer. Recognisance of £20 to be levied etc on his lands and chattels and church goods in the city of London.
>
> Condition, that he shall abide and keep the award of John Stopyndoun, clerk, keeper of the Chancery rolls, concerning all debts, trespasses, debates etc between the parties to this date, and certain opinions of certain articles of the science of astronomy, so that the award be made before Whitsunday next.
>
> Thomas Gosse to Richard Monke [the same recognisance and condition].

Note that the submission is made by mutual conditional bonds like a *compromissum*. The word used in English and French to translate *compromissum* was invariably *compromesse*.

In medieval England women were occasionally appointed arbitrators. There was no legal bar to that, though social conventions made their appointments unusual.[17]

The resolution of a dispute by arbitration was not primarily a legal outcome. It was more real than that. The parties had publicly acknowledged that their dispute was over.

5. A LINGUISTIC INSIGHT FROM MEDIEVAL OXFORD

The most compelling evidence of the differences between Civil Law arbitration *ex compromisso* and the reality in England comes from an award in a thoroughly English jurisdiction which was nevertheless governed by the Civil Law. The University of Oxford in the fifteenth century had wide jurisdiction over both civil and criminal matters, not restricted to members of the University. No Common Law was taught there, only Civil Law and Canon Law. The University's courts applied the Civil Law in a society imbued with traditional English values and ways.

In 1446 two halls, the forerunners of colleges, were in dispute.[18] There had been violence between their fellows. Each party appointed two arbitrators, by a deed which has every appearance of a Civil Law *compromissum*, and charged them to bring a violent dispute to an end, by an agreed settlement as mediators, *amicabiles compositores*, if they

16. *Medieval Arbitration* Chapter 5.
17. *Medieval Arbitration* Chapter 14.
18. Anstey II pp552-554.

could, or if not as arbiters by an award, *laudum* or *arbitrium*. They formulated an award which both sides then *agreed* to.

The choice of language is significant. It followed the precedent of awards upon a *compromissum* already two centuries old in other parts of Western Europe, but with a tiny difference. The Latin copulative *seu*, like the English word 'or', is as often found between near synonyms as opposites, as in *laudum seu arbitrium*. The standard phrase in the appointment clause of a *compromissum* in all times and places is *arbiter, arbitrator vel amicabilis compositor*, in which each noun is an equal alternative.[19] Why then would the creator of this document write *arbiter seu arbitrator et amicabilis compositor*? Because in his English mind he wanted to distinguish clearly the role of an *arbiter* who adjudicated from an *arbitrator* and an *amicabilis compositor* who did not. This is evidence that third parties first (and continuously throughout the proceedings) tried to bring the parties to agree to a settlement and imposed a decision upon them only as a last resort. These arbitrators worked out a settlement which the parties are then recorded as having agreed to. That was what they had anticipated when they made the submission and together agreed to abide by what the arbitrators, the friends of both sides, agreed on. It was not imposed against their will, or willy-nilly by the powers bestowed on the arbitrators in their submission. The parties had stayed in charge throughout. They had got what they wanted. Peace had been restored by an agreed settlement.

The arbitrators described themselves as acting 'on behalf of' their respective appointing parties. However partisan they may have been, they worked out a settlement between them without the help of any objective outsider. They expected to. The parties expected them to. However much the parties, the lawyers who drafted the *compromissum*, and the arbitrators were influenced by and followed the forms of the Civil Law, they were English and their culture prevailed.

Of course the English had no monopoly of even-numbered tribunals. They are found in the multicultural jurisdiction of Cretan Candia in 1305, where Venetian, Greek and Jew lived and worked in harmony.[20] About the same time, in Venice itself, two arbitrators were common.[21] And even as late as 1785 in Geneva.[22]

---

19. Karl Heinz Ziegler 'Arbiter, Arbitrator und Amicabilis Compositor' (1967) 84 *Zeitschrift der Savigny-Stiftung für Rechtsgeschichte: Romanische Abteilung* 376-81.

20. AM Stahl ed *The Documents of Angelo de Cartura and Donato Fontanella Venetian Notaries in Fourteenth-Century Crete* Washington, Dumbarton Oaks 2000 p14 no36 and p191 no492.

21. Fabrizio Marrella and Andrea Mozzato eds *Alle Origini dell'Arbitrato Commerciale Internazionale: L'Arbitrato a Venezia tra Medioevo ed Età Moderna* Milan, Cedam 2001, who at p57 say that 'some modern jurists – perhaps wrongly – call the umpire a British invention'.

22. Jacques Drouin *Catalogue des Factums Judiciaires Genèvois sous L'Ancien Régime*

6. TODAY'S LINGUISTIC REALITIES

What about now? Can historical insights help in any way to illuminate, if not to resolve, contemporary problems? In ordinary English, mediation and conciliation have the same meaning. They are synonymous and inter-changeable. This linguistic reality is recognised in the UNCITRAL Model Law on International Commercial Conciliation,[23] which is intended to provide uniform rules for mediation, which it calls conciliation, to encourage its use, and to ensure greater predictability and certainty. Article 3 defines 'conciliation':

> 3. 'Conciliation' means a process, whether referred to by the expression conciliation, mediation or an expression of similar import, whereby parties request a third person or persons ('the conciliator') to assist them in their attempt to reach an amicable settlement.

But brave efforts have been made to insist on a distinction between mediation and conciliation. The Swiss Rules of Commercial Mediation proclaim, in their English version:

> Mediation is an alternative method of dispute resolution whereby two or more parties ask a neutral third party, the mediator, to assist them in settling a dispute or in avoiding future conflicts. The mediator facilitates the exchange of opinions between the parties and encourages them to explore solutions that are acceptable to all the parties .... The mediator does not make proposals like a conciliator.

So at first sight there appear to be three current usages: 1. 'conciliation' includes both; or 2. 'mediation' includes both; or 3. a distinction is made. The choice between 1 and 2 is unimportant. Of course it would be pleasanter and give us greater self-respect, no doubt, if we could all agree to one or the other, as chemists effortlessly do with sulphur dioxide. But the practical problems arise when we create two categories and have to choose into which we put phenomena, when that allocation has practical effect.

Unless the categories are both comprehensive of all relevant phenomena and are mutually exclusive, and the criteria for allocation of all the phenomena between them are not only clear but agreed, the

Geneva, Société d'Histoire et d'Archéologie de Genève 1988 p84 no274. But not in Louis XIV's Paris, Derek Roebuck *The Charitable Arbitrator: How to Mediate and Arbitrate in Louis XIV's France* Oxford HOLO Books, 2002 p194.
23. Adopted by UNCITRAL 24 June 2002.

process is not only flawed but dangerous. History can at least show that distinctions are culturally specific.[24]

A good example comes from Mongolia:[25]

Conciliation and mediation can be differentiated – the former referring to settlement efforts made during the court proceedings, whereas the latter refers to out-of-court settlement processes, i.e. mediation in its classical sense as employed, for example, in the United Kingdom.

That should not be assumed to be an oriental aberration. A Dutch mediator cites the European Mediation Directive art3(a):[26]

[Conciliation] includes mediation conducted by a judge who is not responsible for any judicial proceedings concerning the dispute in question. It excludes attempts made by the judge seised to settle a dispute in the course of judicial proceedings concerning the dispute in question

and suggests that: 'maybe mediation practitioners and scholars should agree that the word "conciliation" should be exclusively allocated to this type of judicial settlement activity'.

There would appear to be no obvious direct route for cross-fertilisation between Mongolia and The Netherlands. How could what seems to be an idiosyncratic definition sprout in such different climates? Was it born in the European Mediation Directive or has it a history? Why should it matter whether or not the mediation process is carried on by a judge during the litigation? An answer may be found in the separate histories of the *compromissum* in practice in France and England and in the quite different influence which the jurists had.

The confusion does not arise from reality but from an insistence on forcing language into unnatural shapes. In reality, in all our cultures, those we now call mediators have commonly moved backwards and forwards, using whatever skills they had to help to bring about agreement. The parties would not complain, if they got a mutually acceptable settlement.

No agreement on meaning is likely that makes the Mongolian-Dutch distinction, or any other definitional difference between mediation and

---

24. For a quite different approach: The People's Mediation Law of the People's Republic of China 2011.
25. Sanja Tseveenjav 'Mediation in Mongolia' (2011) 77 *Arbitration* 332-336, 332.
26. John M Bosnak 'The European Mediation Directive: More Questions than Answers' in Arnold Ingen-Housz ed *ADR in Business II* Alphen aan den Rijn, Wolters Kluwer 2011 pp625-657, 642.

conciliation, even in English, whether English English, American or reduced. And every flourishing language is historically and potentially a language of ADR. How are·prescriptive definitions going to work in Chinese or Arabic – not unimportant languages of international commerce? No legislation can control the developments, not even Swiss Rules or EU Directives, which can only define for the purposes of their own rules. In something so consensual as alternative dispute resolution, what the parties want and what they think their community should offer them will prevail over any top-down prescriptions.

One thing is integral to everyone's definition of mediation: that mediation is voluntary, at least in the sense that either party may walk away from the mediator and is not bound by anything a mediator determines. But that would not be true of a Korean mediation, where the culture still provides a process of dispute resolution – usually translated into English without more as 'mediation' – which, once the parties have chosen to use it, cannot be escaped without unbearable social pressure.

7. CONCLUSIONS

We will all continue to use words as best we can to communicate what we hope to get the recipient to understand. Of course, there is nothing wrong with defining your terms for scholarly purposes and sometimes lawyers need to when drafting a contract – as long as you don't let the categories determine your thinking, as long as you say what you mean and are sure that the other side accepts that meaning.[27]

Lawyers are skilled users of language. They always have been. Now more than ever, though, their world is multilingual. The paradox is that the more the use of English dominates business and its law, the more diverse the influences on that English are and the more pervasive are the forces which push towards the creation and use of a new language, a reduced language for non-native speakers of English. With the spread of this new apparently simplified language come increased dangers of partial comprehension and blurring of necessary distinctions. Every speaker of reduced English has a mother tongue which colours and expands the reductions. The way that happens is not likely to be the same for speaker and hearer with different mother tongues.

Lawyers are good at other things, too, like creating and exploiting a professional monopoly. Where governments have recently tried to take advantage of the benefits of mediation but have failed to see the dangers of making it a mandatory condition for litigating, the civil justice

---

27. Douglas Yam 'The Death of ADR: A Cautionary Tale of Isomorphism Through Institutionalisation' (2003-2004) 108 *Penn State LR* 929.

system has suffered from excessive bureaucracy and popular backlash. Where lawyers have been astute to try to make mediation fall within the definition of legal practice or otherwise give them an advantage over others, the development of mediation has been skewed and crippled. Even if court-attached mediation needs some control, there is no reason to assume it should extend to mediation generally.

Problems have arisen in Greece and Italy, and there are suggestions that they will in Bulgaria.[28] It may not be wise to introduce into quite different societies answers to problems in the civil justice system of the United States. I have only a hunch that Romania has a tradition of resolving disputes – even the most violent ones – by means which do not require the involvement of lawyers. If I'm wrong, I'm sure someone reading this can put me right or direct me to the appropriate sources. If I'm right, Romania is in danger of making fundamental errors. We are all lawyers and have a special responsibility to ensure that we think clearly and do our best to avoid them.

The more I try to understand how people – individuals and communities – have managed their disputes, the more I am convinced that the answers must be sought by interdisciplinary enquiry. Comparative research is essential. It has already been justified by the insights that have come from working out why processes are alike or different in communities separated by time or space. But comparative research is richer and has more colour if it is viewed not through the monocular microscope, however powerful, of a single discipline, whether law, history, anthropology, psychology or even language. If we are to work most effectively, we shall not only have to draw on every obviously relevant discipline but also constantly to keep an eye out for developments in those we have not yet recognised as potentially fruitful. How much more shall we learn if we try to use together the tools and skills and experience of all those arts and sciences we have not yet explored. And how much more rigorously shall we be able to test and so rely on the results of one another's work.

In the multilingual and multicultural world of modern alternative dispute resolution, is it not obvious that the disciplines of language and history demand our attention?

---

28. Andrew Colvin 'Mediation in Italy: A Progress Report' to appear in (2012) 78 *Arbitration* in November [appeared in (2018) 78(4) *Arbitration* 340 – SH].

First published as part of Chapter 18, 'Neil Kaplan – Patron of Learning' in Chiann Bao and Felix Lautenschlager (eds), *Arbitrators' Insights: Essays in Honour of Neil Kaplan* (London: Sweet & Maxwell 2012, 317–325). Reproduced by kind permission of the publisher.

6.   THE MEDIEVAL IDEA OF ARBITRATION

Historians have discovered the importance of arbitration only recently. Arbitrators have yet to discover the importance of history. It is time they did. Good history may not teach much but there is plenty of evidence that bad history leads astray.

The evidence of the rich surviving sources is more than enough to show that life in medieval England was permeated by not only the idea but the practice of arbitration; that it was a normal means of ending disputes; that it regularly and naturally began with an attempt at mediation; and that its aim was to produce peace through compromise.

For us the distinction between mediation and arbitration is sharp and essential. But, in the Middle Ages in England, the common process was for contending parties first to ask friends to mediate and then to arrange an arbitration if no settlement could be reached. I suspect that many reports of arbitrations fail to disclose the preliminary mediation. For example, the Year Book report of *Bloundelle v Akeley* in the Common Pleas in 1470 makes no mention of mediation; but the excerpt from the record on the De Banco roll describes it fully. John Bloundelle and his son John sued Robert Akeley on a written obligation for a debt of £40. Robert's defence was that, before the written obligation:

> There were various actions, controversies, differences and disputes between them, so, to concede and pacify them, … by the mediation of their friends amicably intervening between them, they put themselves on the arbitration, award and decision of [four named arbitrators],

Those words 'by the mediation of their friends amicably intervening between them' appear so often that they look like a stock phrase.

Nowadays much is made of the need for mediators and arbitrators to be neutral and impartial. In the United States there are elaborate rules which discourage the appointment of those with previous acquaintance of either party. In medieval England it was quite different. It is usually clear by implication and often expressed that the third parties were chosen just because they were already 'friends to both sides'. Not only were they often expected to know something about the dispute, they were rarely rewarded and it was assumed they were giving their services out of goodwill to both sides, or as part of the responsibilities attached to their position in the community. That was why they laboured to bring about a lasting comprehensive reconciliation.

As the arbitrators declared themselves in the great land dispute between Burton Abbey and Thomas Okeover in 1418: 'the arbitrators having the great desire and goodwill, from the affection they have for the parties, to make a final accord between them'. To improve the chances of success, even when the rights were plainly all on one side, arbitrators would give something to the loser, to assuage ill-feeling and wounded pride, if nothing else. As in this case: the abbey got the lands, Okeover had to pay rent for them; but the abbey was to pay him five marks for a general release of any claims he might have. Everybody knew he had no valid claims.

Mediation and arbitration were not necessarily sequential. Either could follow the other, more than once in the process, and the parties might well agree to settle at any time, even after an arbitration had resulted in a solemn and authoritative award. Of course, that still happens today in Hong Kong.

It is not easy to keep in mind that throughout the Middle Ages those who performed judicial functions never lost their responsibilities for good administration. The judges of the Year Books are memorable for their idiosyncrasies and love of legal quibbles but they knew their place in the government. They did not have to worry about limits to their jurisdiction. They were required to deal with their business efficiently. The fundamental law was whatever the king wanted, and there was little legislation to trammel their efforts. The modern bureaucrat's satisfaction with any excuse for passing on responsibility had not yet been born. Courts were Government offices for getting problems solved. They found arbitration a useful tool for many of their tasks.

The Government was not always prepared to leave it to the courts to get things done the way it wanted them. Wolsey's work is a good example of an energetic government using all the means at its disposal, including new institutions with a penchant for arbitration, to get the desired result – the termination of discord.

THE STATE AND OTHER COMMUNITIES

When the parties considered their difference to be serious enough to count as a dispute needing outside intervention, they could be sure that some community to which they belonged had an interest in its resolution. Communities other than the state provided means of resolving disputes: the hundred and shire; groups of magnates like the Marcher lords; city and borough authorities; religious and craft guilds, the University of Oxford; the Church; and separate religious communities like the Jews. The king's own Council and even Parliament, representing the central government, offered mediation and arbitration as alternatives to litigation.

THE MEDIATORS AND ARBITRATORS

All kinds of people were chosen as mediators and arbitrators from the highest in the land, kings themselves, to the most ordinary: men, lay and clergy, and occasionally women. The parties and their community were entitled to expect them to have certain qualities, well understood but not sharply defined. A court might require them to be respectable and law-abiding, *probos et legales homines* or *bouns genz*, though sometimes it was enough to be sensible, *discretos*.

Any number could be chosen, from one to the four usual in arbitrations arranged by the cities of London or York, to the twelve who looked so like a jury that they have been called by that name. Occasionally there were even more. Usually the parties chose their arbitrators, regularly two by each side; but often an authority appointed them, king or Council, or a parliament, or mayor, or overlord.

There is plenty of evidence of arbitrations spoiled by improper influence, bribery and corruption, even violence. Submissions were not always voluntary. Arbitrators could be ignorant, idle or careless, or even rapacious. But, on the whole, the processes were acceptable. Perhaps not all those involved would agree – losing parties often have less happy memories than the winners – but most seem to have chosen alternative methods of resolving their disputes willingly, rather than rely upon litigation. I have found no criticisms of the processes themselves or calls for their improvement. After all, the parties, and the third parties they chose to help them, could usually fashion the processes as they wished. And those ways of resolving disputes were the old and tried methods, an integral part of most communities' customs, well known and respected.

Neither an arbitrator's award nor a mediated settlement was impervious to determined attack, sometimes generations later. But what was concluded 'in love was as strong as a judgment'. That had been the law since the tenth century and still is. Indeed, as present-day arbitrators and parties know, thanks to the New York Convention an award may now be better than a judgment. At least it is easier to enforce in most foreign jurisdictions.

THE SUBJECT MATTER: ARBITRABILITY

The concept of arbitrability was well known to medieval lawyers. Roman law is full of restrictions. But that did not bother anyone in England. It might be hard to settle a treason charge or, in the Church courts, one of blasphemy, but the scope which the courts allowed to arbitration included a whole range of disputes which would not be arbitrable today: not only disputes over ownership of freehold land but questions of status – free or servile – and even serious felonies, quite regularly including rape and murder.

ARBITRATION CENTRES

Perhaps even more surprising is the evidence of the regular operation in London, York and Bristol of what can without anachronism be called arbitration centres. They regularly offered their services in arranging mediation-arbitration to all comers. In London English and foreigners alike availed themselves of the scheme provided by the Lord Mayor, which even provided its services in relation to disputes with no connection to England. Not only great merchant companies used these schemes. My favourite party is Aynour Johnson, a Yorkshire labourer, who on 24 September 1484 is recorded as defending his interests in an arbitration arranged by the York authorities. The Mayor of Bristol, on taking office, swore an oath that he would personally keep an office open for the purposes of arranging arbitrations every day of the working week. The Privy Council took a special interest. In 1549 it even sat on a cold Sunday morning to set up an arbitration under the Lord Mayor of London's scheme.

ADVANTAGES

In his edition of Spelman's Reports, writing of the sixteenth century, Sir John Baker wrote: 'the vast majority of cases commenced in the central courts never reach trial'. Not now, not then. He has since provided some startling numbers, in the *Oxford History of the Laws of England* VI p331.

> In 1535, for instance, when an estimated 10,000 to 12,000 new suits were being commenced in the Common Pleas each year, only about 400 judgments were entered and fewer than 900 other cases were pleaded to issue without determination. In other words, around 90 per cent of the suits – perhaps 9,000 or 10,000 cases a year, were discontinued before issue was joined.

But those who have disputes do not pay court fees for nothing. What is the explanation for the discontinuance of litigation? Why was that normal? Official records do not reveal why but one can guess. One convincing reason was that the plaintiff never intended the proceedings to do more than give notice of the claim to the defendant and to set the scene for resolution of the dispute by negotiation, mediation or arbitration. That would allow the plaintiff all, or at least some, of the advantages which can now be set out. But another reason for the lack of records of conclusions in the reports must surely have been that the parties, faced with litigation which was taking their dispute ever further away from reality, from the merits into a world which existed only in the lawyers' imagination, must have seen advantages in settling. There are many sources which provide evidence of accords and concords and lovedays and they may well have been just a fraction of the reality.

Choice of Decision Maker

The parties to mediation/arbitration were usually able to choose or at least influence the choice of the third parties who would decide both law and facts. Juries might be subject to local political influence, particularly of the sheriff who decided their composition. Moreover, there were times when there were judges who could not be trusted. Gifts were commonplace and the demands for them, or unspoken expectations, were hard to distinguish from corruption. Much better to allow 'friends of both sides' to choose arbitrators who could be trusted and who were already likely to know and understand the background.

Day in Court

Arbitration allowed parties to air their grievances, which is one of the merits of mediation today. Parties who feel badly done to may want more than anything to let the other party – and as many others as possible – know how wronged they have been. Judges, then and now, cannot allow the 'day in court' to be extended just for the purpose of letting off steam. Mediation and arbitration had no such fixed limits.

Freedom from Precedent

In mediation there were no decisions to report, only agreed settlements. Even arbitrators had no authority to lay down the law. Neither mediators nor arbitrators were in any way bound by what their predecessors had done. They were usually unfettered by the strictness of the Common Law. Unlike the Year Books and later the Nominate Reports, there were just no records of awards accessible to be pleaded as precedents.

Equity and Merits

Mediators were concerned to bring the parties together in a settlement. Parties would usually have a good idea of what they might expect if they went to law but their powers of fixing a solution were untrammelled. Arbitrators were usually appointed to decide not according to Common Law but *ex aequo et bono*, according to what they reasonably thought was fair and good. Judges had limited discretions to decide on the merits, though the Year Books show how a determined judge could bend the law when moved by the urge to avoid injustice. That was not enough for the parties, who seem regularly to have shown their keenness to substitute fairness for strict law.

Comprehensiveness

Submissions were usually of all differences between the parties. The standard terms of a bond expressly included everything that could possibly be in dispute from the dawn of time to the date of the submission. It also empowered the arbitrators to use whatever means of resolution they could imagine. The catchphrase 'in high and low', '*alto et basso*', '*en haut et en bas*', seems to have had different connotations at different times but, if the parties ever had to think what it meant, they might have included not only all disputes, whatever and whenever, but also all means of resolving them.

Language

Mediation and arbitration were transacted in whatever language the parties wanted, not in Law French, the patois only lawyers understood. Bonds and awards were usually kept in Latin, because that was the language for all records.

Cost

Though varying greatly from time to time, the cost of litigation was always something most parties had to consider. Mediation always, and arbitration usually, was cheaper. In 1431, the Abbot of St Alban's declared he had saved a thousand marks by going to arbitration rather than litigating.

Speed

Arbitration was comparatively quick. Not always! It could be exploited as a trick to delay a settlement, as in Exeter where the dispute was said to have lasted 160 years, or Lincoln Cathedral's little bother which lasted many centuries. But in most cases the parties relied on mediation and arbitration for a quick result. This was especially important to merchants whose goods might be perishable and whose capital certainly could not withstand inaction.

A splendid example comes from the London Mayor's Court. On 6 November 1413 Agnes Brightwell claimed a debt of £60 from William Rody, mercer. On 22 November the parties agreed to the arbitration of the Mayor and Aldermen. They told the parties to bring 'all evidence, written and unwritten' before them on 24 November (The *Calendar of Plea and Memoranda Rolls* [*CPMR*] for 1413-1437 records, p10).

On that day, as it appeared from the evidence and arguments put in by both parties that the defendant had sealed letters of payment to the plaintiff for £60, and that the plaintiff had received 16 pipes of salt and other goods to the value of £7 8s 4d, they awarded that the defendant pay the plaintiff the balance due, viz £52 11s 8d.

All done in less than three weeks!

The regulations of some craft guilds set short periods, after which the parties might be free to sue at Common Law – six days for the Barber Surgeons. Perhaps there could never have been greater celerity than in an arbitration where the Mayor of London sent a dispute to arbitrators on 17 July 1439 and it was settled the next day (*CPMR 1381-1412* pp140-142).

Process

Arbitration typically meant that each side would choose two persons – always called arbitrators – whose first job was to try to work out between the four of them a solution which would be 'fair and good, *ex aequo et bono*' – and would therefore be acceptable to the parties. In the process it was their duty to make proposals to the parties for what seemed to the arbitrators to be reasonable. They had been chosen because they were good, law-abiding, discreet and wise and the parties had directly told them to be reasonable.

If necessary the arbitrators would decide. If they were of even number and no majority could agree, an umpire would be appointed. Even after the award had been declared, the parties might discuss it further and, then as now, come to a different agreement. It might have been understood from the start that the award would bind only if both parties accepted it.

Two examples show mediation and arbitration at their best. The first is a quite simple resolution of a commercial dispute. In 1451 John Delaber, the Bishop of St David's, who combined considerable business interests with his pastoral responsibilities, was in dispute with Patrick Devy, a Bristol dyer, over the ownership of the *Mary de Montrigo*, which was laden with merchandise and trimmed for war. Each side had nominated two arbitrators. They awarded that the bishop should 'warrant and quitclaim' the ship and its contents to Devy for a year and a day in any court of law and drop all actions against him. Patrick too would release all actions and pay to the bishop 200 marks, twenty down and the rest by instalments. The record was engrossed as a tripartite indenture, one part for each party, one to be kept in Chancery. Arbitration did what litigation could not – but the courts were there to give authority to the award and ensure its enforcement. An apparently happy symbiosis!

The second example shows how the advantages of mediation and arbitration could be expanded by the imagination and adroitness of the peacemakers. In 1408 Hugh of Hodsock died leaving lands scattered all over the place. Half of his estate was to go to his sister Katherine and her husband and children, the other to Sir John Markham, widower of his other sister Elizabeth, and their children. No directions had been given as to who should have what. No particular aggregations of the land had a special logic. Hugh's family and neighbouring gentry helped to sort out the differences before they could become a conflict.

Nowadays the proponents of mediation stress the advantages of a process which, as they would say, provides an opportunity for a 'win-win' solution. With care a settlement may be crafted which will allow both sides to do well, if not making a profit out of the transaction in dispute, at least opening up possibilities for the parties to have mutually profitable deals in the future. I have no evidence of the conversations which went on between the parties in my last example. Such evidence would not survive today. But it makes one wonder.

Authority to Settle

A problem which besets mediators today is that those negotiating may not have the authority to settle. Officers, particularly of state agencies, may appear to be clothed with powers which they deny when agreement has been reached. That difficulty was recognised in England in the Middle Ages, and its solution provided, in a way which drafters of modern arbitration clauses would do well to note. A 'little clause' was inserted into the arbitration agreement giving the agents express authority 'to conciliate, reconcile, compromise and finally bring to agreement, by way of friendly composition or otherwise in whatever way seems most expedient to my agents'. That made any agreement stick and protected the agents from any allegation that they had exceeded their authority. It thereby made negotiations between the parties more likely to succeed.

Finality

Reconciliation gave a chance that the dispute would be finally resolved, whereas a disappointed litigant was often unlikely to give up.

WHAT HAPPENED NEXT?

Mediation and Arbitration in the Middle Ages [published 2013 – SH] ends in 1558, with the accession of Elizabeth I. Much changed in her reign. The nominate reports tell of the development of the law of arbitration. When the history of arbitration in practice in that period comes to be written, no doubt there will be a wealth of primary sources which have not yet been recognised as evidence. They will need to be considered by historians who have a sound understanding of the place of law in our society. So far most have assumed that the growth of the grasp and power of the Common Law could be taken for granted as a good thing in every way – a part of that natural progress of society in which how we organise ourselves to deal with conflict improves in much the same way as how we treat disease. The evidence of our own times might not support that assumption.

We need to know why and how the communities whose members resolved their own disputes came to lose their cohesion and their place in dispute resolution. We cannot summon them back from the past but that knowledge may just provide some clues for future generations, to help them organise themselves so that they can find ways to resolve differences peacefully, if possible before they become disputes; and permanently and satisfactorily once they have.

In the Middle Ages there seems to have been in most communities a saying like the Italian:

> *Meglio e magro accordo che grassa sentenza.*
> Better a slim settlement than a fat judgment.

Perhaps we should wonder why it was so popular. Anyone who wants to take up the challenge would do well to take advice from that patron of learning, and lover of all things Italian, Neil Kaplan.

The Leah and Alexander Woolf Lecture, 2013, Institute of Advanced Legal Studies, University of London. Reproduced by kind permission of the Institute.

7. JEWISH DISPUTES IN ENGLAND 1066 TO 1290

INTRODUCTION

This lecture has a simple ambition: to bring what is knowable about the resolution of Jewish disputes in medieval England into the general body of knowledge on the history of Jewish mediation and arbitration.[1] That Rabbinical learning is a formidable corpus, the result of centuries of scholarly effort. As Sir Bernard Rix said in his lecture to the Three Faiths Forum in 2007:[2]

> From the time of their exile in Babylon …, bereft of a home, the Jews turned inwards to their law … to scholarship, to analysis, to interpretation, and to education ….

Yet, as far as I know, the part of that remarkable treasure house of interpretation which concerns itself with dispute resolution has not been enlightened by comparative insights from the experience of Jews in medieval England.

As far as they were allowed by the external restraints of their hosts and their own cultural and religious requirements, Jews here abided by what Sir Bernard Rix called:

> The second act of great wisdom … the profound advice of Jeremiah: 'Seek the welfare of the city to which you have been carried and pray to God on its behalf, for if it prospers, you too will prosper'.

The primary sources show that Jewish practices contributed to the development of English practices and that their interplay has left traces. In return, now may be a good time for mainstream Jewish learning to take in whatever is useful from English history, from when Jews first settled here after the Norman Conquest until Edward I expelled them in 1290.

---

1. It is based on work now published in *Mediation and Arbitration in the Middle Ages: England 1154 to 1558* Oxford HOLO Books 2013.
2. Bernard Rix 'The Jewish Contribution to the English Legal System' London, 10 October 2007 (2008) 74 *Arbitration* 247-253, 247.

Any such offering had better be humble, especially from a Gentile with no Hebrew, who has never even heard the Hebrew words voiced. So, despite the unfailingly patient help of my old friends, I fear you will find much to forgive in my pronunciation of words I have only ever read.

Everybody with the slightest interest in dispute resolution is familiar with the conceptual distinction between settlement, where the parties come to their own agreement; mediation (or conciliation – I treat the words as synonyms), where they call in a third party to help them; and arbitration, where they hand over the decision of their dispute to one or more arbitrators. But it is wise to keep in mind that these are conceptual categories, not always kept distinct in practice. Boaz Cohen's book, *Jewish and Roman Law*, has given me many references to Jewish learning. He wrote:[3]

> In Tannaitic times, the term *Pesharah* was used to convey the meaning of conciliation or compromise as well as arbitration. In the word *Pesharah*, the Rabbis have launched a term rather than a single clearly defined idea, for invariable consistency is incompatible with the nature of things.

That makes the essential point that the parties, when seeking to resolve a dispute, will make use of all the techniques at their disposal. Until the creation of artificial prohibitions in modern times, the parties and their advisers moved in and out of private negotiations, mediation and arbitration as it suited them. Even now, how often do arbitrators find that their awards have not been enforced, the parties preferring to come to a different arrangement?

But the Rabbis have always insisted on distinguishing an arbitral award from the judgment of a court, with this at first surprisingly clear pronouncement:[4]

> The strength of a compromise is greater than the strength of adjudication according to strict law.

There is divine authority, from Genesis no less and therefore as old as time:[5]

> When God judges Jews, he makes a compromise, *Mefasher ba-Din*; but, when he judges Gentiles, he applies strict law, *Medaskdek ba-Din*.

3. Boaz Cohen *Jewish and Roman Law: a Comparative Study* New York, Jewish Theological Seminary of America 1955 p654.
4. *Dinei Mamonos Bishloshah: Sanhedrin* Chapter 1 5b.
5. *Genesis Rabbah* 82.8; Boaz Cohen p674.

I had better tread carefully.

To return to England. Evidence for the presence of Jews in England is unreliable before the Norman Conquest, though it cannot be doubted that Jews had traded into England before then, possibly even before the Romans, and some may have settled here.[6] A spurious law of Edward the Confessor proclaimed:[7]

> Let it be known that all Jews, wherever they may be in the kingdom, must be bound by allegiance and under the tutelage and protection of the king. Nor can any of them subject himself to any rich man without the king's licence, because they the Jews and everything of theirs belong to the king. So that, if anyone shall have taken possession of them or their money, the king may claim them as his own property, if he so wishes and is able.

Though that law was interpolated no earlier than 1096,[8] it at least shows legal opinion then.

By a charter of 10 April 1201, King John had granted rights to all Jews. They could travel and trade freely. They were exempted from tolls and customs and subject only to the royal courts. There they could swear an oath on the Pentateuch, which would prevail against a Christian's oath unless that was supported by compurgators [a sworn witness to the innocence or good character of an accused person – SH]. As Rigg wrote in his Selden volume:[9]

> The intention was to use the Jewry as a reservoir equally open to receive and close to retain the surplus wealth of the surrounding population, so that the Crown might never lack a fund on which to draw in the hour of need.

Christians could not compete, being forbidden to lend money upon usury, though like today's tax-dodgers they achieved the same by stratagems.

6. H.S.Q. Henriques *The Jews and English Law* Oxford, Oxford U.P. 1908; reprint Clifton N.J., Kelley 1974 p.52, citing references in the *Liber Poenitentialis* of Theodore, Archbishop of Canterbury AD668-690 and the *Exceptiones* of Ecbert, Archbishop of York AD 735-766.
7. Not in the accepted canon but accessible in Benjamin Thorpe *Ancient Laws and Institutes of England* 3rd reprint Clark N.J. 2004 p.195. J.M. Rigg ed *Select Pleas, Starrs, and Other Records from the Rolls of the Exchequer of the Jews AD1220-1284* (1902) 15 Selden Society ix-xliii is an invaluable repository of sources but his Introduction is suffused with Gentile attitudes of his time.
8. Felix Liebermann *Uber die Leges Edwardi Confessoris* Halle, Niemeyer 1896. B.R. O'Brien *God's Peace and King's Peace: the Laws of Edward the Confessor* Philadelphia, U. of Pennsylvania P. 1999 argues convincingly for a date in Stephen's reign (1135-1154); Derek Roebuck *Early English Arbitration* Oxford, HOLO Books 2008 p.197.
9. J.M Rigg *Select Pleas* p.xii.

One was to take ownership of property for a period in return for a sum, effectively a loan, and to keep the income produced by the property until the loan was repaid. English law considered that to be concealed usury and, if the king found out, the lands of the lender would be forfeit to him.[10] It was contrasted with the open and much more efficient *usura publica* of the Jews. As the *Dialogus de Scaccario* [Dialogue about the Exchequer – DR] put it c1179:[11]

> Therefore we call usury public or customary when, in the Jewish way, by contract someone gets back more (in the same specie) than he lent, for example a pound for a mark or two pence a week for a silver pound, in interest as well as the principal.

The king profited most by great impositions of all kinds upon Jews. Edward Coke made an estimate, who knows on what evidence:[12]

> A great revenue by reason of the usury of the Jews came to the Crown; for between the fiftieth year of Henry III [1266] and the second year of Edward I [1273], which was not above seven years complete, there was paid into the king's coffers four hundred and twenty thousand pounds.

That would have been a considerable part of the government's income, perhaps nearly half. But it is usually unwise to rely on the testimony of Coke. After all he says that the Jews left of their own accord once usury was forbidden.[13]

By the thirteenth century the king's courts were creating a Common Law. They were quite familiar with arbitrations and made use of them, setting up arbitrations and providing rules of law as they became necessary.[14] The same Latin phrase was used for submission to arbitrators as to a jury. The parties submitted to, *posuerunt se super*, literally put themselves upon, those they allowed to decide for them.

Indeed, the policy of both courts and arbitrators was the same. Cold adjudication of the parties' legal rights was not primary. What mattered most was that there should be a final and peaceful settlement. The parties

10. By 1263 'papal usury', as the Chief Rabbi called it, was common, J.M Rigg *Select Pleas* p.xxxiv.
11. Charles Johnson ed *Dialogus de Scaccario: The Course of the Exchequer* Oxford, Clarendon P. 1983 Bk 2 X pp.99-100.
12. Edward Coke *Institutes* III 151.
13. H.S.Q. Henriques *The Jews and English Law* tells the story of the Jews' later return.
14. The reports known as the Year Books did not begin until the 1260s but the Curia Regis Rolls provide some evidence of cases heard at this time, D.E. Murray 'Arbitration in the Anglo-Saxon and Early Norman Periods' (1961) 16 *Arbitration Journal* 193-208 gives examples, with translations from the Latin by an Italian friend, with comic results.

should end up as friends and the disturbance the dispute had caused in the community should be dissipated. As Van Caenegem has written:[15]

> What was usually expected of a law court was not a clear-cut decision, of right and wrong, on an issue on which the parties had failed to agree, but much more something in the nature of an effort to bring about a settlement of the litigation by an acceptable, honourable compromise .... by the mediation of the court or the good offices of some doomsmen or various people present at the session, or jurors from the neighbourhood or arbiters.

Certainly studies of the later Middle Ages show that verdicts were rarely taken: one per cent in King's Bench and few in Common Pleas.[16]

Compromise was the wisdom proclaimed as forthrightly by Christians and Jews alike. Of course, there were always those who insisted on what they perceived to be their legal rights. In this too Jews and Christians may not have been far apart.

TECHNIQUES

To discover what people did nearly a thousand years ago, the techniques of every relevant discipline must be applied. To find out how they dealt with their differences, those disciplines must include history and law, of course, but also anthropology and, in first place, language. My first question is always: 'What language were they using?'

A letter from the last decade of the twelfth century, preserved in the *Res Gestae* of Richard I, purports to have been sent by a Jewish merchant in France to a young friend who was intending to settle in England. He advised him to avoid the cities where larger Jewish communities had already been established, like Oxford, Norwich, Lincoln, York and Durham, and to plump for Winchester, applying a simple criterion, language. He wrote, presumably in French, though recorded in Latin:[17]

---

15. R.C. Van Caenegem *Royal Writs in England from the Conquest to Glanvill* (1959) 77 Selden Society 42. This had been the aim of courts in England from Anglo-Saxon times.
16. Marjorie Blatcher *The Court of King's Bench 1450-1550* London, Athlone P. 1978; Margaret Hastings *The Court of Common Pleas in Fifteenth Century England* New York, Cornell U.P. 1947.
17. *Disputes and Differences* p226 citing Richard of Devizes *De Rebus Gestis Ricardi I* London, Bohn 1841 III p437. There is a wealth of scholarship on the Jews in England before 1290, RR Mundill 'Out of the Shadow and Into the Light' (2011) 8 *History Compass* 572-601 and relevant background in Christoph Cluse ed *The Jews of Europe in the Middle Ages (Tenth to Fifteenth Centuries)* Turnhout, Brepols 2004 and Patricia Skinner ed *Jews in Medieval Britain: Historical, Literary and Archaeological Perspectives* Woodbridge, Boydell P 2003 [Skinner] (pb 2012).

Oxford has scarcely enough to keep its scholars alive ... York is full
of Scots, dirty and treacherous fellows – or dwarves rather .... In
Durham, Norwich or Lincoln, you won't find many of your sort among
the leaders of society – not a soul speaks French.

We know that was not quite true but the sources show that the Jews from
the start spoke French to their Christian hosts. Government records were
kept in Latin. Jews kept their own records in Hebrew. They learned the
English they needed for their livelihood and social intercourse. At first
they took French surnames but some changed to English equivalents.

The first reliable evidence of Jews settled in England comes from just
after the Norman Conquest. Jewish communities were established in
London and in many provincial towns, to which they were restricted by
law. By the time they were expelled in 1290, there may have been two
or three thousand Jews in England, out of a population of perhaps three
million. All estimates are guesses.

During that period of just over two centuries, Christians in Western
Europe transformed their religious beliefs into the violent action of the
Crusades. In 1099, Godfrey of Bouillon raised his flag in Jerusalem. Not
until 1290 were the last of the Normans driven out. While they were
there, and elsewhere in their Mediterranean colonies, they legislated for
all those within their jurisdiction, whatever their religion. The Assize of
Jerusalem and other codes derived from it provided for arbitration.

The Normans in England needed no such legislation. Mediation and
arbitration had always been customary, universal and ordinary.[18] And
from the start William the Conqueror insisted that he was the rightful
heir of the Anglo-Saxon kings and was adamant that he was basing his
restoration of law and order on his confirmation of the good old laws of
Edward the Confessor. His successors expressly repeated that claim and
that promise. Therefore, no legislation was needed.

The first question, then, is 'how did disputes involving Jews fit
into the customary usages?' There are abundant sources which testify
that mediation and arbitration were regularly used to resolve disputes
among Jews themselves and with Christians, most of which arose out
of the moneylending and pawnbroking by which many of the better-off
Jewish men and women made their living. Though the English had
then no scholars who might have created a common body of learning
commensurate with their comprehensive and routine practices, there is
plenty of evidence to show that the involvement of Jews has left its mark
on the way dispute resolution developed in England.

18. *Early English Arbitration* Oxford, HOLO Books 2008.

SOURCES

Most of the surviving records[19] relate to moneylending against security in land or goods, but there were other Jews working in skilled crafts, as gold- and silversmiths;[20] and in the professions as physicians[21] and lawyers, both attorneys and advocates.[22] Jews were not supposed to join guilds, which were avowedly Christian organisations, though at least one did. Opportunities for trade were restricted. When in 1275 the Statute of Jewry forbade usury, some moneylending deals were expressed as trade in commodities – corn or wool – but that was a subterfuge.

Starrs and Chirographs

Jews recorded their own transactions in a Hebrew deed, a *shetar*, in English a starr. It was commonly drawn up in three identical parts in the form of a T, called a chirograph, with one wing for each party and the stem, or foot, for the record.

The security of a loan depended on its starr being physically safe. It was in the Government's interest for Jewish bonds to be secure, and at some time after 1190, after the Jews had contributed largely to Richard I's ransom, and perhaps as a result of the destruction of Jewish bonds in the massacre of Jews in York, a system was instituted for the registration and safekeeping of starrs in royal chests, called in Latin *archae*, in the cities where there were major Jewish communities. Each chest had its own chirographers, two Jews and two Christians, appointed by royal command. They created Latin chirographs, kept them in the chest with

---

19. Thomas Madox *The History and Antiquities of the Exchequer of the Kings of England* 2nd edn London for William Owen and others 2 vols 1769 [Madox]; MD Davis [*Shetaroth*] *Hebrew Deeds of English Jews before 1290* London, Jewish Chronicle for the Anglo-Jewish Historical Exhibition 1888 [Davis]; for the Jewish Historical Society of England [JHSE]: JM Rigg ed *Calendar of the Plea Rolls of the Exchequer of the Jews Preserved in the Public Record Office* I 1218-1272 London, Macmillan 1905 and II 1273-1275 Edinburgh, Ballantyne, Hanson 1910 [EJ I and EJ II]; Hilary Jenkinson ed *Calendar of the Plea Rolls of the Exchequer of the Jews Preserved in the Public Record Office* III 1275-1277 London, Spottiswoode 1929 [EJ III]; HG Richardson ed *Calendar of the Plea Rolls of the Exchequer of the Jews Preserved in the Public Record Office and the British Museum* IV 1272, 1275-1277 London, JHSE 1972 [EJ IV]; Sarah Cohen ed *Plea Rolls of the Exchequer of the Jews Preserved in the Public Record Office* V 1277-1279 London, JHSE 1992 [EJ V]; Paul Brand ed *Plea Rolls of the Exchequer of the Jews Preserved in the National Archives (formerly the Public Record Office)* VI 1279-1281 London, JHSE 2005 [EJ VI]; JM Rigg ed *Select Pleas, Starrs, and Other Records from the Rolls of the Exchequer of the Jews AD1220-1284* (1901) 15 *Selden Society* [Rigg *Select Pleas*].
20. EJ VI p280 no1146.
21. Jacob *medicus* in York in 1275 EJ I pp1 and 2 and Isaac and his son Solomon in 1249 in Norwich, and again Davis p132 no52 (1266).
22. Isaac of Southwark, who appears often as attorney, is once expressly called advocate, *narrator*, Rigg *Select Pleas*, pp53-54; EJ VI p43.

four locks, and allowed access to them only formally, particularly for their discharge on payment or on settlement. Behind many of the settlements one can discover mediation and arbitration at work.

Plea Rolls

At some time about 1198, Richard I's government created a new court, within the Exchequer, its organ of general administration. The Exchequer of the Jews was set up to deal with cases between Jews and Christians.[23] Its plea rolls are full of the records of disputes, some of which provide evidence of mediation, occasionally of arbitration, sometimes express but more often clearly implied from the wording and the context. Though their stated purpose was to deal with debts which Christians owed to Jews, they provide ample evidence of the management of disputes between Jew and Jew, and even between Christian and Christian.[24]

The records of the Court are voluminous, thousands of accounts of individual matters. There is an important difference between these records and those of other royal courts, where surprisingly few cases seem to have come to judgment. The Exchequer of the Jews regularly and frequently took the verdict of a jury and declared and recorded its judgment.

Legislation of 1239 required the chirographers or their clerks to write in the parties' presence every bond recording a debt to a Jew from a Christian.[25] This has preserved the evidence on which this lecture is largely based,[26] most of it drawn from the Plea Rolls of the Exchequer of the Jews.

An undated starr from Norwich is some evidence that a chirographer might himself play a role in resolving disputes. The memorandum contains an oath by Isaac that Richard's debt of 2 marks is owed to him and Jekuthiel jointly, Jekuthiel's share being one quarter. Isaac and Richard swore, holding a Torah scroll, that they would act in unison in recovering the debt, bearing the expenses of recovery in proportion to their shares. And Hayyim, the chirographer, would keep a copy of this memorandum and deal with any dispute arising between Isaac and Richard 'as umpire'.[27] Hayyim is similarly given the responsibility of

---

23. At least in part to ensure the collection of impositions on Jews; OHLE II p543; HG Richardson *The English Jewry under the Angevin Kings* London, Methuen 1960; SR Wigram *The Cartulary of the Monastery of St Frideswide at Oxford* Oxford, Clarendon P for the Oxford Historical Society 1895 [Wigram] pp218-221 nos294-298.

24. EJ III p31; EJ VI p12 fn93.

25. EJ VI (see fn19) gives all the details.

26. The basic editorial work was done by Davis, who has been supplemented by Ann Causton *Medieval Jewish Documents in Westminster Abbey* London, Jewish Historical Society of England 2007.

27. Davis p192 no 76.

'umpire' in another undated starr recording the disposition of another debt involving Isaac and Jekuthiel.[28] Another starr from Norwich in 1264 provides for the peaceful and equitable settlement of future disputes by a third person 'to act as arbitrator and umpire'.[29] Here are agreements appointing a Jewish arbitrator in future disputes between Christian and Jewish parties.

As if that were not a sufficient surprise, look at their form! These are precocious manifestations of what would not become prevalent for centuries in England and what was unacceptable in France until modern times. They are arbitration clauses, not submissions: they do not submit to arbitration a dispute which has already arisen. They provide for *future* disputes which may or may not arise. The idea must have come from somewhere. Not from Roman law. It could be indigenous but there is no sign of it elsewhere. So, could the arbitration clause have come from a Jewish tradition, which I have been unable to trace but which one of you could lead me to?[30]

THE LEGAL POSITION OF JEWS

Before we look at those records in more detail, it is important to determine precisely what the legal status of Jews was then. Jews were not full citizens. They were free not servile[31] and their status in feudal law was peculiar to them. Henry III declared by statute in 1253 that: 'no Jew shall stay in England unless he does service to the king', which could mean 'is of some use to' but is more likely the technical term for 'is the direct feudal dependant of'.[32] It has been said that they did not fit into the feudal system because they could not swear allegiance, being barred by Jewish law from swearing a Christian oath. But English practice accepted Jewish oaths then and, in any case, the feudal *system* is an anachronistic creature of later historians and we can stick to the facts to be found in the sources.

If anyone in the thirteenth century ever thought in terms of a legal system, which is unlikely, they would have done what all good science

---

28. Davis pp205-206 no 85. Another starr from Norwich in 1264 provides for the peaceful and equitable settlement of future disputes by a third person 'to act as arbitrator and umpire'.
29. Davis pp116-117 no47. A starr could arrange in advance for any dispute about the value of improvements to rented property to be put to a panel of experts, Davis pp94-95 no40.
30. There have been suggestions that the chirograpph may have Jewish origins but I know of no evidence.
31. Maitland thought otherwise and his opinion has led many astray: 'From Normandy, brought hither as the king's dependants and (the word will hardly be too strong) the king's serfs', F Pollock and FW Maitland *The History of English Law before the Time of Edward I* 2nd edn SFC Milsom ed 2 vols Cambridge, Cambridge UP 1968 p468.
32. Madox I pp248-249: '*nullus Judaeus maneat in Anglia nisi servitium regi faciat*'.

requires and incorporated the reality of Jewish landowning into their scheme, rather than excluding it as anomalous, an exception to rules which did not exist.

Jews did not pay ordinary taxes. But every Jew, male and female of twelve years and up, was subject to a poll tax, called chevage, *capitularium*, of 3d a year.[33] The king also required enormous sums for his favours, for example Henry II in 1186 required 1,800 marks from Jurnet of Norwich for permission to live in England with the king's goodwill.[34]

Because it has sometimes been assumed that Jews could not have full ownership of land, it is worth digressing to provide copious proof that they did.[35] Restrictions on their ownership changed from time to time and even from one person to another, but own land they did, by any acceptable definition of ownership. That is important because many of the disputes were about land, and not just about land held as security.

Perhaps from as early as the 1150s there survives a conveyance by Gervase of Cornhill to Isaac, son of Rabbi Josce, of a house and land in London.[36] The Jewish community was allowed to buy land to build a synagogue.[37] And conveyances by Jews gave as good a title as any.[38] For example, in 1241 Josce, grandson of Aaron of York, sold land to Malton Priory: 'Take note that I have ceded and conveyed to the Prior and Convent of Malton six bovates of land in Little Edstone'.[39] And Jews could sell land to one another: 'Samson, son of Isaac, to his son Abraham land in the Parish of St Laurence.'[40] There are half a dozen documents from Oxford between 1220 and 1260, including straightforward conveyances from Christian to Jew.

The best evidence there could be that Jews could own land is the statute of 1271 which forbade them thenceforth to do so.[41] But even that was not observed and in 1272 Edward I legislated to allow Jews to buy houses in those towns where they were allowed to reside. In 1275 Hagin, a prosperous financier in Lincoln, sold to Stephen Chenduit properties he owned in Lincoln and York. The next year Stephen sold a house in

33. Madox I p221 describes and itemises the tallages.
34. Madox I p228.
35. King John's Charter of Liberties 1200, to the Jews of England and Normandy, Madox I p255.
36. Richardson *Jewry* pp237-240: '*in feodo et hereditate de me et meis heredibus illi et heredibus suis....*'
37. Richardson *Jewry* p134.
38. Richardson *Jewry* Appendix X.
39. Richardson *Jewry* p281.
40. Richardson *Jewry* p241.
41. Cecil Roth 'Oxford Starrs' [Roth *Starrs*] p70.

London to Hagin's nephew.[42] Another Hagin was 'formally enfeoffed with the manor of Childewick'.[43]

If their title was impugned, Jews had access to the king himself to protect it. HG Richardson declared:[44]

> We find them suing and being sued before the justices in eyre as well as in the exchequer and sometimes before the king himself.... for the possession of land.

And he supports that statement with many authorities.

The estate of a Jew passed on death automatically to the Crown. A mixed jury of Jews and Christians fixed its value, with the cooperation of representatives of the deceased's family. After the deduction of one-third of that value, which went to the king, the remainder went according to the deceased's will or Jewish customary law of intestacy. The family might buy back the third share from the king and often did.

Women

The position of Jewish women is of special interest. They worked as moneylenders and pawnbrokers in their own names. There are almost as many women as men in the records of the Exchequer of the Jews. Single women, widows and married women had for these purposes the same status as men, though married women could not dispose of their property without their husband's consent.

In 1220 Chera of Winchester distrained on the lands of Margaret de Craye for a debt of 16 marks.[45] That is a simple example representative of hundreds in the plea rolls of the Exchequer of the Jews. Husband and wife could be treated as one. In 1275 Robert Colingham owed Iveta, daughter of Bonefey, 5 marks (66s 8d) on a bond which the king had taken for tallage. Robert produced a receipt for 10s from Josce Bullock, Iveta's husband. Robert paid 56s 8d to the king and was discharged of the debt; that is, the payment to Josce was treated as a payment to Iveta.

Women were often identified by their mother's name: Belina, daughter of Mirabil.[46] More surprising, to me at least, is that a man could be identified by the name of his mother – in 1244 Deulesant, son of Chera,

42. Roth *Starrs* p68; text at Richardson *Jewry* pp239-240.
43. Roth *Starrs* p70, who discusses the family relations, particularly of Abraham son of Vives.
44. Richardson *Jewry* pp112-113 with copious citations to the Pipe Rolls from Henry II.
45. EJ I p26.
46. EJ I pp37, 53 and Comitissa and Genta *passim*.

is named as a creditor and a summons is recorded against Simon, son of Chera[47] – or even his mother-in-law: Moses, son-in-law of Antera.[48]

Attitudes to Jews

The role Jews played as moneylenders coloured the attitudes of Christians. *We* live in a world of credit. The adherents of no religion now take the clear prohibition of usury more seriously than to take care how they get round it. But then as now moneylenders were not loved. The rate of interest for Jewish loans was up to 2d per £1 per week, 42½ per cent per annum. That is much less than Wonga, the widely advertised 'payday loan' company, charges now: 4,214% APR or just under 1% a day.[49] Like us, thirteenth-century borrowers were glad of the chance to use other people's money. The king was no doubt happy to be able to confiscate Jewish bonds by a tallage whenever he needed to. But no one *enjoys* paying that kind of interest or thinks well of those who lend to them. If they can be identified as culturally different, especially if they are of a strange religion when religion is a powerful influence, they are likely to be ill treated. Christians heard no other propaganda than the sermon they were required to listen to every week and the Church insisted until recently that all Jews, past and present, were Christ-killers.

Ill-will easily turns to violence. From their first arrival in England, Jews had been subjected not only to bigoted envy and royal greed but increasingly to physical brutality.[50]

The Expulsion of 1290

In 1289 Edward I expelled all Jews from Gascony. In 1290 he extended his ethnic cleansing to England. Many left for Poland and other parts of Eastern Europe. Most of Catholic Western Europe was scarcely more hospitable than England; those who got to France were soon driven out.

Until their gradual return under Cromwell in 1655, there are few official records of Jews on English soil except in connection with the *Domus Conversorum*, in Chancery Lane, where converts lived up to

47. EJ I pp75 and 77 and p248, Moses, son of Belia.
48. EJ II p209. Of course, this practice was not unknown among Gentiles. Henry II was known as Henry fitz Empress but Matilda was no ordinary mother. But the Pleas Rolls of the Exchequer of the Jews record Christians: John son of Beatrice, Robert son of Susanna, Roger, William and John, sons of Margery, and John son of Juliana, EJ I pp 5, 9 and 24.
49. Wonga, the widely advertised 'payday loan' company, charges 4,214% APR or just under 1% a day.
50. RR Mundill *The King's Jews: Money, Massacre and Exodus in Medieval England* London, Continuum 2010.

1551 and even later.[51] There were also a few Spanish Jewish merchants in London who had ostensibly converted, and some occasional visitors.

DISPUTE RESOLUTION WITHIN THE JEWISH COMMUNITIES

Now to dispute resolution, first among Jews themselves. The Jewish communities were consistently careful to observe Jeremiah's precept of rendering unto Caesar. The obverse of that expedient was their preference for mediated settlements or judgments within their own community. But the sources show that the abhorrence of litigation between the faithful before the courts of the Gentiles, enjoined by the clearest of doctrine, could wane before the attractions of expediency.

The Beth Din

The traditional English assemblies of hundred and shire and the feudal courts were not normally open to Jews, nor could they use the royal courts without the king's permission. Government policy was to interfere as little as necessary in their internal affairs. They should handle their own disputes and could be relied on to have more effective social sanctions against the recalcitrant.

That did not stop the Government intervening when it saw fit. Then as now, the Common Law courts enforced the judgments of the *Beth Din*. A few traces have survived of the *Beth Din*'s work and of the Masters of the Law who advised it and the parties.[52] A starr from 1264 records the decision of a *Beth Din* on a marriage jointure relating to property in Norwich. The land was declared to belong to Cuntasse. That allowed her to transfer it formally to her son-in-law Judah, at the customary rent of one nail of cloves.[53] And other starrs from Norwich record the outcomes of similar disputes about the rights of widows to jointures.[54] These are not arbitrations but rather settlements formalised by the *Beth Din*. Jewish law drew a clear distinction between the judges of the *Beth Din* and arbitrators, who need not be qualified in Rabbinic law or be three in number. But the Common Law courts enforced their awards and judgments alike.

A Private Arbitration

We are fortunate to have direct documentary evidence of a Jewish arbitration from the middle of the thirteenth century, preserved in the

---

51. YT Assis and Yosof Kaplan eds *Jews and Conversos at the Time of the Expulsion* Jerusalem, Zalman Shazar Centre 1999; RC Stacey 'The Conversion of Jews to Christianity in Thirteenth-Century England' (1992) 67 *Speculum* 263-283.
52. Rigg *Select Pleas* pp65-67; Lipman pp150-153.
53. Davis p109 no45.
54. Davis p136 no53, p143 no55, p178 no66, pp298-299 no156 and p336 no180.

earliest surviving manuscript recording a private arbitration of any kind in England since Roman times.

Two Jewish brothers, Isaac and Hayyim, had problems in physically dividing into equal shares the property in Norwich they inherited from their father Meshullam.[55] Two unnamed arbitrators declared their award in Hebrew in July 1249.[56] The badly damaged manuscript is one part of a chirograph.

My friend Victor Tunkel, secretary of the Selden Society [retired 2016; d. 2019 – SH], brought the document to my notice. He has edited and translated what can be read, with the learned assistance and additions of Dr Zefira Rokeah and her husband, the Hebrew scholar Professor David Rokeah. All credit is theirs, though not the responsibility for the shortcomings of my interpretation.[57]

The whole plot seems to have lain alongside two other properties owned by Jews, Eliav ben Jacob to the south and Samuel to the west. To the east lay the land of William of Beltham, a Christian; to the north a public way. Isaac was a doctor. He and his son Solomon were in general practice as physicians. They would have made use of the herb garden which lay immediately south of this property.[58]

The award gives every appearance of following a common form. That is more likely to be evidence that arbitration was commonplace among the Jews of Norwich (and probably more widely) than that the precedent was taken from some non-Jewish source for this arbitration particularly. This is yet more evidence that Jews could then *own* land for their own occupation. Lines 17 and 19 read: 'lands from the creation of the world until its end …. to exchange and to bequeath …. selling to whomever.' As an old conveyancer, that looks to me as good as a fee simple.

Line 18 is incomplete but, depending on the disputed translation, may contain the common form requirement that the parties accept the award in friendship. The dispute may have been heated at the start. We do not know the circumstances. It would not be unusual for brothers to fall out over their inheritance. On the other hand, the difference could just as easily have been amicable, the family preferring impartial friends to make the allocation to avoid the possibility of the difference becoming a dispute. The even number of arbitrators might justify a slight preference for this being a friendly distribution.

55. Lipman pp117-118.
56. Westminster Abbey Muniment WAM6816.
57. Lipman between pp116 and 117.
58. Lipman p118.

THE EXCHEQUER OF THE JEWS

Protection of the Jews

So much for differences between Jews for which they had their own arbitration practices. What about disputes between Jews and Christians? About 1198, the Government set up a court to deal with them, the Exchequer of the Jews. Its purpose was to protect the bonds recording loans from Jews to Christians: to give Jewish moneylenders the security they needed if they were to function at all. But its jurisdiction was wider than that; it did whatever the Government wanted it to do.

When the king wanted the Court to do something on his behalf, he addressed his writ thus:[59]

> Greetings to the treasurer and barons and justiciars assigned to the care of the Jews, *thesaurario et baronibus et justiciariis ad custodiam judeorum assignatis.*

Now in Latin *custodia* has a range of meanings. In English they include guardianship and safekeeping and looking after, but there is no element there of custody in the sense of restriction of freedom. The Plea Rolls provide plenty of evidence that the Government, for whatever reasons, did take care to protect Jews from violence and wrongful accusations when it wanted to. Its motives were no doubt mixed.[60]

For example, no authority could claim any customary right to exact a toll on Jews. As late as 1281, when feelings were high against Jews, the Court punished seven Christians for toppling over a Jewish hearse and taking away a tabard as a toll. They pleaded that they had stopped the procession in their office as bailiffs and taken the tabard to pay the 2s toll to which they were entitled by custom on the trappings of a Jewish funeral carriage. Because he had no royal warrant, and 'since all the Jews in all the kingdom of England by royal charter should be relieved of every kind of custom', their leader was imprisoned until 'he satisfied the king and the Jews'.[61]

The *archae* system and the processes of the Court seem to have worked well. There is plenty of evidence of Jews and Christians cooperating efficiently. The Court regularly swore a panel, in Latin *inquisitio*, of six Jews and six Christians, sometimes twelve of each, to decide matters

59. EJ V p160 no865; there are many other examples.
60. EJ I pp157-158; EJ III p5.
61. EJ VI pp274-275 no1124. A Christian debtor before the Exchequer of Jews might lose a defence which he would have had at Common Law such as infancy, EJ II pp288-289.

of fact,[62] to estimate the value of chattels,[63] to decide who owned what land,[64] to authenticate a starr,[65] sometimes to hear criminal charges. They usually seem to have been able to agree on their verdict. Jew and Christian even sat together as arbitrators.

Mediation

The records of the Court provide plenty of evidence of mediation. Parties do *not* take their dispute to court and pay the required fees if they can resolve the matter themselves, with or without legal advice. The mere fact that there is a record proves that the parties had a dispute which they could not resolve without third party intervention. It is true that, once the matter was before the court, the issues might have been clarified for the first time sufficiently for the parties to sort them out for themselves. But they knew that it was usual for the court, once involved, to demand a fee to allow (and record) a settlement. The court might forgo the fee, if a party was poor,[66] but the liability to pay it was never overlooked.

Hundreds of concords are recorded in the Plea Rolls. The Latin phrase used to record them is ambiguous: *concordati sunt* can equally mean they came to an agreement themselves or they were brought to an agreement by others. It did not matter to the Court or much to the parties perhaps. But it means that in most cases we can only guess whether mediation was involved in any way.[67] But there are examples where there is no ambiguity. Thomas Madox records such a settlement in *The History and Antiquities of the Exchequer*.[68]

> For instance: in the 9th year of K Richard I, the Justices of the Jews settled an account between Richard de Bitebroc and Samuel the Jew of Stanford, touching a mortgage …

In another passage he puts beyond doubt the meaning of *concordati sunt*. He describes an unusual example of how officers of the Exchequer of the Jews could exploit their privilege of bringing their own disputes before the court:[69]

---

62. EJ VI p238 no943.
63. EJ VI eg pp239-240 no947.
64. EJ VI eg p244 no968.
65. EJ VI pp247-248 no985.
66. The non-Jewish party. EJ I p221. '1 mark *condonatur per judicios*' EJ V p33 no218 marginal note.
67. The different usages are shown in *Dictionary of Medieval Latin from British Sources* London, Oxford UP Fascicle II C 1981.
68. Madox I p235.
69. Madox I

Robert de Fulham, a Justice of the Jews, came into the Exchequer and complained of a violence done to his person in Westminster Hall by Robert de Coleville, a Sergeant at Law ... . The Treasurer and Barons summoned the Sergeant to appear before them ... . And there, in the presence of the Treasurer and Barons, and of Gilbert de Preston and Robert de Messinden, Justices of the Bank then sitting in the Exchequer, the Sergeant made an entire submission to the Justice of the Jews. Whereupon, by mediation of the other Sergeants of the Bank, it was settled, *concordatus est*.

Coleville had to appear again before the same assembled persons, with his tunic loose and his head uncovered, and submit to the will of de Fulham, life and limb and all his land and goods. The offended Justice of the Jews forgave him all and sealed it with a kiss. *Et concordati sunt*.

Christian Against Christian

There all the parties were Christians. The circumstances were special but, though no legislation gave the Court jurisdiction over actions between Christians, hundreds of instances are recorded. Some are understandable: for example where one of the parties had succeeded to an obligation arising originally out of a Jewish moneylending bond;[70] or when the king stood to gain.[71] But a dispute about a Christian will might be heard, not only where a loan from a Jew was involved, but where there was no Jewish involvement at all and the Court was clearly usurping the jurisdiction of the Church.[72]

Another general exception seems to have been the privilege granted to officers of the Court. William de Middelton was a clerk of the Court from 1265 and given custody of the rolls in 1276.[73] It was part of his job to receive money paid into court.[74] There is evidence that he was himself a moneylender.[75] He certainly used the court to recover his own debts,[76] as did other clerks, serjeants and even the senior justiciar, Hamo

---

70. EJ I pp243 and 244.
71. EJ I p269.
72. EJ V pp39 no 256 and p40 no 257; EJ V p58 no 356. The Court might even deal with a dispute about tithes in which the parties were Christian clergy, EJ VI p179 no584; or the apportionment of Christian lands, EJ VI pp219-220 no818; or with a will, giving instructions to the Archbishop of Canterbury's seneschal, EJ VI p214 no785. There are too many other matters between Christians to cite, but e.g. EJ VI pp222-224 and *passim* pp284-297.
73. EJ VI p40 gives full details of his career; he later became a Baron of the Exchequer; Madox I p234.
74. EJ I pp307-308, from Rosamund de Ernham.
75. EJ I p201; also pp203, 214.
76. EJ I p316 against the presumably Christian Peter Chaplain.

Hauteyn.[77] In 1275, the Court allowed de Middleton a loveday in his claim of trespass against two Christians.[78] He helped others to recover debts, in matters in which he was not personally involved. In 1272 he laid before the Court the claim of Ralph, son of Adam of the Chamber, against Walter of the Chamber and his wife Emma. A settlement was arranged: '*postea Willelmus de Middleton et Radulfus de Camera concordati sunt*'. It was de Middleton, acting perhaps as Ralph's attorney, who settled with Walter and Emma, the creditors.

Jew Against Jew

The Exchequer of the Jews was set up to deal with disputes between Jews and Christians but there are enough examples of Jew suing Jew there to show that the policy was not exclusive and easily and often circumvented.[79] No religion has a monopoly of hypocrisy and it was easy and routine to get round the Biblical prohibition of one Jew lending to another on usury by pretending that there was a Christian intermediary.[80]

A bond entered into by a Christian might later become the subject of dispute between Jews and be ended by a court-mediated settlement.[81] An undated starr from Norwich records that Abraham was indebted to Jechiel. If he failed to follow the agreed repayments, the debt would be converted to a debt on a bond between them 'through a Christian hand, paying interest thereon'.[82]

The intervention of third parties might break the deadlock of a fixed debt wholly repayable on a due date, by arranging payment by instalments, even after the Court had worked out a compromise and the parties were *concordati*.[83] That might result in the Court removing a block in the way of repayment from Jewish debtor to Jewish creditor. Nicol de Randworth's debts to Jacob ben Eliab had been 'compromised for 13 marks' in the Court. But an undated starr from Norwich relates that Jacob's brother Judah later swore on oath that he had a claim to the debt.

77. EJ VI p187 no633, p222 nos830, 831. He was later suspended for maladministration in his accounts, Madox *Exchequer* I pp254-255.
78. EJ II p256.
79. The Court was given jurisdiction in Crown Pleas between Jew and Jew, EJ I pp50-52. There is ample evidence of accusations of crimes committed by Jews, particularly of coin-clipping, J Thorold Rogers ed *Oxford City Documents: Financial and Judicial 1268-1665* Oxford, Clarendon P for Oxford Historical Society 1891 pp186-187; and of murder e.g. Wigram pp221-223 nos 97, 98.
80. Deuteronomy xxiii 20; Davis pviii, pp46-47 no20, p50 no22, pp63-64 no28, p72 no 31, p74, no 32 (AD1252).
81. EJ I pp83-84 and pp250-251 the detailed account of the concord 'by leave of the justices' between Rosamund of Ernham, Benedict of Winchester and Wlliam le Tailor.
82. Davis p202 no83.
83. E.g. Madox I pp250-251.

A private arrangement provided that Jacob should have 3 marks forthwith and at a future date a further 5 marks, plus 32s which he had lent Judah. From the balance Judah must repay 2 marks to Abraham.

The Court assumed that it was for the *Beth Din* to say whether one Jew could take interest from another. Madox cites an entry on the Great Roll of the Exchequer without a date:[84]

> Judas the Jew of Bristol owes two ounces of gold for an inquiry to be made in the *Beth Din* whether a Jew ought to take usury from a Jew.

In 1278, the Court explicitly decided that such a loan was legal and that it had jurisdiction to enforce it. Josce had sold debts to Aaron:[85]

> It will be perfectly legal, *bene licebit*, for Aaron to have a writ from the king against Josce.... If Josce goes back on this agreement in any way, it shall be perfectly legal for Aaron to have him distrained in any court, Christian or Jewish, for the debts, plus interest and all expenses, for which Aaron's own word will be sufficient evidence.

An action brought by a Jew to recover a debt on a transferable instrument, drawn by a Jewish drawer payable to a Jewish payee or bearer, shows how the procedure worked in 1272.[86]

The Court even took cognisance of matrimonial disputes between Jews and, after hearing expert evidence on Jewish law, declared a purported marriage invalid.[87] And the king used the Court to protect a Jewish woman's dower.[88]

Arbitration

The evidence so far has been of *mediated* settlements. What evidence is there of arbitrations? At their very start, the records provide an example of an arbitration arranged by the Court.[89] One of the leading Jewish families in England were the descendants of Jurnet and Muriel of Norwich.[90] From about 1175 they lived in a great town house, later owned by the Pastons and then by none other than Edward Coke. Jurnet had a brother and partner Benedict, who made a loan to Walter of Raveningham. In

84. Madox I p244: '*Judas Judaeus de Bristo debet ii uncias auri, pro inquisitione facienda in Capitulo Judaeorum si Judaeus debet capere usuram de Judaeo*'.
85. EJ V pp49-50 no 313.
86. Rigg *Select Pleas* pp65-66, from the Latin.
87. EJ I p152 (1267).
88. EJ III pp316-317.
89. EJ I pp3 and 5.
90. Lipman pp95-112.

1218, after the deaths of both Walter and Benedict, Pigone, presumably Benedict's widow, sued Walter's son Roger for repayment of the sum of £81, producing a starr to prove the terms of the loan. The court referred the matter to two Christian knights and two Jews to bring the parties to a concord. If not by agreement, then their award was to be final. If they could not agree on their award, a date was set for the case to come back to the Court.

An award of 1277[91] records that Henry Pyle had agreed with Isaac of Camden and Meyr of Bruges to submit their dispute to Walter de Sterchesl' and Aaron son of Vives, who had awarded that Isaac and Meyr should pay Henry 7 marks, by two instalments of 20s and 42s 8d, Roger de Croft taking the balance of 24s if he claimed it, with subsidiary questions also determined, including the possession of a brass pot.

CONCLUSIONS

What then can be learned of general importance from the study of how Jewish disputes were settled in the two centuries when Jews were such a part of English life? The evidence is clear that Jews within their own communities used mediation and arbitration in much the same ways as Christians then did. Moreover, their special status under royal protection opened up many kinds of opportunities for enforcing their legal rights and taking advantage of defences which were not open to Christians. Whatever kindly interpretations can be put upon *custodia* though, Jews were in fact both exploited and discriminated against. Yet there were individuals with more wealth and influence, like Aaron son of Vives, who must have been able to use not only the courts but other ways of enforcing debts, well enough to count themselves successful.

As arbitrators and members of juries, as clerks and chirographers, even occasionally as lawyers, Jews also played a full part in the business of their own Exchequer Court, taking the same responsibilities and being trusted in the same way as Christians there.

The total absence of any panel with an odd number of members in itself shows that, in all these third-party interventions, mediation was primary, with arbitration only if mediation failed. The even number arises from the appointment of usually two persons by each party, who would first try to mediate a complete settlement to which the parties would agree but, if they failed to do that, could at least agree together to suggest arbitrators who the parties would agree should dispose of the differences still in dispute.

91. EJ III pp289-290.

How different the development of dispute resolution might have been if the Jews had been allowed to stay. There is still much to be discovered. What allowed Jews to swear oaths on the Torah scrolls, even together with Christians? Why is there no sign in the English sources of the need for a *kinyan*? The requirement of the exchange of a token has prevailed in Jewish law from the earliest times to the present day, from the shoe which Boaz gave to secure the purchase of the land and Ruth who came with it, through the traditional Rabbi's handkerchief and then, when Rabbis started to use tissues, the token pen which itself has given way now, so I am reliably informed, to today's mobile phone.

There is so much more work to be done by others with a better grasp of Jewish traditions. I hope this lecture will stimulate it.

[*TAILPIECE – SH*
I have had to work on two different drafts of this text: one is, apparently (from Derek's insertions in ink), the one he intended to use to deliver his lecture on 19 February – it is on a memory stick dated 13 February. At the end of that original text is a handwritten note ready for the end of the lecture. In it, Derek not only noted that the lecture was in honour of Leah and Alexander Woolf, but also wished to dedicate it to their son Harry, Lord Woolf, 'whom everyone holds in the highest esteem who knows him as a judge, a mediator and a man. He cannot be here tonight but will respond to my invitation to increase our knowledge by commenting critically on the text I've sent him'. Given the changes to the later text (on a memory stick dated 19 February), I surmise Lord Woolf may, indeed, have commented.]

8.   ODDS OR EVENS: HOW MANY ARBITRATORS?

1. INTRODUCTION

There is now a lively debate, among those who know most from their
own experience, about the proper role of the party-appointed arbitrator
in international commercial arbitration.[1] If all goes well, it will produce
results based on clear thinking about what is best for the parties, those
for whom the whole machinery of international commercial arbitration is
required to function.[2]

Leaving aside the quite easily separable problems of disputes arising
under bilateral investment treaties and the like, this short article will
concentrate on arbitrations in which the parties have untrammelled
control over the choice of arbitrators and the scope and procedure of the
arbitration. It will not suggest for a moment that there are lessons from
history which offer solutions. It will be content to ensure that those who
continue the debate understand better how we have got to where we are.
That knowledge can do no harm and may just throw occasional light
where assumptions have obscured the discussion.

2. ARCHIVES OF ARBITRATION PROJECT

At the end of 2012 the Chartered Institute of Arbitrators financed the
Archives of Arbitration Project, a small pilot study with limited aims,
completed in July 2013.[3] It sought to recover and archive documents
relating to arbitration which would be of value in programmes of

1. There is a rich and extensive literature, too large to list here. The arguments are made
in the special issue of the ABA Section of International Law, International Arbitration
Committee *Newsletter* (2013) 1: 1.
2. Sir Peter Cresswell 'The Future of Arbitration in the Changing World of Dispute
Resolution' (2013) 79 *Arbitration* 285-294 is a clear statement of current policy.
3. The directors were William Twining and Derek Roebuck, assisted by Magdalene
D'Silva on Part 1 and Francis Calvert Boorman on Part 2. I thank Dr Boorman not only
for that research but for his critical comments on a draft of this article. [In order to provide
an update, I asked Dr Boorman to do so for this footnote. He replied, 'The pilot study
developed into two successful projects, 'The History of Arbitration' and 'Legal Records at
Risk', both based at the Institute of Advanced Legal Studies – SH]

research and teaching. Though interested in documents of all kinds, it has concentrated on records in the English language.

The Project had two parts. Part 1 sought to identify records of international commercial arbitration, to consider problems of privacy and confidentiality, and to do the preliminary work which would allow the creation of the necessary databases. It will be reported on separately.

Part 2 sought to survey the published literature on arbitration records from 1558 to *c*1700; to start an inventory of archives which already hold significant arbitration records; to find and catalogue all other relevant materials, and to set up systems for their continuing retrieval. That research has provided the material for this article.

Dr Boorman searched public archives to find documents relating to arbitration; 32 repositories produced results and a database has been created of records from across England and throughout the period. It will be published and made available to all when resources allow. It includes agreements to submit to arbitration (usually bonds) awards and letters and other background material.[4]

The records show that all kinds of dispute were submitted to arbitration: commercial, criminal, ecclesiastical, family and inheritance, but above all about the ownership of land. Every condition of person could be a party, infant or centenarian, woman or man, labourer or Bess of Hardwick. The arbitrators could be anyone from the humblest husbandman to Elizabeth I. Women were appointed occasionally and in particular circumstances.

The parties often chose lawyers, including some of the most distinguished judges of their time, but sometimes they expressly disqualified them. Two documents from the Shakespeare Archive are sufficient illustration.[5] A deed from 1596 insists that the arbitrators be gentlemen and not lawyers 'in study or in practice'. A suggested arbitrator makes clear in 1633 that he will accept appointment only if the other arbitrator is determined to put an end to the matter 'for I would have him no rangler'.

Many things are to be learned from these private documents but none more informative than the clue they reveal to understanding what our ancestors, parties and arbitrators, assumed to be the function of the party-appointed arbitrator. That clue is the preferred number of arbitrators.

3. EARLIER EVIDENCE

The clue demands that we follow it backwards, picking up what had previously been overlooked in *Mediation and Arbitration in the Middle*

---

4. Research has also begun on other sources, e.g. the Privy Council records considered below; also Derek Roebuck 'The London Centre for the International Commercial Mediation and Arbitration in the Reign of Elizabeth I' (yet to be published). [It was published in 2014 and is, indeed, included in this volume as Chapter 11 – SH.]
5. The Shakespeare Centre DR5/1316 and DR10/1723.

Ages.[6] An odd number seems to us to have such obvious advantages that we may take it for granted that parties would always and naturally have preferred it. Yet in England, at the latest from when a state legal system can be seen to be well established until modern times, that has not been so.[7]

As early as 1278, James Le Roy, a Flemish merchant, claimed £500 from the English wool merchant, John de Redmere, in a matter which had been running since 1267 and was not disposed of until 1284.[8] William of Norbury, one of the royal judges, was appointed together with 'any one of our faithful subjects whom you shall have associated with yourself for this' to make enquiries and correct any error they found and 'to do justice according to the mercantile law (*secundum legem mercatoriam*)'. William co-opted five merchants: a tribunal of six.

In 1290 Peter Arnold of Bayonne petitioned the king to instruct the Seneschal of Gascony to compel Arnold and Peter De Monte to swear to abide by the arbitration of Sancho de Sanguineto and William of Paris, to declare their award between Peter Arnold and the De Montes. A writ was issued to the Seneschal.[9] All parties and the arbitrators appear to be foreigners: a tribunal of two.

A dispute arose in 1299 under the Statute of Merchants 1285 whether Ralph's debt to Reymund had been paid and whether Reymund's receipt was valid. The parties submitted to the arbitration of four named worthy and law-abiding men, *probos et legales*, in respect of all existing disputes between them, a fifth to be added if they could not agree. The four agreed in their award.[10]

In 1353, the Statute of Staples designated eleven English towns, one Welsh and four Irish to have exclusive rights in the trade of wool, fleeces, leather, lead and tin. Chapter 24 provided for six experts to arbitrate in matters of quality, four aliens (two from Germany and two from Lombardy) and two English, good and faithful men, *bones gentz et de foi*. The statute gave their awards the force of law.

On 14 February 1388 in the Lord Mayor's Court John Burwell claimed from his partner Nicholas Horne 86 tuns and one pipe of Rochelle wine.

6. Derek Roebuck *Arbitration and Mediation in the Middle Ages: England 1154-1558* Oxford: HOLO Books, The Arbitration Press pp70-84 (*Middle Ages*), under the subheadings Commerce and Maritime.
7. The research, which has not gone beyond 1714, has so far not shown when the change took place.
8. Hubert Hall ed *Select Cases Concerning the Law Merchant 1239-1633 II* (1929) 46 Selden Society ppxxxiii-iv, 18-27.
9. *Rotuli Parliamentorum I* p58.
10. Hubert Hall ed *Select Cases Concerning the Law Merchant 1251-1779 III* (1932) 49 Selden Society pp17-18.

The mayor appointed four arbitrators, apparently of his rather than the parties' choice.

In *Costace v Forteneye* (1389) the Mayor of London's Court had to deal with a dispute arising from the London buyer's refusal to accept and pay for wine delivered in London from Gascony:[11]

> The defendant admitted the agreement but declared that the plaintiff was not prepared to deliver the casks as agreed ... . Instructions were given to summon a jury, of whom half should be Gascons, according to custom ... . The parties agreed to put themselves on the arbitration of four men of the mistery of vintners.

The *Black Book of the Admiralty* is a collection of documents compiled probably in the thirteenth century.[12] It includes the Laws of Oléron, possibly introduced to England under the patronage of Eleanor of Aquitaine, who died in 1204. Its introduction reads:

> Here are the good ordinances and the good customs concerning maritime matters, which the wise men, who travel the world, began to give our forebears, which they took from the books of the knowledge of good customs.

Those customs included submission of disputes to arbitration. On disputes about loading:[13]

> If the ship which has been chartered is required to load in that place where the charterparty, *contracte del nolit*, was made, it should be submitted to two good men of the art of the sea, *dos bons homens de la art de la mar*, who are worthy of trust; and whatever they say should be followed.

When disputes arise about the price of freight of timber,[14] or about replacement of a ship's lost gear,[15] or unnecessary expenditure on fitting out the ship,[16] they should similarly be submitted to the arbitration of two *bons homens*. They are also to decide questions of salvage:[17] 'salvors

---

11. AH Thomas ed *Calendar of Select Pleas and Memoranda of the City of London ... AD1381-1412 [CPMR]* pp162-164.
12. Travers Twiss ed *The Black Book of the Admiralty with an Appendix* London, Longman [Rolls Series] 4 vols 1871-1876 [*Black Book*].
13. *Black Book* III p116.
14. *Black Book* III p632.
15. *Black Book* III p302.
16. *Black Book* III p405.
17. *Black Book* III p618.

should be paid appropriate remuneration by the award of *bons homens* of the place.' If a ship has to be run aground and the parties, the master and the merchants whose goods were aboard, cannot agree on the value of the vessel and its cargo, the dispute should be submitted to two *bons homens* who know and understand well the art of the sea.[18] They will fix the price to be paid by those whose goods survive, if the parties cannot agree. They can hold an auction and let the arguing parties bid.

So a manual, from a culture quite distinct from that of England in the Common Law's infancy, was there recommending a tribunal of two as the best practice.

Technical problems might require specialist skills. The master of a ship might hire, for a time or a voyage, casks for the transport of wine. Their owner might stipulate that they be at the master's risk and that the freight be paid in advance of the voyage. If the casks were lost, the master would be liable to the owner for their value plus the hire. Any dispute between them was to be submitted to two good men 'who are coopers and of the coopers' guild'.[19]

In the fourteenth century the London Sheriff's Court disposed of maritime disputes by referring them to the Mayor's Court, which arranged an arbitration. The roll for 10 June 1386 records that John Bedon of Calais, owner of the 'Mary of Exeter', claimed profits from Hugh Richardson of Southampton, its captain and helmsman, *custos et gubernator*.[20] They agreed to the arbitration of two 'good citizens'.

The Court of Admiralty followed not the Common Law but the procedures of the Civil Law. An entry for 16 April 1444 records a *compromissum* by which the parties agreed to submit their dispute then before the court to Thomas Burgh and Simon Pygot, merchants of King's Lynn, chosen by the claimants, and Thomas Salesbury and John Scyle, chosen by the defendants.

The King's Council also took an interest in maritime disputes. On 4 January 1454 Robert Bretlond, bailiff of Harwich, entered into a bond of £100 to John Bullock, master of the 'Nicholas', and three other Aberdeen merchants. They had made a general acquittance to Robert and put it into the hands of a Chancery master, to hold until they certified that Robert had restored to them the ship and its cargo. Meanwhile Robert must enter into this bond, to stand by the arbitration of two, the Chancellor and Viscount Beaumont, to fix what damages and costs the Scots had suffered as a result of Robert's detention of the 'Nicholas'.[21]

18. *Black Book* III p266.
19. *Black Book* III p294.
20. *CPMR 1381-1412* pp121-122.
21. *CCR 1468-1476* no676; *Rotuli Parliamentorum I* p32.

In 1539 the Court of Admiralty appointed two arbitrators in a matter arising from a collision at sea;[22] and in 1540 four arbitrators appointed to dispose of a dispute about seamen's wages were able to mediate a settlement.[23]

Just one contemporary example from a quite different culture, that of Malta, then part of the Kingdom of Sicily before the time of the Knights, shows that the even number of arbitrators appointed by a standard form of *compromissum* was no English aberration. Notary Zabbara of the tiny island of Gozo recorded on December 9, 1496 a land dispute submitted '*in egregios Andream de Falsono et Marcum de Brancato … arbitros, arbitratores et amicabiles compositors*'.[24]

Many more examples of submission to an even number of mediator-arbitrators could be produced but they would not allow any comparison of odds and evens. That is possible only when larger collections of private documents become available which can be compared with the records of the Privy Council.

4. THE EVIDENCE OF THE PRIVATE ARCHIVES

A striking feature of the documents in private archives is their evidence of the number of arbitrators appointed. Ordinarily each side appointed one (or two) and those two (or four) together resolved the dispute. Sometimes, if they could not, they would appoint a third, or fifth. They knew the difference between one who was appointed to make up an odd number, so that a majority might prevail, and one appointed as umpire, to make the final decision himself. They might even provide for the third or fifth in an arbitration clause intended to deal with disputes which had not yet arisen.

The figures cannot support any statistical analysis but, for what they are worth, 23 archival repositories produced 405 documents between 1558 and 1700 from which it was possible to be sure how many arbitrators were appointed. There was nothing to suggest that any hidden element might skew the figures.

In 81 a single arbitrator was appointed; in 206 two; in 30 three; in 61 four; in 3 five; in 11 six; in 1 seven; and in 2 twelve – therefore 115 odd

22. (1892) 6 Selden Society pp90-91.
23. (1892) 6 Selden Society p101.
24. Stanley Fiorini (ed.) *Documentary Sources of Maltese History* Pt 1 Notarial Documents, 3 vols (Valletta University of Malta, 1996, 1999, 2005) Vol. II p 376 no 390. It is hoped to publish the results of research based on Giacomo Zabbaro's records as 'Mediation and Arbitration in Medieval Malta'. [This was published in 2015 in *Melita Historica* 16 115-140 and is published below as Chapter 10 – SH.]

to 280 even. So, why should parties have preferred two rather than three by seven times (206:30) and four to three by twice (61:30)?

The preference for a single arbitrator was usually where the matter in issue was of comparatively little value. Other single arbitrators held a special position of power over the parties which made their award and its enforcement acceptable: for example their common landlord or other social superior. But other evidence from the period shows that the submission to an even number was the norm. In 1596 the Court of Chancery in *Vysey v Walton*, wishing to end strife between two brothers, referred their dispute to two knights to arbitrate;[25] and in *Wentworth v Knightley* asked Edward Coke, then Attorney-General, and George Croke, of *Croke's Reports* and then Recorder of London, to mediate a particularly difficult land dispute. In 1624 the House of Lords delegated a dispute between adjoining manors to two arbitrators: the Earl of Bridgwater and Lord Russell.[26]

William West, in his book of precedents published in 1641, provides a standard Chancery form (in Latin) for the submission of a matter to be examined and mediated or arbitrated:[27]

Commission to hear and determine a matter on petition, and response, and to examine witnesses

... we grant you, or two of you, the power and authority to hear and examine ... and to determine it finally according to your sensible discretion if you can. Therefore we order you, or two of you, at a fixed time and place ... to call witnesses before you, or two of you ... to put an end to this if you can ... under your seals or those of two of you ...

The subject matter of the dispute does not seem to have determined the number of arbitrators. County archives contain quite a few documents relating to commercial disputes of all kinds. They arise from contracts for the sale of coal, wood, grain and tin; for house building and painting and decorating; all submitted to panels of two or four. The guilds, which had regularly resorted to arbitration in earlier times,[28] maintained their preference, and submitted disputes to a panel of two.[29] There were

25. JP Dawson *A History of Lay Judges* Cambridge, Mass, Harvard UP 1960 p167, citing *Reg Lib 1596* (A) fol l650b. At the start of the reign of Elizabeth I, the Court of Chancery referred 48 matters before it to arbitrators. A search is being undertaken to see the number in each case but a reference to two seems to be the most common practice.
26. JS Hart *Justice upon Petition* London, Harper Collins 1991 p51 and fn178 citing HLRO Main Papers HL 14 April 1624; *LJ* iii pp303, 415.
27. William West *The Second Part of Symboleography* pp191-192, s58.
28. *Middle Ages* especially pp217-234.
29. Cornwall Archives BHEL/259.

disputes arising from foreign trade, with what is now Germany,[30] or in the West Indies or Africa.[31] The subject matter of the trade covered everything that was traded then, not only cloth, timber and grain but jewellery, furs and wine. Arbitrators were asked to settle disputes over bills of exchange.[32] A panel might be appointed consisting solely of foreign arbitrators, for example French and Dutch merchants.[33] The brief descriptions of items in the National Archives do not usually allow the number to be ascertained; further examination of the originals is needed. When the number appointed can be discerned, it is usually even.

If we were studying modern arbitration records, we would not expect to find documents which expressly declare the parties' reasons for choosing their party-appointed arbitrator or for preferring the standard tribunal of three. But, by a stroke of luck, there survive a couple of unrelated ones from Lancashire which do reveal, if not in so many words then by clear implication, what the parties wanted from their party-appointed arbitrators. The first is a bond from 1562:[34]

John More of Bank House near Liverpool Esq to John Crosse of Liverpool Esq.

BOND in forty pounds, payable at Lady Day [25 March]. Dated 25th of February 5 Elizabeth [1562].

CONDITION: To abide and observe the award of the following arbitrators, viz: Richard Fazakerley, Thomas Bastwell and Alderman Robert Corbet, all of Liverpool, on behalf of John More; and John Maynwaring of Liverpool, merchant, John Jolie of Leigh, yeoman, and Laurence Breres, of Up-Walton, gent., on behalf of John Crosse, concerning the division of certain parcels of land in a close, croft, or hey in the Dale Street, called Asshe Heyghe.

The Award to be made in writing before Lady Day   Liverpool

It could be objected that the words 'on behalf of' are not clear enough to show that the parties meant their arbitrators to act for them. But that objection fades when the next document is set against it. This is a settlement arrived at by the arbitrators and agreed by the parties.[35]

30. National Archives SP46/176/fo273.
31. National Archives PRO 30/24/49/1 Barbados; C 6/407/63 Jamaica, also Old Calabar, Guinea Coast.
32. National Archives E134/4 Wm and M/Mich 49 and E134/5 Wm and M/ East30.
33. National Archives PRO 30/34/14.
34. Lancashire Archives DDSH 1/191.
35. Lancashire Archives Record Office DDF 1028.

AGREEMENT William Farington of Wourden Esq and Thomas, his son and heir; and Elizabeth Benson of Hugill, Co Westmoreland, and Mabell her daughter, widow of John Preston of Holker, by the mediation of Thomas Talbott of Basshall, John Bradley of Bythome, Esqs, John Talbot of Whalley, James Braithwate, Thomas Brigges and Gawen Braythwate, gents, arbitrators indifferently elected by every of the said parties.

Thomas was to marry Mabell and William Farington to pay her mother an annuity of fifty pounds with provision for a moiety of certain land and a jointure.

Now what is the difference between arbitrators appointed 'on behalf of' one party and those 'indifferently elected by every of the parties'? The former were expected to act as friends of one side, the latter as friends of both. If asked, those involved at the time could no doubt have written an essay on the functions of the party-appointed arbitrator.

The even number cannot be simply because mediator-arbitrators were then considered to be the agents of the party appointing them, because many of the arbitrations were arranged by a court, or by the Privy Council which chose the arbitrators. The Privy Council might allow or even encourage the parties to add their own choices. Sometimes the parties might object to the arbitrators selected for them. But, when a court appointed the arbitrators, it almost always chose two or four.

5. A SAMPLE OF APPOINTMENTS BY THE COUNCIL

A contemporary and plentiful source allows comparative insights.[36] Just one volume of the *Acts of the Privy Council* has been chosen, IX 1575-1577.[37] It records the work of the Privy Council, sitting at Westminster or Hampton Court, or following the queen around the country. A clerk recorded every substantial activity, from the grant of a passport or the return of an absconding wife to orders dealing with the troubles in Ireland, the fortifications of Ostend or the chronic problems of pirates and plague.

All the entries, a total of 1251, have been read to pick out those setting up arbitrations, 50 in all, and to find where possible the number of arbitrators appointed. Each individual entry has been counted once, though many produced multiple acts, such as one instruction to send the

36. JR Dasent and others eds *Acts of the Privy Council of England* [*APC*].
37. Not because they can be shown to be specially representative but for no better reason than that I happen to have those odd volumes and I find the hard copy easier to read than even the splendid on-line source.

same letter to four recipients, though none of those were instructions to set up an arbitration.

One entry does not disclose the number of arbitrators appointed and can be discarded. Of the 59 in our sample, there were:

9 with 1 arbitrator
18 with 2
9 with 3
13 with 4
1 with 5
4 with 6
1 with 8
1 with 12
1 with 2 or 4
2 with 4 or 6

That would mean that the Council appointed an even number 40 times and an odd number 19 times. But the appointment of a single arbitrator may perhaps be discounted for comparative purposes. There were usually sufficient reasons for the single appointment: the Vice-President of the Council in the Marches, or the Lord President of the Council in the North, or the Captain of Portsmouth, or the Earl of Pembroke, or the Master of Requests (twice) or the Admiralty judge (3 times). They were required to dispose of a controversy, but out of court, often in an administrative manner. Dr Dale, the civilian, was asked once to sort out part of the accounts in a composition with creditors. Where the Council appointed more than one arbitrator and therefore had reason to choose between an even and an odd number, it preferred an even number 40:10.

The subject matter did not affect the number of arbitrators the Council appointed. An even number was preferred, whether the dispute was commercial or within a family, whether between English parties or foreigners, whether to judges or laymen.

Arbitration was common in maritime disputes.[38] In 1575 the Court of Admiralty delegated a dispute about general average to four arbitrators 'elected and chosen to deem and judge.'[39]

The practices of insurers (and their underwriters) and those they insured are enlightening about attitudes and assumptions of merchants generally to dispute resolution. In 1573, the Council committed 'a

38. RG Marsden *Select Pleas in the Court of Admiralty I* (1894) 6 Selden Society and *II* (1897) 11 Selden Society [*Marsden*].
39. *Marsden II* pp39-40.

complaint against certain merchants of London for the assurance of a ship', to six merchants (or any four of them) to mediate a settlement.[40]

The Council's response to a foreigners' petition in 1576 was:[41]

> To the Master of the Rolls, Southcote, Harper and Jeffreys JJ, touching the matter in controversy between George Monnoux and certain merchants assurers. Forasmuch as the matter is of some weight and therefore doubtful whether it may be tried by the Common Law or not, the Lord Chief Justice and Dyer LJ are required to join with them the above-named, and to examine the said controversy anew; considering that the circumstances require the advice and opinion of such as are learned in the Civil Law, they should call unto them Dr Lewis and Dr Drurye, as so willed from the Lords, to join with them in the hearing and examining of the said cause, and upon the examination thereof to bring the parties, if it may be, to some good composition, which, if they shall not be able to do, to certify them particularly of their proceedings therein, and from which of the parties the stay groweth, that if the matter cannot be by them accorded, some final end may be taken further therein as appertaineth.

All even numbers: four judges to start with, then add two more, then another two civilians.

6. FURTHER WORK

This article has attempted no more than to show that for centuries some parties to disputes assumed that it was normal to have an even number of arbitrators. It may be possible to draw the conclusion that they generally assumed that their party-appointed arbitrators would act on their behalf during the proceedings of the tribunal, at least at the preliminary mediation stage. There could be other explanations. Much more work needs to be done and this article will have achieved one of its purposes if it leaves those who read it with a sense of unease until resources are provided for that purpose, while thanking again the Chartered Institute of Arbitrators for the generous grant which started off this line of research.

Just one topic may be bait enough: arbitration clauses have been assumed to be a modern invention. In some jurisdictions until recently, the Civil Law has refused to recognise a clause which binds the parties to submit future disputes to arbitration. Yet parties in England have been including such clauses in their agreements since the thirteenth century and frequently since the seventeenth.

40. JR Dasent ed *Acts of the Privy Council of England I* [*APC*] *1571-1575* p167.
41. *APC 1575-1577* p230.

Research already completed shows that mediation-arbitration, not litigation, was the process of dispute resolution preferred not only by the parties but by the government, at least up to the Restoration. When did that change? And why? More insights are readily available. If there is an 'arbitration community', and it has sufficient interest in its family history, it should be possible to persuade some of its members to provide the resources to support the work of a new generation of scholars prepared to devote a part of their lives to the necessary research.

[TAILPIECE – SH
Although the foregoing was published in 2014, it was completed on 7 October 2013. Instead of conclusions, it ends with the need for further work, in particular on arbitration clauses. The chapter that follows (9: 'Arbitration Clauses in England AD 1258 to 1600') shows that Derek complied with his own implicit exhortation. It was completed on 23 June 2014. He gave no publication details in either of his draft tables of contents, and I have been unable to find any.]

There is no evidence that this essay has ever been published.

9. ARBITRATION CLAUSES IN ENGLAND AD 1258 TO 1600

INTRODUCTION

Edward Coke [1552-1634 – SH] knew a lot about law reports:[1]

> I have often observed that, for want of a true and certain report, the case that hath been adjudged, standing upon the rack of many running reports (especially of such as understood not the state of the question) hath been so diversely drawn out, as many times the true parts of the case have been disordered and disjointed, and most commonly the right reason and rule of the judges utterly mistaken.

He had a genius for making what the judges were reported as having said lay down the law as Coke wanted it to be. Some of the best known reporters, like Dyer and Plowden, and Coke himself, were busy arbitrators.[2] When Dyer CJCP reported his own awards, he may well have expected them to have authority equal to his judgments. There are other reports which remain in manuscript, some of which have been considered worth editing and publishing recently, including Dyer's own previously unprinted notes.[3] But the whole corpus of the law reports, even if all the manuscripts were edited and published, would, by itself, be insufficient, even if not misleading, evidence of the law which was applied to dispute resolution. Nor should a narrow interpretation of legal history as the story of the development of legal rules be allowed to obscure the reality of what was happening in practice.

Law may exist before it is ever declared by a court. Some would argue that it must, but here it is enough to state the obvious: the opportunity for a court to make law arises when lawyers argue for it to win their

---

1. 1 Coke's Rep preface.
2. LW Abbott *Law Reporting in England 1485-1585* London, Athlone P 1973 pp176 and 204.
3. JH Baker ed *Reports from the Lost Notebooks of Sir James Dyer* 2 vols (1994) 109 and (1995) 110 Selden Society; WH Bryson *Cases Concerning Equity and the Courts of Equity 1550-1660* 2 vols (2000) 117 and (2001) 118 Selden Society; those of William Dalison (2007) 124 Selden Society and Sir John Spelman (1976) 73 and (1977) 74 Selden Society are from before this period.

case. Before then, it may for years have been applied in practice by generations of lawyers who were confident that the courts would so decide when they were given the chance.[4] Lawyers cannot wait for a case to be reported on a doubtful point before they advise a client. Historians may need to look elsewhere than in law reports to find out what the law was in practice.

THE ASSUMPTION

An example of a mistaken assumption arising from reliance on the evidence of the law reports is that the use of arbitration clauses, agreements to submit future disputes which may never arise, in English contracts began in the eighteenth century. From the lack of reported cases, it has been argued that arbitration clauses are modern inventions.[5]

> Until the first half of the eighteenth century, submissions ... were invariably *ad hoc* ... . The first agreements in which the parties promised that *future* disputes would be arbitrated appeared before the courts in the first half of the eighteenth century in commercial agreements.

The first statement does not follow from the second. It could be true that the first reported cases dealing with arbitration clauses appear in the eighteenth century. If no litigation arose from arbitration agreements – which would mean that they had done the job for which they were intended – or, more accurately, if no report exists of such litigation, evidence would have to be sought elsewhere. Fortunately enough documents have survived which contain arbitration clauses from as early as the middle of the thirteenth century.

EARLY EXAMPLES

A document in the Nottinghamshire Archives from 1633 records a disposition by the Archbishop of York dated 5 May 1258 resolving ecclesiastical disputes, with an arbitration clause providing that the sacristan should deal with any future disputes.[6]

---

4. An example would be that any competent lawyer would have advised a client to settle rather than rely on what was usually accepted to be the statement of the law on acceptance of a smaller sum in discharge of a debt in *Pinnel's Case* (1602) 5 Co Rep 117a in the three centuries and more before *High Trees* [1947] 1 KB 130.
5. MC McGaw 'Travels in Alsatia: "Judges of the Parties' Own Chusing", "Monstrous Powers", and the Role of the Courts' in Anthony Thornton and William Godwin eds *Construction Law: Themes and Practice* London, Sweet & Maxwell 1998 pp131-187.
6. Nottinghamshire Archives DD/SR/234/125.

In 1260 a clause in a Jewish starr appointed three men to assess the value of improvements should any dispute arise:[7]

> Should any additions have been made to the property, by which it has been materially improved, three good men of the city are to be called in to assess the value.

Two other contracts from around the same time contain arbitration clauses, appointing the chirographer who recorded them to deal with any future dispute as 'umpire'. And another, also from Norwich, provides for the peaceful and equitable settlement of future disputes by a third person 'to act as arbitrator and umpire'.

There are examples, too, from the fifteenth century. In 1420 William, Lord Botreaux, and Sir Walter, the future Lord Hungerford, entered into marriage contracts for their children. They delegated to their counsel the supervision of the necessary conveyancing and in an arbitration clause provided that any differences that might arise should be determined by Serjeant John Juyn, who was 'of counsel and friendship' to them both.[8]

In 1430, when English lords were about to set off for Henry VI's coronation in France, they anticipated disputes. They all agreed that the lords who were not parties would act together as arbitrators for those who were in dispute, to:[9]

> stand whole, united and knit together; and the lords between whom peradventure the difference shall arise shall stand in every respect, in high and low, to the redress and rule of the others.

STATUTORY ARBITRATION IN THE FIFTEENTH CENTURY

The Treaty of Utrecht 1473 required all disputes arising in the future between Hanse and English merchants to be submitted to two or more merchants.[10] For centuries, at least from the middle of the thirteenth century until they were expelled in 1597, the Hanse, merchants from a dozen or more Western European towns, had been privileged residents in

7. Derek Roebuck *Mediation and Arbitration in the Middle Ages* Oxford, HOLO Books p248.
8. Carole Rawcliffe and Susan Flower 'English Noblemen and Their Advisers: Consultation and Collaboration in the Later Middle Ages' (1986) 25 *Journal of British Studies* 157-177, 167 citing HL Hastings mss HAP box 2.
9. Ian Rowney 'Arbitration in Gentry Disputes of the Later Middle Ages' (1982) 67 *History* 367-376 citing *Rotuli Parliamentorum* V p415.
10. JR Dasent ed *Acts of the Privy Council of England* New Series London, HMSO 32 vols 1890-1964 [*APC*] 23.21.

London. The Privy Council was required by statute to arrange arbitrations of their disputes. The record for 9 July 1592 reads:[11]

A letter to Dr Aubrey and Dr Caesar. Complaint hath been made unto us by Wilkin Haynes, merchant of Hamburg, whereby he doth declare that in March last he did exhibit a petition unto us together with the information made by you, the Judge of the Admiralty, concerning the loss of 52 butts of sweet wines which were sunk and so quite lost by one Captain Cannett, set forth and freighted by Sir Thomas Pullyson and others, wherein we gave order that the cause should be determined by the Judge of the Admiralty and two other doctors to the contentment of both parties, if it might be, or otherwise, if they could not compound, to remit the cause to the proceeding of the common law ... . The merchants have obstinately refused to perform the same, not willing that the cause should receive the examination of indifferent persons but do delay the same on the pretence to be ordered by course of law, and by a special article contained in the covenants made between this realm and the cities and states of Hanse in the 5th year of King Edward IV in the treaty of Utrecht, and confirmed by Act of Parliament, as in the enclosed note may appear unto you, it was then covenanted, concluded and agreed that, at the petition of any of the merchants having cause of controversy in this realm against any of the subjects of the same, two indifferent arbiters should be named to end the controversy without going to law.

THE UBIQUITY OF ARBITRATION CLAUSES IN THE SIXTEENTH CENTURY AND AFTER

By the sixteenth century arbitration clauses appear not infrequently and by the seventeenth they appear to be common. In 1586 Edmund Pelham of Gray's Inn was appointed to arbitrate any disputes which might arise under the grant of a royal charter.[12] The Nottinghamshire Archives provide two more examples. A grant of water rights in 1581 had an arbitration clause providing for what should happen if the rights should be disturbed by digging.[13] A will in 1590 appointed Southcote J and the Master of

---

11. *APC* 23.21. There is no trace of any express provision for arbitration in the statutes as recorded in *Statutes of the Realm*. Volume II p413 has the statute (1465) 4 Edward IV c5, which confirms the privileges of 'the merchants of the Hanse'. The matter is discussed in detail in Derek Roebuck *The Golden Age of Arbitration: Dispute Resolution under Elizabeth I* Oxford, HOLO Books [*Golden Age*] due January 2015 Chapter 11, with the relevant texts [published – SH].
12. East Sussex Record Office (no individual ref, part of WIN) for 1586.
13. Nottinghamshire Archives 157/DD/P/94/3 25 August 1581; there are other relevant entries in the next century: Nottinghamshire Archives 157 DD/P/48/24 1625/6;

the Rolls and directed that: 'if there shall arise any trouble between the executors, or between any person and them touching my will, they should have the hearing and determining of such matters, without any suit of law'.[14] One might have thought that the Earl of Shrewsbury's experiences would have left him with a poor view of arbitration,[15] but his will of 1590 contained an arbitration clause, providing that four arbitrators, among them Cecil, Lord Burghley, were to deal with any disputes that might arise, and each was to be paid £100 for their services.[16]

The Privy Council might insert an arbitration clause in its order enforcing the award of its commissioned arbitrators. On 28 February 1600 it wrote to the Attorney General, the Solicitor General and Francis Bacon:[17]

We have considered the report you have made and the order you have taken in the cause between the aquavitae and vinegar makers and the patentee, whereof we do like the better in regard both parties have given their consents. And because we have been often troubled with the complaints of these men, we have thought good to require you (if any other difference do arise between them and the patentee) that you in your discretions will order the same in such sort as you shall think to be agreeable to equity and reason, that no further occasion of trouble be given unto us. And so we bid you very heartily farewell.

COMMERCE AND INSURANCE

Merchants signing an ordinary partnership agreement might, apparently routinely, insert an arbitration clause. The Government took care to see that such clauses were effective.[18] In 1593 John Soame, a London merchant, complained to the Privy Council that his partner, John Baker, would not account. When they had made their agreement, five years before, they had provided:[19]

DD/E/105/180 23 December 1673; East Sussex Record Office DYK/614; West Yorkshire Archive Service WYL100/NE/71 20 April 1693. And, on 24 May 1689, John Locke insisted on an arbitration clause in his contract with the publisher of *An Essay Concerning Human Understanding*.

14. FG Emmison *Elizabethan Life: Wills of the Essex Gentry and Merchants* Chelmsford, Essex Record Office 1978 p302.
15. *Golden Age* Chapter 9 describes Elizabeth's mediation attempts and the final arbitration of the disputes between Shrewsbury and his indomitable wife, Bess of Hardwick.
16. Nottinghamshire Archives DD/4P/46/1 will of George, Earl of Shrewsbury, 24 May 1590.
17. *APC* 30.132.
18. *APC* 24.109; *Golden Age* Chapter 10 under *Partnerships*.
19. *APC* 24.109; 24.315.

if any controversy should at any time arise in the course of their proceeding, it should be referred to the decision of merchants or others exercised in the affairs of their trade, to be indifferently chosen by them.

Soame had been wise to have that provision, because now Baker refused not only to hand over his share, amounting to 2,000 marks, or to account, but even to submit to arbitration, well knowing that 'the contract of partnership grew and was made beyond the seas, which can receive no trial here at the common law'. The Council commissioned arbitrators to 'use your uttermost endeavours to order and compound the controversy according to equity and conscience'.

Perhaps the most telling evidence that such clauses were routine as early as 1555 comes from an insurance policy. One of the earliest surviving policies, known as the Salazar/Santa Cruz, contains the clause: 'We promise to remit to honest merchants and not to go to the law'.[20] Is it justified to see that not as a unique phenomenon but rather as representing clauses which were common, if not standard, at that time? Contracts were hand-written then, not printed, but further research in the archives of insurance companies may provide evidence of regular practice.

Arbitration clauses may not have been commonplace among merchants but nor were they rare. Parties availed themselves of them whenever it occurred to them such a clause would be useful.[21] All these different kinds of arbitration clause seem to have done the job for which the parties intended them. That is no doubt one reason why no litigation arose from them, or more accurately, if there was such litigation, no report of it has survived.

THE ORIGIN OF THE ASSUMPTION

Elizabeth I favoured the settlement of disputes without litigation. The arbitration scheme which she established through her Privy Council regularly commissioned arbitrators to mediate and, if unsuccessful in that, to arbitrate all kinds of disputes.[22] Though she had little respect for the Common Law courts, which she recognised as sluggish and inexpert in business matters, she was happy that the Council should commission the judges to arbitrate disputes relating to the title to land or the family. But

---

20. JP Van Niekirk *The Development of the Principles of Insurance Law in the Netherlands from 1500 to 1800* Cape Town, Juta 1999 p231 fn156.
21. David Ibbetson 'Law and Custom: Insurance in Sixteenth-Century England' (2008) 29 *J of Legal History* 291-308 [*Ibbetson*], 297: 'a compulsory arbitration clause in the policy would not have been worth the paper it was written on', though his evidence suggests the contrary, p294 and fn24.
22. *Golden Age* tells the story in detail.

for commercial matters she preferred the appointment of civil lawyers, the Doctors of the Civil Law whose expertise came from their education and their practice in the Admiralty Court. They dealt with commercial cases in the Admiralty Court itself, where they had a monopoly; in the Court of Requests; as individual arbitrators, especially Dr Julius Caesar; and as members of arbitral tribunals.

Nowhere in the records of their work is there any sign of them being influenced by what may have been one element in the development of the assumption of later scholars that arbitration clauses came late to England.

The Romans allowed a binding submission to arbitration only of existing disputes.[23] The *Digest* is clear:[24]

> An arbiter may make a decision on those matters and calculations and disputes which were in existence between the parties at the time they made the *compromissum* but not those which arose later.

That was because the law required the submission to be in the standard form, the *compromissum*, before the state would intervene. There was nothing to stop parties agreeing that future disputes would go to arbitration. It was just that their agreement would not be a *compromissum* and would therefore have no legal effect. There was no readily available action to enforce any other agreement to submit to arbitration, though Cicero describes an arbitration clause intended for disputes which might arise in the future, limited to one particular potential source of trouble, submitted to the arbitration of a named person.

Jurisdictions which have based their law on the Roman have been known to refuse to recognise arbitration clauses similarly, as in France until modern times.[25] The modern policy was to restrict arbitration clauses to commercial contracts, where the parties would be presumed to bargain equally. Elsewhere there was a perceived danger of a stronger

23. Derek Roebuck and Bruno de Loynes de Fumichon *Roman Arbitration* Oxford, HOLO Books 2004. There was no such problem in Ancient Greece or in Ptolemaic Egypt, as the papyri show, Derek Roebuck *Ancient Greek Arbitration* Oxford, HOLO Books 2001, e.g. the arbitration clause in a marriage agreement of 310BC from Greek Egypt, pp308, 309; and they were common in interstate arbitration treaties, p157, citing Thucydides.
24. Justinian *Digest* 4.8.46.
25. 'The possibility of submitting future disputes to arbitration has passed through many vicissitudes. And there is no doubt that they are not yet finished': Jean Robert *L'Arbitrage* p47, paragraph 58. Who could withstand such a clear statement of the rule from René David: 'La clause compromissoire n'est devenue courante qu'à une époque récente', *L'Arbitrage dans le Commerce Internationale* Paris, Economica 1982 p274? The primary sources do not support him: Derek Roebuck *The Charitable Arbitrator: How to Mediate and Arbitrate in Louis XIV's France* Oxford, HOLO Books 2002 p237 Chapter XXXV 'How to make commercial contracts and avoid Litigation'. And the Code de Commerce art 332 expressly provides for arbitration clauses in marine policies.

party forcing a weaker into a method of resolution the stronger could control and exploit, outside the state's benevolent supervision. Civilian doctors in France might extrapolate from that, that an agreement to submit future differences to arbitrators was theoretically repugnant. There is no sign that their English counterparts had any such notions.

Perhaps the differences in the way submissions and awards were enforced explain the English practice. Governments of all kinds approved of arbitration, as they would of any procedure which reduced the possibility of disorder, fear of which concerns all governments. But in France arbitration was seen as a private matter, and parties were expected to arrange their arbitrations so that the resulting awards would be performed without the state's intervention. The state did offer a procedure which would add its sanctions to enforcement, but only if the parties adopted the state's form and formalities, which were not onerous but could not be made to include future disputes. In France, as in Rome, that form was the *compromissum*, which required the parties to submit to and rely on the standard procedure, rather than their contract.

In England it was the agreement that mattered. Even if the parties chose the *compromissum* form, which many did, and would have satisfied all the Roman and French requirements, that was not relevant. Whether their submission worked or not depended on their agreement. They could make it by deed, supported by mutual bonds, not much different in effect from the penalty of the *compromissum*. Or they could rely on the remedies for breach of contract, which in most cases came down to a Common Law action in trespass on the case, *assumpsit*.

CONCLUSIONS

According to all the available evidence, arbitration clauses may not have been commonplace in the five centuries from 1200 to 1700, but nor were they rare. Parties seem to have availed themselves of them whenever it occurred to them that such a clause would be useful.

First published in (2015) 16 *Melita Historica* 115-140. Reprinted by kind permission of the publishers.

10. MEDIATION AND ARBITRATION IN MEDIAEVAL MALTA FROM THE RECORDS OF NOTARY ZABBARA (1471-1500)

Derek Roebuck[1]

INTRODUCTION[2]

Malta has been independent since 1964, a republic since 1974 and a member of the European Union since 2004. It acceded to the New York Convention on 22 June 2000 and now has a lively arbitration centre and new legislation to support dispute resolution.[3] It also has a recorded history of mediation and arbitration, with a cultural tradition which underpins peaceful settlement.

Just one short period, of no more than thirty years, has been chosen to provide the proof, based on the records of one notary, Giacomo Zabbaro published in three volumes of the series *Documentary Sources of Maltese History*, Part I nos 1, 2 and 3, cited here as Z1, Z2 and Z3, with the number of the document.[4]

1. Derek Roebuck is a Research Fellow at the Institute of Advanced Legal Studies. He was formerly professor of law (comparative law) in Australia, Papua New Guinea, China and Hong Kong and is editor emeritus of *Arbitration*. He has published over forty books on law, legal history and language including (part author and editor) *Credit and Security in Asia* 10 volumes Queensland UP; 7 volumes Peking UP bilingual texts on Hong Kong contract, criminal law and criminal procedure; latterly on the history of dispute resolution: *A Miscellany of Disputes* (2000), *Ancient Greek Arbitration* (2001), *The Charitable Arbitrator: How to Mediate and Arbitrate in Louis XIV's France* (2002); *Roman Arbitration* (2004); *Early English Arbitration* (2008); *Disputes and Differences* (2010); *Mediation and Arbitration in the Middle Ages* (2013) (*Middle Ages*). The *Golden Age of Arbitration:Dispute Resolution Under Elizabeth I* (2015) and introductions to 2009 reprints of Matthew Bacon *The Compleat Arbitrator* (1731) and Stewart Kyd *A Treatise an the Law of Awards* (1799).
2. It would not have been possible to make this attempt but for the generosity of Neville Cardona, who makes his general knowledge of Malta and his scholarly command of its history available to his guests at the Hotel Phoenicia. I thank the peer reviewer much more than formally for a meticulous examination of this text and the corrections and suggestions, as helpful as they were necessary.
3. Jotharn Scerri Diacono 'Malta: Arbitration and Enforcement of Foreign Arbitral Awards', (2001) 67 *Arbitration*, 321-324.
4. Stanley Fiorini ed. *Documentary Sources of Maltese History* all published by the

The last quarter of the fifteenth century was as quiet and settled a period as Malta was ever to enjoy until recent times, though it suffered repeated corsair raids. By 1450 Malta and Gozo were at peace.[5] The Knights of St John would not arrive for another 80 years, by which time the population of the two islands has been estimated to be about 17,000.[6]

NOTARIES

There were notaries in Malta appointed by the Pope to handle ecclesiastical affairs but this paper is restricted to the notaries who acted in ordinary matters, who were appointed by Malta's overlord, the King (or Queen) of Sicily. There were usually at that time perhaps half a dozen practising in Malta.[7]

Though the records do not show notaries acting regularly as mediators or arbitrators, notary Ingomes de Brancat acted as an expert valuer in Z2 131 below. There is a reference as early as 1391 to notary Francesco Gatto[8] acting in 1391 as one of two mediators between the King of Sicily and the rebels but I have not been able to follow up the cited manuscript in the State Archives at Palermo.

Professions ran in families in Malta then, as they still do. Doctors and lawyers passed their skills and their businesses to their sons and nephews. Zabbara must have been born some time before 1430. His mother was from the Sansone family of Gozitan notaries. Zabbara sometimes signed himself in full: Jacobus Sabbara de Sansone.[9] He is likely to have served his apprenticeship to a notary in Sicily, learning the necessary Latin and picking up the Sicilian language to which he sometimes reverts in his deeds. A note survives saying simply: 'Of notary Jacobus Zabara 1451 Indiction 14 9 October', nearly twenty years before the first surviving record in his books.

University of Malta: *Part I Notarial Documents No 1 Notary Giacomo Zabbara R494/ l(I): 1486-1488: Part I No 2 Notary Giacomo Zabbara R494/l(II-IV): 1494-1497: Part I No 3 Notary Paula Bonello* MS. *588: 1467- 1517 Notary Giacomo Zabbara MS 1132: 1471-1500.* Anyone who wants to know anything about Malta at that time owes a great debt to the industry, knowledge and above all the scholarly generosity of the editor, Stanley Fiorini.
5. Unless the context makes the contrary clear, Malta includes Gozo, though then, as now, its people insisted on their separate customs and customary law.
6. B W Blouet *The Story of Malta* Allied Publications revd edn 2007, 86.
7. Their identities are discussed in Z3, xlvi-1.
8. In Z3 pxxi citing the State Archives at Palermo, *ASPRCIDoc* 229 (4v1398), Doc 233(31v1398).
9. Zl px. His spelling of his own name was not consistent. Names of people and places present difficulties for a translator with little first-hand knowledge of Malta. The manuscripts are not consistent. I have followed the editor as best I could, usually retaining his Latin version.

From 1471 to 1500, Zabbara practised as a notary throughout Malta, living first in Gozo and later in Mdina, Malta's main city. Fiorini suggests, Z2 xxi:

> Zabbara never really settled permanently in Malta but kept going back to his native Gozo for appreciably long stretches in spite of making two serious attempts to settle down in Mdina by taking a wife there twice, in 1467-68 and again in 1492-93.

He also made trips to Sicily. His practice was interrupted in 1480, when corsairs captured him on his way home. He was not ransomed till 1486. His last record is of a deed dated 30 April 1500. He must have died some time between May 1501 and October 1503.[10] Not all of his notarial registers have survived. Of the 972 documents, 27 record settlements of disputes. They will be considered in three main sections: settlements by the parties themselves without the assistance of a third party; mediations; formal arbitrations. Other short sections will deal with grants of power to compromise and valuations.

All the passages quoted are my translations, redacted to omit notarial repetitions and anything else which might burden the reader and inhibit the transmission of meaning accurately. The omissions have not been indicated unless they need explanation. I have depended on the editor's helpful glossaries for words in the Sicilian or Maltese into which the writer has frequently lapsed for want of a Latin word or expression.

JEWS

Jews played an important role in the commercial life of the islands at that time. In 1495 there may have been as many as 500 Jews, perhaps 3 per cent of the population of the island of Malta and 5 per cent of Gozo. Even a third of the inhabitants of Malta's largest city Mdina, the *civitas Melite*, could then have been Jewish.[11] Jewish law was recognised in family matters. On 10 March 1477 the Vicar-General's Court in Malta recognised a Jewish divorce; Jews were allowed to practise their traditional polygamy.[12] Jewish notaries were officially appointed for transactions between Jews;[13] but Zabbara's books show that Jews regularly made use of Christian notaries, sometimes as mediators. A tithe record declares:[14]

10. Z1, xii.
11. Godfrey Wettinger *The Jews of Malta in the Late Middle Ages* Malta, Midsea 1985 [*Wettinger*], 9 and his 'Honour and Shame in Late Fifteenth-Century Malta' (1980) *Melita Historica*, 67-77, 69.
12. *Wettinger*, 64.
13. Z3, xlvi-xlvii.
14. *Wettinger*, 35.

Xellule Bracha owes me for the year of the Fourth Indiction, according to a receipt under the hand of Jacubu as mediator between the Jew and me. I have a white handkerchief as security.

All the Jews who would not convert were expelled in 1492 and their property was confiscated. Even conversion did not save some of those who later fell into the hands of the Inquisition.[15]

SETTLEMENTS

The first technique of resolution was for the parties to settle the dispute themselves without outside help. Zabbara's notarial records contain five examples of such agreements.[16] The earliest record, Zl 44, dated 1 August 1486, is of the simplest kind of transaction. The noble Donna Becta de Habica of Mdina had been in partnership with the commoner Bertus Mintoff of Gozo. Together they owned a mule, according to Gozo custom, *iuxta usum Gaudisii*, sharing all profit and loss. That was all. They disputed what each was entitled to when they terminated the partnership. Without anyone else's intervention, they agreed that Bertus would pay Donna Becta an agreed sum and keep the mule for the next two years to allow him to make payments from the profits of its use, each party retaining half-ownership until then.

Eight years later, on 23 October 1494, a settlement is recorded, Z2 24, of a dispute between the noble Nicolaus de Caxaro and Randinus Busuttil. Nicolaus had a judgment of the civil court of Malta against Randinus, who was his shepherd, *mandrarius* from the Maltese word for a flock.[17] Randinus was opposing Nicolaus's attempt to execute that judgment. The deed records Randinus' payment and their *concordia*.

The notary concluded by adding a formula from Roman law, the antique *Aquiliana stipulatio*, or *acceptilatio*, a formal discharge of oral obligations. The debtor asked the creditor: 'What I promised you, have you received it?' The creditor replied 'I have'. The formula took its name from the ancient jurist Aquilius Gallus, who devised it. Later documents show that the notary Zabbara was in the habit of explaining what he was doing to his clients and that they sometimes expressly declared they understood. One can only wonder what a shepherd, anywhere and at any time in history, or even the noble Nicolaus, would have made of the

---

15. *Wettinger*, 286 gives the authority for Deydac being racked. Cecil Roth 'The Jews of Malta' (1928-1931) 12 *Transactions of the Jewish Historical Society of England*, 187-251 is still necessary background reading.
16. The records of notary Paulo Bonello provide an earlier example, Z3 98 from 22 October 1467.
17. Z2 Glossary.

references to the *Aquiliana stipulatio*, but no doubt both parties would have been impressed by the solemnity.

On 3 December of that year Nicolaus Zammit and Slejtu Mallia settled their dispute about wine and cotton, Z2 54. Nicolaus had a judgment of the civil court of Malta but 'wanting to live peacefully together and to behave towards one another like brothers, each released all claims to the other', with promises not to take any claims further.

Not all settlements were so straightforward. The record for 17 July 1495, Z2 139, shows that the noble Nardus de Vaccaro's dispute with the honourable master Geronimus Callus had many elements. Nardus owed Geronimus two uncie, ten tareni and ten grani in Sicilian gold coins.[18] That included 17 tareni which Geronimus had lent to Nardus so that he could redeem a donkey distrained on by the *Secretus*, the civil authority representing in Malta the King of Sicily, for a debt Nardus owed 'to the Jews'. Geronimus had already brought an action in the civil court of Malta. Now all was settled by Nardus giving Geronimus the donkey, valued at seven florins, the balance to be paid when Nardus got the inheritance due to him from the estate of the noblewoman Francia de Vaccaro.

Nardus may have been noble but he was the illegitimate son of Petrus de Vaccaro. On 11 May 1496 he settled his differences with the noble Antonius Falzon, acting as agent of his wife, Petrus' legitimate daughter Catherina, over their inheritances, Z2 283. Petrus had left Nardus an orchard, *viridarium*, in Mgarr near Mdina, called the Little Garden, *Lu Jardinu Pichulu*, and a vineyard and other neighbouring land. He also left him his house in Mdina and land nearby. There had been litigation already in the civil court of Malta, so now 'wanting to avoid the costs and expense of litigation and the turmoil of legal proceedings' they came to an agreed settlement, which they signified by touching the notary's pen. Nardus relinquished all rights to inherit his father's estate, except for the Mdina house and the Little Garden in Mgarr.

MEDIATIONS

Parties who could not come to an agreement might seek the help of third parties. Though the results of a successful mediation are so often recorded in the stock phrases of notarial Latin, the records give more than a hint that mediation was a regular process of resolving disputes, not only within the family but in all kinds of commercial relations.

The earliest record of a mediation, Z1 37 of 8 June 1486, is of a dispute arising from a Jewish marriage settlement. All the parties were Jewish but they had chosen Zabbara, a Christian notary, and Christian witnesses.

---

18. 1 uncia=30 tareni; 1 tareno=20 grani; 1 grano=6 denari, Z1 pxvii. I have not translated the adjectives which were often added, e.g. 'Sicilian' or 'golden'.

Hannuna, widow of Hauad Cussu, had two daughters, Chineyna married to Sadi Cussu, and Ster (or Esther), betrothed to Melchi Ketib. Hannuna and Sadi had promised Esther as her dowry 'certain goods described and specified in Hebrew script'. Esther and Melchi had recently begun an action on the grounds of their dissatisfaction with that dowry, seeking part of the property which Hannuna inherited on her husband Hauad's death.

This notarial act then includes a formula, found in one form or another in many records of mediations, not only in Malta but other jurisdictions of Western Europe, which shows how disputes were traditionally resolved: 'by the mediation of those who were related to and friends of both sides', *'communium consanguineorum et amicorum interventu'*.[19] Not just mutual friends and relatives, the mediators were accepted because they were all either friends of both sides or related to both sides. No wonder they were successful in persuading the parties to agree to a settlement.

And so Hannuna – with the advice and approval of Sadi – and the betrothed Esther and Melchi unanimously came to an agreement. Esther and Melchi gave up all actions and claims and happily accepted in full satisfaction the various marriage settlement goods, including clothes and animals, set out in the Hebrew list, but reserving to Esther's brother Moshe his rights if the marriage did not take place. Hannuna added a house in Mdina, reserving to herself a life interest. The betrothed gave her a mattress, an article which seems to have had special significance in Maltese marriage settlements.

Zabbara the notary heads the next settlement *concordia et debitum*, recording not only the agreement but the creation of the resulting debt, Zl 139 of 8 March 1487. Again, one of the parties is Jewish.

> The Egregius Andreas de Fauczono, acting as guardian for the children and heirs of Johannes de Fauczono, and Abias Sabaha a Jewish citizen of Malta, declare that Master Abias is the creditor of Johannes.

Johannes had had a slave, Martinus, whom Johannes had pledged to Abias to secure a guarantee Johannes had given him on behalf of Albanus Formusa and Matheus Nihayse alias Farrugia. Granata, Johannes' widow, laid claim to Martinus, whom she said belonged to her separately, alleging she had married Johannes according to the custom of the Romans, *secundum usum Romanorum*, which gave her the right to him as her separate property, which had been confirmed by an action in the civil court.

---

19. The translation of *interventus* as mediation is justified. It has the authority e.g. of Gaius *Institutes* 3.176 and of Justinian *Digest* 24.1.50 and 14.4.7.1.

By the mediation of friends of both parties, *comunium amicorum intervently*, and to avoid the costs and expenses of litigation, they have come to this concord or contract: Andreas will pay Abias 30 florins at the next grape harvest and another 30 florins at the following one (four florins worth in must). And vice versa Master Abias, declaring himself content with this concord and contract, gives up his right of action against the sale of the slave.

Abias also renounced any claim against Albanus and Matheus and a later marginal note records that Abias had been paid in full.

In any case, Abias also renounced any claim against Albanus and Matheus and a later marginal note records that Abias had been paid in full. In any case Martinus had run off. Another Jewish creditor had got him, Haninus Inglixi, acting as guardian of the children of Azar Marsani. Haninus had a shop in Mdina and is mentioned in the arbitration quoted below, Zl 141. He had an order of the civil court in his favour. But Granata was not giving up and was now trying to establish her ownership of Martinus against Haninus too, by Roman custom, *ala Romana*, just as she had against Abias. An entry for 20 March 1487, Zl 152, records a mediated settlement between Andreas Falzono, acting in Granata's name, with the formula: 'wishing to avoid the expenses of litigation, by the mediation of friends of both sides, they unanimously came to the following settlement, *concordia*': Andreas would pay Haninus eleven florins in three instalments for some oil bought from Azar. Haninus had already given up the judgment of the civil court and transferred or released, *scapulavit*, the slave to Andreas.[20]

Haninus was a leader of the Jewish community in Malta, busy not only in financial transactions, lending money and guaranteeing loans, but trading from his own warehouses.[21] Then as now in Malta the name Inglixi would have been pronounced 'English'. His family may have been one of those who two centuries before in 1294 had been banished from England by Edward I. He suffered the same fate, being expelled from Malta with all the other Jews in 1492; his lands were sold up.[22]

On 30 April 1487 the record begins, Zl 181:

20. *Scapulare* is not a Latin ward, neither classical nor medieval. It is Sicilian and must mean something like 'to release from a burden'. It is not even necessarily related to the Latin *scapula*, shoulder, and the sense of shrugging off, or the Maltese ward *skapula*, avoid, because there is a Sicilian ward *skapuli*, which means fallow land, Z2 glossary, 418.
21. Zl, 16, 45, 176, 180, 293; Z2, 381.
22. Z2, 381.

> We certify that, since a lawsuit and question is pending in the court of the Magnificus Lord Captain of the State of Malta, between Ylagia, widow of Franciscus de Caxaro, of the one part, and his brother Matheus, his mother Mica, his brother Nicholas and sister Perna, of the other part, about a house and adjoining fields, an apiary and other property there in Ghajn Qajjed ... today, by the mediation of friends of both sides, they have unanimously come to the following settlement.

Ylagia may be presumed to be a young widow because her brothers and sister-in-law were still under age. She was happy to transfer the legal ownership of all the property she had received from her husband back to his family, provided she could enjoy possession and use of the house and land for her lifetime.

On 4 July 1487 the mediated settlement, Zl 209, was of a dispute so ordinary that it must have arisen often and have been disposed of in this way. Yet our experienced notary Zabbaro had to resort to a strange mixture of Sicilian and Latin to express its resolution. Periyannes de Carmona and his wife Francisca disputed rights to water from a cistern in Axac, now Rahal Ghaxaq, with Nellus Grixti. Litigation was pending. Unanimously they declared their settlement. The de Carmonas would have two thirds, Nellus one third. The mixture of Latin and Sicilian reads:

> *Li conducti et miatus per li quali divi discurriri lacqua pluviali et andari intra la dicta cisterna stayanu et restanu acussi comu ab antiquo foru et apparinu ... intra lu cortiglu di lu dictu Nellu.*

For their expenses Nellus had given the de Carmonas the choice of one of two pigs and eight *thumini* of grain, about 150 litres. All declared themselves content.

The documents quoted already show the regular participation of women both in the mediated settlements and the transactions of all kinds that gave rise to them.[23] Usually, though by no means always, when something as fundamental as the sale of land was involved, a woman was accompanied by a man, often called her *mundualdus*, a Lombard law term commonly translated 'guardian' but in Malta better as 'the man under whose protection the woman lives', because the woman was carrying out the legal act in her own right. There are scores of records like this of a woman, in this case Jewish, selling her own land in her own name, Zl 51:

---

23. The legal and social status of women is discussed in more detail in Susanna Hoe *Malta: Women, History, Books and Places*, Oxford, HOLO Books: The Women's History Press 2015.

Sappora, widow of the Jew Rubin Ketib, with the advice and approval of David Inglixi, ... in her own right and name, for herself, her heirs and successors forever, has sold ... an enclosure of arable land ... at Gudja ... to her brother-in-law.

Zl 228 of 31 July 1487, is a good example of women acting on their own account. Garita was the wife of Frankinus Mullica and the mother of Catherina and Jacoba. Garita's mother, Contissa, had had a dispute with Fridericus Buras over arable land at Rahal Pessa. Before the start of legal proceedings, the parties came to a unanimous agreement, this time after the mediation of not only common friends but relatives of both sides, *comunium consanguineorum et amicorum interventu*.[24]

It might be thought that where male members of the family were appointed to represent the female in a mediation, that was evidence that women were in some way legally disabled. On 14 January 1488 the noble Petrus de Vacaro settled a dispute with the Venerable Don Amator Zammit. Petrus's wife Francia was Amator's sister. Amator was acting for another sister, Catherina, and for Imperia and Ysabella, the daughters of his brother Johannes. Land in various parts of the island of Malta had been in dispute in the Captain's Court, judgment had been pronounced and now an appeal was pending before the Maltese court of first appeal. The record, Zl 315, reveals a motive for reconciliation often expressed and even more often implied in mediation in many jurisdictions, the avoidance of ill-will within a family:

Bearing in mind the close blood relationship and affinity between them, by the mediation of friends and relatives of both sides, they came unanimously to the following contract and settlement, *transaccionem et concordiam*.

Amator 'so far as he could and had power and authority' to do so, made concessions and Petrus, as Francia's legal administrator and 'in the name of his wife' did the same.

Could there be evidence more express that the legal actors in substance were the women, the men their agents? Where a man is acting as guardian, the deed expressly says so, *curator* in Zl 139 or *tutor* in Zl 152. In Roman law, 'a procurator is someone who administers someone else's affairs with the authority of the master', '*procurator est qui aliena negotia mandatu domini administrat*'.[25] There is no doubt who is boss. Procurators were

---

24. The verb *laudare* may mean 'arbitrate' but here, in a phrase which follows *omnia acceptante et laudante et confirmante* it means 'approve'.
25. Justinian *Digest* 3.3.1.

usually freedmen and sometimes slaves. They had all the powers which the principal gave them and no more.'The principal could change or end those powers at will. There is no element of "guardian" in the word or in practice. The nearest equivalent institution in English life and law is the attorney, as in "power of attorney".' But, because that word now usually means a lawyer, procurator will remain untranslated here.

There is a gap of some years in Zabbara's records. The next relevant entry is Z217 for 24 September 1494. Paulus Mangion had been murdered. He had left property to his sister Catherina. Their brother Bartholomeus claimed a third of it. Michael Mangion, her husband, acted on her behalf. They settled:

> By the mediation of friends of both sides, wishing to be spared the expense of litigation and to live in agreement together in peace, they came to this agreement ....

Michael, 'for himself and on behalf of his wife' agreed to pay Bartholomeus twenty Sicilian florins in two instalments. Bartholomeus agreed to transfer to Michael and Catherina land near Zebbug, subject to the building of a wall and access to water.

There was a difference between the promises to settle and the document which transformed those promises into legal acts. The *concordia et transactio* might produce a balance to be paid from one party to the other, a simple debt which the parties were content needed no further document, though the notary sometimes recorded the debt in a separate document. But it might be more complex and need a formal transfer of property or acceptance of continuing obligations.

A dispute about land in Malta had been heard in the court of the Maltese consul in Licata, Sicily. The Sicilian Petrus Calarca, acting as procurator for his wife Antona and her sister Lucia, had won an order distraining on the land of Garita, wife of Laurencius Magro. Garita and Laurencius opposed that order. The parties came to an agreed settlement, 'through the mediation of friends' who also valued the land.

On 6 November 1494 the parties recorded their mediation, Z2 31, and then the formal settlement, Z2 32. It was drawn up between Petrus Calarca, of Licata in Sicily, 'acting as procurator' of Lucia and Antona, and Laurentius Magro of Malta, acting for himself and as legal administrator of his wife Garita. It recorded that Laurencius for himself, *pro se et sponte sua etc*, and Petrus as procurator, *procuratorio nomine*:

> To avoid the expenses of litigation and be spared the bother, for the sake of peace and quiet, through the mediation of friends, they have arrived at this settlement, contract and final pact.

And once again, according to Maltese notarial custom, they symbolically touched the notary's pen to signify that this was their act: '*dedit, tradidit et per tactum penne mei notarii assignavit*'.

Another family dispute over land had come before the Captain's Court, Z2 71 of 23 January 1495. Henry Cauchi had sued the Honourable Lucas Zammit. The action had been only partly successful and Henry appealed. Henry died and Andreas, his son and heir, took the case over and agreed to settle for a payment of six uncie:

> Wishing to avoid the expenses of litigation and be spared the bother, and most important because the outcome of litigation is so uncertain, by the mediation of friends and relatives of both sides, unanimously and in cooperation, they have come to the following settlement, contract etc.

On 4 July 1495 the settlement is recorded of another land dispute. Egregius Judge Marcus de Brancato had a field in Wied il-Busbies, Z2 128. The Honourable Nicolaus de Calabachio claimed half of it. Through the mediation of friends of both sides Nicolaus gave up his claim in return for 2 uncie and 15 tareni.

Ventura and Catherina were sisters. They fell out over their inheritances. On 15 March 1495 their mediated settlement was recorded, Z2 242, reciting the various legal actions they had started and their agreement:

> With the intention of contracting, concording and agreeing ... wanting henceforth to treat one another with fraternal love and to avoid the turmoil of legal proceedings, as well as all the attendant cost and bother, most of all because the outcome of litigation is uncertain, through the mediations of their family and friends on both sides, for the sake of peace and concord, unanimously and in cooperation, they have come to this agreement ...

They made various exchanges of land, agreed that Ventura was not liable for her share of their father's funeral expenses, and dealt with rights to the grape harvest. They ended by both of them renouncing the *exceptio doli*, the right to attack this settlement on the ground of fraud, called there the *excepcio decepcionis enormis*; and the right to *restitutio in integrum*, the equitable right to be restored to the legal position one had before some unfair transaction took it away; and any other legal advantages which might be available specially for women.

Not all mediations began as family disputes. On 8 August 1496 the record, Z2 239, shows a dispute between many parties. The Venerable

Don Lanceas Desguanes had found time from his religious duties to take part in overseas trade. He and his partner Jacobus Hakem had brought an action which had gone on appeal to the Magna Regia Curia, the high court of Malta. The original defendant was Manfridus de Bonello, who had undertaken to build a brigantine for them. All three original parties were now dead. Hakem had left his rights to a half share in the ship to the hospital at Rabat, Malta. His widow Ylagia, now married to Andreas Falzono, was contesting that bequest. Chicca, the widow of Manfridus, was now married to Matheus Bertelli, who was now representing her and all the others who claimed an interest in Manfridus's estate. They all came together to approve a settlement, 'through the mediation of friends of both sides, bearing in mind that the outcome of litigation is uncertain', with payments to the hospital and the family of Jacobus, who dropped all further claims against the family of Manfridus. The deed ended with the *acquilliana stipulacio*, by which the parties were mutually absolved of all debts.

Four days later, on 11 August 1496, another settlement ended a dispute which had reached the stage where witnesses presented their evidence, Z2 331. Fridericus Heleu was suing Jorlandus Cauchi over arable land adjoining the church of Santa Maria de la Gructa. The settlement, through the mediation of friends and relatives of both sides, provided for Jorlandus to pay Fridericus 4 uncie in return for ownership of the land, some of which had already been paid in barley and half of which would be forgiven in gratitude for the kindness of a third party.

One of the last entries in Zabbaro's books, Z3 171 for 27 November 1499, is a mediation, described simply as *amicorum interventu*, by which Nicolaus Kinzi transferred land to Nicolinus Theuma in return for a further payment of 7 uncie, with Nicolaus promising Nicolinus to protect him from claims by Nicolaus's brothers and sisters.

ARBITRATIONS

The best attempts of family and friends could not resolve some disputes. Sometimes the parties could agree no more than that the matters be placed in the hands of arbitrators, whose judgment would be final and unappealable. Then the submission followed the medieval form of the Roman Law *compromissum*. It was common for each party to choose one and for both to act as arbiters, arbitrators and friendly mediators, *arbitros, arbitratores et amicabiles compositores*. As mediators they would try to bring the parties to a settlement which took its force purely as a contract, from the parties' own agreement. If that attempt failed, as arbitrators they had the parties' authority to continue the process and, if all else failed, the parties had given them power as arbiters to decide all the issues between them, whether the parties liked their award or not.

The fullest surviving record, Zl 141 and 142 dated 9 March 1487, is of the award of arbitrators in the distribution of the estate of Bayhunus and Zambita Mehyr. Because of its usefulness to historians of arbitration more widely than in Malta, despite its length and detail, it has been translated and redacted to remove the notary's surplusage and added as an appendix. It contains all the standard elements of arbitration as it had developed in Malta to that time and illustrates the extent and complexity of one Jewish family's estate. When the grandparents died, the family was geographically divided, Xamuel living in Mdina in Malta and Pinhas in Syracuse in Sicily. They had extensive landholdings in Malta and considerable property in Sicily. They also had a company carrying on business as merchants in Malta. How would a Jewish family come to own 38 separate properties in Malta in the 1480s? They lived in Mdina but the holdings were all over the islands, including Gozo. There is only one convincing explanation. The Mehyrs were not only merchants, they were also moneylenders.

It is clear from the conveyances of land in Malta then, as represented by the scores of transactions recorded by notary Zabbara alone, that one common form gave the seller the right to repurchase within a time limit. It was so usual that it was sometimes expressed to be 'according to Maltese custom' (e.g. Zl 112). That may go back to a time when land belonged to families rather than individuals, so that, even when an individual could grant a good title, others had some kind of residuary customary claim. That might account for the other customary right, of adjoining landowners to have first option when land next to theirs was sold.

The Church in Malta as elsewhere then took usury seriously as a sin, at least intermittently and sufficiently for a Jewish moneylender to be concerned about security. There was no security like land, scarcely any other worthwhile security at all. Why not then take advantage of the Maltese culturally acceptable institution to create mortgages, or rather gages by which ownership of the land could pass to the lender while the borrower retained it physically and worked it to pay back the loan? It is not so surprising that the Mehyr family, with its merchandising business in Mdina and its homes there and in Syracuse, should own 38 plots of land, if more than 30 of them represented security for loans.

The only other award in Zabbaro's books was formally recorded on 7 May 1496, Z2 280. No doubt the parties assumed that it had finally sorted out their differences. The noble Don Lanceas Desguanes and his wife Agatha had a daughter Violans, stated to be illegitimate, *naturalis*, though it is not clear why. An order of the Captain's Court had appointed

Orlandus de Bordino her guardian but in practice Agatha had shared that responsibility until her death, for both income and expenditure. On Violans' marriage to Nicolaus Saguna, Orlandus accounted for his guardianship and also as far as he could for Agatha's, who was dead by then.

Through the mediation of Manfridus de Caxaro the parties settled their differences and by this deed Violans and her husband gave up any claims Violans might have had against Orlandus, for a debt of 22 tareni, for fire damage to her house in Greek's Gate, Mdina, and for the death of her slave, Preciosa. In return Orlandus forwent any claim he might have had for his services or expenses. Not only Manfridus but five other lawyers and laymen witnessed this elaborate, repetitive and solemnly formal document. But the hoped-for peace and concord did not last long. On 9 December 1496 Nicolaus, 'acting as husband and legal representative of Violans', and Orlandus, acting similarly for his wife Imperia, submitted their revived and new differences to arbitration, Z2 390.

They compromised and made a compromissum to Andreas Falzono and Marcus de Brincat, who are present and accept, and chose them to be their arbiters, arbitrators and friendly mediators, *arbitros*, *arbitratores et amicabiles compositores*, to whom they have given authority and full power, *plenarium potestatem*, for the said differences and lawsuits, arisen now or to arise, each to other, to be propounded, awarded and determined by the arbiters, as they see fit within the next fortnight.

The arbiters could ask for another month to complete their work, which a marginal note shows they did. They did not need to take advantage of the power given them to add a third arbiter if they could not agree. The parties promised to accept the award as final and to renounce any right to appeal or to resort to *arbitrium boni viri*, a Roman law procedure which would have been quite out of place but presumably needed to be mentioned if the notary's precedent was to be faithfully followed. Finally, after reciting the formula of *acquilliana stipulacio acceptilacio*, Zabbaro switched to a mixture of Latin and Sicilian, which must have been to make sure the parties got the message: 'they promise in future to rest content *di tuctu quillu ky sirra declaratu per li dicti arbitri et non moviri plui quistioni ad invicem di li negocii preteriti et iterum juraverunt ...*, in every detail with what has been declared by the arbiters and not to raise further questions against one another in relation to this business, and again they have sworn ...'.

There is just one other document of interest, Z2 213. It bears no date but Fiorini suggests that it comes from c1487. It is headed *Annotatio*

Compromissi. Notary Zabbaro had been sitting as a judge in the civil
court in Gozo. He had referred some part of a matter in contention before
him to *arbitros et arbitratores*. That meant that they had the authority
to decide that part. Zabbaro would then incorporate their award in his
judgment. The manuscript is fragmentary. The bits worth quoting are
([I…] signifies a gap):

> First it is provided by the arbiters that the said […] And also […] And
> also it was reserved [...] And they wished [...]
>
> On [date] my judgment was given, declared and published, sitting with
> the arbiters, with the witnesses and both parties present ... intervening
> and acting in the name of T, of the one part, and also the honourable
> [...] and the noble […] with Simon Histese? of the other part; they
> offered and presented to us copies or documents in a cotton carta, of
> two contracts, put out in the said town in the hand of T between T and
> Simon the Jew, with the following meaning:
>
> […] by which contracts written and declared to them by the
> honourable […] and T per Magnificus […] and, they said they well
> understood; and accepted and approved by Simon, so T and [...] of their
> own free will and accord, ... obliged themselves as joint debtors with
> [...] and [...] even if absent, at the request and by the stipulation of [...]
> in the debt contained and declared in the two contracts, subject to the
> contracts, pacts, clauses, obligations, renunciations on oath inserted
> into the two contracts, more broadly and one by one, the meaning and
> content of the two contracts being understood more fully so that
> payment of half of the debt at least, and when that part has been paid,
> […] will be released, free and immune from the obligation, T and Simon
> remaining bound, severally, jointly and together, for the other half.
>
> GENERAL PROCURATION FOR THE CONTRACTS OF DEBT
>
> With a pact that it is not possible to oppose, defend or take exception
> to this, nor seek any remedy of fact or law against the contract or by
> taking monastic vows?, *promissionarie*, and vice versa, without first
> paying off the debt, and not otherwise and in no way can the parties be
> adjudged and vice versa.

No attempt has been made to add sense where there is none in the
original or to produce an elegant result. The text is too partial for that.
But it is reasonably clear that Zabbaro had made use of the arbitrators,
whose names are missing, to do what judges have asked arbitrators to do
for them in many other times and places, to sort out the financial details
of the parties' mutual transactions.

POWERS TO COMPROMISE

Zabbaro's records provide more evidence of the use of arbitration in the documents which give power to others to make compromises. The Maltese bireme, the *Sancta Maria*, had been captured by Venetians and taken to Mytilene. Johannes de Nava, Castellan of the Castrum ad Mare, appointed Petrus de Pignero his procurator, by a document recorded on 9 May 1486 (Zl 26), to take his armed bireme and get the *Sancta Maria* back. He was given powers not only to carry on litigation but to make a settlement, *cum potestate concordandi*, to choose a *iudicem*, presumably an arbitrator rather than a judge, and to take an interlocutory or final judgment, *sentenciam*, totally – from top to bottom, *alte et baxe*, the equivalent in Malta of *alto et bassa*, the standard form in a *compromissum* found in other contemporary jurisdictions. Though litigation is foremost in the wording, it seems that arbitration was envisaged.

VALUATIONS

Parties with differences could take advantage of the services of friends to do the more mundane job of valuing disputed property. Ventura Falca wanted to give her niece Ventura property to the value of 30 uncie for her dowry. She set out a list of items to that value – mattress, bed linen and other belongings according to Maltese custom – and arranged for it to be valued by friends – *per comunes amicos estimandas* (Zl 66 of 30 November 1486).

Manfridus and Ysabella Axac had promised Salvus Falzono a dowry when he married their daughter, Imperia. It included land and no less than 400 uncie worth of other property, with dresses, jewels and ornaments to be valued *extimandis per comunes amicos iuxta usum Melite* (Zl 341 of 6 March 1488). Another Falzon marriage required a similar valuation, which was carried out according to Maltese custom by *probos viros* notary Ingomes de Brancat, Manfridus Axac himself, Michael Vassaldu, Lucas Hellul and others (Z2 131 of 9 July 1495).

Manfridus Axac also had a part to play as assessor when Jewish property was to be valued, after their expulsion in 1492. Peri Caruana had been appointed to administer Jewish property and had started to collect everything he could of value. The debtors to the Jews on Gozo had already, for example, paid him more than 29 gold uncie (Z2 140). On 24 September 1495 (Z2 164) he had got his hands on one of Xamuel's vineyards, that at Habel Libilac, and needed it valued. He appointed the *expertos et probos viros* Inigo de Cantore and Manfridus Axac as experts in this kind of business – *tamquam experti in huiusmodi negotiis*.

There was no suggestion there that the assessors should be friends of both sides, nor the experts in a lease of land (Z2 166) nor in the sad story of Luna, who had to sell back to her father-in-law part of her dowry. She needed the money to get her husband out of prison. She took one uncia on account and a promise of the balance of the value after valuation *iuxta extimacionem expertorum* (Z2 250 of 2 April 1496).

NOTARY BONELLO

All the texts considered have been those in the books of Giacomo Zabarra. The records of Paulo Bonello, which start earlier in 1467 and end later in 1517, contain nothing that requires separate treatment. Z3 37 of 16 September 1467 is a full record of a mediation in the form used by Zabbaro, with the formula:

> The parties for the sake of peace and concord and to avoid the costs and expenses because the outcome of litigation is uncertain, by the mediation of friends of both sides, came to this settlement.

Z3 84 of 16 October 1467 is the record of a valuation *per duos amicos comunes expertos*, similar to Zabbar's Z1 341 above.

COMPARISONS

How did the practice in Malta then compare with that elsewhere in the Catholic Western world? It would be unwise to attempt a comprehensive survey here but it may be possible to get a worthwhile insight from just two English jurisdictions, the London Lord Mayor's Court, working within the Common Law, and the University of Oxford, which applied the Civil Law.

On 13 November 1470 arbitrators appointed by the Lord Mayor of London made this award:[26]

> Award of arbitrators between Roger, a citizen and tailor of London, and Peter, a merchant of Venice, concerning two barrels of Romany wine given to Lady Brice, the shearing of cloth, upon which the advice of William Eame, shearer, was taken, the sale of cloth, and various exchange transactions in Messina, Palermo and Majorca, mentioning Leonard Camarda, notary of Messina, the consul of the Venetians in Messina, the consul of the English nation in Palermo, and various foreigners.

26. Derek Roebuck and Bruno de Loynes de Fumichon *Roman Arbitration* Oxford, HOLO Books 2004 Chapter 5, 46-66.

So Sicily was not then *terra incognita* in London. Notarial deeds from Malta could well have been found occasionally there and *vice versa*.[27]

The Church in England had its own notarial practice, sadly allowing such self-indulgent drafting as this, in the *compromissum* in a dispute between the Dean and Chapter of Lincoln Cathedral in 1439:[28]

> We the Canons Residentiary ... chose and appoint you ... *arbitrum et arbitratorem, diffinitorem, arbitralem sentenciatorem, et amicabilem compositorem, preceptorem, ordinatorem, dispositorem, pronunciatorem et declaratorem to restore peace and concord and as arbitrum* [repeats the whole list again] we submit, *compromittimus* to you *alte et basse* ....

Even Dr Roget might have balked at a request to find synonyms in English.

A better example comes from the University of Oxford. By the middle of the fifteenth century it had become a powerful religious institution with wide-ranging jurisdiction not only over its members. It had its own courts, to which in the first instance all its members were subject, to the exclusion of any other forum. The authorities were expert in the practice and theory of both systems of law: the Civil Law, which they also taught, and the Common Law, which they did not.[29] Their documents avoided the worst excesses of ecclesiastical drafting. They were as comparatively economical as Zabbaro's, and in slightly more elegant Latin.

In February 1465, John Caldbeke, Professor of Theology, appointed by a *compromissum* to deal with a dispute between two University halls, White Hall and Deep Hall, ordered the parties to forgive each other of all their quarrels, of law and fact, and to be forever silent, leaving the Chancellor to deal with a dispute over a desk. The four parties, together with four others from each hall, should meet at a time to be fixed and:[30]

> Each side shall pay for a gallon of wine and do what is necessary to carry out these instructions and, before they leave, they shall clasp one another's hands ... and we order all these things to be done upon the penalty of £20 which was put into the compromissum, half to

27. Derek Roebuck and Bruno de Loynes de Fumichon *Roman Arbitration* Oxford, HOLO Books 2004 Chapter 5, 46-66.
28. *Middle Ages*, 289.
29. Henry Anstey *Monumenta Academica, or Documents Illustrative of Academical Life and Studies at Oxford* London, Longmans, Green (Rolls Series) 1868 (*Anstey*) 535-541; *Middle Ages*, 205.
30. *Anstey*, 714-715.

the party who has abided by our order and requests it and half to the Chancellor's office.

Two gallons of wine to be shared among the dozen of them, just short of a bottle each. That was the Oxford way of ensuring the Maltese equivalent of oil on troubled waters, 'for the sake of peace and concord'.

CONCLUSIONS

In quite different settings, mediation and arbitration seem to have been such a normal way of ending disputes in the 15th century. Malta, then as now, was an integral part of Western European culture. The survival of primary sources of such revelatory richness demands the recognition of Malta's contribution to social and legal history. Maltese scholarship has made them available, so that even foreign scholars with no knowledge of Maltese language may attempt to exploit them. This paper has found there ample evidence of a sophisticated system of resolving conflict without violence or even litigation, in the search for amity within the family and wider social cohesion. I hope it will lead others to find there the stimulus to work on other topics.

APPENDIX

THIS DEED WITNESSETH *testamur*, that Salamon Mehyr, a Jewish citizen of Mdina, of the one part, and Xamuel Mehyr and Sabatinus Sacerdotu, Xamuel in his own name and Sabatinus as husband and procurator of Hanina, his wife and Xamuel's sister, and Xamuel and Sabatinus as procurators of Sabatinus Mehyr, Xamuel's brother, and by a procuration established by a public document made in Syracuse under the hand of notary Francisco de Buctaro on 30 October 1486, with Xamuel Caglariso intervening as guardian of Zambita, the infant sister of Xamuel Mehyr, ordered by the court of the Captain of Mdina, to the distribution written below, to be solemnly performed, as laid down by the intent of a document recorded in the acts of that court dated the 6th instant, of the other part.

They explained that there had been litigation between Salamon and Xamuel Mehyr, Sabatinus Sacerdotu, and the others about property inherited from Bahyunus and Zambita Mehyr, the parents of Salamon and grandparents of Xamuel and his brothers and sisters, Sabatinus, Xamuel, Hanina and Zambita, and about a business carried on by Salamon and Pinhas, his brother, and the father of Sabatinus, Xamuel, Hanina and Zambita.

They had agreed to submit those lawsuits and differences to the arbitration of Rabbi Bias Sabaha, Xamuel Nifuso and the said Xamuel Caglariso, as *arbitros sive arbitratores et amicabiles compositores*, as set out in the *compromissum*.

Rabbi Bias, Xamuel and Xamuel, as *arbitri sive arbitratores*, having listened to what the parties wanted to say and allege, came to a final and definitive award, *sentenciam*, recorded in the deeds of the learned, *providus*, notary Gracian de Vassaldo, declared in Malta on 12 January of the present Fifth Indiction. Both parties approved and acquiesced in the meaning and content of the award (in their various capacities) in relation to the inheritance from Bahyunus and Zambita and the business carried on by Salamon and Pinhas and Bahyunus, their father.

Salamon's Share

First, it fell to Salamon to have first choice of the lesser half of the property of his parents, Bahyunus and Zambita, and Pinhas to have the greater. That is to say, a dwelling house in Mdina adjoining the houses of notary Paulus de Bunello and the houses of notary Corradus de Laymo.

Item, another tenement or household in Mdina adjoining the house of Nicolaus Xara and the city walls and the houses of the Reverend Lanceus Desguanes.

Item, a shop, *apotheca*, in Mdina, adjoining the shop of Master Abia Sabaha and the shop of Hanini Inglixi and the houses of the Abbey of St Peter.

But with the liability that Salamon be required from his own pocket to pay or restore one uncia to Xamuel Mchyr and the children of Pinhas.

Besides, from the property acquired from the business previously mentioned, by lot cast between them, all the vineyards or land planted with vines belonging to Cataldus de Lazarono in a place called Habel Libilac.

Item, half the arable land called Habel Libilac ... (measurements)

Item, a piece of arable land called Bita il Hagem in the district, *contrata*, of St Zacharia.

Item, half the land which belonged to Andreas Candiotu near the church of St Zacharia adjoining the land of Paulus Allegrectu.

Item, three pieces of land in the district of Ras il Hued, one called Bita il Basala, others of Masus Galia and the rest of Paulus de Ayona.

Item, an undivided half of the land in the district of Guardia of which the other half belongs to Gaddus Casaha.

Item, a piece of land in the district of Tafalia, called Bita il Hajarat, belonging to Antonius Heleu.

Item, two pieces of land, in the district of St Paul alu Mahasel, which belonged to Nicholaus Cassar.

Item, a piece of land on the island of Gozo, adjoining the land of David Bualus Bualus on the road which leads to Cala Marsalfurni, which belonged to Yski Safaradus.

Item, half the land in the region of Xeukia called de Bonsignuri, that is to say half of those lands from the east side, with half the houses and adjoining rights with the territories of the royal court called il Fiden, with a field there called Bita il Bahal and other fields on the rocks, with two folds, of which one is called De ill Ginnen, another De il Bacar and another Bita Segeyrat, and the houses called I Dar il Kibire and Sihyra, with the entry that was there in the first place and with a space called Msirah behind the house which Salamon surrounded with a wall behind the field, which was of the vineyard behind the oven there.

Item, of the animals: ten *sumerini* and six *vachi* but with the liability to pay from his own pocket the Pinhas family 4 uncie and 15 tareni.

Item, there falls to Salamon *tucti li stigli li quali si trovaru ala putiga de ipsu Salamuni* in Malta, where he ran the business, with all the tools and furniture to be found in the house of Salamon in Malta but with the liability to reimburse and pay one good uncia from his own pocket to the Pinhas family.

Item, there has fallen to Salamon one Hebrew book called *Macdixie*, which is found written in the inventory of Pinhas' movables in Syracuse.

Salamon has accepted as his half all the property described generally and in particular above, having had first pick according to the lot cast between them, but with the addition of the 6 uncie and 15 tareni paid from his own pocket by Salamon to the Pinhas family.

Item, on the other hand, from the property described above there has fallen to the Pinhas family, *filiis et coheredibus*, *Pinhas*, for their half, jointly and in common, as successors to their grandfather and to the company business formerly carried on by Salamon and Pinhas and Bayhonas the following property, that is to say:

First, a dwelling house in the city of Syracuse, *in capite de la mastra ruga*, adjoining the houses of Master Daniel Rah and the houses of Master Nicolaus Politu and the houses of Johannes Tramontana.

Item, one vineyard in the territory of Syracuse in the district of St Masus, adjoining the orchard of Masus Pelliczerus, with the vineyard of Master Johannes *mastru de axa* and the aforesaid property is the inheritance of Bahyuni and Zambita, the grandparents of the Pinhas family.

Besides, out of the property acquired by the business, divided by lot as set out above, to the Pinhas family have fallen the following:

The remaining half of the lands called St Zaccaria which belonged to Andreas Candiotu, from the lands below those adjoining the lands of Henricus Seykel.

Item, the remaining half of the arable lands called Habel Libilac, belonging to Cataldus de Lazarono, adjoining the vineyard of Paulus Manduca, so far as the valley described above in Salamon's part.

Item, a piece of land in Malta in the district of Rahal Luca called ta Lampa.

Item, four pieces of land in the district of Rahal Curmi, in a place called Mirahal, of which one is called Bita il Lihudi and another two fields called Bita Turbe which belonged to Girardus de Vassaldo, and the remaining one called de Bertelli, which belonged to Thomas Camenzuli.

Item, a piece of land in the district of St Nicolaus in Malta which belonged to Antonius Bigenus.

Item, four fields or enclosures in Malta in the district of Calet il Habid, adjoining and together surrounding the vineyard of Sadie Inglixi.

Item, a field or enclosure in the district of Bita Gebelde il Guardia called de Sandar which belonged to Johannes Galia.

Item, another enclosure in the district of Guardia, which belonged to Aloysius Skembrus.

Item, four fields or enclosures called Bita Midauhara in the district of Mihatab and another field called de Kylment and two fields *ala* Madalena called Bita Derrun and Bita Misbah.

Item, the remaining half of the lands in the district of Xeukie de Bon Signuri with half of the house *zoe la banda ki esti lavuri* (on the cultivated side?) At the present season with Lineyder, the Gineyn di Dueli and the market garden, *gructa*, and the field Bita Sigira within which is the house *de lapi*.

Item, the field of Lueyze with the house without a roof and the common entry between the field of Chirmet and that of Gineyn.

Item, all the goods described in the inventory prepared in Syracuse in the hand of Rabbi Rabaattan, with all the books described there except the book called *Macdixie* which has fallen to Salamon's portion.

Item, from that inventory shall be excepted the silver apples and *la mippie* ...[31]

All the property described above, with the exception of the apples with *la mippie*, fall to the share of the Pinhas family, the son and coheir of Bayhunus and Zambita and brother of Salamon, being present as above and accepting for themselves and on behalf of [all the other parties).

---

31. The following few lines, in a baffling mixture of Latin, Sicilian and Maltese, deal with these silver apples and *la mippie*, whatever that is. They are clearly intended to leave these objects out of the distribution.

Pact and Contract

In addition, the parties, for themselves and [the others] ... declare themselves debtors for 55 uncie and creditors for 20 uncie, according to the calculation made by the arbiters, and the parties have agreed with one another that Salamon should accept a quarter of the debts of 20 uncie subject to this agreement that, if he should recover more than the 20 uncie out of the quarter or any other debt not mentioned in that quarter, the excess would be divided, one half to Salamon and one half to the Pinhas family, out of the 35 uncie the balance of the debt of 55 uncie. Salamon agrees to pay 20 uncie and Xamuel Mehyr and his associates agree to pay the balance of 15 uncie, as if they were the Pinhas family, to current creditors in the city of Syracuse ....

Another Pact and Contract

Item, the parties further agree that, of the 30 uncie and 3 tareni the Pinhas family are owed from the company, according to the award of the arbiters, they have deducted or failed to pay 10 uncie which Salamon was owed by the company for his wife's dowry and in satisfaction of the 20 uncie and 3 tareni owing to Salamon, which is 10 uncie and 3 carlini, for which Salamon is bound to the Pinhas family for his part of the 20 uncie and 3 tareni, the balance of the 30 uncie owing to the Pinhas family.

Unpaid Sale with Right to Repurchase

By touching my notarial pen, Salamon has formally sold on credit to the Pinhas family the Hebrew book *Macdixie*, subject to the right to buy it back whenever he wishes on payment of 10 uncie and 3 carlini, within a year from today, and subject to agreement that during that year it stays here in Malta in the hands of Master Abia Sabaha, and that neither the Pinhas family nor anyone in their name should be able to remove it from Mdina within the repurchase period.

Another Pact

Item, the parties agree that Salamon should be obliged and owe and promises to pay on behalf of the Pinhas family 5 uncie and 15 tareni out of the sum of 6 uncie and 15 tareni which Salamon owes the Pinhas family, the addition required to equalise the division for the personal creditors of the Pinhas family by which they bought certain merchandise on credit, to be paid within a year from today, and Salamon should make himself the principal debtor of the 5 uncie and 15 tareni and the remaining 1 uncia in settlement of the 6 uncie and 15 tareni Salamon binds himself to pay on behalf of the Pinhas family for their part of the legacies to pious causes outstanding from Bahyonus their grandfather and Salamon's father.

Pact of Avoidance

It follows from the pact between the parties agreeing in the distribution that Salamon is bound as to one half to the Pinhas family to give up the property which has gone to them as their portion and conversely the Pinhas family are bound as to one half to Salamon to give up the property which has gone to him as his portion.

Acceptance of the Arbiters' Award

Moreover, the parties in every way and in all things submit themselves to the award of the arbiters willingly, accepting that it should stand and remain for ever and all future time continuously and firm. The parties each to the other promise, agree and bind themselves by solemn stipulation always and for all future time to be legally bound by all and every of the aforesaid.

(Then follow the usual formulaic clauses, by which the parties reiterate their obligations, including pledging all their property for the payment of damages on breach of any of the stipulations, and one, introduced by the phrase *consencientes prius*, by which the notary, because a party was outside the jurisdiction, in this case in Sicily, assumed responsibility for performance of the contract, that party making the necessary commitments to the notary.)

11. THE LONDON CENTRE FOR INTERNATIONAL COMMERCIAL MEDIATION AND ARBITRATION IN THE REIGN OF ELIZABETH I[1]

1. INTRODUCTION

Elizabeth I approved of mediation and practised it herself. Among the manuscripts preserved by the Marquess of Salisbury at Hatfield House is the agreement between the Earl of Shrewsbury and his wife, Bess of Hardwick, dated 7 August 1586.[2] The queen herself presided over the mediation, which she put into the hands of Lord Chancellor Bromley and the head of her administration, Lord Treasurer Cecil, Lord Burghley:[3]

> **1.** ... these things being reported to her Majesty by the Lord Chancellor and Lord Treasurer, her Majesty called the Earl and his wife unto her, and in many good words shewed herself very glad thereof, and thanked the Earl, for that she knew he had conformed himself to this good act for her sake and at her request, adding that she took it to tend much to her honour that by her mediation they both were thus accorded. And with many good comfortable speeches required them both to proceed and persevere in this godly act of reconcilement. And so they both shewed themselves very well content with her Majesty's speeches, and in good sort departed together.

That had been a bitter matrimonial dispute, which threatened the tranquillity of the queen's closest circle and had wider political implications. More important for the history of commercial mediation and arbitration

---

1. The Mayor of London provided an earlier arbitration centre for foreigners and Bristol and York had their own schemes, Derek Roebuck *Mediation and Arbitration in the Middle Ages* Oxford, HOLO Books 2013 [*Middle Ages*] pp179-185.
2. Mss preserved at Hatfield House III 1583-1589 no326 p165, 7 August 1586, MC4305400327. A fuller treatment by my colleague Dr Francis Boorman, with a wider range of sources, is awaiting publication. The details of the settlement, down to the last crumpled curtain, are at Calendar of the Cecil Papers in Hatfield House, Volume 3: 1583-1589 1889 pages 155-170.
3. The full quotations are advisable and justified by the need to provide evidence to subvert established assumptions. Each has been given a number in bold for easy reference. I have translated into modern English and redacted to get rid of surplus 'saids' and such.

are the records of the work of Elizabeth's Council. The *Acts of the Privy Council* are now accessible online.[4] Volumes VI to XXXII cover the years 1558 to 1603. They show that throughout Elizabeth's reign the Privy Council acted as a modern arbitration centre does, offering dispute settlement services to anyone who petitioned it, including disputes between foreigners as well as between foreigners and English merchants.

Government policy was consistently and expressly in favour of foreign trade. As is usual, war was closely connected. Spain was the enemy. The Dutch were usually allies but always rivals. France had to be watched. But the merchants of every friendly country were to be nurtured and their governments kept on side. The Privy Council took on every kind of task, judicial as well as administrative. Its workload greatly exceeded that of any other royal court. Its records show that few then expected the Common Law to work. The Council was easy of access by simple petition, acted quickly, cost less, and made good use of the best lawyers without allowing them to warp its processes.

This article is part of a larger study of court-ordered mediation-arbitration between the accession of Elizabeth I in 1558 and the death of Anne in 1714, itself part of an even more ambitious study of all aspects of dispute resolution in that period. It is hardly more than a preliminary skirmish, confined to the Privy Council's own records of its activities to assist foreign merchants between 1558 and the accession of James I in 1603.

It begins with close attention to just one year, 1576, in the middle of Elizabeth's reign.[5] It then moves on twenty years to 1596 and the years around it, for examples of the service provided for foreign merchants. Further work on the other volumes has already begun to show that these years are fairly representative of the whole period. Even if they prove to be aberrant, that itself may be significant. In any case, this glimpse may be enough to generate more interest in the period.

2. THE PRIVY COUNCIL AT WORK IN 1576

Volume IX of the Acts starts in 1575 and ends in 1577. It shows that the Government was having to deal with serious disturbances in Ireland. New

---

4. JR Dasent et al eds *Acts of the Privy Council of England New Series* 46 vols London, HMSO 1890-1960 Kraus reprint 1974 [*APC*] accessible at http://www.british-history.ac.uk, last searched 7 October 2013. 'Council' and 'Privy Council', though technically terms which may refer to different institutions, are used indiscriminately here.
5. I learned of this source from JP Dawson's two-part article 'The Privy Council and Private Law in the Tudor and Stuart Periods: I and II' (1950) 48 *Michigan LR* 393-428 and 627-656, rich both in insights and references, particularly pp408-409 and fnn53-57. I have imposed the present calendar, with the year starting on 1 January, though until 1752 it did not begin until Lady Day (25 March); the records of 1576 cannot be fully representative, because the records are lacking from 13 March to 15 April.

groups of immigrants were arriving from the Low Countries, refugees from Catholic persecution who also had an eye on opportunities in the textile trades. There was then, as now, not only resentful xenophobia but the Samaritan instincts represented in the contemporary ballad:[6]

> Thou shalt be none the worse,
> O England, if thou nurse
> These exiles come of late.

Pirates, like the notorious Beggars of the Sea, with their base in Flushing, now Vlissingen, strained relations with the Dutch, not helped by the many English freebooters who worked all sides for themselves. A visit from the Prince of Orange facilitated a settlement. The Government was not distracted from its responsibilities by any ideology of free trade: grains, textiles, import of wine and export of beer, import of books and export of gold were everyday concerns and subject to Government control. There was no other venue than the Council for the insurance matters which were growing in number and importance.

Meanwhile, Martin Frobisher was about to try to find a north-west passage and Francis Drake was fitting out his old *Pelican* as the *Golden Hind*. To all this human bustle were added the ever-present threats of plague and typhus. Yet the Council took time to give instructions for Christopher Saxton to be helped to extend his map-making into Wales, from 'any tower, castle, high place or hill', with 'a horseman who can speak both Welsh and English to safe conduct him'.

The record begins on 2 January with a board sitting at Hampton Court made up of the Lord Treasurer, the Lord Admiral, the Lord Chamberlain, the Earls of Warwick and Leicester, the Treasurer and the Comptroller, Mr Secretary Smith and Mr Secretary Walsingham. Lord Treasurer Cecil was in the chair as usual. Their first task was to authorise payment of £20 for two theatre evenings which the queen had enjoyed on Boxing Day and New Year's Eve. The last entry is on 28 December, with almost the same board, lacking only the Lord Chamberlain and Mr Secretary Smith, Cecil presiding, issuing a warrant to all the queen's subjects 'presently upon the seas, as also such as serve under other princes being in amity and league with Her Majesty', to assist a small bark, the *Catherine* of

---

6. HE Rollins ed *Old English Ballads 1573-1625* Cambridge, CUP 1920 no26 p182. Nothing changes: 'Very strict control was imposed on building workers who, "more reasonable in their takings, and lesse wasters of time by a greate deale than our owne", invariably aroused strong native jealousy', H Hearder and HR Loyn eds *British Government and Administration* Cardiff, U of Wales P 1974 p129 citing William Harrison *An Historical Description of the Iland of Britaine* London, New Shakespere Society 1877 p238.

Marseilles, on its voyage to London with merchandise from Provence belonging to subjects of the French king.

In that year, the Privy Council probably dealt with more than a thousand matters. Records for the five working weeks from 13 March to 15 April have not survived. The 627 matters which were recorded produced some action, a letter or order which needed to be noted, if only the simple grant of a passport. Internal evidence refers back to acts, of no less importance, of which no record survives, for example previous references of the same matter to arbitrators. The numbers can only be rough; the categories are not exclusive; but they include: arbitrations 24 (17 with a foreign element, 7 private English); foreign merchants 22; pirates 24; passports 14; insurance 7; refugees 2; guilds 2; matrimonial 1; property settlement 1; plague 1; physician 1; enclosure 1; arms trade 1. Of most relevance here are the 22 disputes involving foreign merchants.

Amongst all its multifarious work, the Privy Council set out, actively and expressly, to deal with the problems of foreign merchants, in the records called 'strangers', by offering a dependable, consistent and efficient process of international commercial arbitration. All aspects of the process can be illustrated in a letter sent to the Master of the Rolls and the Solicitor-General from Westminster on 13 March 1576 appointing them arbitrators:[7]

2. Whereas there is a matter in controversy between Richard Peagrim, merchant of London, and Philip Macchiavelli, an Italian, concerning two bills of debt, they are required to call both the parties before them and to examine substantially the matter between them … and, according as it shall stand with equity and justice, to make some good end between them, so that their Lordships be no more troubled. If they are not able to do so, then to tell their Lordships who is at fault, so that they can make the appropriate further order.

Almost without exception the submission, as here, was to an even number of mediator-arbitrators.[8] The Privy Council did not hesitate to require a senior judge-administrator and a busy law officer to take from it the mundane task of resolving what seems a straightforward mercantile dispute. They were required to mediate, 'to make some good end between them', examining all the relevant facts and making suggestions for a compromise, according not to the Common Law, the

---

7. *APC* IX p307 (1576).
8. I have discussed the significance of the preference for an even number of mediator-arbitrators in 'Odds or Evens: How Many Arbitrators?' [to be] [published in (2014) 80 *Arbitration* no1 pp8-15. [Reproduced as Chapter 8 above – SH.]

technical rules of equity, or commercial custom, but 'as it should stand with equity and justice', that is on the merits. If, after what must have been a time-consuming task, they could not get the parties to agree to a settlement, then they were to report back their opinion on who was at fault. That would not be an award, in the modern sense, because it did not conclude the matter. It was an opinion. The Council kept for itself the authority to make the decision.[9]

There are dozens of variations on this form of letter. The Council never adopted a common form. But the working parts were constant, whether the dispute was between English parties, between an English party and a 'stranger', or between two 'strangers'. The last two categories are our concern, with most examples taken from twenty years later, the years around 1595-1600, which provide an even richer choice of examples of the Council's concern to provide a forum of easy access to 'strangers'.

3. AN ARBITRATION CENTRE FOR FOREIGN DISPUTES

The first examples are of disputes between foreigners, with no English parties; then disputes where only some of the parties are foreign.

Between Foreigners

A good example of the readiness of the Council to offer its arbitration services to foreigners is this from 1595:[10]

3. A letter to Philippo Corsini, Marco Basigli, Giovanni Baptista Messenghi and Giovanni Baptista Giustiniani, Italians. We have heard the complaints and allegations of Marino de Gozzi and Nicholo de Menza, your countrymen, … concerning the goods of Nicholo de Gozzi, late deceased, and the quarrels arisen between them which, because we are desirous to bring to an end and perfect agreement without process and lawsuit, which would be inconvenient for strangers not well acquainted with the laws of our nation, for the better expedition and for the special regard we have to dispatch the causes of strangers, we have thought it good to commit the hearing and examination of the matter between them to you … whom the parties have nominated and accepted as indifferent [impartial] men to take knowledge of their cause.

In justice toward Menza, who is Nicholo de Gozzi's executor, we have ordered that he be restored to possession of the house and goods

9. As the *basileus* did in ancient Greece, and, through his deputy the *strategos*, in Ptolemaic Egypt, Derek Roebuck *Ancient Greek Arbitration* Oxford, HOLO Books [*Ancient Greek*] pp30-31 and 318-343.
10. *APC* XXV pp127-128 (1595).

which unjustly and directly against law Marino de Gozzi had taken from him; but, so that Marino de Gozzi may not be defrauded of the inheritance intended for him by his kinsman, nor wronged in any part of it, we require you by this letter to call both parties before you, to examine all points of reckoning, controver[s]y, quarrels or difference between them ... and to endeavour to order, agree and compound the same according to equity and good conscience, so that neither of them shall have cause either of lawsuit or further complaint.

If you find just reason, cause Menza without further trouble and with convenient speed to consign and deliver up to Marino de Gozzi the inheritances, debts, bills, obligations and all such things thereto belonging, which, if you can effect with the contentment of both parties, we shall well approve. If not we require you to certify to us your opinions etc.

All the Italians may be assumed to be merchants. This dispute was not about commerce but inheritance, yet the Council was keen to help.

On 2 June 1596 the Council sent this letter to the Lord Mayor of London:[11]

4. Whereas a humble petition has been presented to us on behalf of Balthazar Lowbitch, a stranger and jeweller of the city of Augsburg, wherein he complains that he has been cunningly overreached and most fraudulently dealt with by Bartholomew Shorer, a stranger likewise, for a jewel of great price and value, which Shorer has not only, by false pretences and specious means, got into his possession from the suppliant (as alleged) but also has since unjustly imprisoned him and otherwise injured him by many undue vexations. We have therefore thought it good to require your Lordship with convenient expedition to call the parties on both sides before you and, using our names and your Lordship's authority, in their presence to nominate and appoint four discreet and indifferent persons of the city to hear and examine the details of this complaint and if they can bring the matters between them to agreement to the complainant's satisfaction or, if they shall not be able to do so, to report to us on their proceedings, so that we may make such a further order as seems convenient.

In the meantime, we think it appropriate that you take good bonds from Shorer, with sufficient sureties in the sum of £[blank], so that he does not depart the realm or absent himself out of the way until the matter has been heard and ordered by you, or you have returned to us your certificate.

11. *APC* XXV 427-428 (1596).

On 27 August 1596 the Lord Mayor was required to deal with the complaint of another foreigner, Adrian Peterson of Middleburg, against his factor in London, with the foreign name of Martin Beremans.[12]

The name Menza appears again a little later. On 29 September 1600 the Council wrote to two Italian merchants, the Philippo Corsini already mentioned in **3** and Emanuel Demetrius:[13]

5. We send you the petition of an Italian, Francisco de Menze, presented to us today, because we think it better that a cause between strangers about merchandise should be examined and determined by some indifferent and sufficient persons of the same sort than to be put to a lawsuit. As you can see from his petition, Menze complains that John Francisco Soprani and Philip Bernardi, having in their hands certain goods of his (being 31 pieces of fustian or thereabouts), as security for certain money he received of them, are suing him to recover that money, but they will neither restore the goods to him nor give him a due account or satisfaction for them.

The particulars of this question between them you will understand more perfectly from the petition or the parties themselves, so, in order that the matter may be ordered without trouble of law, we pray and require you to call before you the Italians Soprani and Bernardi, together with the petitioner, and upon examining the claim make the best order you can to end the controversy between them in whatever way you find agrees with good right and conscience. If Soprani and Bernardi would like to join any other one or two merchants with you in the examination of this cause, then admit them with yourselves ... and proceed all together, or any two or three of you, each party having one merchant of his own choice or acceptance... and, if you fail to make an agreement between them, then certify to us in whom you find the wrongdoing.

The Council was concerned to ensure that the shortcomings of the legal system should not inhibit trade, even if that meant subverting the legal system of the Common Law and recent legislation, which had created a new court of Exchequer Chamber in 1585.[14] Nothing could be more explicit than its statement of intent in a letter in 1597 to all the judges of that court, which had been set up to hear appeals by writ of error from the King's Bench:[15]

---

12. *APC* XXVI 134 (1596).
13. *APC* XXX 698-699 (1600).
14. 27 Elizabeth c8 amended 31 Elizabeth c1.
15. *APC* XXVI 452-453 (1597). It was called King's Bench in Elizabeth's time.

6. To the Lord Chief Justice of the Common Pleas, the Lord Chief Baron, and to the rest of Her Majesty's judges appointed for the examining of errors upon judgments given in Her Highness' Bench.

Whereas Hans Hunger, a merchant stranger, has for a long time had an action on an account against Guilliam Vermaiden and Garrett de Mallines,[16] his factors, which he has prosecuted now for four years, in different ways at great cost, and at last has brought it to a condemnation of Vermaiden and Mallines in the sum of £5,300 sterling, by two several verdicts and judgments in the King's Bench, and to an execution of the judgments, and yet notwithstanding finds himself frustrated of his long travail and suit by a writ of error, which his adversaries have procured and follow before you in the hope of reversing the former proceedings:

Forasmuch as the cause of Hunger has, by letters from the Estates General of the United Provinces in the Low Countries and from Count Maurice [of Nassau, Prince of Orange], been often and earnestly recommended to Her Majesty and to us, we cannot but have regard that justice be done to him in such a way as we would wish it to be done to any of our own nation in a strange country, and therefore we have thought it good, because the matter has come into your hands, to commend it to your care and trust, so that Hunger may not be wronged by any over-scrupulous and nice point of error, but that you will diligently and uprightly consider the alleged error to see whether it is of sufficient moment to make the former proceedings void or not, and that he may have the trial hereof with expedition and such favour as is fit to be afforded to a stranger in a cause so recommended as explained above, which we pray and require you to do.

In other words, the Privy Council was instructing the judges, who had been given jurisdiction by act of parliament to hear this appeal by writ of error against a judgment of the King's Bench, not to find an 'over-scrupulous and nice point of error', which could be expected to take years, but to get on and come to a conclusion not only 'with expedition' but 'with such favour as is fit to be afforded to a stranger in a cause so recommended'. A wink was no doubt expected to be as good as a nod.

When the Council had to deal with Malynes again, it appointed two London aldermen and two merchants with English names, Archer and Woodward, though all parties were foreigners:[17]

---

16. The father of the Gerard de Malynes, author of *Lex Mercatoria*; Derek Roebuck 'Gerard Malynes, Arbitrator' (1996) 62 *Arbitration* 12-15. The father had been born in England, emigrated to the Netherlands and returned to work in London, so all parties were strangers. His more famous son was notorious for his procedural stratagems put forward to avoid paying his debts, *APC* XXXVI 163, 267 (1618).

17. *APC* XXVI 556 (1596).

7. To hear a cause in controversy between Garret de Malynes, a stranger and prisoner in the Fleet [the debtors' prison] and Abraham van Herwick and Deryck Lipson, merchant strangers, and thereupon to make a friendly and final order between them, or else to report to their Lordships how the case stands and who is at fault. And if the parties should choose anyone else to be commissioners for them, they were required to admit them, to join with them and proceed accordingly to hear the cause.

Between Foreign and English Parties

The Council was just as ready to intervene to protect foreign merchants against English parties. In 1596 it wrote to two English merchants, Gerrard and Barnham, and two Italians, the Giovanni Baptista Giustiniani mentioned in **3** above and Horatio Franchiotti:[18]

8. requiring them to examine the complaint of Paulo Gondola, a merchant stranger, against Alderman Houghton ... for £1,926, for he pawned to him certain satins and taffetas of great value ... . They are required to order and end the matter if they can, or to certify their Lordships, and, if Mr Houghton wishes to name some commissioner of like quality with them for more indifferency, they are to admit them.

Scotland was then, of course, a foreign country. A letter to the Bishop of Durham in 1596 asks him to intervene in a dispute between a Scottish merchant and one from Durham, over a consignment of lead, because that is what we would expect if a similar wrong were done 'by any Scot to men of our nation' – 'the King of Scots having taken knowledge of this', as he had also done in a dispute between a Scot and an Englishman, referred to the Lord Mayor of London a little later in the same year, and again when the Council asked the Lord Mayor of London to choose 'some honest and discreet citizens' to deal with the claim of a 'poor merchant', William Scott of Kirkaldy. He had sailed to the Azores on behalf of London merchants, leaving a chest for safe custody with John Lawson, a shipwright of Wapping, who would not give it up. Scott's claim had been 'recommended to Her Majesty by the Scottish king'.[19]

The Council was ever ready to help foreign creditors to collect debts from recalcitrant English debtors. On 9 April 1601 it wrote to the Mayor of Southampton:[20]

---

18. *APC* XXVI 363 (1596).
19. *APC* XXVI 29 (1596).
20. *APC* XXXI 271 (1601).

9. We send you enclosed the petition of Michel Sherland, a merchant of Bordeaux in France, containing a complaint of very devious dealing which he alleges is used against him by Thomas Beele of that town [i.e. Southampton], to whom he alleges he sold a certain quantity of wine but, because another third person (since become bankrupt) was used in making the bargain between them, would disclaim to be answerable for payment for the wine, and would refer him for his satisfaction to the other party who is insolvent.

Whereupon the suppliant, having made humble suit to us through the French Ambassador, to procure a remedy against that wrong, we have decided to refer the examination of his complaints to you ... to examine carefully whether Sherland's information is true ...

All the evidence shows the Council's generous concern for foreign merchants. But the converse was a determination that no English merchant should flout English jurisdiction by bringing an action in a foreign court against another Englishman about matters justiciable in England:[21]

10. A letter to Mr Doctor Caesar,[22] Mr Thomas Smithe, Clerk of the Council, and George Southerton, esquires. Upon a complaint and information given us by the merchants trading into Levant that Michael Locke did commence suit in Venice against some of them for matters of accounts and reckoning, and other demands alleged to be due to him by them while he was used and employed in their affairs, because we did not like the way that the subjects of Her Majesty were suing one another on matters determinable in the realm, we did enjoin him to cease that suit.

Nevertheless, because in his letters to us he alleges that various sums are due to him from that company, we require you to call before you such persons as the merchants of Levant shall appoint, and such also as shall be instructed in the matter on behalf of Locke, and consider Locke's demands and what the merchants allege on their side, and we shall be very happy if you can manage to set down some good agreement between them. But, if you have any difficulty, we require you to certify to us the state of the controversy and differences between them, and what course you think most appropriate to decide them.

Parties who had begun litigation abroad might ask the Council to take over their dispute. On 30 April 1600 it asked four London merchants

---

21. *APC* XXVII 29 (1598).
22. Julius Caesar was then master in the Court of Requests and MP for Windsor. He was the son of an Italian immigrant, Queen Mary's doctor.

to sort out the problems of two English merchants about 200 tons of alum, which the French king had allowed to be exported to France free of customs dues:[23]

> **11.** Forasmuch as the parties are now here together and happy to refer the matter to arbitration, for a full end and order to be set down, and by consent have chosen you to be their arbitrators, and if you cannot agree to stand to the determination and award of a fifth as an umpire, appointed by you … . cause them to enter into a bond of £1,000 each … . If you find any matter needs to be opened and revealed to you by learned counsel, you may use the advice of such learned counsel as the parties shall think good … and proceed to the award either by yourselves or with the assistance of the umpire if you cannot agree … .

In that case, the parties' own agreement provided that the arbitrators' award should be final and no reference back to the Council was necessary.

Sometimes the Council itself gave the arbitrators the authority to make a binding award. In 1596 it asked the Lord Keeper, Sir Thomas Egerton, and the Chancellor of the Exchequer, Sir John Fortescue, to dispose of the complaint of John Van de Wall, merchant of Amsterdam, against Englishman Jerome Horsey:[24]

> **12.** to make such good and final order between them … agreeing to the equity of the cause.

Usually no more is heard but occasionally a party was obdurate, either in refusing mediation or in failing to conform with the settlement or award.

One of the Council's concerns was to alleviate the plight of debtors, particularly to encourage compositions with creditors. Debtors were routinely imprisoned for default, which did no good to either side, except in the cases, probably including Malynes senior, when the debtor was playing tricks.

The Council knew how to deal with recalcitrants. In 1590 it advised Abraham Turnour:[25]

> To be contented for charity's sake to take his debts of two poor men, Bale and Woodley … with that reasonable respite of time that their other creditors agreed to. And let him understand that not only would he be doing a good and charitable deed, but would ease a poor woman,

23. *APC* XXX 273-274 (1600).
24. *APC* XXVI 350 (1596).
25. *APC* XX 90 (1590).

Bale's wife, who has been following their Lordships, of the further trouble and labour of renewing her complaint, which, if it should happen, their Lordships would be constrained to take that course against him as otherwise they would be loth to do.

Anyone receiving such a reproof would be unlikely to mistake its gentle tone for a reluctance to strike hard.

4. OTHER COURTS

The Privy Council had no monopoly of arbitration. Its use was widespread and normal. Other courts regularly delegated disputes for mediation and arbitration, sometimes to one or more of their own judges, or to lawyers associated with the court, but frequently to laymen. Contemporary examples from two courts, Admiralty and Chancery, must suffice.

Arbitration was common in maritime disputes, in particular about general average claims. The *Elizabeth* of London had arrived in Elsinore laden with cloth, a quarter of a century before Shakespeare wrote *Hamlet*. The King of Denmark had demanded a toll. The amount could only be met by handing over some of the smaller rolls. Any larger one would have been worth more than the toll and there was no way of giving change. Those whose smaller rolls had been taken asked the Court of Admiralty to require contributions from those whose bigger rolls had not. In 1575 the Court delegated the dispute to four arbitrators chosen by the parties, who made their award according to the rules of general average:[26]

13. We David Lewes, Judge of the Admiralty, Thomas Yale, Judge of the Court of the Audience of Canterbury, Robert Fourthe and John Hamonde, doctors of the law, arbiters elected and chosen to deem and judge ... every man ... ought by law and equity to make contribution ... according to the rate of his goods delivered.

In 1596 the Court of Chancery in *Vysey v Walton*, wishing to end strife between two brothers, referred their dispute to two knights to arbitrate;[27] and in *Wentworth v Knightley* asked Edward Coke, then Attorney-General, and George Croke, of *Croke's Reports* and then Recorder of London, to mediate a particularly difficult land dispute.

---

26. RG Marsden *Select Pleas in the Court of Admiralty II* (1897) 11 Selden Society pp39-40; and e.g. in vol *I* (1894) 6 Selden Society p101, a dispute about wages was determined by four arbitrators.
27. JP Dawson *A History of Lay Judges* Cambridge, Mass, Harvard UP 1960 p167, citing *Reg Lib 1596* (A) fol 1650b.

5. CONCLUSIONS

This article has made use of just a handful of examples, taken from only two volumes of the *Acts of the Privy Council*, with one or two other sources, but enough perhaps to provide answers to these questions: what kinds of dispute were handled; who were the arbitrators; what law did they apply; what procedure did they follow; how were awards enforced?

The most striking characteristics of all aspects of the Privy Council's work were its omnivorous reach and its flexibility, with no effort spared to provide tailor-made responses to whatever needs the petitioner could substantiate. Though most appointments contained the same elements, no standard forms were ever adopted, despite the bureaucratic pressures there must have been to save trouble by creating them.

The Arbitrators

The Privy Council took it for granted that it could call on anyone it deemed appropriate to serve as mediator-arbitrators. The appointees, almost always two or four, were often judges or law officers. Laymen as well as lawyers were chosen, and sometimes justices of the peace from the place where the dispute had arisen. The Council might pass the task of appointing to someone who could be relied on to know better, the Lord Mayor of London or the Bishop of Durham. It did not hesitate to call on anyone it thought could best help. On 17 September 1599 it wrote to Francis Bacon, then a busy QC and Member of Parliament, short of money and desperate for any judicial office, applying for every one that came vacant. He had turned on his patron Robert Devereux, Earl of Essex, and pleased the queen by writing a justification of Essex's execution, but still she would not give him any kind of post as judge or law officer. The Council gave him the job of sorting out a property dispute between the Bishop of London and the son of his predecessor.[28]

Though the records show the Council appointing arbitrators of its own choice, there is plenty of evidence that it was happy for the parties to have a say in the selection: if the parties 'would like to join any other one or two merchants … each party having one merchant of his own choice', **5**; and 'if the parties should choose anyone else … they were required to admit them' **7**; and 'if Mr Houghton wishes to name some commissioner of like quality with them for more indifferency', **8**.

---

28. *APC* XXIX 136-137 (1599); Bacon was perhaps the cleverest man in Europe, already with a substantial list of publications, theatrical as well as theological, legal and political works, including *Maxims of the Law* (1596) and *Essays* (1597).

Procedure

The arbitrators were instructed to examine the parties in person: 'to call both the parties before them and to examine substantially the matter', **2**, **3**, **4** and **5**. They were given full authority to call witnesses and examine documents. They might be given permission to seek the advice of counsel, whose selection would have to be agreed by the parties, **11**.

The arbitrators were almost invariably expressly instructed to mediate a settlement.[29] Only if they failed as mediators were they to adjudicate, which they did on the evidence, of the witnesses and of any documents. They then had to report back, certifying their opinion – it seems to have been assumed they would be unanimous saying who was at fault. Occasionally they were authorised to make a binding award, **11**. There the parties had set up the arbitration themselves. That was not so in **12**, where the Council directly authorised the arbitrators: 'to make such good and final order ... agreeing to the equity of the cause'.

Equity and Good Conscience

'The equity of the cause', **12**, and 'good right and conscience', **5**, can only mean 'according to the merits', however surprising that may seem to us. Even when the Council was addressing the most senior judges, it expressly made its meaning clear: they were to take 'no over-scrupulous and nice point', **6**. That would always require the arbitrators to be fair to both parties in every way, though favour should be shown to those recommended by foreign powers, **6** and **9**.

No More Troubled

The Privy Council was always busy, busier than it is easy for us to imagine now. It sat for long hours and most working days. One of the advantages of submitting disputes to arbitration was that it usually finished them off. Mediation worked. The submission made its intention clear, as did the queen's own attempt, **1**. The usual instruction was some variant of: 'so that their Lordships be no more troubled', **2**.

6. FINALE

It has been generally assumed both that mediation is a modern procedure and that arbitral institutions are modern inventions. I hope this preliminary survey of the primary sources has added further evidence and argument

---

29. This procedure has a respectable history. Governments used it in ancient Greece and in Ptolemaic Egypt: *Ancient Greek* pp108, 328. It was common before Elizabeth's time: *Middle Ages* pp147-148.

to earlier attempts to disprove both.[30] Most legal historians have written as though the Common Law prevailed in this period, and the Queen's Courts were the final arbiters. Even more dangerously, they have taken it for granted that the slow development of what we now accept as an integral part of what we call the 'rule of law', with a decision in favour of one side the only and optimum outcome, is the best answer to the problems caused by private controversies. Perhaps we should consider whether, when one assumption has been shown to be unreliable, it would be unscientific not to wonder whether the edifice is shaky which has been built on it.

---

30. Most substantially in *Ancient Greek*, *Early English Arbitration*, and *Middle Ages* and recently in 'Time to Think: Understanding Dispute Management' (2011) 77 *Arbitration* 342-350. ['Time to Think' follows as Chapter 20 – SH.]

12. ITALIAN ARBITRATORS IN ELIZABETHAN LONDON[1]

> By this mode of settling disputes, lawsuits are nipped in the bud, the restraints of forms of process are thrown aside, and the mind of the merchant is not distracted from his own business by the conduct of the suit.
>
> Ascanio Baldessaroni[2]

INTRODUCTION

Elizabeth I (1588-1603) did all she could to encourage foreign trade. The customs duties [trade] produced were a major part of her essential income. She governed through her Privy Council, keeping a close watch on all its manifold activities, from waging war to dealing with gypsies. Fortunately for the historian, the Council kept a record in which many but by no means all of its activities were reported. Those records have been edited and published as *Acts of the Privy Council*; they provide most of the material for this article, where they will be cited simply by volume and page, e.g 13.15.[3]

One of the Privy Council's responsibilities was to provide an arbitration scheme to deal with all kinds of disputes, which Elizabeth I was well aware her courts were incapable of handling expertly or expeditiously. She not only offered her Government's services alike to English merchants and 'strangers', as all non-English were called, even Scots; she also often asked foreign merchants to act as arbitrators. And the strangers, like their English colleagues and rivals, not only usually preferred their differences to be adjudicated according to their own law

---

1. The work on which this article is based has been expanded to include merchants in London from other European countries – France, Germany, the Netherlands, Scandinavia, Spain, Portugal and Scotland – in Chapter 11 of *The Golden Age of Arbitration: Dispute Resolution under Elizabeth I*, Oxford, HOLO Books forthcoming end of 2014. [It was published in 2015 – SH.]

2. Ascanio Baldessaroni, *Delle Assicurazione Marittime Trattato* Nella Stamperia Bonducciana, 1786.

3. JR Dasent ed *Acts of the Privy Council of England* New Series London, HMSO 32 vols 1890-1964 [*APC*].

merchant rather than the Common Law; they also preferred mediation and arbitration by their own kind.[4]

Foreign merchants were perhaps better acquainted than the English with the Civil Law *compromissum*, by which they were in the habit of submitting their disputes to private arbitration, but the Privy Council and the English merchants were well aware of its procedure and documentation and took its validity and value for granted.[5]

The Council's unconcerned and unspoken assumption seems to have been that its jurisdiction was as great as its power to enforce its orders. Certainly there is no evidence that it concerned itself with legal niceties of jurisdiction.

When a dispute arose between foreign and English parties, the Privy Council would sometimes appoint a mixed tribunal, chosen from London merchants, English and foreign, commissioning experts to 'see the accounts and reckonings' of foreign merchants. In 1578 it chose two London Aldermen with three Italians – Horatio Palavicino, Benedict Spinola and Philip Corsini – and some whose nationality is not so obvious: John Calvette, Vincent Gingerdyne and Jerome Danalie.[6] Those three Italians will be given further individual scrutiny here; others will also be considered together.

The Privy Council consistently showed that its main concern was efficiency. It was prepared to deal with a dispute between foreign merchants about a matter with no connection at all with England, even where the disputed property was abroad, if that would dispose of the matter fairly and promptly. On the other hand, it would refer a dispute to a foreign power, if it thought that would be more appropriate. In 1571 it wrote to the Lord Mayor of London, reminding him that a dispute between members of the Fortuni family of Florence had been committed to 'certain persons, as well English as strangers', but the Council had changed its mind, because 'the reformation of this matter did belong rather to the Duke of Florence, unto whom they are subjects'.[7]

But in 1597 the Privy Council made it clear that it was not so happy to allow the same licence to English merchants abroad. It dealt with a complaint from the Levant Merchants that Michael Locke had 'commenced suit in Venice against some of them for accounts and reckoning and other demands ... while he was employed in their affairs'. It told Locke that they were not happy that 'subjects of Her Majesty should sue one another [abroad] for matters determinable here', and it

---

4. The earlier history is described in Derek Roebuck *Mediation and Arbitration in the Middle Ages* Oxford, HOLO Books 2013 pp70-86.
5. 13.15.
6. 10.156.
7. 8.41.

commissioned Dr Julius Caesar, Master of Requests and Admiralty Judge (himself of Italian parentage), with two others to 'set down some good agreement between them, if they could', or to report back for the Council to decide.[8]

Among all his other commitments, Caesar acted as arbitrator in scores if not hundreds of disputes, usually commissioned by the Privy Council, which made frequent use of civil lawyers, the Doctors of Civil Law, who practised in London then out of Doctors' Commons in Chancery Lane, in matters within the jurisdiction of the ecclesiastical and admiralty courts.

DR JULIUS CAESAR

Julius Caesar was born in London about 1558 the eldest son of Dr Cesare Adelmare, born in Venice but by then a naturalised English citizen. Under the name of Dr Caesar he was physician both to Mary Tudor and Elizabeth I, who was one of Julius's godparents. Julius graduated from Magdalen Hall, Oxford, in 1575 and then studied in Paris, took a doctorate in law there in 1581, and a DCL from Oxford in 1584. In that year he was appointed deputy judge of the Court of Admiralty, and judge the next year. In 1591 he became an extraordinary Master of the Court of Requests and in 1596 a permanent Master. He had been a Master in Chancery since 1584. After Elizabeth I's death he first played a more political role as Chancellor of the Exchequer and then from 1614 until his death in 1636 he was Master of the Rolls, the senior Chancery judge.

He sat as a Member of Parliament for no fewer than seven constituencies at different times. He had many business interests, including the Mineral and Battery Company, the Northwest Passage Company and the French Company, and invested in the voyages of discovery of Thomas Cavendish and Sir Martin Frobisher. He was also a member of the commission which in 1624 drew up the statute which constituted the first colony of Virginia.

And all through Elizabeth's reign he was a busy arbitrator. All in all, not a bad contribution to English life from the son of an Italian immigrant! His gifts to charity justified his description by a contemporary as 'a person of prodigious bounty to all of worth or want, so that he might seem to be almoner-general of the nation'.[9]

THE ITALIAN MERCHANTS

The records of the *Acts of the Privy Council* are full of Italians, as parties and arbitrators, some names recurring over again. They include simple commissions, for example to make enquiries and report back for the

---

8. 27.29.
9. Thomas Fuller *History of the Worthies of England* III 26.

Council itself to make the necessary order, on the petition of the Italian Rizzo.[10] Others more complicated stretch over decades.

There were close-knit family groups, for example of Genoese, who were merchants in London, aristocrats in their own country.[11] In the Prerogative Court of Canterbury is a copy of the will, dated 6 July 1580, of Benedict Spinola. One of the witnesses was Horatio Palavicino, like Spinola from Genoa and probably related on his mother's side to Spinola. Spinola calls him his 'very trusted confidant'. Another witness was Giovanni Battista Giustiniano, for many years Palavicino's agent, who appears in various capacities in the *APC* and was Palavicino's executor.

There were in London then merchants whose families had lived there for generations, some for centuries like the Corsini family of Florentine bankers, whose descendants are still to be found there. The same names recur as parties, arbitrators and experts. Three will receive special attention here, serving as the more outstanding and well-documented examples for the rest: Horatio Palavicino, Benedict Spinola and Philip Corsini.

Horatio Palavicino

Horatio Palavicino, who was born in Genoa about 1520 and died in 1600, came from an Italian aristocratic family. His mother was a Spinola, also from Genoa. He was granted English citizenship in 1585 and knighted in 1587. As a young man he had made a fortune by collecting the various taxes due to the Pope and, when the Roman Catholic Queen Mary died and the Protestant Elizabeth I succeeded her, choosing to show his loyalty by keeping for himself what he had accumulated for the Pope and lending it to the new queen. Perhaps it is some explanation, even if no justification, that the Pope had tortured his brother. In 1584 the Inquisition condemned Horatio and he was excommunicated.

Palavicino and his family traded in alum, the crystalline ore used in the processing of woollen cloth. They exploited their monopolies, engrossed supplies and manipulated markets, usually successfully. For much of the early 1580s Horatio lived in France to supervise the business. He also travelled freely, adding to his usefulness and his position of influence by spying for the Queen's head of security, Francis Walsingham, who more than anyone was responsible for Elizabeth I surviving all the Catholic conspirators' attempts to assassinate her.

Horatio became very rich and with cash to lend came political influence. For whatever reason, he was able to get close to the Queen.

10. 25.75.
11. National Archives Prob 11/62 ff294-5 1 tr Nina Green http://www.oxford-shakespeare.com.

He must have had considerable charm. He even managed to promote himself as a fighting man, fitting out a ship against the Armada. His freedom to travel and his many contacts throughout the business world of Western Europe made him especially useful. From March 1586 to April 1587 he was entrusted with an embassy to the German princes, to try to persuade them to support Henri of Navarre against the Guise and the Catholic League. The Queen sent him again in March 1590 to negotiate the support of the German princes but, despite his success, she blamed him for later setbacks and he fell from favour.

Palavicino was sought after as an arbitrator. On 26 September 1598 he wrote from his Cambridgeshire estate at Babraham to Sir William Cecil:[12]

If second thoughts are no better than first ones, it befits me to take my stand on the declaration made by you, but as I have no wish to trouble you I will only say about my journey to France that I have two reasons for going. First, that my brothers have quarrelled over this debt, in which the elder has a larger interest than the younger, and have asked me to arbitrate, which I cannot do so far off. In the next place, I am anxious once more to serve the Queen, and I think I can be more useful there than here … . At any rate you will be able to judge, when once I am in Paris, and if I find all as I hope, the Queen can authorize me then and not before. So that I ask that my passport may be made out in the form that I had when I went to Holland four years ago.

Palavicino died of old age in 1600, worth £100,000.

Benedict Spinola

The power of the rich in English politics can at no time be overestimated. Another wealthy foreign merchant in London at that time was Benedict Spinola, born in Genoa about 1519. Related to Palavicino's mother's family, he became his friend and business associate. He was granted English citizenship in 1552. His business interests included exporting woollen cloth and importing wine. He was well known to those at the top of society as the man to go to for the best deals in fine fabrics, which he got from his three brothers who dealt with such stuff, importing it through Flanders, where they lived, from Italy, where it was made. The Earl of Leicester bought new hangings from Benedict for the dining hall when he was building Kenilworth Castle, because he was 'able to get such stuff better cheap than any man'. He also asked Walsingham to favour Spinola

---

12. Calendar of the Cecil Papers in Hatfield House 8 1598 pp348-373. URL: http://www. british-history.ac.uk/report.aspx?compid=111744, accessed 11 May 2014.

in his 'great cause', whatever that may have been, because he was 'my dear friend and the best Italian I know in England'.[13]

Where the dispute involved an Italian, the Council's practice was to appoint at least one Italian arbitrator, as it did Emmanuel Demetrius to join three Londoners or Spinola with two doctors of the civil law, an alderman and the Admiralty judge to deal with a regular petitioner, John Baptista Sambitores. A month later, the Council added two more English merchants when there was trouble enforcing the award.[14] Spinola was appointed again with Guicciardini, in a 'controversy lately grown between Diogenes Francischini and Alvigi Securro'.[15]

On 24 June 1574 various creditors owed Spinola debts totalling the enormous sum of £27,879 9s 8d. In 1578, he and Palavicino were together able to arrange a great loan to the Union of Brussels. Benedict Spinola died of plague in London in 1580.

Philip Corsini

The Corsinis ran the oldest and biggest bank in London. Since the 14th century they had been reputed to be able to deliver a letter from London to Florence in three days. The Privy Council often called on Philip Corsini for help with arbitrations. In 1600 it commissioned him and another Italian merchant resident in London, Emmanuel Demetrius:[16]

> We send you the petition of an Italian, Francisco de Menze, because we think it fitter that the cause betwixt strangers in a matter of merchandise should rather be examined and determined by some indifferent [which then meant 'favouring neither side'] and sufficient persons of the same sort than be put to suit of law ... . To the end that the matter may be ordered without trouble of law ... take the best order you can to end the controversy in such sort as you shall find agreeable to good right and conscience.

Not according to law of any kind, it should be noted, not even the merchants' own *lex mercatoria*, but 'good right and conscience', the Privy Council's preferred criteria. The defendants were invited to nominate one or two arbitrators of their own, so long as there was an even number from each side.

Philip Corsini and his family appear in the Privy Council records as parties as well as arbitrators. Bartholomew Corsini, 'merchant stranger

13. BL Harley MS 260 f363.
14. 20.215; 8.195; 8.211.
15. 9.169.
16. 30.698.

resident in London', complained he had consigned twelve packs of kerseys [coarse woollen cloth] to two London merchants to carry to Livorno, which they had misappropriated. In April 1580 the Council ordered the Lord Mayor and three London aldermen to compound the matter or report their reasons for failure; and it added a postscript telling the arbitrators to deal similarly with the claim of Nicholas Gozzi, Philip Corsini's partner, relating to a consignment of lead, which the English merchants had similarly failed to deliver, and meanwhile to attach the respondents' ship, the *Mary Flower*. Two days later it gave further instructions that, because the cargo on the *Mary Flower* was perishable, it should be unloaded and sold and the proceeds kept to await the award.[17]

Later that year Philip Corsini was respondent in a claim for his share in a dispute over average after Turkish galleys had captured the *Ughera Salvania*. And in May 1586 he, Gozzi and others complained that Ralf Griffin, a London merchant, had failed to pay his debts to them, that they had been compelled to make him bankrupt, that they had been persuaded to give him more time, but that he had not kept his promises. Dr Caesar and two aldermen were charged to 'end and determine the cause between them according to equity and conscience'.[18]

Six years later, on 23 January 1592, the Privy Council appointed new arbitrators in Philip Corsini's claim against Robert Middleton and Erasmus Harbie for the 'uncasing and false marking' of 25 bags of pepper; and on 22 March it made a detailed order for enforcement of the award in Corsini's favour, acting on behalf of 'the Italians', but taking a bond from him in case any of the pepper was proved to belong to Spanish merchants.[19]

There is just a note on 12 July that the Privy Council itself dealt with Philip Corsini's claim against Middleton and Harbie about the goods taken in the *Ughera Salvania*. The record for 2 August shows that a committee of four members of the Council sat to deal with this 'cause that hath so long time depended in controversy'. The parties had agreed that all their litigation and other claims would cease and all their differences would be referred to that committee, 'and some others learned in the civil laws to be assistants to them, finally as arbitrators to order and end'. The parties chose Dr Ford and Dr Cosen, and the committee coopted Dr Aubrey, all civil lawyers. 'Ready money and plate to the value of the goods which either of them have received' was to be deposited with two of the Tellers of Her Majesty's Receipt, in 'coffers whereof there shall be two locks,

17. 13.16; 13.20; 13.27; 13.103; 13.128; 13.171.
18. 13.194; 14.95.
19. 22.199; 22.351; 23.26; 23.92; 24.196; 24.385-24.393; 24.403; 24.405.

and each of the parties to have a key'. The record required that the award be made by All Saints Day [1 November].

On 18 April 1593 the Privy Council complained to Dr Aubrey and Dr Caesar that, though they had each sent in a report, what it wanted was a joint award. On 14 July it wrote three letters to 'the Mayor of Dartmouth and the Customers and Searchers there', to Sir John Hart and Alderman Saltenstall, and to James Bagg and John Blithman, telling them 'we have now set down a final order' and giving them detailed instructions about how to handle the pepper and sugar. Then followed the award of 3 July, signed by the final arbitrators – the Lord Treasurer, the Lord Admiral and Lord Buckhurst – all members of the Privy Council, setting out with great particularity each consignment with its distinguishing mark.

There was just one more matter to be attended to, and the Privy Council did so in a letter to Sir John Hart and Alderman Saltenstall on 17 July. There was the chest with two locks. Harbie held the key to one and would not hand it over. If he still refused, the Council gave them authority to break it open; and it repeated its instructions to the Mayor of Dartmouth James Bagg and John Blithman, telling them to make haste.

Philip Corsini was also defendant to the claim of Martin Heigthowzen of Dansk, which the Privy Council committed to Dr Aubrey and Dr Caesar, Masters of Requests, 'for the matter of freight of a ship'. On 9 June 1592 it wrote to them:[20]

> We are since given to understand that the matter is of such nature as cannot well be decided without the advice of some well experienced seamen; we have therefore and for the speedier expedition of that cause thought good to require you by virtue hereof to call some of the Wardens and Assistants of the Trinity House unto you for the better satisfaction in such points and doubts as shall need their resolution ... and set down some good order and end betwixt the parties.

The maritime experts from Trinity House would be master mariners.

In December 1595 Philip Corsini complained against three merchants of Totnes. The matter was referred to the mediation of Dr Caesar and Anthony Ashley, one of the Clerks to the Council, who, if they were unable to produce a settlement, were to enquire whether the dispute had not already been resolved in an earlier arbitration.[21]

By then Corsini's partner Nicholas Gozzi was dead and his nephew, Marino Gozzi, had taken over his business. Nicholas de Mensa complained that Marino had also taken his goods and books of account, letters of exchange and bonds. London aldermen were commissioned to 'examine the controversy and make some end thereof'. The Privy Council summoned the parties and made what would now be called an interim order, telling Marino to restore what he had wrongly taken. It then ordered the arbitration to continue before the parties' chosen Italian tribunal: Philip Corsini, Marco Bassegli, Giovanni Baptista Messinghi and Giovanni Baptista Giustiniani. It told them that they had been commissioned:[22]

> Because we are desirous to bring to end and perfect agreement without process and suit of law, the same being inconvenient for strangers not well acquainted with the laws of our nation, for the better expedition and for the special regard we have to despatch the causes of strangers … . endeavour to order, agree and compound the same according to equity and good conscience.

The Privy Council later extended the time for de Mensa to deliver accounts. A week later it told the Master of Requests, Dr Caesar, to take a bond of £200 from de Mensa, by which he must undertake 'to perfect the accounts' and to stand to the award of 'Philippo Corsini or any three of the commissioners'. The amount of the bond was left to Caesar's discretion. And it wrote to the arbitrators explaining what had been ordered. But there was worse to come. Marino Gozzi was a thug. Accompanied by 'certain desperate persons he brought over with him, fit for such purposes' he had made violent attacks on de Mensa. The Council therefore wrote to Sir Richard Martin, previously 'appointed by us to deal in those matters in controversy between them' and 'being a Justice of the Peace in London, to take such order for the security of de Mensa against Gozzi and his followers as the law of this realm doth appoint'.

The Privy Council was as industrious as it was open to petitioners of all kinds. It sat nearly every day, including Sundays, even when twice Sunday fell on Christmas Day. On Sunday 21 November 1596 a full board of the Privy Council wrote to Dr Caesar, Philip Corsini and Baptista Giustiniani, saying that it found their report on the Marino Gozzi and de Mensa dispute too brief; and it sent it back for them to do a better job.

Philip Corsini became the defendant to a complaint brought by a Dutch merchant, John Adrianson. The Deputies of the Low Countries were visiting the Council and it was eager to accommodate their concerns. Adrianson alleged that Corsini had sent him and his freight to Palermo and on the voyage he had been captured by Turks and held prisoner for three years. He also asked that Corsini be made to account for over

22. 25.101; 25.120; 25.127; 25.190; 25.213; 25.214; 25.324; 26.314.

£1,000 which he said he had delivered to Corsini's account in Venice. The Council commissioned Dr Caesar and two others to examine the parties and make an order agreeable to equity and reason.[23]

It is remarkable that so much evidence has survived of Philip Corsini's manifold activities. It is fair to speculate that there was much more of interest of which no record remains.

Other Italians

In 1577 the Master of the Rolls and the Solicitor-General were informed that there was 'a matter in controversy between Richard Peagrim, a merchant of London, and Philippe Macchiavelli, an Italian, concerning two bills of debt'. They were asked to seek information from the Recorder of London about a possible acquittance and then 'according as it shall stand with equity and justice to make some good end between them, that their Lordships be no more troubled', or to report back so that the Council might finally dispose of the dispute.[24]

In 1596 Paulo Gondola complained that he had 'pawned certain satins and taffetas of great value' to Alderman Houghton, who would not let him redeem them except by payment of £400 more than he had received from him. The Council commissioned two London aldermen and Giovanni Baptista Giustiniani and Horatio Franchiotti to 'order and end the matter if they can'. If Houghton wanted to name some other 'commissioners of like quality for more indifferency, they are to admit of them'.[25]

Giustiniani was often used by the Council. Shortly after that commission he was said to be 'an Italian merchant of good sort that hath remained many years in the realm and behaved very honestly'. But he lost all his money when the King of Spain failed to pay his debts to those who owed Giustiniani large amounts. The Privy Council could be relied upon to come to his aid. It instructed the Lord Mayor and Sheriffs to arrange a compromise with his creditors. He would pay them all half now and the rest in time, when he collected his own debts. Meanwhile they should protect him from harassment and all claims against him would be stayed.[26]

A dispute between Venetian merchants, John Bassadona and John de Riveira, 'wherein Michael Hixe claimeth interest', had been disposed of by Dr Caesar. He had ordered that part of the goods in question should be sold to pay mariners' wages, and the rest, being perishable, sold by John Woodward, who would hold the proceeds as trustee: 'to the use of the

23. 28.381.
24. 9.307.
25. 26.363; 26.525.
26. 26.391.

parties to whom the goods should be found to appertain'. But de Riveira had appealed to the Privy Council. So now, 'upon letters to Her Majesty from the Duke of Venice', the Council wrote to the Judges Delegate, asking them either to remit it back to Dr Caesar or set down a final order themselves. The interim order for the sale of the perishable goods should stand in any case, to be handled by John Woodward, or some other of their choice.[27]

John Plademo, master of the galleon *Tyson of Venice*, was in dispute with Martin de Frederingo, wine merchant, about the freight and average of certain wines. The Privy Council instructed the Admiralty judge to call 'two such merchants as he shall think to be skilful and experienced' and 'to set down some final end and order such as they shall see agreeable with equity'. If Frederingo refused to conform, they should 'cause so much of the wines to be appraised and sold as shall satisfy Plademo'. They should likewise end any other controversy touching the ship, so that it might be discharged and suffered to depart.[28]

CONCLUSIONS

The Council did not restrict its protection to business matters. On 13 April 1581 it commissioned the Master of the Rolls and the Recorder of London to look into the complaint of John Swigo, an Italian merchant, against two other strangers, Franchot and Domain, presumably French, for slander and assault. The arbitrators were to try first to mediate, 'to compound the matter between them in good sort with both their consents', but if that failed, 'to order it so in justice as the parties culpable may receive due punishment'.[29]

The evidence is clear: merchants of Italian families were playing a full part in arbitration in London in the sixteenth century and seem to have been welcomed and accepted, some as honoured citizens.

27. 25.387.
28. 18.72.
29. 13.19.

First published in (2016) 2(5) *Journal of Dispute Resolution* 1–26 and reproduced by kind permission of the publisher. Reprinted in Neil Kaplan and Robert Morgan eds *Lawyer, Scholar, Teacher and Activist. A Liber Amicorum in Honour of Derek Roebuck* Oxford: HOLO Books: The Arbitration Press 2021.

13.   THE ENGLISH INHERITANCE

What the First American Colonists Knew of Mediation and Arbitration

Derek Roebuck[1]

> How extensive the practice of arbitration was among private citizens
> with no involvement of lawyers or the courts we will probably never
> know, as the only records of such practices will be happenstance.
> James Oldham and Su Jin Kim[2]

I. INTRODUCTION

It seems fair to assume that the first American colonists took with them attitudes and practices from home, including the ways in which they routinely resolved disputes. For example, on November 11, 1647 the General Court of the Massachusetts Bay Colony authorized the purchase of Edward Coke's *Reports*, *First and Second Institutes* and *Book of Entries*, "to the end we may have the better light for making and proceedings about laws."[3] But does that mean it was natural then for parties with differences to look to litigation for an answer? This Article provides ample evidence of a preference for other ways of resolving their disputes. Its main purpose is to show what dispute resolution attitudes and practices

---

1. Professor Derek Roebuck, Senior Associate Research Fellow, Institute of Advanced Legal Studies, University of London. This article was presented at the University of Missouri School of Law's Center for the Study of Dispute Resolution and *Journal of Dispute Resolution* Fall 2016 Works-in-Progress Conference, which ran in conjunction with the Fall 2016 Symposium entitled, *Beyond the FAA: Arbitration Procedures, Practices, and Policies in Historical Perspective*. For Symposium articles, see 2016 *Journal of Dispute Resolution* 1. For a more complete discussion of the points raised in this article, please see DEREK ROEBUCK, ARBITRATION AND MEDIATION IN SEVENTEENTH-CENTURY ENGLAND (Oxford HOLO Books: The Arbitration Press, 2017).
2. James Oldham & Su Jin Kim, *Arbitration in America: The Early History*, 31 LAW & HIST. REV. 241, 245 (2013) hereinafter Oldham & Kim].
3. RECORDS OF THE GOVERNOR AND COMPANY OF THE MASSACHUSETTS BAY IN NEW ENGLAND 212 (Nathaniel Bradstreet Shurtleff, ed., 1853) at 212, *available at* https://archive.org/details/record-sofgoverno01mass.

prevailed in England that could have been transported to the American colonies. It ends by providing, from English sources, names of one or two individuals, namely Nathaniel Bacon and Francis Bacon, who could have been particular conduits, leaving it for others to find and assess the American evidence.[4]

Throughout the 17th century England expanded its interests in the Americas. The colonists brought to North America the dispute resolution practices they had known in England.[5] These practices included mediation and arbitration. [6] There is something to be learned from the English cases reported in the 17th century, but contemporaries thought little of their law reports. As their most disparaging critic concluded, describing in detail the processes by which those reports came to be published:[7]

As if to avenge the seclusion in which this knowledge had been held, the nation dragged to light every thing [sic] which bore so much as semblance to the aspect of law. 'Then came forth', says a historian of the time (5 Mod viii), 'a flying squadron of thin reports', and past doubt there must be meaning in the sudden and unexampled increase of this sort of publication at the epoch of which we speak.... Most of these reports are *posthumous, were printed from MSS not original; and*

4. Oldham & Kim, *supra* note 2, though concentrating on the adoption of the Arbitration Act 1698, contains much more of relevance to the 17th century, particularly on Maryland and Pennsylvania, and is as authoritative for that century as Henry Horwitz and James Oldham *John Locke, Lord Mansfield and Arbitration During the Eighteenth Century*, 36 THE HISTORICAL J. 137 (1993) are for the 18th century. *See also* Bruce Mann, *The Formalization of Informal Law: Arbitration Before the American Revolution*, 59 N.Y.U. L. REV 443, 446 (1984). Mann features Connecticut. Its reliability can be judged by such generalizations, impliedly of England: "For all practical purposes, arbitration awards were unenforceable." For Massachusetts, *see* DAVID THOMAS KONIG, LAW AND SOCIETY IN PURITAN MASSACHUSETTS: ESSEX COUNTY 1629-1692.
5. MORTON HORWITZ, THE TRANSFORMATION OF AMERICAN LAW: 1780-1860, 145-48 (Harvard University Press, 1977); Mann, *supra* note 4, at 443; Eben Moglen, *Commercial Arbitration in the Eighteenth Century: Searching for the Transformation of American Law*, 93 YALE L.J. 135 (1983); Carli N. Conklin, *Lost Options for Mutual Gain: The Lawyer, the Layperson, and Dispute Resolution in Early America*, 28 OHIO ST. J. ON DISP. RESOL. 581, 583-84 (2013); Carli N. Conklin, *A Variety of State-Level Procedures, Practices, and Policies: Arbitration in Early America*, 2016 J. DISP. RESOL. 55, 60-66; Oldham & Kim, *supra* note 2, at 241, 244-251, 266; James Oldham, *The Historically Shifting Sands of Reasons to Arbitrate*, 2016 J. DISP.RESOL. 41, 41-42.
6. For an overview of mediation and arbitration in early America, see generally JEROLD S. AUERBACH, JUSTICE WITHOUT LAW? (Oxford University Press 1983). See also references *supra* note 4 for works on English-style arbitration in specific British colonies in North America.
7. JOHN WILLIAM WALLACE, THE REPORTERS, CHRONOLOGICALLY ARRANGED: WITH OCCASIONAL REMARKS UPON THEIR RESPECTIVE MERITS (T. & J.W. Johnson, 2nd rev. ed. 1845) (emphasis in the original) *available at* https://archive.org/details/cu31924024518346.

that even the originals were not designed for the press. Ignorance and interest and accident all combined to produce error.

The first writers on arbitration law tried to make the best of what they had, but lawyers turning to them for guidance would find them thin sustenance.[8]

There are, however, ample primary sources in the form of records preserved in national and local archives of the work of practicing mediator-arbitrators. Any account of the period must try to take advantage of all of them. This Article relies on the voluminous collection of just one, Nathaniel Bacon (1546-1622), the son of Sir Nicholas Bacon, Elizabeth I's Lord Keeper and the older half-brother of the more famous Francis.[9] Nathaniel was a busy Justice of the Peace (JP)[10] in Norfolk and, as will be shown below, was often commissioned as arbitrator by the government, but often too by private parties who were happy to rely on his reputation for integrity and expertise in private mediation and arbitration. Each side could appoint a single arbitrator or several arbitrators.[11] It was not uncommon for the sides to appoint a single arbitrator when, like Bacon, both sides trusted him.[12]

After Trinity College Cambridge, Nathaniel Bacon entered Gray's Inn, one of England's Inns of Court, but he was never called to practice as a barrister before the courts.[13] Instead, as soon as he could, he settled into the life of a country squire on the family estate at Stiffkey, Norfolk.[14] In addition to serving as JP, Bacon was a Member of Parliament (MP) for King's Lynn, High Sheriff of Norfolk and Steward of the Duchy of

8. Perhaps the best example by the author is REGULA PLACITANDI, ARBITRIUM REDIVIVUM: OR THE LAW OF ARBITRATION; COLLECTED FROM THE LAW-BOOKS BOTH ANCIENT AND MODERN, AND DEDUCED TO THESE TIMES, (Rich. & Edw. Atkins, 1694). Unfortunately, the identity of the author of REGULA PLACITAN-DI is unknown. *See also* JOHN MARCH, ACTIONS FOR SLANDER AND ARBITRE-MENTS (1648); JOHN MARCH, THE SECOND PART OF ACTIONS FOR SLANDERS, WITH A SECOND PART OF ARBITREMENTS (William Brown ed., 3rd ed. 1674).

9. Nathaniel Bacon lived from 1546-1622 and served as a member of parliament. *Nathaniel Bacon*, THE HISTORY OF PARLIAMENT, http://www.historyofparliamentonline.org/volume/1604-1629/mem-ber/bacon-nathaniel-1546-1622 (last visited Dec. 10, 2016). His younger half-brother, Francis Bacon, lived from 1561-1626. *Francis Bacon*, THE HISTORY OF PARLIAMENT, http://www.historyofparliamentonline.org/volume/1604-1629/member/bacon-sir-francis-1561-1626 (Last visited Dec. 10, 2016).

10. *Francis Bacon*, *supra* note 9.

11. For English law on the number of arbitrators required for arbitration, see Carli N. Conklin, *A Variety of State-Level Procedures, Practices, and Policies: Arbitration in Early America*, 2016 J. DISP. RESOL. 55, 60-62.

12. Such an appointment would be a sign of esteem. BACON PAPERS IV, *infra* note 18, at xliii.

13. *Nathaniel Bacon*, *supra* note 9.

14. *Id.*

Lancaster's lands in the county.[15] He fulfilled his duties as MP but gave priority to the obligations, religious and civil, he considered essential to create an orderly and godly community within his jurisdiction.[16] He devoted much of his time to settling disputes, and he submitted his own disputes to private arbitration.[17]

Bacon's enormous collection of manuscripts, preserved and edited under the title, *The Papers of Nathaniel Bacon of Stiffkey*[18] provides the primary sources for an understanding of routine practices and attitudes to dispute resolution in his country at that time. Indeed, they themselves show that some extrapolation may be justified to the rest of England then. As the following account will demonstrate, most of the documents in the *Papers* refer to his work as a JP, many of them commissions to mediate from a great range of authorities, from the King, Parliament and Privy Council, and the various Courts, to individual authorities.[19] But there is also plenty of evidence of his popularity as a private arbitrator, where with no official interference both parties were content for him to sit alone.[20]

This article draws on edited volumes of the *Papers*, beginning towards the end of Elizabeth I's reign and ending with the latest volume in 1607.[21] The volumes contain two hundred or more documents relating to Bacon's activities as resolver of disputes.[22] As the following discussion will demonstrate, mediation was an essential component of keeping law and order. There was no effective police force; as the editors of volume IV of the *Papers* write, Bacon's brother-in-law was injured in a duel and his son-in-law and later his stepson were to be killed in duels.[23] Mediation and

15. *Id.*
16. *Id.*
17. BACON PAPERS IV, *infra* note 18, at xlii-xliii.
18. THE PAPERS OF NATHANIEL BACON OF STIFFKEY, of which five volumes have so far appeared: Volume I 1556-1577 (A. Hassell Smith, G.M. Baker and RW Kenny eds., (XLVI 1978/1979)) [hereinafter BACON PAPERS I]; Volume II 1578-1585 (A. Hassell Smith & G.M. Baker eds., (XLIX 1983)) [hereinafter BACON PAPERS II]; Volume III 1586-1595 (A. Hassell Smith & G.M. Baker eds., (LIII 1990)) [hereinafter BACON PAPERS III]; Volume IV 1596-1602 (Victor Morgan, Jane Key, & Barry Taylor eds., (LXIV 2000)) [hereinafter BACON PAPERS IV]; and Volume V 1603-1607 (Victor Morgan, Elizabeth Rutledge & Barry Taylor eds., (LXXIV 2010)) [hereinafter BACON PAPERS V]. Two earlier selections will remain useful until the greatly superior Norfolk Record Society edition is complete: NATHANIEL BACON, THE OFFICIAL PAPERS OF SIR BACON OF STIFFKEY, NORFOLK, AS JUSTICE OF THE PEACE 1580-1620 (H.W. Saunders ed., 1915) and SUPPLEMENTARY STIFFKEY PAPERS (F.W. Brooks ed., 1936).
19. *See generally* BACON PAPERS, Volumes I-V, *supra* note 18 (detailing Nathaniel Bacon's work as a JP and the commissions he received to serve as a mediator or arbitrator from the King, Parliament, Privy Council, various Courts, and individuals).
20. *Id.*
21. *Id.* BACON PAPERS I-V, *supra* note 18.
22. *Id.*
23. BACON PAPERS IV, *supra* note 18, at xlii.

arbitration existed as alternative modes of dispute resolution. Bacon's status in the community was reflected in his selection by community members for assistance in peacefully resolving their disputes:

> Resolution of minor local disputes may have been tiresome and time-consuming but the seeking out of a local gentleman such as Bacon as an arbiter by individuals in the locality or the referral to him of disputes that had reached the centre did two things. First, it reflected his existing standing in both local society and in the estimation of those at the centre.... Second, every act of mediation or arbitration helped to spin out yet further filaments of obligation.[24]

Social class expected privilege. Obligations were more readily accepted on the understanding they would generate reciprocity. Bacon's selection as an arbitrator or mediator to resolve disputes was integral to this system.

This article explores Bacon's role as a mediator and arbitrator, and the implications of that role for the practice of mediation and arbitration in the American colonies, in three parts. Part II explores Bacon's official commissions to arbitrate, which he received from the King, Parliament, Privy Council, Chancery and the Chancellor, the Court of Requests, in his role as High Steward, and from the pre-eminent English jurist, Sir Edward Coke. Bacon's communications with Coke, in particular, are worth looking at in depth as they demonstrate the high value placed on mediation and arbitration in this period.

Bacon also received private commissions to mediate or arbitrate disputes; these commissions will be discussed in Part III. Bacon's selection to serve as mediator or arbitrator for private dispute resolution most likely stemmed from his reputation in the community and his authority as Justice of the Peace. This Article explores several such commissions, including a dispute over land and debts between the widow Elizabeth Earle and her late husband's son, Robert, and disputes between neighbours over conflicts as varied as the use of well water, the payment of rents and tithes, and the killing of a boar. The variety of private commissions received by Bacon provides evidence not only of the broad use of mediation and arbitration to resolve disputes, but also of the great value community members placed on mediation and arbitration for settling controversies and restoring the peace. Indeed, in a surviving letter describing a dispute that Bacon was selected to help arbitrate, arbitration is described as a "pathway to peace" and the arbitrator is lauded as "blessed peacemaker".

Part IV concludes this article with a discussion of exportation of mediation and arbitration to the British colonies in North America. That

---

24. BACON PAPERS IV, *supra* note 18, at xliii.

exportation included not only the practice of mediation and arbitration to resolve disputes, but also the high value placed on those dispute resolution processes by individuals and entities as varied as individual colonists and the Privy Council. Part IV ends with a call for future research in this area, in hopes that the uncovering and exploration of archival materials, like the papers of Nathaniel Bacon, might provide a more complete and nuanced understanding of how the English forms of dispute resolution played out in the early American colonies.

II. OFFICIAL COMMISSIONS TO MEDIATION AND ARBITRATION IN 17TH CENTURY ENGLAND

A. Commissions From The King

It was not uncommon for Bacon to receive an official commission to arbitrate a dispute. The endorsement at the foot of a commission might reveal the King's own hand.[25] For example, Martin Hambleton had mortgaged his land for one year to John Mingay and his son Henry, for £60 at 10 percent interest.[26] The land was leased to Edward Murton.[27] Murton and the Mingays took possession of the house and evicted the Hambleton family, even though Hambleton had offered them all he owed.[28] Hambleton specifically asked for Bacon and four others, or any two or three to examine his petition for redress.[29] The petition dated 16 May 1604 is endorsed with an order from King James I that, if the case was not being dealt with judicially, the arbitrators, or some of them, with two or more chosen by the other parties, should settle it equitably.[30]

Julius Caesar, one of the two Masters of Requests, was the conduit through which the King's instructions were usually sent.[31] On June 24, 1603 he wrote to Bacon and Sir Christopher Heydon, referring to them the petition of Nicholas Ringold to the new King, who had asked that Ringold's cause be sent to "some indifferent gentlemen" of Norfolk:[32]

> His Highness' good pleasure is that you should call both him and his adverse parties before you and examine the differences between them, and thereupon mediate such good end and order between them as you

25. BACON PAPERS IV, *supra* note 18, at 108-109.
26. BACON PAPERS V, *supra* note 18, at 108-109.
27. *Id.*
28. *Id.*
29. *Id.*
30. *Id.*
31. BACON PAPERS V, *supra* note 18, at li-lii, 38, 135, 153.
32. BACON PAPERS V, *supra* note 18, at 37-43.

shall find to be agreeable to good conscience and dignity, that His Highness be no further troubled.[33]

The request was expressly to mediate an outcome, not according to law, but according to conscience and dignity.

Not all Bacon's efforts to mediate were successful. A matter referred to him and others on a petition to the King "concerning a messuage and 103 acres in Briston" was returned on May 1, 1604 when they were unable to persuade the parties to a settlement.[34]

B. Commissions From Parliament

Parliament, too, might send a matter to arbitration, even when it was the subject of a bill before it. For example, Arthur Penning of Kettleburgh, Suffolk died in 1594.[35] His heir and executor was his elder son Anthony.[36] The will provided for his younger brother Edmund to receive £4,000 from the estate.[37] The intention was that Edmund should have a substantial share of the family lands.[38] As it would be impossible to convey land of exactly £4,000 in value, there would be a balance to be paid in cash.[39] A difference as to valuation might have been expected to be a simple matter. It was not.

A committee of the Commons appointed arbitrators: Bacon and Sir Charles Cornwallis for Edmund and Sir John Higham and Robert Kempe for Anthony.[40] Sir Robert Jermyn was appointed umpire but later replaced Kempe as arbitrator.[41] Their many attempts produced considerable heat, partly because Edmund's wife Anne was a determined woman who took over the conduct of their claim from her husband and stood up to Anthony's appointed arbitrators, who tried to bully her.[42] Bacon was magisterial when they tried to insist on their preferred award.[43]

Whatever the law might say about title not being arbitrable, arbitration or mediation was through the centuries the preferred method of dealing with disputed ownership of land.[44] Once the arbitrators had decided the

33. *Id.*
34. BACON PAPERS V, *supra* note 18, at 107.
35. BACON PAPERS V, *supra* note 18, at 17, at 222, n.612.
36. BACON PAPERS V, *supra* note 18, at 221-22.
37. BACON PAPERS V, *supra* note 18, at 222.
38. *Id.*
39. *Id.* The balance to be paid was 560 pounds. *Id.*
40. BACON PAPERS V, *supra* note 18, at 221-22.
41. BACON PAPERS V, *supra* note 18, at 222.
42. BACON PAPERS V, *supra* note 18, at 240-43, 250-51, 261-63.
43. BACON PAPERS V, *supra* note 18, at 261-63.
44. DEREK ROEBUCK, THE GOLDEN AGE OF ARBITRATION: DISPUTE RESOLUTION UNDER ELIZABETH I, at 244-58 (2015).

question of title, they would get the necessary conveyances drawn and, when executed, they were as good as any title any court could give.[45]

Anthony Penning wrote to Bacon on 8 September 1606 that he had received a draft conveyance from Edmund and that he had taken exception to it.[46] He had had his own draft prepared by counsel and submitted both to Bacon and whatever was acceptable to him, Higham and Jermyn he would willingly perform.[47]

Higham got in first. He wrote to Bacon on 9 September 1606 to say he had perused both drafts and preferred Anthony's: "I hold it not reasonable that the woman, if she survive her husband, should hold the land without impeachment of waste."[48] Nor should Edmund have a life estate that he could dispose of, "for then he may, through his want of experience, be brought to pass away that interest and live full meanly all his life after."[49] Better he should have only the profits from the land.[50] Was Higham worried that the woman would manipulate her husband?

A letter from Higham and Jermyn to Bacon dated 30 October 1606 appears in The Papers of Nathaniel Bacon preserved in the Folger Library.[51] Anne had been to see them at Bury St Edmunds.[52] They had not enjoyed her visit.[53] She had shown "great mislike" of their preference for the land to remain in trust, with discretion in the trustees as to where the profits should go in Edmund's lifetime:

Her importunity was so great as we sent for Mr Anthony Penning to come to us at Bury, where we laboured him to yield so to assure the lands as his brother might have the very land itself during his life a counsellor-at-law (whom the gentlewoman entertained) did affirm that it might be safely done. Mr Anthony Penning desired to be advised by his own counsel, who fully resolved us that, if the land were assured for life as to the husband as it should be to the wife, with remainder to the issue etc, that then the husband and wife might then by recovery cut off the entail, and so in a short time the husband's estate would quickly be overthrown. The gentlewoman misliked of this and urged us to a certificate, and we perceiving her disposition and that nothing will content her but the sale of the land, we have in a letter set down the whole truth and ascertained my Lord Chancellor thereof, whereof

45. *Id.*
46. BACON PAPERS V, *supra* note 18, at 255.
47. *Id.*
48. *Id.*
49. *Id.*
50. *Id.*
51. *Id.* at 261-62.
52. *Id.*
53. *Id.*

if you like we pray you to subscribe, to prevent the malicious purpose of the woman.[54]

Nothing in all the five volumes of *Papers* shows Bacon's qualities as an arbitrator so well as his reply of 1 November 1606:

Sirs, I have perused the certificate sent unto me under your hands and have considered also of your letter yet I must entreat you to excuse me though I forbear now to join in the certificate. You have had your judgments satisfied by hearing the parties on both sides to speak before you, and it may be I shall be of your judgment when I hear the like. But I am doubtful at this present how to judge this point, *viz* how far forth Edmund Penning shall be barred during his life. I allow well that he be barred to do no act to overthrow the inheritance, and this seemed on our first meeting to be agreed upon between us, and the other point was left doubtful. Therefore, I think it best that a cause of this importance be at London determined upon, where the best counsel in law may be had, and where you, Sir John Heigham, and I are like shortly to meet, and then upon more advice we may certify Sir Robert Jermyn what there falleth out best to be allowed upon and in the meantime the causes may rest as they be.[55]

A model, even for today.

C. Commissions from Privy Council

James I's Privy Council used arbitration to deal with petitions just as Elizabeth I's had done, and Bacon's *Papers* reveal commissions from Privy Council. In giving instructions to those it commissioned, Privy Council rarely made a distinction between mediation and arbitration, or even between an order to resolve a dispute themselves or just to report back, such as in the commission dated 12 November 1604 to Bacon with Sir Miles Corbett, Thomas Cromwell and Owen Sheppard (or to any three or two).[56] They took extensive evidence of the rights of warren over Castle Rising, which were disputed by the Earl of Northampton's tenant and, among others, Sir Henry Spelman, the antiquary's father.[57] The arbitrators were instructed: "upon examination and perusal of such proofs and matters

54. *Id.*
55. BACON PAPERS V, *supra* note 18, at 262-63.
56. BACON PAPERS V, *supra* note 18, at 137-38.
57. BACON PAPERS V, *supra* note 18, at 137-41.

of evidence as they shall have severally to end the controversy if you can, or otherwise certify us of your whole proceedings."[58]

Sir John Popham often referred to Bacon matters that came before him when he was Chief Justice of the King's Bench (CJKB).[59] For example, in 1601 he directed Bacon, Henry Spelman, and Thomas Layer, or any two, to arrange a settlement between Katherine Barr, widow, and the executors of a foreign merchant, Adam Kindt, whom she accused of cheating her of her trading goods.[60] Kindt had died and his executors would not pay his debt.[61]

The *Papers* do not always make it clear whether Popham was acting as CJKB or on behalf of the Privy Council. It made no practical difference to Bacon. Popham appointed Bacon sole arbitrator to determine all the disputes between the Reverend Edward Slynne and Robert Younger, gent, except for a matter between them in the Star Chamber.[62] The parties entered into bonds to abide by his award, which survives.[63] On 3 October 1601 he awarded that Slynne should allow Younger to enter the disputed land, of which some was copyhold in the manor of South Burlingham, and to release all actions other than that in the Star Chamber, to hand over the deeds and pay compensation.[64] Younger must allow Slynne to enter land in South Burlingham and release actions and deliver assurances on request, i.e. to execute the necessary conveyances.[65]

Popham's commissions included one about trespasses to land and a stolen boar "to end if he may"[66] and a petition from the poor inhabitants of Wiveton against John King, a man of great wealth, who had got his hands on funds intended for the poor "now ready to starve," which Popham had himself endorsed to Bacon and Henry Spelman, to "examine this cause and, if you may, take some course that the poor may have their due, otherwise to certify me the true state of the matter at the next assizes."[67]

From the Privy Council Popham sent a dispute between two aldermen of Lynn, Baker and Gurlyn, to Bacon and Sir Miles Corbett, "to mediate matters between them and if you may finally to accord them."[68] In June 1602 John Atkins of King's Lynn wrote to Lord Keeper Egerton, on behalf of himself and his neighbours, complaining of the "unjust malefactions" of Alderman Thomas Baker, and asking him for permission to petition

---

58. BACON PAPERS V, *supra* note 18, at 137-38.
59. BACON PAPERS IV, *supra* note 18, at 206.
60. *Id*.
61. *Id*.
62. BACON PAPERS IV, *supra* note 18, at 209.
63. *Id*.
64. *Id*.
65. *Id*.
66. BACON PAPERS IV, *supra* note 18, at 324
67. BACON PAPERS IV, supra note 18, at 269-70.
68. BACON PAPERS IV, supra note 18, at 273.

the Privy Council for "letters to be directed to 3 or 4 knights or gents in the county to call all the parties grieved before them… whereby some good order may be had for reformation according to their godly wisdoms agreeing with equity." By letter from Popham the Council appointed "the right worshipful my very loving friends Sir Miles Corbett and Nathaniel Bacon Esq":

> With my very hearty commendations. Where there are certain controversies and suits depending between Mr Baker and Mr Gurlyn, two of the aldermen of the town of Lynn, which occasioneth some division in the town to the hindrance of the good governance of the same, I have thought good thereby to pray you to take the pains at this my entreaty to mediate matters between them and if you may finally to accord them wherein in mine opinion you shall do a very good office not only in making peace between these two in particular but in furthering thereby the continuance of the good government of that town.[69]

D. Commissions from the Chancery and the Chancellor

In addition to receiving commissions from the King, Parliament, and Privy Council, Bacon regularly received appointments resulting from petitions to the Chancery, like the one from Thomas Pearce to Lord Keeper Egerton, which Egerton passed to Bacon to deal with alone in June 1600:

> I pray you take the pains, calling both him and his mother before you to examine the matter and by some quiet order agreeable to equity and justice, to prevent and stop these farther suits which were unfit to be between parties so nearly bound to one another in love and duty, and which the petitioner seems to desire to have by this course prevented.[70]

When he became Lord Chancellor Ellesmere, Egerton continued his habit of commissioning Bacon to mediate an end to matters before the Court of Chancery. Thomas Fairfax was plaintiff in a Chancery suit against John Rust. On 15 February 1605 Rust petitioned the Chancellor expressly to appoint Bacon and by a letter of 18 February he was asked "to make some quiet and friendly end between them according to equity and good conscience."[71] But meanwhile Edward Coke had jumped in and sent Rust to Bacon with a letter dated 17 February, asking him:

---

69. *Id.*
70. *Id.*
71. BACON PAPERS V, *supra* note 18, at 152.

to hear and understand the controversy, and thereupon to do your friendly endeavour to end and determine the same between them . . . if by your good persuasion and means you cannot bring them to accept of such order and agreement as you in your wisdom and conscience shall think fit for them, then I pray you to certify to me the true state of the controversy and in whom you find the default to rest, that such order may be taken as is according to justice and equity.[72]

A memorandum of 5 March explains that the dispute was about mutual bonds and that the parties were brought to a settlement, except that Fairfax would not agree to Bacon's finding that he should bear the costs of the Chancery suit.[73] So Bacon had to certify and return the commission, which he did by a letter of 8 April not to Coke but to Ellesmere LC.[74] He explained that the bonds had arisen out of liability for customs duties on barley exported to the Low Countries.[75] Fairfax had had no cause to start proceedings in Chancery, so he should bear the costs of them, £3 or £4.[76] Fairfax could not be persuaded.[77] And so Bacon was certifying and returning the commission, as instructed, "submitting my judgment to your Lordship's wisdom and grave consideration."[78]

On 22 April 1605 Bacon wrote to Coke enclosing a copy of the certificate he had sent to Ellesmere LC on 8 April 1605, and "referring the poor man [Rust] to your further favour for his relief."[79]

E. Commissions from the Court of Requests

Some commissions to mediate went to Bacon through the Court of Requests. For example, after a detailed memorandum of disputes between Robert Barnard and Thomas Clarke relating to corn, oats, straw, malt, peas and a horse, the settlement is recorded:

It is agreed 6 August 1604 between Robert Barnard gent and Thomas Clarke as followeth *viz* Robert Barnard doth accept in full discharge of a debt of £250 due to him from Thomas Clarke the £239 14s 6d demanded by Thomas Clarke, and in discharge thereof, as also of all other demands,

72. BACON PAPERS V, *supra* note 18, at 153.
73. BACON PAPERS V, *supra* note 18, at 156.
74. BACON PAPERS V, *supra* note 18, at 169-170.
75. BACON PAPERS V, *supra* note 18, at 170.
76. *Id.*
77. *Id.*
78. *Id.*
79. BACON PAPERS V, *supra* note 18, at 173-74.

agreeth to seal him a special acquittance. And Thomas Clarke agreeth to seal the like acquittance unto Robert Barnard.[80]

F. Commissions Received by Bacon as High Steward

Among his many other public offices, Bacon was High Steward of the Crown and Duchy of Lancaster in Norfolk.[81] He received commissions to serve as arbitrator in that capacity, as well. For example, in November 1604, Thomas Edwards of Wisbech complained to him as High Steward of the King's manor of Walpole that the brothers Griggs had by a suit in the manor court wrongly taken his copyhold land.[82] On 14 November 1604, Ellesmere LC made an order referring the case to Bacon as High Steward "to decide in law and conscience," "as the fittest person to decide this controversy" but "to make a quiet and friendly end between them according to law and conscience."[83] This made for a nice little conundrum of categorization for the conceptual purist.

Bacon heard the matter as High Steward and wrote forthwith to both counsel that he had considered the legal title and what could be alleged in equity for Edwards and had asked each of the parties whether either would be prepared to renounce the land to the other and for what price.[84] Edwards was willing but the Griggs were not, insisting on their title.[85] Bacon told counsel that he would therefore certify to the Lord Chancellor that a trial be held at the next assizes.[86] Edwards assented but the Griggs said they needed further advice.[87] So Bacon asked counsel to give him their opinions as soon as possible.[88] But even at this stage he made his preference clear: "I incline rather to have the cause mediated than referred to the law if the Griggs would be ruled by me."[89]

Bacon settled another dispute, referred to him by the Duchy Chamber with the consent of both parties. Musket surrendered his rights in a tenement and orchard to Bretland, who agreed to pay him two instalments of £3 6s 8d "in full satisfaction of money due under any cause now depending in the Chamber."[90]

---

80. BACON PAPERS V, *supra* note 18, at 121-24.
81. *Nathaniel Bacon*, *supra* note 9.
82. BACON PAPERS V, *supra* note 18, at 136.
83. BACON PAPERS V, *supra* note 18, at 136, 141-42.
84. BACON PAPERS V, *supra* note 18, at 175.
85. *Id.*
86. *Id.*
87. *Id.*
88. *Id.*
89. *Id.*
90. BACON PAPERS V, *supra* note 18, at 268.

As Chief Steward of the Duchy Lands, Bacon had jurisdiction to decide disputes in his own court. He also performed other judicial functions. For example, if copyhold land was held by a husband in the right of his wife, the wife's agreement was necessary for any transfer.[91] A memorandum of surrender recites that Alice was examined in the absence of her husband by Sir Nathaniel Bacon, Chief Steward, and then John and Alice surrendered the land to Bacon.[92]

G. Commissions from Sir Edward Coke

Edward Coke dominates the legal world of this period. The *Papers* preserve three documents, trimmed and redacted here, which illustrate his involvement with Bacon in the settlement of disputes.[93]

On 8 September 1602 William Cobbe, whose land adjoined Edward Paston's, wrote to Bacon seeking a private arbitration:

Sir, I must confess my presumption to be far greater than my deserts, so as I cannot challenge that interest in your love I so greatly desire. Yet, knowing that it hath been agreeable with your good disposition not to think that time lost which is spent in so good a work as ending of controversies and dissensions, and making of peace and amity between gentlemen and your neighbours, pardon me if I seem troublesome, that am so wrongfully troubled (as I suppose) being not led thereto with self will, yet willing to defend my poor patrimony to my power, being resolved of my right by them of judgment and learning, as also by divers trials lately passed at the common law to my great trouble, charge and hindrance; which by your good means I hope shall now receive a friendly and quiet end (and the rather for that it hath pleased Mr Attorney General [Coke] so earnestly to move the same).

Sir, the sincerity of my cause is to be censured out of your wisdom to which I do appeal, desiring our cause may be weighed in equal balance. I covet not that which I never had, but what my ancestors time out of mind have quietly enjoyed without interruption of them that had the right Mr Paston now hath. Neither build I upon bare presumptions (as shall plainly appear unto you) but upon divers depositions which will be verified by ancient evidence.

---

91. BACON PAPERS V, *supra* note 18, at 292-93.
92. *Id.*
93. BACON PAPERS IV, *supra* note 18, at 284-88.

I wish the state of my body were such as I might safely adventure to attend you myself, but my cousin Athow [the barrister Thomas Athow] and my wife will be ready at all times to attend your leisure for the same, and what you and they shall agree I will most willingly perform, and acknowledge myself bound to you in bonds of perpetual friendship. William Cobbe.[94]

His wife Mary took over. She wrote to Bacon on 21 September 1602, referring to a visit she had made to him with a Mr. Mingey, a relative of Coke's, with Coke's "request that you should take pains to hear and end (if it may be) certain causes betwixt Mr. Paston and Mr. Cobbe, my husband."[95] If they could not mediate a settlement, the matter would go back to Coke, "that he by his wisdom and better persuasions may effect that which you cannot."[96] She suggested possible dates.[97] She had spoken to Paston and got his agreement to submit to Bacon and Henry Wyndham, "to perform without delay what shall be then ordered by you and Mr. Wyndham, and consented to by him, my cousin Athow and myself."[98] So William Cobbe had authorised his wife, with the lawyer Athow, to consent to a binding settlement.

Mary wrote to Bacon four days later.[99] She had received his answering letter (which has not survived) and letters from Coke which she had not read but presumed were attempts to fix a date.[100] She pressed for a date before the start of the legal term.[101] Shortly thereafter Bacon and Wyndham wrote to Coke, responding to his request for them to work for a peace between Cobbe and Paston touching certain land.[102] They reported that they had "had a meeting at Appleton, Mr Paston's house, with the allowance of Mrs Cobbe in the absence of her husband, and there we saw the ground in question and did after see their evidence and hear the depositions read."[103]

Both sides had deeds, which conflicted as to whether rights of common were attached to Babingley manor or Newton manor, "and this we left undetermined, with a consent that the same should be used for the graving of flags and such like as hath of late years been most accustomed."[104] Differences as to who should have rights to feed sheep and rabbits were

94. BACON PAPERS IV, *supra* note 18, at 284-85.
95. BACON PAPERS IV, *supra* note 18, at 285-86.
96. *Id.*
97. *Id.*
98. BACON PAPERS IV, *supra* note 18, at 286.
99. BACON PAPERS IV, *supra* note 18, at 286-87.
100. *Id.*
101. BACON PAPERS IV, *supra* note 18, at 287-88.
102. *Id.*
103. BACON PAPERS IV, *supra* note 18, at 287.
104. *Id.* at 288.

not a major point of contention.[105] But the arbitrators had to listen to all the complaints of both sides' tenants, and that may have been the scarcely concealed collusive object: to get rid of the bickering between their tenants over rights of common and pasture, then a general source of more contention even than the pews in their churches.[106]

They wrote a similar letter to William Cobbe, to tell him of their judgment, adding though that Athow, "your counsellor in the cause" was at the hearing.[107] Would you call that a private mediation, or arbitration, or did Coke's intervention make it Government-ordered? However it may be classified, it seems to have worked. The Cobbes were recusants, as were the Pastons. Religious differences did not inhibit wealthy neighbours from seeking Protestant Bacon's intervention, or affect his willingness to provide them skilled and experienced services.

Coke wrote fairly often and informally to Bacon.[108] He sat with Bacon as a Commissioner for Sewers in 1605.[109] Because of the leading part he played in the creation of the modern law, the *Papers'* evidence of his involvement as a party in mediation and arbitration deserves particular attention.

A letter dated 2 March 1603 from Henry Warner, a friend of both sides, asked Sir Miles Corbett to arbitrate in a land dispute between Edward Coke, then Attorney General, and the same Edward Paston.[110] The disputed land in Flitcham may have adjoined both their properties.[111] Bacon agreed to be the other arbitrator.[112] Coke's confidence in Bacon as a mediator is shown time and again in the commissions he sent him, but this, of course, was a purely private arbitration.[113]

The relevant records begin again with a letter of 1 September 1604 from Coke to Bacon and Sir Miles Corbett, which included:

I being desirous not only of quietness between ourselves (whereof I made no doubt) but also between our posterities afterwards, and that suits (that commonly are mothers of unkindness) might stay, desired you (as likewise my cousin Paston did) to inform yourselves of the true state of the matter in variance; and by your good mediation to end the same. Whereupon (as I am informed) you have taken the pains to view the

105. *Id.*
106. BACON PAPERS IV, *supra* note 17, at 287-88.
107. BACON PAPERS IV, *supra* note 17, at 288.
108. BACON PAPERS V, *supra* note 18, at 143-44.
109. BACON PAPERS V, *supra* note 18, at 187.
110. BACON PAPERS V, *supra* note 18, at 11-12.
111. *Id.*
112. *Id.*
113. BACON PAPERS V, *supra* note 18, at 11-12, 128-129.

ground, and to hear the allegations and proof of either party. These are to desire you to proceed in so good a work, and to the end your labours already taken may not be lost, and that either party may receive the better satisfaction, that you would be pleased to meet again at Flitcham some time this next week, and to set down the proof and matters tending to the maintenance of the claims by either party, and to the manifestation of the right touching these matters in variance, wherein as you shall do a charitable and friendly work, so shall you make us much both beholden to you for your pains and indifferency herein. And so I commit you to the blessed protection of the Almighty.[114]

That letter was enclosed with the following, dated the next day:

Sir, you shall perceive by these enclosed what a desire I have of quietness, and how bold I am to require your further travails. Sir Miles sent me word by the messenger that any day after tomorrow he would give meeting about the finishing of your former travails. Whereof I am the more desirous, because I would have it driven to an issue before I depart. What day it please you to appoint, this bearer shall give notice thereof to Sir Miles. It was my cousin Paston's resolute request that the reasons and proofs of either side should be set down or else he would no further proceed. And so with my very hearty commendations to you and your good lady I commit you to the blessed protection of the Almighty and ever rest, your assured friend.
Godwike 2 September 1604 Edw Coke[115]

Sadly, the *Papers* tell us nothing more of how this matter was resolved, so research must continue elsewhere.

Coke took pains to encourage Bacon's mediation of a dispute between Jerome Alexander, a King's Bench attorney and Alexander's brother-in-law Robert Plandon over copyhold land.[116] On 16 February 1604 he wrote to Bacon:

After my very hearty commendations. I have received knowledge that there are very many suits betwixt this bearer my servant and one Plandon, his wife's brother. And that there are commissions awarded to you and others directed to examine witnesses and to end and determine the same suits. And forsomuch as I heartily wish a peace between them, lest the one should consume the estate of the other, and in the end feel

114. BACON PAPERS V, *supra* note 18, at 128-29.
115. *Id.*
116. BACON PAPERS V, *supra* note 18, at 74.

the sharpness of their own faults to their great hindrances. Therefore I heartily pray you in the behalf of both their goods to take the more pains at my request to reconcile all questions betwixt them, so shall you do a work of much piety betwixt them, and give me occasion to be heartily thankful to you for your travail therein to be taken . . . .

Your very loving friend [signed] Edward Coke.[117]

Unfortunately, the later correspondence shows no signs of a successful settlement.[118]

In the summer of 1606 Coke referred to Bacon to end or certify a petition he had received as Chief Justice of the Common Pleas about a dispute over money deposited with Thomas Thetford in trust for the two brothers and five sisters of John Moretoft.[119] It asked for "some course to come by their money, being very poor and unable to sue for their rights."[120] Four sisters were married and one was a widow.[121] Bacon's own notes show that he addressed the problem, comparatively trivial in financial terms, with as much care as he had the Pennings' £4,000, with the result that: "Mr Thetford agreed to disburse presently 20s apiece" to the three husbands and the widow, and the rest "their portions out of the said remainder" on Thursday at the house of Bacon.[122] A memorandum dated 21 August 1606 sets out the final settlement in detail.[123] Thetford was also a party to a dispute, this time with no less than Sir Christopher Heydon, Bacon's partner in so many arbitrations. Coke as Chief Justice of Common Pleas (CJCP) similarly referred petitions for wrongful possession of a house and – a grandiloquent effort with many Biblical references, some apposite – from "your poor orator . . . whose cry ascends to God."[124]

On 13 August 1606 Bacon's reply to a Coke commission relates that he had tried to mediate a settlement of a claim against the heir of the debtor, who was answering that he had administered the estate and the claim was too late.[125] Bacon wrote:

In conscience (in my judgment) he ought to pay, both in respect of the poverty of the man, who lent the money to old Lambart, and also of the portion of land which was left to the young man by his father being of the

---

117. *Id.*
118. BACON PAPERS V, *supra* note 18, at 74-75, 77.
119. BACON PAPERS V, *supra* note 18, at 243-44, 249-50
120. BACON PAPERS V, *supra* note 18, at 244.
121. BACON PAPERS V, *supra* note 18, at 243.
122. BACON PAPERS V, *supra* note 18, at 250.
123. BACON PAPERS V, *supra* note 18, at 253-54.
124. BACON PAPERS V, *supra* note 18, at 244-45.
125. BACON PAPERS V, *supra* note 18, at 251.

value of £40 by year being copyhold. I would have had him repair unto your Lordship with the bearer but he refused to do it without warrant. I have thought fit to certify thus much unto your Lordship referring the poor man to your considerations.[126]

On 5 November 1606 Bacon reported failure to Coke on a matter Coke had referred to him from the Norfolk Assizes: "Bullen, notwithstanding his consent given to abide my arbitrement, refuseth to enter into a bond to perform my arbitrement as touching the matter passed by verdict for him before you Thus leaving the cause to your Lordship's further consideration, I take my leave."[127]

A year later, on 2 November 1607, Bacon's letter to Coke reveals the work he was prepared to undertake to resolve a dispute, and the limitations he laboured under, even with Coke's authority as Chief Justice behind him.[128] He had tried again but:

Bullen refused and withdrew himself in a froward and obstinate sort … I moved Bullen to a most reasonable course (as I thought) for end. But his wilfulness was such as he would not be conformable in any sort, which will breed him great trouble from others of his neighbours as well as Laseby.

Thus, being sorry that my labour hath brought forth so little fruit, I yet hope that the wisdom and consideration of your Lordship and the rest will bridle this Bullen, who spareth not to hazard his own undoing for the trial to have his will.

And so I take my leave.[129]

The closeness of their relationship is shown by a letter from Coke to Bacon asking him to play the detective.[130] Joan Cooke had been remanded in custody, charged with poisoning her husband Thomas, parish officer and overseer.[131] Bacon had examined her.[132] Coke commended his actions, particularly in not allowing bail, for poisoning one's husband was the

---

126. *Id.*
127. BACON PAPERS V, *supra* note 18, at 263.
128. BACON PAPERS V, *supra* note 18, at 300.
129. *Id.*
130. BACON PAPERS V, *supra* note 18, at 257-58, reply at 269-70.
131. BACON PAPERS V, *supra* note 18, at 257-58.
132. BACON PAPERS V, *supra* note 18, at 257.

most damnable crime and therefore petty treason.[133] He made specific suggestions:

> It were in mine opinion necessary to get that black stone that was supposed to be brought out of Iceland and to sift out that matter of the ratsbane . . . and to re-examine the widow, where and when she bought it. The matter of unkindness between her and her husband would be thoroughly examined. Your true and loving friend. Edw Coke

> Item   Whether he chewed any tobacco that morning and whether he had any in the house.

> Item   Who were those that saw the body to know it after he was dead.[134]

H. Between Half-Brothers: Nathaniel Bacon and Francis Bacon

The *Papers* provide little evidence of brotherly relations between Nathaniel and Francis, but arbitration crops up even here. In fact, the only substantial record is of Nathaniel intervening to remind Francis of his obligation to arbitrate impartially in a dispute in which he had acted as counsel for one of the parties.[135]

The inhabitants of Southwold had petitioned the Council against Richard Gooch.[136] The matter came by bill before the Star Chamber, which referred it to Francis for report.[137] It was alleged that Gooch had maintained the unfounded complaints of Margaret Raphe, widow, against named persons and other inhabitants of Southwold, twenty persons in all, by bringing frivolous suits in Star Chamber and Chancery.[138] The petitioners introduced what would today be objected to as irrelevant matter: a third of the town had been destroyed by fire, what was left had been ravaged by plague and pirates (Dunkirkers) and "hostile enemies of Spain" and "hard voyages in fisher fare and bad markets whereon the state of the town wholly dependeth" had taken their livelihoods away.[139] They pointed out that Francis had been Gooch's counsel when bringing the bill in Chancery, and Gooch had worked for Francis and Nathaniel's brother Nicholas.[140]

---

133. *Id.*
134. BACON PAPERS V, *supra* note 18, at 257-58.
135. BACON PAPERS V, *supra* note 18, at 256-60.
136. BACON PAPERS V, *supra* note 18, at 256-57.
137. *Id.*
138. *Id.*
139. *Id.*
140. BACON PAPERS V, *supra* note 18, at 257.

He was hardly likely to be impartial.[141] So they asked Nathaniel to write to Francis, asking him either to recuse himself or, if not, to act judicially rather than as an advocate.[142]

On 21 October 1606, two of the petitioners wrote a note to Nathaniel, asking for an answer to their request and setting out the details of their petition.[143] For two years Gooch had wrongfully occupied town lands worth £50 a year in rent and cut and sold timber, with other wrongs, some of them "continued by reason of an injunction grounded upon a report made by a doctor being one of the Masters of the Chancery."[144]

So, on 25 October Nathaniel wrote to Francis:

Good brother, I understand that there is a reference made unto you out of the Court of Star Chamber, of a bill there exhibited by the township of Southwold in Suffolk against R Gooch, my brother [Nicholas] Bacon's servant and your client. And they of the town being not very rich, by reason of the great pestilence which hath been lately amongst them, and by other occasions of piracy and fire, are loth to hold on a chargeable contention, and therefore have entreated me to be a means unto you in their behalf, that some good course might be taken whereby there might be no continuance of the suits between them.

The consideration hereof causeth me hereby to be a suitor unto you, that you will take knowledge of the grievances of both sides and, as a judge, advise and move such a proceeding as a peace may be concluded between them. And in so doing, as well Gooch as the townsmen of Southwold shall have great cause to hold themselves beholden unto you, and will be ready to do you any kindness or service for your travail so bestowed, and I also take it kindly at your hands.

When I was at the last parliament I did hear some of them, and R Gooch also speak touching the differences between them, and I then thought Gooch in fault and did tell him that I would complain to his master for the unquiet carriage of himself.

So I commend you to the grace and favour of God.[145]

While hardly affectionate, it was quite straightforward.

141. *Id*.
142. *Id*.
143. BACON PAPERS V, *supra* note 18, at 259-60. Letter is to Nathaniel Bacon's clerk, Martin Man. For Man's designation as Bacon's clerk, see BACON PAPERS V, *supra* note 18, at 350.
144. BACON PAPERS V, *supra* note 18, at 260.
145. BACON PAPERS V, *supra* note 18, at 260-61.

III. PRIVATE COMMISSIONS FOR MEDIATION
AND ARBITRATION

Bacon's authority as a JP, and no doubt his reputation for integrity and impartiality, led not only to official commissions but also to many private requests to resolve disputes. Perhaps, too, his special skills as a mediator were recognised at all levels within his community, as well as by the several government authorities.

On 13 November 1601 Bacon mediated an end to a dispute over land and debts.[146] Elizabeth, widow of Robert Earle, agreed to pay £100 in two instalments to John Earle, Robert's son, presumably by a previous marriage, who agreed to release her from all claims and convey to her all his father's lands.[147] She also agreed to pay to Robert's married daughter, Margaret Slye, "besides her legacy 20s after three years."[148]

Richard Foster, rector of Burgh Parva, wrote to Bacon to ask him to resolve a dispute between his former servant, poor but honest, and a John Bacon – no relation – who was accusing him of trespass.[149]

In September 1604, Bacon took detailed and rambling evidence in successfully mediating the settlement of a dispute between John Girdlestone and Ellen Howes, a widow.[150] On 25 September the neat and straightforward agreement is recorded: The parties were to exchange bonds, John and his brother were to make payments to her, and she was to allow John to farm her copyhold land until her son was 14 – "and all reckoning clear."[151]

Two settlements were recorded on one day, 25 August 1606.[152] One was a simple exchange of a money payment for the release of a bond.[153] The other was of a dispute over Mundy's liberty to draw water from his neighbour King's well:

> King shall pay 10s unto Mundy towards the making of a well in his own ground. And Mundy to forbear to draw water at King's well hereafter. And the 10s is agreed to be left in Robert Walker's hand, and 5s thereof to be paid to Mundy so soon as he doth begin the well and the rest after it is finished. And each party releaseth the peace taken against one another and against the rest contained in the warrants made and granted by Sir Nathaniel Bacon and Mr Gwynne.[154]

146. BACON PAPERS IV, *supra* note 18, at 219-20
147. BACON PAPERS IV, *supra* note 18, at 219.
148. BACON PAPERS IV, *supra* note 18, at 220.
149. BACON PAPERS V, *supra* note 18, at 129-30.
150. BACON PAPERS V, *supra* note 18, at 126, 130.
151. *Id.*
152. BACON PAPERS V, *supra* note 18, at 254.
153. *Id.*
154. *Id.*

Bacon and Gwynne had referred to themselves and mediated a settlement of a matter, which had come before them as JPs, arising from mutual allegations of breaches of the peace.[155] Has there ever been a legal system, which could have produced a more refined resolution?

But sometimes it was arbitration that was expressly required. As Christmas approached and 1602 came to an end, Bacon was as busy as ever. As sole arbitrator on 9 December 1602 he declared his award in a private arbitration between neighbours, Roger Bulwer (and his sons Edward and George) and John Athill.[156] Athill must pay Roger 30s before 1 February 1603, for a boar he had killed.[157] Disputes between Roger and Athill over rents and tithes were to be decided by John Fountaine and if Mr. Fountaine could not reach a decision that both parties agreed to, the matter would be referred to Bacon.[158] "The demand of tithe hay from Mr George Bulwer by Mr Athill in the right of the vicar is referred to a trial at the Assizes in summer next," and Bacon added: "Memorandum: I have promised that no advantage shall be taken of bonds which have been formerly passed for abiding by this my order."[159]

In December 1594, the *Papers* had recorded a violent tithe dispute with a vicious mastiff and heavies imported from Kent with long pikestaffs which the parties had submitted to local mediation.[160] Bacon's role was limited to fixing and allocating costs and acting as umpire if called on.[161] The matter arose again eight years later. On 27 December 1602 Bacon had signed a memorandum of evidence in disputes between Armiger and Franklin, which spilled over into the new year.[162] The land dispute was deferred until the following Whitsuntide, "when a sight shall be had of the survey made in the meantime."[163] Certain trespasses were referred to the judgment of the arbitrators, Mr. Holland and Mr. Warde, "on Monday next . . . and if they do not order it then it shall be decided by Nathaniel Bacon esquire."[164] Franklin's demands for tithes and wool and sheep were also "referred to their examination and ordering."[165] "Costs of suit and

---

155. *Id.*
156. BACON PAPERS IV, *supra* note 18, at 301.
157. *Id.*
158. *Id.*
159. *Id.*
160. BACON PAPERS III, *supra* note 18, at 285-87. *See also* BACON PAPERS IV, *supra* note 18, at 302-303, nn.638-639.
161. BACON PAPERS III, *supra* note 18, at 285-87. *See also* BACON PAPERS IV, *supra* note 18, at 302-303, nn.638-639.
162. BACON PAPERS IV, *supra* note 18, at 302-303.
163. BACON PAPERS IV, *supra* note 18, at 302.
164. PAPERS IV, *supra* note 18, at 303.
165. BACON PAPERS IV, *supra* note 18, at 302-303.

for battery with costs of suit, referred to Nathaniel Bacon when the other matters be brought to order."[166] On the same day Bacon signed an order for the hearing the following Monday.[167] On time, an agreement between Armiger and Franklin was mediated and signed by Holland and Warde on 3 January 1603:[168]

First Mr Armiger is to pay unto Mr Franklin for the tithe hay 15s.

Item Mr Armiger is to pay him for the tithe rakings five combes barley.

Item Mr Armiger is to pay him for the tithe of tenscore couples of ewes and lambs sold to Mr Buggin 52s.

Item for grasses occupied by Mr Armiger of the parsonage glebe for every acre 16d.

The day of payment of the said sums of money and barley to be set down by Mr Bacon his worship.[169]

One undated letter must suffice to show in detail how a submission worked and how arbitration was valued then:

Good Sir Nathaniel Bacon, mortal men should not have immortal suits, and suits commenced by fathers and continued by their children in an unchristian and uncharitable succession do often times ravel up and undermine the fathers' estates before they die, and in the end do utterly undo their heirs by descent, when they be dead, a cross and a curse, that contention by God's wrathful ordinance brings with it, which you in your wisdom and experience hath seen to fall upon divers families. Not far off – *sic obdurit cor Pharaonis* ['so he hardened Pharaoh's heart' *Exodus* 7.13 and 14] through the which, by excessive fees disbursed upon exceeding lawyers, both Mr Bulwer's family and mine, shall hereafter fare the worse, for prevention whereof at the first, before any suit was set on foot between him and me, I for my part made an overture of peace unto him, above 10 years since, to submit all intended controversies to any men of worth and wisdom in all Norfolk to decide and censure the same.

---

166. BACON PAPERS IV, *supra* note 18, at 303.
167. *Id.*
168. BACON PAPERS V, *supra* note 18, at 1.
169. *Id.*

But Mr Bulwer then, before the walking spirit of the lands in question was any wise conjured, utterly refused that my peace offering, saying that he would not put his coat to dyeing, to never a man in England. But now of late (and somewhat too late for us both) he hath changed his mind and out of his own voluntary, (the pleasingest motive that may be), it hath pleased him to come walking unto me in the pathway of peace, protesting to embrace that peace now which long since was offered unto him, before any money was spent, or rather spoiled, at law. Requesting at my hands a submission and a compromise of all matters in difference betwixt us, to some men of worship in the country (lawyers excepted, the minters of other men's coin, out of their true owners' purses into their own). Gladly I condescended to this his motion, as proceeding from God, and did put upon him first to choose one for himself and I would second it, suit and sort another of like quality and condition. He, for him, chose Sir Nathaniel Bacon, a knight in his opinion without exception. And I, purposing to choose one that was *omni exceptione major* [above all objection] and in all respects suitable and sortable that never would dissent in judgment, nor jar in the proceeding, chose for me your worship to be the judge, the justicer and *honorarius arbiter* of all our controversies. At which my seconding choice Mr Bulwer was so well pleased that presently off went our hats, on went our hands and hearts to a pacification, which was the first time that ever we two shook either hands or hearts together, making you by mutual and reciprocal consent our judge, if you please to assume that office upon you, *beati pacifici, exuenda est persona amici, et induenda judicis* [the blessed peacemaker must doff the character of friend and don that of judge] to end as in a moment ten years tedious and costly suits, thereby to give better satisfaction to Mr Bulwer, concerning his supposed right and title to the lands in question by delivering your opinion therein, than either the Lord Chancellor or the high court of the Chancery by decree, injunction and commission could do, or than I can do by paying 200 marks out of the said lands to his sister for her marriage portion, and by spending in suit or otherwise 400 marks more *in toto* paid and spent out of my poor purse, twice as much money as the recovered lands be worth. Thus stand I, *de damno vitando* [for avoidance of loss], a loser at the close, although I got somewhat at the crush. Thus contendeth he, *de irreparabili damno* [in relation to loss which cannot be recovered], for lawyers have irrevocably got his money. *Omnia vestigia antrorsum, nulla retrorsum, opera et impensa periit* [if every track leads forward, none back, then the toils and the costs have vanished]. Fearing tediousness I submit myself to your censure, and you and yours I do recommend to the protection of the Almighty, together with my duty remembered to the good Lady Bacon.[170]

Both parties signed, though it was penned by Dr John Hunt, himself a civil lawyer and Master in Chancery (c1596-1615), a JP in Suffolk and an expert devotee of arbitration.[171] If no other record had survived, that fortuitous product of Nathaniel Bacon's determination to hoard every scrap of evidence of his daily work would stand as colourful proof of how mediation was regarded then. It repays the most careful reading.

Nathaniel Bacon was a busy man. He had to arrange for troops to be mustered, taxes collected, and for the support of unmarried mothers and their children.[172] In a footnote to the Papers of Nathaniel Bacon, the editors reveal that Bacon must have acted as mediator in many more disputes than the *Papers* document: "Entries in Bacon's recognizance books suggest that this procedure was widely used but rarely figures in the formal records." [173] He may well have dealt on average with two or three matters every month, which might require him to ride for a day, stay at least two nights away from home, spend a day to inspect many acres of land and perhaps another to hear dozens of witnesses' inexpert testimony.

Many awards make orders, which apply to non-parties. A good example is that of 28 June 1603, in a tithe dispute between Richard Boulter on the one hand and Gyles Mychell and Thomas Grene on the other, referred to arbitrators from the Consistory Court.[174] The calendar reads: "Concerning covenants in a pair of indentures for land lately bargained and sold to Boulter by Mychell, Boulter may reasonably require Mychell's son Mardocheus, at his comng of age, to release to him all title and interest."[175] No quibbles about whether the son was a party could be allowed, even if they were noticed.

There was no bar against women being parties to arbitration, whether they were single or married. The *Papers* are weighty testimony of the routine involvement of women in all kinds of dispute, including the ownership of land. For example, Margaret Bosom had no need to involve her husband Adam in a complex claim on a bond involving her son by a previous marriage.[176] She gave evidence and signed her deposition herself.[177] Anne Penning's determination exasperated Higham and Jermyn, who rudely

170. BACON PAPERS V, *supra* note 18, at 113-114.
171. BACON PAPERS V, *supra* note 18, at 114.
172. *Nathaniel Bacon*, *supra* note 9.
173. BACON PAPERS V, *supra* note 18, at 52, n.137.
174. BACON PAPERS V, *supra* note 18, at 39.
175. *Id.*
176. BACON PAPERS V, *supra* note 18, at 121-23.
177. BACON PAPERS V, *supra* note 18, at 121.

referred to her as "the woman."[178] The evidence from America is the same. I still search, though, for women who resolved disputes in this period.

IV. EXPORTATION TO THE AMERICAN COLONIES

Just a cursory reading of some of the secondary sources has been enough to show not only that a systematic study is wanted, but that there must be primary sources surviving in the United States which have not yet been discovered or fully exploited. The tasks for new generations of scholars will be pleasurable and satisfying. They will know that their work is worthwhile if only to ensure that future practising mediators and arbitrators will not grow up believing, as many of their forebears have done, that: "Arbitration did not become an integral part of the early social and economic development of the country nor a recognised institution of any consequence."[179] Though they may accept as a challenge: "Arbitration literature of this period is exceedingly sparse and enquirers are therefore handicapped in examining the somewhat vague course taken by arbitration and the causes of its inaction."[180]

There is only one way of combatting such apparently complacent ignorance! The American story must be left to American authors. But Connecticut Colonial Records declare that in 1645 that state's General Assembly suggested that trials could be prevented if arbitrations were held privately.[181] There are examples such as George and Christopher Sanders, two brothers who were partners in a commercial venture to Jamaica and England.[182] "When they could not settle their accounts themselves, they submitted their dispute in 1677 to the arbitration of four men."[183] Oldham and Kim's section on "The Maryland Experience" gives the full text of an award of 1668 and comes to the conclusion: "The Maryland archival records demonstrate an early American endorsement and continuation of English arbitration practices."[184]

So there is evidence (and there are tantalising clues to more) of arbitration's early start in North America. No doubt there is more work to be done on Dutch influence in New York and perhaps Swedish in Delaware, following the example of John Locke, the architect of the Arbitration Act 1698, whose role Horwitz and Oldham have described so well. Two letters

178. BACON PAPERS V, *supra* note 18, at 255.
179. FRANCES KELLOR, AMERICAN ARBITRATION: ITS HISTORY, FUNCTIONS AND ACHIEVEMENTS 6 (1948).
180. Frank D. Emerson, *History of Arbitration Practice and Law* 19 CLEV. ST. L. REV. 155, 158 (1970).
181. Mann, *supra* note 4, at 452.
182. Mann, *supra* note 4, at 453, n.41, 454 n.43.
183. Mann, *supra* note 4, at 453.
184. Oldham & Kim, *supra* note 2, at 262-65, 262 n.109 for references.

from Benjamin Furly, the English merchant of Rotterdam who promoted the first German emigration to America,[185] show his comparative scholarship and merit further attention.

Some evidence from England can contribute. There are a few references in this period to the Americas in the *Acts of the Privy Council (APC)*.[186] The Privy Council might appoint a committee of its own members to resolve a dispute; although that might not be comprehended in anyone's definition of arbitration, it shows an attitude. The best evidence comes from *APC* entries relating to Virginia.[187] In 1627 Sir George Yeardley, the Governor of Virginia, died leaving by his will to his widow and sole executrix, Dame Temperance, always known through three marriages as Temperance Flowerdew, her maiden name, all the household goods in his house in St. James City, later Jamestown, and all his other estates in Virginia to be sold.[188] The proceeds were to be divided, one-third to Temperance, two-thirds to his three children. She then married Francis West, the next Governor, who left to her Yeardley's estate. Temperance could be trusted. She had left England in 1609 with her new first husband Richard Barrow in the *Falcon*, part of that ill-fated community of whom all but a few perished. She was one of those who survived the terrible "Starving Time." Barrow apparently did not.

Yeardley had been in the same convoy but his ship, the *Sea Venture*, was wrecked on Bermuda. No lives were lost and two ships were built from the wreckage. They made it to Virginia in May 1610. Soon thereafter three ships arrived there from England. Temperance married Yeardley. They had three children, Elizabeth, Argoll and Francis. He became Deputy Governor in 1616. In 1618 he and Temperance were in London. He was knighted and appointed Governor and granted 300 acres of land. They returned to Virginia and created the Flowerdew plantation of 1,000 acres, producing tons of tobacco annually. He died in 1627. Forthwith Temperance married his successor as governor, Francis West, but she died the next year.

185. JULIUS FRIEDRICH SACHSE, BENJAMIN FURLY, AN ENGLISH MERCHANT AT ROTTERDAM, WHO PROMOTED THE FIRST GERMAN EMIGRATION TO AMERICA, PRINTED FROM THE PENNSYLVANIA MAGAZINE OF HISTORY AND BIOGRAPHY (1895), *available at* https://archive.org/details/benjaminfurlyane00insach.
186. ACTS OF PRIVY COUNCIL OF ENGLAND. For the Acts of Privy Council of England, see http://www.british-history.ac.uk/search/series/acts-privy-council [hereinafter ACTS OF PRIVY COUNCIL].
187. On Lady Wyatt's petition against the Virginia Company: "take such effectual course for the petitioner's relief as in justice and equity you shall find cause," see 39 ACTS OF PRIVY COUNCIL 360 (J.V. Lyle ed., 1933). For the petition of Elizabeth Barwick, see 45 ACTS OF PRIVY COUNCIL 104-105 (R.F. Monger & P.A. Penfold eds., 1960).
188. For the following account of Sir George Yeardley, Francis West, and Temperance Flowerdew Yeardley West, see 46 ACTS OF PRIVY COUNCIL 38-39 (P.A. Penfold ed., 1964).

Temperance had sent the tobacco to Yeardley's brother Raph, apothecary of London. When he knew Temperance was dead, under the pretence of affection for the children, he took possession not only of his brother's but also of Temperance's estates. He refused to account to West or come to any agreement with him. The Council, "considering the difference between them rests chiefly upon matter of account," referred it to four merchants, "persons experienced in business of this nature . . . to mediate and settle such an end (if they can) as shall be indifferent and equitable, or certify in writing in whom the default is."[189] That is good early evidence of a mediation relating to the North American colonies.

Ensign Edmond Rossingham was Temperance's nephew. He had asked the Council for "relief and satisfaction out of the estate of Sir George Yeardley in the possession of Raph Yeardley as his administrator."[190] He claimed he had left cattle and goods in Sir George's hands and had performed services for him there.[191] The Privy Council had referred the matter to "certain persons of judgment and experience in the affairs of that Plantation," who had certified that those services had been beneficial, and the cattle worth £360, and that Raph had confessed that the estate in his hands was worth £1,200.[192] Therefore on 19 February 1630, "rather for that by dissolving the Company (the government thereof being assumed by his Majesty into his own hands) the Petitioner was left without remedy in the ordinary course," the Privy Council ordered Raph to pay Rossingham £200.[193] The order would be a sufficient discharge against any other claimants against the estate, "for that it did not appear there were any debts at all."[194]

Another Governor of Virginia was John Potts.[195] He and his wife Elizabeth sailed from London aboard the *George* in March 1619 and arrived in Jamestown in May. In 1623, he prepared the poison which killed 200 native Americans attending a "peace ceremony" at Jamestown. He became a member of the Governor's Council in 1625 and Governor in 1629. On 9 July 1630 he was convicted of cattle theft and dismissed. He may have lived until 1645. On 30 September 1630 the Privy Council wrote to the Governor and Council of Virginia:

189. *Id. See also, A Tale of Two Houses in Virginia and Kirkcudbright*, 74 TRANSAC-TIONS OF THE DUMFRIESSHIRE & GALLOWAY, NAT. HIST. & ANTIQUARIAN SOC'Y 120-22 (3rd series, 2000) *available at* http://www.dgnhas.org.uk/transonline.php.
190. 45 ACTS OF PRIVY COUNCIL, *supra* note 187, at 285-86. For the following account of Edmund Rossingham, see *id*.
191. 45 ACTS OF PRIVY COUNCIL, *supra* note 187, at 285-86.
192. *Id.*
193. *Id.*
194. *Id.*
195. For the following discussion of John and Elizabeth Potts, see 46 ACTS OF PRIVY COUNCIL, *supra* note 188, at 85-86.

Complaint hath been made both to his Majesty and this Board against you in a petition presented by the brother of Dr Pott But we are not apt to give credit to any complants of this kind against a man that is entrusted by his Majesty in a place of government as you are. Therefore we have sent you the Petitions take it into consideration and thereupon proceed according to justice and the orders established in that Government with convenient expedition so that there may be no further just cause for complaint.[196]

Eleven members of the Privy Council signed that letter. The *APC* show no further activity in relation to Dr Potts but later the same day it wrote again to the Governor and Council of Virginia.[197] It had received a complaint from Thomas Grendon that he had spent £1,400 in various parts of Virginia, and learned from him that planters only planted tobacco and this did not help the plantation and planters did not have permission to do so. Grendon had supplied "divers ingenious artificers for the making of artificial mills, useful for sundry commodities, and saws for sawing timber," and "people skilful in making rape oils and soap ashes," all "for the good of the Common Weal."[198] The Council "earnestly recommend his good endeavours" and ask the Governor and Council to help Grendon in getting in his debts.[199]

The last record of Privy Council's interest in the colony is a letter of 30 June 1630.[200] John Woodhall was a speculator in the colony who never left England.[201] He had bought land from the estate of Sir Samuel Argoll, famous among other things for kidnapping Pocahontas and bringing her to England. Lawsuits ensued. Woodhall complained that "the chief detainors of his land and cattle are both parties and judges" in his cause.[202] The Privy Council's response was to tell the Virginian Council:

As we cannot but marvel at such your neglect of the commands and recommendations from this Board and have just cause not only to blame you for the same but for your partial and dilatory proceedings (if they be such as informed) in the administration of justice we expressly require you to afford the Petitioner expedite justice.[203]

---

196. *Id.* at 85.
197. For the following account of Thomas Grendon, see *id.* at 88.
198. *Id.*
199. *Id.*
200. *Id.*
201. For the following discussion of John Woodhall, see 46 ACTS OF PRIVY COUNCIL, *supra* note 188, at 88.
202. *Id.*
203. *Id.*

Another example of early American arbitration occurs with Francis Poythress, who went to Virginia c1633 as agent for the London merchant Lawrence Evans.[204] Evans later charged Poythress with breach of trust.[205] In March 1639 the Governor and Council appointed four merchants in Virginia to arbitrate; they decided in Poythress's favour.[206] The Privy Council's committee for the foreign plantations "directed a further enquiry when Evens was to go to Virginia himself."[207]

There is a Canadian reference to arbitration, as well. In 1628 Charles I himself referred to the Privy Council a complaint by two Frenchmen that another Frenchman had "taken them at sea in a voyage they were making for a Plantation in Canada."[208] The Council formed a committee of three of its members (or any two) to report "that thereupon such final order may be taken . . . consonant to justice and equity."[209]

Another example of 17th century arbitration comes from Barbados. The National Archives preserve the record of an award made on 18 June 1652 in a private arbitration between Sir Anthony Ashley Cooper, and Gerard Hawkaine, (probably Hawkins), about a plantation in Barbados.[210] Cooper became the first Earl of Shaftesbury, a member of Cromwell's Council of State and one of the founders of the Whig party.[211] He was John Locke's patron and collaborated with him on the Fundamental Constitutions of Carolina.[212]

V. CONCLUSION

I shall be happy if this Article, with all its inadequacies and perhaps false starts, does no more than attract the attention of scholars, perhaps especially younger Americans, to fill the blanks and correct the errors in what all must agree is at this stage a patchy and inadequate history of dispute resolution in the early American colonies.

204. TRANSACTIONS OF THE DUMFRIESSHIRE & GALLOWAY, *supra* note 189, at 120-22.

205. *Id.*

206. *Id.*

207. William B. Hall, *The Polythress Family: A Study of Francis, Francis, Francis, and Francis*, 14 WM. & MARY Q., 77, 77 (1934).

208. 44 ACTS OF PRIVY COUNCIL 359 (R.F. Monger ed., 1958).

209. *Id.*

210. *PRO 30/24/49/1 Award of the arbitrators between Sir Anthony Ashley Cooper and Gerard Hawkaine*, NAT'L ARCHIVES (June 18, 1652), http://discovery.nationalarchives. gov.uk/details/r/C6757225.

211. See *Anthony Ashley Cooper, 1st Earl of Shaftesbury and successors: Papers*, NAT'L ARCHIVES, http://discovery.nationalarchives.gov.uk/details/r/C11970 (last visited Dec. 10, 2016).

212. *Id.*

14. INTRODUCTION TO *THE COMPLEAT ARBITRATOR OR THE LAW OF AWARDS AND ARBITRAMENTS 'BY A GENTLEMAN OF THE MIDDLE TEMPLE'* [MATTHEW BACON] (1731)

1. THE BACKGROUND

In 1731 George II, the unpopular German, had been king of England for four years. In the first years of his reign, smallpox, influenza and other diseases with vaguer names had reduced the population of the United Kingdom to a little over 5 million, what Scotland's or Wisconsin's is today.

> The sense of sickness which pervaded the period was more than physiological. The greed, fraudulence, and hysteria which had characterized the South Sea Bubble were denounced both in the press and from the pulpit as the ruling vices of the years which followed.[1]

Tory government had given way to the Whigs. Sir Robert Walpole was the astute but financially dodgy first Prime Minister, though not yet called by that name, and had just taken up residence in Downing Street. He it was who created the present system of government, by which Prime Ministers control Parliament so long as their party has a majority of members.

Judicial offices fell vacant on the death of the king.[2] The incumbents could have been reappointed but the opportunity was taken to dismiss the Tory judges and ensure that supporters of Walpole's Whig Government were preferred. Lord Parker, the Lord Chief Justice, was appointed Lord Chancellor. He became the Earl of Macclesfield and held the office of Chancellor until 1725, when he was dismissed on 21 articles

---

1. Kenneth O Morgan ed *The Oxford History of Britain* Oxford, Oxford UP 1984 p415.
2. John, Lord Campbell *Lives of the Lord Chancellors and Keepers of the Great Seal of England from the Earliest Times till the Reign of King George IV* London, John Murray 4th edn 1857 vol. 5 pp294-6 quotes in full Lord Cowper's letter to the king, setting out his recommendations; a rich source of gossipy insights.

of impeachment charging him with corruption in the aftermath of the South Sea Bubble. He had sold appointments, even at the judicial level of Master in Chancery.

Macclesfield's trial in the House of Lords had been presided over by Sir Peter King as Speaker. King was then Lord Chief Justice of the Common Pleas and not a peer. He had little experience of Chancery practice but in June 1725 he was made Lord Chancellor and was in office in 1731 when *Compleat Arbitrator* was published. Lord Raymond was Chief Justice of the King's Bench, Sir Robert Eyre of Common Pleas, James Reynolds Chief Baron of the Exchequer and Sir Joseph Jekyll Master of the Rolls.

In 1731 Handel's *Acis and Galatea* was first produced, in Lincoln's Inn. Its libretto was by John Gay, whose *Beggars' Opera*, the scandalous success of three years before, had satirised the corruption of George II's court. In that year too, the Abbé Prévost published *Manon Lescaut* and Voltaire his *History of Charles II*. In America, Benjamin Franklin opened the first free public library, in Philadelphia. John and Charles Wesley had just begun to spread the influence of their group, which others called Methodists. Their efforts were to be rebuffed, when they set off as missionaries to America, by those whose Christian charity did not extend to slaves.

Many merchants in London preferred to have their disputes determined by men of their own sort whom they chose themselves. They hoped, then as now, for a speedy, cheap and sensible process. Arbitration, which then comprised mediation, was readily available and supported by the legal system, up to a point.

2. THE AUTHOR

When he wrote this book, his first work to be published, Matthew Bacon (or Mathew – spelling was inconsistent then) was an Irish law student, about thirty years old, making his way in London. Neither the date of his birth nor death is known but his will, in favour of a brother, was proved in March 1757.[3] He was admitted to the Middle Temple in 1731 but not called to the Bar until 24 November 1732, the year after this book was published, anonymously, as by 'a Gentleman of the Middle Temple'.[4] Presumably he and his publisher thought it better not to disclose that the book was written by a student, though that cannot be the reason he continued to write anonymously. Five years later he produced the first

3. The best account of his life is by Neil Jones in the *Oxford Dictionary of Biography* which supersedes P R Glazebrook 'Bacon, Matthew' in AWB Simpson ed *Biographical Dictionary of the Common Law* 1984.
4. WS Holdsworth *A History of English Law* London, Methuen vol. 12 1938 (Holdsworth) p393.

two volumes of *A New Abridgment of the Law*, a third in 1740.[5] Those too were anonymous, though there never seems to have been any doubt who wrote them and by then he must have been established as a legal author. The fourth (1759) and fifth (1766) were published after his death. Most of the material for the *Abridgment* was probably taken from the published or unpublished work of others. By 1832 it was in its seventh edition in eight volumes. It was published in Dublin from 1770 and American editions followed, by Bird Wilson,[6] and John Bouvier.[7]

Bacon also almost certainly wrote *Equity Cases Abridged* 1733.[8] JD Cowley[9] cites the marginal notes of Sir William Lee in his copy: 'NB This abridgment is wrote by Mr Bacon, a gentleman of Ireland, and, as I have been informed, a student at the time of its publication'. Its fifth and final edition was published in 1793.

There is another title, anonymous but attributed to him because it seems to have been drawn from relevant titles in the *Abridgment*. Bacon could have had nothing to do with its publication in separate form, as *Leases and Terms for Years, with an Appendix of Precedents*,[10] because the only edition was published in 1798, at least 40 years after his death.

3. THE BOOK

The Compleat Arbitrator is an early and admirable exemplar in a line of monographs devoted to arbitration. Before it there were the titles in the abridgments, usually Arbitration, Arbitrement (or Arbitrament) and Award, some detailed and substantial like those in William Sheppard's *Grand Abridgment* of 1675.[11] There was occasional treatment of the topics in more general works on commercial law, such as Gerard Malynes' *Consuetudo vel Lex Mercatoria*.[12] Six times Bacon cites the second volume of William West's *Symboleography*[13] (1594), an

5. WH Maxwell and LF Maxwell eds *A Legal Bibliography of the British Commonwealth of Nations Volume 1: English Law to 1800* 2nd edn (1955) (Maxwell and Maxwell) 16, 286.
6. The 1st American from the 6th London edn with the addition of the later English and the American decisions by Bird Wilson, Philadelphia, Farrand and Nicholas 1811.
7. Philadelphia, Thomas Davis 1846.
8. Holdsworth vol. 12 pp171-2 provides the evidence. Maxwell and Maxwell 286.
9. *A Bibliography of Abridgments, Digests, Dictionaries and Indexes of English Law to the Year 1800* London, Quaritch for the Selden Society 1932 (Cowley) lxviii, 56, 59–68.
10. Maxwell and Maxwell 479.
11. *A Grand Abridgment of the Common and Statute Law of England* London, John Vaughan 1675.
12. Gerard Malynes *Consuetudo, vel, Lex Mercatoria, or the Antient Law-Merchant* London, Adam Islip 1622, 1629, 1636, 1656, 1685 and 1686 (Malynes).
13. William West, *The First Part of Symboleographie: Which may be Termed the Art, or Description, of Instruments and Presidents* Miles Flesher, last edition 1647, unpaged; *The Second Part of Symboleography, Newly Corrected and Amended, and Very Much Enlarged*

early encyclopedia of forms and precedents. He makes much use – 90 references – of _Rolle's Abridgment_ (1668). Sir Henry Rolle was Chief Justice of the King's Bench 1648-55 and Bacon spells out his respect for his _Abridgment_ as an authority: 'But my Lord Roll, in his Abridgment of this Case, is not satisfied with the Reason here given, although he says the Court relied on it.'[14]

Perhaps surprisingly, Bacon does not refer to the two earlier monographs: John March _Actions for Slaunder ... to which is added Awards or Arbitrements_ 1647,[15] or the anonymous _Arbitrium Redivivum_ 1694.[16]

Bacon, who was perhaps living on his legal writing at that time and who never made a name at the Bar, must have seen a market for a handy text, with all the relevant cases, something more and better than the available dictionaries and abridgments and more up-to-date than the monographs which had been superseded by the 1698 legislation, by then more than a generation old and well established in routine commercial practice.

He declares his good intentions:

By laying down the whole learning of awards and arbitraments, which has hitherto lain dark and obscure, and as intricate and perplexed as any general head of our law, to assist mankind in making them better friends and neighbours, and in securing to them their fortunes and possessions, and to prevent that even this method of determining controversies may not be (as it often happens) the foundation of new broils and contentions.

---

in All the Foure Severall Treatises ... of Compromises and Arbitrements ... Miles Flesher and Robert Young, last edition 1641, 360pp, reprinted Lawbook Exchange 2008 (West).

14. p132.

15. The title page declares it to be 'By Jo. March of Grayes-Inne, Barister, London, Printed by FL for M Walbank and R Best'. The part on arbitration starts on p149 and ends on p241. References to _March_ on pp66, 152 and 153 of _Compleat Arbitrator_ are not to _Actions for Slaunder_ but to _March's New Cases_ (KB) 1639-42. The title page of the third and last edition reads: 'March's Actions for Slander and Arbitrements The First, ... where an Action _De Scandalia Magnatum_ will lie: and of the Nature of a Libel. The Other, a Discourse, shewing what _Arbitrements_ are good in Law .... First Written by Jo. March of Grayes-Inn, Barrister, in the Year, 1648 And now Reviewed and Enlarged with many useful Additions: By W.B. London, Printed for Elizabeth Walbanck, at Grayes-Inn Gate in Grayes-Inn Lane 1674.'

16. _Arbitrium Redivivum:_ or the Law of Arbitration; collected from the Law-Books both Ancient and Modern, and deduced to these Times: Wherein the whole Learning of Awards or Arbitrements is methodically treated with Several Forms of Submissions by way of Covenants and Bond; As also several Forms of Arbitrements or Awards. By the Author of _Regula Placitandi_. London, Printed by the Assigns of Rich. and Edw. Atkins Esquires, for Isaac Cleeve at the Star in Chancery-Lane near Serjeants-Inn, 1694. Unfortunately, the identity of the author of _Regula Placitandi_ also seems to be unknown.

And he hopes that his 'plain and easy method' will be enough not only for lawyers but also for the many arbitrators who are not. Holdsworth considered *Compleat Arbitrator* to be 'a good straightforward and up-to-date account of the law'. It was not cribbed from the work of others, as far as one can tell from internal evidence, and there is none external.

There were three editions, the last posthumous:[17]

[**Bacon** (Matthew)] Compleat Arbitrator; or, Law of Awards and Arbitraments. By a Gentleman of the Middle Temple. vi + (6) + 308pp., 12mo, 1731; 1744; 3rd ed., vi + (6) + 281 + (42) pp., 8vo. 1770

My copy of the first edition is leather bound, octavo, 7¾ x 5¼ inches (20 x 13cm), used, spines beginning to split, but in good condition. It is nicely printed. I found only three typographical errors.[18] The title page, as can be seen from the facsimile, shows the publisher to have been 'John Worrall, at the *Dove* in *Bell-Yard*, near *Lincoln's Inn*' and the printers the brothers E and R Nutt, with R Gosling.

The second edition is almost identical with the first. The third and final edition, published about thirteen years after Bacon's death, provides the precedents in English and adds new cases.

Though he follows the arrangement adopted by some of his predecessors, Bacon's treatment is fuller and better organised. He divides the work into 'five things', the categories which Sheppard and others had used before him, originally from Dyer:[19]

Matters of Submission
The Submission
Parties to the Submission
The Arbitrators
The Making and Delivering the Award

Though he cites many of the same cases as Sheppard and other predecessors, with similar emphasis, for example *Samon's Case* 5 Co Rep 77b on awards, his treatment is clearer and often more analytical though, as we shall see, not always accurate. As many textbook writers have done since, he gives his readers what he believes they want and expect, the law as it appeared to prevail in the opinions of those then practising in the Inns of Court. Bacon did not analyse cases in the modern way, to seek

17. Maxwell and Maxwell 544.
18. On p119, 4 lines up and p142 line 4; and in the Contents, for Chapter VI Section X the page reference should be to p186, not 180.
19. According to March, who cites Trin 4 Eliz. Dyer folio 117 pl 60.

their *ratio decidendi*. It would be as anachronistic as it would be unfair to expect him to have done.

4. GENERAL PRINCIPLES

Definition

Bacon makes a shaky start, with a definition not only manifestly wrong but proved so by many of his own examples:

> 1. *Arbitrament* (*Arbitrium, Laudum, Compromissum*), or an *Award*, is the Determination of Two or more Persons, at the Request of two Parties at least.

Of course, there has never been any problem with having a single arbitrator and many of Bacon's own examples[20] and indeed precedents[21] have a submission to only one, including Sir Matthew Hale CB whose aborted arbitration Bacon describes,[22] though most are to two and occasionally three[23] or four[24]. Where did he draw this error from and why?

There is nothing in the earlier texts to support or explain Bacon's error. Though *Arbitrium Redivivum* regularly refers to arbitration by two arbitrators, one appointed by each side, its whole introduction impliedly allows arbitration by a single arbitrator and its definition expressly refers to it:[25]

> Arbitrement ... is an Award ... by the Arbitrators or Umpire, being such person or persons ....

March in *Actions for Slaunder* gives no definition but cites Year Book cases with a single arbitrator, without comment on the number,[26] and his commentary often refers to arbitrations by a single arbitrator.[27]
Sheppard's 1675 definition is unambiguous:

> Arbitrement is an Award ... made by one or more ....

20. eg pp106-7.
21. eg pp191-2 and 200-1.
22. p222.
23. pp58-9, 106ff, 206-9.
24. p193-6.
25. p1.
26. e.g. on p177, 9 E 4.43 b 44c36 and H 6 8 c11.
27. e.g. on p184.

Bacon's own *Abridgment* from its first publication in 1736 follows closely the text of *Compleat Arbitrator* in its section on arbitrements. It speaks of 'submissions to persons indifferently chosen',[28] 'the authority ... given to the arbitrators',[29] and the plural is most often used, for example 'there must be Arbitrators' and 'the Arbitrators must make an award'.[30] I like to think Bacon would have used the plural today but that would have been for a different reason: to avoid gender-specific language. In substance, though, he shows that the award of a single arbitrator was recognised without comment.[31]

The cause of his mistake may well have been a difference between law and practice. Gerard Malynes, writing as early as 1622, described the practice he knew, at home and abroad, as a merchant who was not a lawyer:[32] 'Some are contented to name foure or six persons on either side .... Consideration must be had also, whether two, three, or all foure shall have authority.' But even Malynes envisages a single arbitrator: 'for example an arbitrator, or many Arbitrators do award.'

What is true is that, in Matthew Bacon's day, the method most common among merchants was for each party to choose its own arbitrator, who would first put its case to the other side's arbitrator, much as if he were an advocate arguing for the best settlement he could get. The objective of both arbitrators, however, was to reach a compromise. If they themselves could agree, they would then together try to get the parties to accept that agreement. If one or both parties rejected the best efforts of the arbitrators, they would then adjudicate. If they agreed on an award, it was final. Only if the arbitrators could not agree, would an umpire be called in to make a final adjudication.

We must take care not to assume that parties and their arbitrators had the same concerns as we have now. They saw no conflict of interest when the same person first acted as a kind of advocate and then, if they could not bring about a settlement, as arbitrator. Any impasse would be resolved by the umpire, who was regularly appointed and waiting in the wings to be called on. In the same way they did not concern themselves with the problems which might arise when the party-appointed arbitrators, having first tried to mediate and failed, then went on to adjudicate. These are problems which arose much later, when lawyers disassociated theory (and law) from practice.

The treatment of arbitration in Bacon's *Abridgment* follows *Compleat Arbitrator* closely. It regularly assumes a submission to plural arbitrators:

28. Vol. 1 p131.
29. Vol. 1 p133.
30. Vol. 1 p151.
31. e.g. vol. 1 p152.
32. Malynes 1636 pp297, 298.

'to persons indifferently chosen',[33] and 'authority ... given to the arbitrators'[34] but the award of a single arbitrator is recognised without comment.[35]

When Bacon was writing, English law had started to interfere in the customary processes of appointment, apparently attempting to outlaw chance, as I describe in the Conclusion below, but it had certainly not restricted the freedom of the parties to choose any number of arbitrators they wished.

Bacon's definition does not work for another reason: it concentrates on the adjudication of the dispute. Any useful definition of arbitration must comprehend the whole process. In his day as now, it cannot have been too different from that in the new *Jowitt*:[36]

> *Arbitration*, the processes (other than litigation) by which parties to a dispute submit it to a third party to resolve and by which that resolution is reached and enforced.

He compounds the error:

> It is called an arbitrament, because that the parties have willingly submitted their differences to others, to determine them arbitrally, and according to their own opinions and judgments, as honest and disinterested men, and not according to law.

Yet throughout the rest of his book he makes it quite clear that arbitrators are bound to follow the law and may not act capriciously. If they do, they risk the intervention of the courts of equity, though the judges are beginning to see the merits of a policy of restrained non-interference. The confusion arises in part from the introduction of notions of *arbitrium liberum*, free will, the other sense in which *arbitrium* is widely found in the writings of religious belligerents, who had been battling about it for centuries.

He goes on to say that an arbitration is called an award, from the French word *agarder*, 'which signifies to judge or decide', which indeed it does in Law French, as many Year Book reports attest,[37] but it is not correct to say: 'It has heretofore been called Love-Day, because of the Quiet and

33. p131.
34. pp133, 137.
35. e.g. p152.
36. Any definition stands or falls according to whether it serves the purpose it is intended for. I have adopted different ones for studies of Ancient Greek, Roman and early English arbitration. The definition in the forthcoming new edition of *Jowitt* is just my latest attempt.
37. William Rothwell *Anglo-Norman Dictionary* 2nd edn London, Maney, 2005.

Tranquillity which usually followed the Ending of the Controversy.'[38] A love-day is not an arbitration but rather an opportunity for parties to a dispute to remove it from the normal course of litigation, so that they may settle it themselves or put it into the hands of arbitrators.[39]

5. THE LAW AND THE PRACTICE

The Use of Cases

But though the Law seems to be thus settled as to this Matter, yet as it is designed in this Treatise, to mention all the Cases reported concerning Awards and Arbitraments, I shall insert the Cases themselves which warrant the above Observations, that the Reader may be the better able to judge of them.[40]

And as our Courts have lately been more liberal in their Constructions of Awards, in expounding them according to the Intent of the Arbitrators, than formerly, I have, as near as possible, set down the Cases according to the Series of Time in which they were resolved.[41]

In all, Bacon cites well over 500 cases from the Year Books and the Nominate Reports. He cites *Rolle's Abridgment* 90 times but no other. There is no more duplication than is needed to ensure comprehension and comprehensiveness. He takes care, when he thinks he should, to point out that a case was decided before the Arbitration Act 1689, for example when he deals with the right of a party to revoke a submission.[42]

Bacon points out that the Court of Chancery, though it commonly follows the law and practice of the other courts of Westminster, differs from them in two important ways. It treats awards as agreements made by the parties and enforces them by decrees of specific performance, a remedy not available to the Common Law courts. More generally, it is readier to set aside awards which it finds 'unreasonable or injurious, by the Ignorance, Partiality, Dishonesty etc of the Arbitrators'. Therefore he is determined to 'set down all the Cases we have reported on this

---

38. pp1-2.
39. JW Spargo 'Chaucer's Love-days' (1940) 15 *Speculum* 36-56; JW Bennett 'The Medieval Loveday' (1958) 33 *Speculum* 351-370; MT Clanchy 'Law, Government and Society in Medieval England' (1974) 59 *History* 73-8; MT Clanchy 'Law and Love in the Middle Ages' in John Bossy ed *Disputes and Settlement* Cambridge UP 1983. WA Morris, *The Early English County Court* Berkeley, U of California P 1926 pp127, 154, 189-230 provides evidence of the Yorkshire County Court allowing a loveday, for a price, in 1259, and selling many licences to settle.
40. p131 para 22.
41. p93.
42. p217.

Head, in our books of Chancery'.[43] Of particular note is *Corneforth v Geer*,[44] where Lord Chancellor Cowper declared that, if it appears from the award that the arbitrators made 'a plain mistake, either as to the law, or in a matter of fact' a court of equity may set it aside. But 'the plaintiff failing to make out his case by proof, bill dismissed'.

Arbitrability

His exposition of the law begins with arbitrability, declaring that 'all matters and disputes whatsoever (except criminal offences, or concerning the enforcing or dissolving a marriage) may be submitted to arbitration'.[45] That is both too wide and too narrow. There were other matters which the law did not allow to be submitted, for example adoption or legitimacy. On the other hand, in practice, many arbitrations concluded disputes which contained a criminal element. Even as late as the eighteenth century a magistrate might allow, indeed encourage, a servant-girl complainant to go off and come to terms, if necessary helped by a third party, with the employer who had raped her.[46] Bacon modifies his rule (citing West again) to limit the restriction to any offence 'indictable at the suit of the King':[47]

> But if the Party injured proceeds by Way of Action, as he may in Assaults and Batteries, Libels etc the Damages he sustained, or he expects to recover, may be submitted to Arbitration.

For the submission of a dispute over freehold land to be binding, it had to be by bond. A bond was advisable in every case, even where the parties made their submission a rule of court and thereby enforceable by a court order attaching the body of the person in contempt of it. That was because the obligation on a bond survived the death of the maker against

43. p212.
44. (1715) 2 Vernon 705; 23 ER 1058.
45. Citing West 2.33: 'Matters concerning the Commonwealth seem not arbitrable, as all criminall offences'. He also cites West 2.163 on the distinction between absolute and partial or conditional submissions. The citations are to the second volume, the section 'Of Compromise and Arbitrements', which starts at page 163 (wrongly printed as 136), continues (numbers only on the recto) with 164, then 146 (which should be 165), then correctly thereafter from 166. Bacon's citation 'West, Symb. 2 Part, 163' refers to that first page. His citation 'West. Symb. Part 2. §.33.' however refers to paragraph 33 on p146 (which should be p165). He develops his view of the law on arbitration of family matters on p29.
46. Ruth Paley ed *Justice in Eighteenth-Century Hackney* London, London Record Society 1991 xvii-xviii, 39.
47. p28.

the estate, while the court order could not be enforced against the dead.[48]
A mere written undertaking, without the formality of a bond, could be
'revoked at pleasure'.

Appointment of Arbitrators

Despite his slip in providing a definition, Bacon provides evidence of
arbitration by a single arbitrator or two, three, four or more. It would
appear that the practice with which he was most familiar was that
described above as normal, where each party nominated one arbitrator
and both parties either named an umpire or gave the arbitrators power to
appoint one if necessary. We have seen that Sir Matthew Hale CB was
appointed sole arbitrator. It was possible to refer a matter by rule of court
to the judges of assize, as a panel.[49] There was also a practice in cases
being heard at Nisi Prius to refer the matter to the arbitration of the three
men who had been chosen as foremen of juries.[50]

Capacity

Bacon states the obvious: that an infant may not make a binding
submission. He follows the common opinion but not the actual practice
of his time in stating that a married woman, *feme covert*, cannot herself
make a binding submission, quoting *Lumley v Hutton*.[51] But this case is
no authority for Bacon's proposition. Lumley alleged that Busfield owed
him a debt of £276. Busfield died. Mrs Busfield was his executrix and
beneficiary. She married Hutton. All parties submitted to the arbitration
of two arbitrators, who awarded Lumley £240 in instalments. Hutton
claimed that the submission covered only what he owed in his own right,
not what his wife owed as executrix. The court held that the submission
gave the arbitrators authority to award 'that which is due by him in right
of his wife as executrix' and that is all on the point of a woman's capacity:
nothing whatever on whether a woman – married or single – may make
a submission.[52]

Women never seem to have been appointed arbitrators, though there
is no evidence of any express restriction on them, let alone a formal dis-
qualification such as they and others suffered in Roman law. But there
are many examples of married women submitting to arbitration with or

48. p34.
49. p227.
50. p228.
51. p.7; (1618) Cro. Jac. 447; 79 ER 383.
52. The court also held that an award to pay a smaller sum in satisfaction of a greater debt
was good. A creditor who refused to accept that smaller sum in satisfaction would forfeit
the bond.

without the participation of their husbands, for example in the London Mayor's Court, and having awards enforced in their favour or against them.

In *Stanmok v Cherche* in 1388, the defendant first pleaded that no action lay in account against a woman and Charlton CJ seemed to agree:[53]

> A writ of account is never maintainable against a woman, for a man may have such a writ sealed in the Chancery against no woman and it is madness for a man to be willing to hand over any money to a woman to account for.

But the court took time to ponder the question and the defendant dropped that argument and pleaded that there had been an arbitration and the question was put to a jury. In *Scrope v Hyk* in 1511[54] the court declared that a single woman could make an arbitration agreement but, if she married before the arbitration, that would make the agreement void, because the arbitrator could not make an award which would bind the husband.

Debt, Damages and Contract

In Bacon's time there survived the notion that there could be no arbitration of a fixed sum, a debt already quantified. This begs the questions, whether any liability existed and, if so, what it was. It was for a time considered that only claims for damages might be submitted to arbitrators. This confuses the nature of the obligation with the forms of action available to enforce it.

Bacon was writing when recent changes in the law on consideration and the procedure for enforcing contracts were still fresh in lawyers' minds. Mutual promises were now recognised as sufficient to make a binding contract – an executory contract as it became known, where neither party had yet performed. That had been decided as early as 1602, in *Slade's Case*,[55] where the fundamental nature of the suggested reform was well recognised.

All the judges of the royal courts met together to hear arguments not only on the existing law but on the policy behind the reforms. This

---

53. '*Brief d'accompt ne fut unqs maytenable vers un femme qar homme n'avera tiel brief enseale en le chauncerie devers nully femme et est le folie d'un homme q'il voilleit bailler ascuns deniers a une femme d'accompter*', YB 12 Richard II Ames Foundation 164-66. The reporter adds an aside: '*Query de ista materia, qar est un estraunge matere come moy semble*', 'Query this matter, for it is a strange matter, as it seems to me.' As well he might, if he had his eyes open to what went on around him all the time in practice.
54. *Caryll's Reports* II (1999) 116 Selden Society 618.
55. (1602) 4 Rep 91; 76 ER 1072. There is a short and simplified treatment in Derek Roebuck *The Background of the Common Law* Oxford, Oxford UP 2nd edn 1990 pp96-7.

extraordinary court, 'all the justices of England assembled at Serjeants' Inn on Ascension Day, being 13 May', had heard Sir Edward Coke put the case for the plaintiff and his rival Sir Francis Bacon (no relation to our Matthew) for the defendant. The only full report is Coke's own, based on his arguments, which the court accepted. Coke does not supply the arguments for the defendant, which are to be found in print only in Professor Baker's study and translation of the manuscripts.[56]

Popham CJ,[57] purporting at least to speak for the whole assembly of judges, despite a detectable split between those of King's Bench and those of Common Pleas, laid down the simple rule: 'every contract executory imports in itself an assumpsit': mere mutual promises, without performance by either party, were sufficient to make a binding contract, each promise being sufficient consideration, the price of the other's promise.

The result of the development of the law of consideration up to our Bacon's time of writing was that by then an award could be pleaded as satisfaction of a claim: 'because the submission is a mutual promise, upon which an action lies; and performance need not be averred'. And he then cites *Boisloe v Baily*[58] where, in an action for trespass, an award was pleaded as a bar. The award had been that:

> The defendant should provide two fowls at his mansion house in Old Bedlam in London, to be eat by the plaintiff and his friends etc, in satisfaction of the said trespass.

The plaintiff objected that this was not a good bar, because the award had not been performed. But the court held that 'as a submission mutual, though not by bond, was of late resolved to be an actual promise of performance, it need not be averred executed'.

There must have been some lingering doubt, because Bacon later rehearses the arguments with many examples, but he puts the matter to rest with a firm statement that the law was now decided:[59]

56. JH Baker 'New Light on Slade's Case' (1971) 29 *Cambridge Law Journal* 51-67 and 213-36, reprinted in JH Baker *The Legal Profession and the Common Law: Historical Essays* London, Hambledon P 1986 pp393-432. Also David Ibbetson 'Sixteenth-Century Contract Law: *Slade's Case* in Perspective' (1984) 4 *Oxford Journal of Legal Studies* 293-317.

57. Sir John Popham, Chief Justice of the King's Bench from 1592 till his death in 1607, as senior judge had convened this unique assembly, despite and perhaps to outflank the appellate jurisdiction of the new Exchequer Chamber, created by statute, (1585) 27 Eliz I c. 8.

58. (1704) 6 Modern Rep 221, 222. But Bacon refers to the report in 1 Salkeld 76 SC, where Powel J was of a contrary opinion.

59. pp246-9, 245.

Of late, indeed, it hath been held, that upon mutual Promises an Action lies, and consequently there being equal Remedy on both Sides, an Accord may be pleaded without Execution, as well as an Arbitrament. *Raym*. 450. 2 *Jon*. 158.

6. PROCEDURE

Bonds and Rule of Court

Bacon makes it clear that the parties must expect to be bound by the awards of their own arbitrators. After all they have chosen them freely:[60]

> For if they are incompetent Judges, the Fault is in those who choose them; but they must, notwithstanding this, have some common Sense as well as common Honesty; for if they err in a Point of Law, or are mistaken in a Matter of Fact, their Award will in many Cases be set aside, particularly in a Court of Equity; so likewise if they exceed their Authority, or are guilty of Partiality, Corruption, or Dishonesty.

In practice, Bacon says, all submissions are now made either by bond or rule of court or both.[61] The first reference to the legislation which settled the procedure for making a compromise agreement a rule of court is right at the beginning of his book.[62] The preamble to what is often called the first Arbitration Act, (1697) 9 & 10 Wm and Mary c15, declares its objects to be:[63]

> for promoting trade, and rendering the awards of arbitrators the more effectual in all cases, for the final determination of all controversies referred to them by merchants and traders, or others, concerning matters of account or trade, or other matters ....

He sets out the whole of the statute in Chapter VIII, where he explains its provenance. It was passed because courts had gone back on their former practice of granting an attachment to enforce a submission which had been made a rule of court. The practice was for the parties, after they had agreed on the submission, to enrol it in one of the courts, usually the Court of Common Pleas, often at Nisi Prius, sometimes King's Bench, so that any breach would be a contempt, enforceable by an attachment. The attachment would allow the injured party to have the other imprisoned.

60. At p9, developed at p73: 'though the Courts of Law have been pretty strict in this particular, yet Awards have, and are often set aside in a Court of Equity, for Corruption and Want of Understanding in the Arbitrators'.
61. p33.
62. p6.
63. Whether the year is stated as 1697 or 1698 depends on the choice of calendar.

Bacon tells the story of a court refusing such an attachment in 1670.[64] A dispute about the ownership of a ship and its tackle, which had started several actions in trespass at Nisi Prius, was submitted to the 'final end and determination' of a single arbitrator, Sir Matthew Hale, Chief Baron of the Exchequer 1660-71.[65] The Nisi Prius court made the submission a rule of court. Hale CB made his award but it appeared that one party had already revoked the submission. The Court of King's Bench refused to accept that that was a contempt, despite having three other of its own decisions cited to it. They said this was a new practice, to put men in prison without a hearing. They rejected the application for attachment and said the other party could litigate if he wished. But the matter was adjourned and there is no record of further proceedings.

Hale CB could not have been pleased that not only his award but a court order had been defied. He had been an influential Member of Parliament with the ear of those in power. He may have argued for the reform which produced the legislation 28 years later, 21 years after his death.

In Chapter VIII 'Of Submissions made a Rule of Court, and Awards made thereupon' Bacon describes the 'new' procedure upon the statute. He then sets out to consider four topics:[66]

I. How the Submission is to be made a Rule of Court
II. What shall be a Breach of the Rule
III. The Method of enforcing the Performance of Awards, made pursuant to a Rule of Court
IV. What shall excuse the Non-performance of the Award

The parties have three ways to make their compromise a rule of court. They may put a clause in their submission. They may make a separate memorandum in the presence of one or more witnesses. Or, when already in court, they may submit the controversy itself to the foreman or members of the jury. Bacon supplies the necessary wording. The parties show their consent by affidavit and the court grants counsel's motion as a matter of course. The award will then have the force of a judgment without further argument.

A party breaches the rule not only by failure to perform the award but also by any act or omission which hinders the arbitrators in making the award. Specifically, it is a breach of the rule to revoke the arbitrators' authority.

64. pp222-3, citing *Tremenhere v Tresillian* (1681) 1 Siderfin 452. Siderfin says he was himself counsel in this case.
65. Friend and follower in his scholarship of John Selden; he edited anonymously the 1668 edition of *Rolle's Abridgment*.
66. p225.

When a party fails to perform the award, the other applies to the court by a motion for an attachment to compel performance. That motion is supported by an affidavit which sets out that the award conforms to the submission and that the applicant has done whatever the award required. On this application the court grants a rule that the defendant should show cause why an attachment should not be granted by a fixed date; otherwise a rule on a second motion will be made absolute.

The sheriff apprehends the defendant, who must give a bail-bond and appear in person and enter into a recognisance to appear whenever summoned until the matter is disposed of. The court gives the applicant four days to file interrogatories, on which the defendant is examined. If the defendant makes a denial, the applicant brings witnesses to prove the contempt – not the original claim – in court, with the defendant answering the charges and the questions put by the court.

The parties have made their own choice. They cannot complain about 'Severity or Inequality in the Award'; there must be some 'notorious Defect in the Award itself, or some Fault in the Arbitrators, such as Partiality'. Bacon gives an example of misconduct:[67]

> An Award was set aside, the Arbitrators appearing to have an Interest in the Cargo, touching which the Award was made, and therefore put too great a Value thereon; and in five Days after the Award made, the Money awarded was attached by the Arbitrators, for Debts owing to them.

The parties may have delimited the authority of their arbitrators, expressly or by implication, for example as to time. The award must be made within any time limits set out in the submission and any requirement of notice must be complied with. If an award demands something impossible, it is void but only insofar as it is impossible to perform.

The big issue remained unresolved. What about a simple mistake of fact or law? Citing a case decided 18 years after the Act,[68] Bacon states the law:

> If it appears that the Arbitrators went upon a plain Mistake, either as to the Law, or in a Matter of Fact, the same is an Error appearing in the Body of the Award, and sufficient to set it aside.

67. p235 citing *Earl v Stocker* (1691) 2 Vernon 251; 23 ER 763, also Eq Cas Abr 50 pl. 5, SC.
68. p236 citing *Corneforth v Geer* (1715) 2 Vernon 705; 23 ER 1058.

But it was not as simple as that, as Bacon reveals in discussing a case decided in 1703:[69]

> *Holt* said, That the Parties being Judges of the Parties own chusing, the Party shall not come and say, they have not done him Justice, and put the Court to Examine it .... However, the Award was examined and confirmed; and the Plaintiff moved for an Attachment for not performing it; and the Court held, That the Non-performance, while the Matter was *sub Judice*, was no Contempt, and then the Plaintiff moved for his Costs, and that was denied; upon which *Powel*, Justice, said, that seeing they could not give the Party any Costs, he should never be for examining into Awards again.

This dilemma has still not been completely resolved, despite almost universal lip-service in favour of non-intervention. Courts in many parts of the world, to different degrees, find it hard to resist the argument, if put convincingly enough, that although the parties have expressly and clearly chosen to submit to the final and unchallengeable award of their own arbitrators to the exclusion of the court, nevertheless, in this instance, they must have impliedly intended to exclude this particular error.

7. PLEADING

A proper understanding of Matthew Bacon's text requires a grasp of the elements of pleading in his day. He himself insisted:[70]

> As Pleading in general is allowed to be the most nice and difficult Part of our Law, and as an infinite Number of Causes of all Kinds have been lost or delayed for want of a right Observance of the Rules of Pleading, it is necessary in the Case of Awards, (which has partaked of these Difficulties as much as any other Branch whatsoever) to be cautious and exact in all the Proceedings.

The pleadings begin with the plaintiff's declaration, which must set out the submission bond rather than, as one might have expected, the award itself. That is because the claim is for the defendant's non-performance of the undertakings in the bond, not directly for refusal to abide by the award. The promise in the bond is to pay a sum of money (or other value) unless the submission to arbitration shall be fully performed according to the terms of the bond, in Latin *ita quod arbitrium fiat de premissis* or *de et super premissis*.

---

69. p229, citing *Morris v Reynolds* (1703) 1 Salkeld 73; 91 ER 69.
70. p236.

A recurring question was whether the submission included disputes which arose after the submission but before the award. Clear words were needed:[71]

> If an Award be made *de & super Premissis*, and the Condition is *ita quod fiat de Premissis*, and the Award is, that one shall make a general Release to the other, of all matters till the Award, and that the parties shall be Friends and loving; this is good, although the Award is void as to Matters after the Submission; and therefore he is not bound to make any Release of them, but of those only which were before the Submission.

The defendant must plead performance of the bond, which of course includes carrying out what the award has determined. This requires the defendant to put the award in evidence unless the defence is that there has been no arbitration, *nullum fecerunt arbitrium*.

The plaintiff may plead in replication that there has been a valid award and set it out.

> The defendant may then put in a rejoinder, which must introduce no new matter. For example, if the defendant's first defence was that there was no award, to which the plaintiff produced the award, a rejoinder that there was an award but that it was void in law is a departure and of no effect.[72]

Either party might at any stage interpose a demurrer, a pleading that it should be given judgment even if the other party's allegations of fact were accepted.[73]

> A Demurrer may be upon a Declaration, Replication, Rejoinder, etc, as well as on a Plea .... The safest Way for the Defendant in most Cases, if he imagines that the Award was not made according to Law, is to demur to the Plaintiff's Declaration.

Although the courts expected the parties to take care with their pleadings and were quick to penalise them if they did not do so strictly, they frowned on what they saw as trickery. *Veale v Warner*[74] began as an action in debt on an arbitration bond. The defendant pleaded that the arbitrators had

---

71. pp135-6 citing 1 *Rolle's Abridgment* 260.
72. p257.
73. p258.
74. pp168-9; (1669) 1 Wms Saunders 323 and 326; 85 ER 463 and 468. Bacon repeats all this again at pp250-1.

awarded that he should pay the plaintiff £3,100 and give him a general release and that he had done that. What he did not plead was that the award required the plaintiff to do anything. The plaintiff replied that the defendant had not paid. The defendant put in an insufficient rejoinder and the plaintiff demurred. The court could not find for the plaintiff, who should have pleaded that he had released the defendant, according to the award. But nor would it give judgment to the defendant:

> because they apprehended it to be only a Trick in Pleading; for which the Chief Justice reprehended [defendant's counsel] *Sanders*, who excused himself, by Reason of the Severity of the Award.

In other words, counsel said his apparently unmeritorious technical objection was justified because the award was manifestly excessive. The court would have none of that and allowed the plaintiff to discontinue, so that he could start his action again and take more care with his pleadings the next time.

8. THE PRECEDENTS

Bacon concludes with 38 pages of precedents of a wide range of the pleadings he has just discussed: declaration upon a bond, oyer of the condition, defence, replication, demurrers of various kinds, joinder in demurrer, rejoinder, refusal of tender.

The pleadings are in Latin, though they recite the arbitration bond in its original English, unless the parties have chosen to 'affect to have the Bond of Submission in Latin', as Bacon drily puts it.[75] In 1731, the very year of publication of *The Compleat Arbitrator*, Parliament had another go at abolishing Latin pleadings.[76] Bacon's second (1740) edition retains them but they are replaced by English versions in the posthumous and last 1770 third edition.

9. CONCLUSION

The purpose of this introduction has been to help the reader of the facsimile not only to understand but even to enjoy reading it.

Many insights can be found in Bacon's text. Some are all the more convincing for not being intentional. In 1731 the legal system was changing. Judges' attitudes were becoming more favourable to arbitration. Latin pleadings gave way to English. The discrepancies between law and practice have been discussed above. The most striking, perhaps, is on the

---

75. p52.
76. (1731) 4 Geo II c.26.

position of women. There are statements of law that would apparently disqualify women, even single women, from being themselves parties to a submission. Yet, wherever there is evidence of practice, for centuries they had been making submissions and suing and being sued on them.[77] The only restriction arose from the general rule that, so long as a woman was married, she could make no valid contract (or dispose of property) – with some broad exceptions – without joining her husband in the transaction.

In his earlier treatise, John March had written: 'submissions are most commonly to illiterate men',[78] by which he did not mean they could not read or write but that they were unlearned. Even as late as 1748, the Earl of Chesterfield could write: 'The word *illiterate*, in its common acceptation, means a man who is ignorant of those two languages',[79] *scilicet* Latin and Greek. Indeed, there would have been little point in March or Bacon or anyone else writing, as they claimed they were doing, for lay arbitrators as well as lawyers, if their words could not be read. Bacon's many examples show that the parties more often than not chose arbitrators who were not lawyers.

Another insight is into the way in which merchants, given the opportunity, resorted to chance if they could not agree on a choice of arbitrators. Gerard Malynes describes how it was done in his day:[80]

Wherefore the maner to elect arbitrators is worthy the observation. Some are contented to name foure or six persons on either side in writing, and refer the naming or electing of foure out of them by reciprocall proceeding, when one named the first person, another the second, and then again the third, and the other the fourth person. Others putting severall names in a paper, are contented that a mere stranger shall upon the back side of the paper pricke their names with a pin, or that (as they are numbred) the dice shall be cast upon them, accordingly by the number.

Others put their names in severall papers, and cause them to be mingled & drawne by way of lot, by an indifferent person; which course may be thought allowable, as we have noted in the chapter of dividing commodities by lots.

Others will do the same by nomination of them, and drawing the longest and shortest straw, or by any other extraordinarie means of

---

77. This is a topic on which I am now working so my authorities are not quite random, but see PE Jones *Calendar of Plea and Memoranda Rolls 1458-82* pp43-4 for Margarete Bate and pp48-9 for Alice Braunche.

78. p246.

79. From his *Letters*, quoted under 'illiterate' in the *Oxford English Dictionary*.

80. Malynes 1636 p297.

pointing, numbring, or describing, al tending to one end, to have indifferencie, and that partialitie may by al means be avoided.

Bacon cites authority that such resort to chance was not allowed by law:[81]

> If by the Submission the Arbitrators have Power to chuse an Umpire, and they not agreeing, throw *Cross* and *Pyle* which of them should name the person; and the Umpire thus chosen makes his Umpirage; the Court will set it aside.

Cross and pyle was what we would now call tossing-up, calling 'heads' or 'tails'. If the parties agreed to that way of selecting an umpire or arbitrator, it would seem mischievous of the judges to refuse to enforce their bond. To resort to chance is not necessarily to take the matter lightly. Indeed it followed the customary law of the merchants, as Malynes vouched.

So what are we to make of this strange intrusion of the judges into the world of commerce? Did the court really decide that a submission was void because the arbitrators were chosen by lot? Our judgment of Bacon's qualities as a legal scholar may be affected by his use of this authority.

The parties had provided in their submission that, if the arbitrators had not made an award within the stated time, the arbitrators should *choose* a third person as umpire. The arbitrators could not agree who should be umpire. Each suggested their own man and they tossed up for it. The arbitrators endorsed the bond that they had *appointed* the umpire. The report says that, among other reasons for his decision, the Master of Rolls, Sir John Trevor, found that the arbitrators had not *chosen* the umpire at all as the submission required but allowed him to be picked by chance, and that that was sufficient cause to set the award aside.

Whatever that meant, it did not decide that the parties could not have provided that the umpire be selected by lot if they had made that clear expressly. It did not decide that there was some policy against that method of picking arbitrators or umpire. Moreover, there are other reasons for hesitating before accepting even the most unambiguous opinions of Sir John Trevor, particularly relating to matters of chance, despite 'the reputation he gained of being the best judge in all gambling transactions, of the tricks and intricacies of which he had personal experience'.

John Trevor was born with disadvantages which other benefits well compensated for.[82] It was said that 'no person ever had a worse sort of

---

81. p217 citing *Harris v Mitchell* (1704) 2 Vernon 485; 23 ER 911.
82. Edward Foss *Biographica Juridica: a Biographical Dictionary of the Judges of England from the Conquest to the Present Time 1066-1870* London, John Murray 1870

squint' but he had an influential uncle, the repulsive Judge Jeffries who on his return from his Bloody Assizes was rewarded with the office of Lord Chancellor. Trevor became Master of the Rolls in 1685 and kept the job until 1717, with a break from 1689 to 1693. He quarrelled with Jeffries and Roger North says that: 'Like a true gamester, he fell to the good work of supplanting his patron and friend'. He was also Speaker of the House of Commons. Foss is savage:

> Trevor with unblushing rapacity participated largely in the corruption that then too universally prevailed .... In the investigation instituted by the parliament .... He was condemned to sit for six hours hearing himself abused, and at last was obliged to put the question and to declare himself guilty of 'a high crime and misdemeanour'... he was expelled the house .... The wits remarked 'that justice was blind, bribery only squinted'.

Foss says that he was a good lawyer:

> He continued master of the Rolls for twenty-two years after his expulsion, possessing so high a reputation as a lawyer that he was frequently appealed to as authority in doubtful points by Lord Chancellor Harcourt.

Yet we must be left with doubts about what may well have been the irascible *obiter dictum* of a judge who had become a figure of fun. His meanness was notorious:

> On a relation calling upon him as he was drinking his wine, he exclaimed to the servant: 'You rascal, you have brought my cousin ... up my back stairs. Take him down again immediately, and bring him up my front stairs.' During the operation the bottle was removed and Sir John saved his wine.

Matthew Bacon may not have had the most analytical approach to the authorities but he must be judged by the standards of his time. His pioneering work has given us unequalled access to the law and practice then. For a truly scholarly treatment we must wait another lifetime, until Stewart Kyd writes the first modern treatise.[83]

673-5. John Trevor was a descendant of John Hampden and an ancestor of the Duke of Wellington.

83. The best edition is Stewart Kyd *A Treatise of the Law of Awards* London, 2nd edn for J Johnson and others 1799. [Derek Roebuck also wrote the introduction to Kyd's *Treatise* for the Lawbook Exchange's 2009 edition. The chapter that follows this (15 – *Stewart Kyd: The Scottish Pioneer*) is not that, but an article based on it – SH.]

15. STEWART KYD: THE SCOTTISH PIONEER

1. INTRODUCTION

In 1791 there was published in London the first modern textbook on the law of arbitration in England. It must have had some success because a second edition appeared eight years later.[1] How did a Scot, a young barrister making his way in London, come to write so expertly and precociously on the subject? What sort of a man was he?

Stewart Kyd was baptised on July 3, 1758,[2] the eldest son of Harry Kid and Helen Fullerton of Arbroath, and educated at Arbroath Grammar School and King's College, Aberdeen.[3] He went to England as a young man and was admitted a member of the Middle Temple in June 1782 and called to the Bar five years later. Probably about that time he became involved in the movement for the democratic reform of Parliament. In November 1792 he joined the Society for Promoting Constitutional Information. On May 29, 1794 he was arrested, examined by the Privy Council and released. On June 4 the Council summoned him again and on June 7 charged him with high treason. On October 25 he stood trial with nine others at the Old Bailey.

They were exciting times. Thinkers had begun to apply reason to the study of society and activists started to do something about what they saw as its ills. In 1776 the Scot Adam Smith had published *An Inquiry into the Nature and Causes of the Wealth of Nations*, which created the new discipline of political economy, and the English writer and activist Thomas Paine published his *Common Sense*, calling for independence for the American colonies. In that year, too, Jeremy Bentham published

1. Stewart Kyd, *A Treatise on the Law of Awards by Stewart Kyd Esq. Barrister at Law, of the Middle Temple* (London: 1791, 2nd edn 1799, reprinted Clark NJ, Lawbook Exchange, 2009), for which I wrote an introduction on which this article is based.
2. *http://www.familysearch.org* [Accessed December 4, 2009].
3. The entry is brief in *Oxford Dictionary of National Biography* (Oxford: Oxford University Press, 2004) and there is little more in AWB Simpson (ed.), *Biographical Dictionary of the Common Law* (London: Butterworths, 1984) and John Hutchinson, *A Catalogue of Notable Middle Templars, with Brief Biographical Notices* (London: The Honourable Society of the Middle Temple, 1902).

A Fragment on Government, criticising Blackstone's conservative views and calling for law reform.

Then in 1789 came the French Revolution. At first the greatest minds in Europe declared their approval and support: Beethoven, Kant, Hegel, Schiller and Pestalozzi among others. In Britain intellectuals welcomed it and poets sang its praises: not only Robert Burns the radical Scot but Blake, Coleridge and Wordsworth. On the day the Bastille fell, the *Morning Post* enthused[4]:

> An Englishman not filled with esteem and admiration at the *sublime* manner in which one of the most IMPORTANT REVOLUTIONS the world has ever seen is now effecting, must be dead to every sense of virtue and of freedom.

The Society for Promoting Constitutional Information had been set up in London in 1780 to promote the reform of parliament but had failed. Its main activity had been the publishing and distribution of radical literature, in particular the works of Paine. It co-operated with the more popular corresponding societies—membership costing one penny a week—which aimed to spread democratic propaganda— educating ordinary people in their democratic rights—through the press and by holding discussions and meetings with itinerant speakers. They called for parliamentary reform: votes for all men (not women), secret ballots and annual general elections. They also trained their members to organise. Membership rose above 10,000 and attendance at their open-air meetings could exceed 100,000.

The Government reacted. Britain was at war with France. The reformers had French ideas and some even had French connections. They must be traitors. In Scotland, in 1792, the Lord Advocate Robert Dundas prosecuted John Morton, James Anderson and Malcolm Craig for sedition. They had toasted 'George the Third and last!' They were sentenced to nine months' imprisonment.[5] Some thought those sentences too light. When 27-year-old Thomas Muir came up for trial in 1793, such clemency was absent.[6] Robert MacQueen, who had a reputation as a good conveyancer, had been appointed Lord Justice Clerk, as Lord Braxfield, in 1787. He is said to have been the model

---

4. *Morning Post*, July 21, 1879, quoted by E.J. Hobsbawm, *The Age of Revolution 1789–1848* (London: New English Library, 1962), p.74.

5. Alan Wharam, *The Treason Trials, 1794* (Leicester: Leicester University Press, 1992), p.48. I have taken much of the background from this excellent source.

6. *The Trial of Thomas Muir, Younger, of Huntershill, before the High Court of Justiciary at Edinburgh on the 30th and 31st days of August, 1793, for sedition*, New edn corrected (London: Ridgeway, Symonds and Edinburgh, Robertson, 1793).

for the cruel father of the hero in Robert Louis Stevenson's unfinished novel, *Weir of Hermiston*. He knew what was expected of the highest criminal judge. 'Bring me prisoners and I'll find you law' was said to have been his cry.[7] He found the problem as simple to answer as it was to state: the Constitution was perfect as it then was; therefore any proposal for reform, however moderate and peaceful, must be seditious. He summed up against Muir:

> Mr Muir might have known that no attention could be paid by Parliament to such a rabble. What right had they to representation? … A Government in every country should be just like a corporation; and, in this country, it is made up of the landed interest, which alone has a right to be represented. As for the rabble, who have nothing but personal property.

And so on. On conviction by a carefully picked jury,[8] Braxfield sentenced Muir to 14 years' transportation to Botany Bay. Not to death, though that was a more than evens chance unless you were hard and fit. The jury were shocked and determined to petition for a prison sentence of a few weeks but they gave up when one received a death threat.

A fortnight later a clergyman, Thomas Fyshe Palmer, was convicted of sedition in Perth and sentenced by Lord Abercromby to seven years' transportation.

Braxfield made the law up, pretending that there still existed an old Scots common law offence when it had had been abrogated by the new Parliament of the United Kingdom after the Union in 1707, which substituted the English Treason Act 1351. He rejected Secretary of State Henry Dundas's pleas that royal mercy might reduce the sentences. By the end of 1793 many of the leading Scottish reformers, later known as the Scottish Martyrs, had been convicted by specially selected juries of 'sowing discord between the king and people' and transported. To another defendant charged with sedition who proclaimed that all great men had been reformers, 'even our Saviour himself', Braxfield reasonably replied: 'Muckle he made o' that—he was hangit!'[9]

---

7. He looks so kindly in the Scottish National Portrait Gallery but Lord Cockburn wrote of him in the *Dictionary of National Biography* that he was a powerful man, coarse, debauched and illiterate (i.e. he knew no Latin), who had probably never read a book except textbooks on the law and two or three works of indecency.

8. He is reported to have said in an aside to one juror: 'Maister Horner, come awa, and help us to hang ane o' thae damned scoondrels': Michael Gilbert (ed.), *The Oxford Book of Legal Anecdotes* (Oxford: Oxford University Press, 1989), pp.210–211.

9. Gilbert (ed.), *The Oxford Book of Legal Anecdotes*, 1989, pp.210–211. In his trial, the democrat Margarot had the nerve to take Braxfield on, asking him whether he had said to a young lady at dinner: 'What should you think of giving Margarot a hundred lashes

In January 1793 the French guillotined Louis XVI despite Paine's arguments against the death sentence in the National Convention: 'Kill the king but not the man!' Marat belittled Paine as a timid Quaker. But printers and booksellers in England were fined and imprisoned for publishing his works.

In May 1793 Charles Grey's motion for a committee of inquiry into the reform of Parliament showed that 71 peers and 91 commoners chose 302 members of Parliament. One constituency, Old Sarum, Pitt the Elder's seat, had seven voters and two seats in parliament. Seats were bought and sold as private property. Pitt and Burke and the Tories made sure Grey's motion was lost, using their political power to prevent democratic reform as that party has always done when it could.

In 1794 prosecutions of the reformers started in London. The Government suspended habeas corpus. The Crown charged some of the more prominent members of the corresponding societies with treason, setting up a special commission of the Privy Council at the Old Bailey to try them before a jury thought at the time to have been rigged in favour of conviction. The first to be tried was Thomas Hardy, a shoemaker from Glasgow.[10] The jury acquitted. Then came the best known, the Reverend John Horne Tooke, the champion and publicist of Tom Paine. He called as witnesses some of the leading politicians, including William Pitt the Younger and Charles James Fox, the playwright MP Richard Brinsley Sheridan and the novelist judge Henry Fielding. Pitt made a spectacularly poor show, prevaricating and pretending that he had forgotten his own part in earlier proposals for reform until Sheridan reminded him.

The Lord President, Chief Justice of the Common Pleas Sir James Eyre, was criticised for the fairness of his summing-up and conduct of the trial.[11] The jury acquitted Horne Tooke after only a few minutes. The cases against the others were dropped. Stewart Kyd had been next but one in line of those whom the Government wanted to hang, draw and quarter.[12]

together with Botany Bay?' On her answering that the mob would never allow Margarot to be whipped, he replied that the mob would be better for losing a little blood.
10. He gave up being a bricklayer after being badly injured in an accident when working for Thomas Roebuck at the Carron Iron Works.
11. T.B. and T.J. Howell, *Complete Collection of State Trials and Proceedings for High Treason and Other Crimes and Misdemeanors from the Earliest Period to 1820* (London: Hansard, 1816–28), 33 Vols. Manoah Sibley, *The Genuine Trial of Thomas Hardy for High Treason...* (London: Jordan, 1795). Mary Thale, *Selections from the Papers of the London Corresponding Society 1792–1799* (Cambridge: Cambridge University Press, 2008).
12. This loathsome practice was imposed by apparently civilised judges on conviction by juries of good Christian men, though by this time the executioners usually ensured that their victims were dead before they disembowelled them. This amelioration was made mandatory by the Treason Act 1814 but the butchery was not finally abolished until the Forfeiture Act 1870, within the lifetime of people I knew as a child, who were well aware of it.

2. PRACTICE AND PUBLICATIONS

Kyd's publications provide some of the evidence for his practice at the Bar. They cover most of the commercial practice developed under the Scot William Murray, later Earl of Mansfield, who, during his time as Chief Justice of the King's Bench (1756–88), had fashioned a new system of commercial law. He had a profound knowledge of the Common Law, which had been evolving for six centuries, and took evidence of the customary law of merchants, which had been developing for much longer and in which the influence of Roman law was stronger and more overt.[13]

Kyd's published works start in 1790 with bills of exchange.[14] Then came the first edition of his book on arbitration.[15] That was quickly followed by his largest but least original work, the third edition of the encyclopedic classic, *Comyn's Digest*.[16] Next was another monograph, the first substantial modern treatment of company law in two volumes,[17] which the legal historian Sir William Holdsworth judged to be[18]:

[A] very complete and learned work. Like his other books, well arranged and clearly written, a remarkably able pioneer treatise on this subject.

Holdsworth says that Kyd wrote the last chapter of *Corporations* in the Tower of London, presumably with limited access to books. He dedicated it to Horne Tooke. His political activities, arrest and trial must have made practice difficult for him in the next few years. Yet, when Pitt first introduced income tax in 1799, Kyd published his text on the topic before the year was out.[19]

Some evidence of Kyd's abilities as a barrister survives in his speech in defence of a poor printer, Thomas Williams, charged with uttering a

---

13. James Oldham, *The Mansfield Manuscripts and the Growth of English Law in the Eighteenth Century* (Chapel Hill: University of North Carolina Press, 1992) 2 Vols.
14. Stewart Kyd, *Laws of Bills of Exchange and Promissory Notes* (London: 1790).
15. Stewart Kyd, *A Treatise on the Law of Awards*, 1791.
16. Stewart Kyd (ed.), *A Digest of the Laws of England by the Right Honourable Sir John Comyns* ... (London: 1792), 6 Vols.
17. Stewart Kyd, *Treatise on the Law of Corporations* (London: Vol.I, 1793; Vol.II 1794, reprinted Clark NJ Lawbook Exchange, 2006).
18. *History of English Law* (London: Methuen, 1938), XII p.400.
19. Stewart Kyd, *The Substance of the Income Act: in a Methodical Arrangement* (London: 1799, 2nd edn 1801). This work, 'printed for, and sold by, Thomas Hurst, and Carpenter and Co. Old Bond-Street' is generally confused in the bibliographies with a distinct publication of the same year: Stewart Kyd, *Arrangement, under Distinct Titles of all the Provisions Relating to the Assessed Taxes* (London: 1799).

blasphemous libel by publishing Paine's *Age of Reason* in 1797.[20] The Scot Thomas Erskine (1750–1823), third son of the Earl of Buchan, prosecuted. He had been called to the Bar in 1778 and won quick success. In 1792 he had been shouted down in his unsuccessful attempt to defend Paine against a charge of treason for publishing *Rights of Man*. He had been Kyd's counsel at his trial for treason. Erskine made much of his own reputation as a champion of free speech. The thrust of his arguments was that it was as right to argue for the reform of religion as it was for political reform, but one must not go too far. Freedom of speech had already been brought 'as near perfection, by the Law of England, as perhaps is consistent with any of the frail institutions of mankind'. Paine had challenged Christianity itself. He might not have been an atheist but he had suggested that knowledge of God might be gained from observation of his creation and could not come from any holy book. In particular, not from the Old Testament, which he called a collection of:

[T]he obscene stories, the voluptuous debaucheries, the cruel and torturous executions, the unrelenting vindictiveness a history of wickedness that has served to corrupt and brutalize mankind I cannot dishonour my Creator by calling it by his name.

Erskine communicated his outrage to the jury. Paine's book was like pornography, 'pointed to debauch innocence, and to blast and poison the morals of the rising generation'. Most telling, it would rob the poor of their only comfort:

I can conceive a distressed but virtuous man, surrounded by children, looking up to him for bread when he has none to give them, sinking under the last day's labour, and unequal to the next, yet still looking up with confidence to the hour when all tears shall be wiped from the eyes of affliction, bearing the burden laid upon him by a mysterious Providence which he adores, and looking forward with exultation to the revealed promises of his Creator.

That 'conceit' was to come back and haunt Erskine.

Christianity justified the legal system, in which everything was founded on the Christian oath.[21] He concluded by making the political point: 'No man can be expected to be faithful to the authority of man who

---

20. The best and fullest account is in Howell, *State Trials*, 1816-28, Vol.26, p.653.
21. It is strange how those who most rely on the Bible as God's word can ignore inconvenient texts, apparently unambiguous, such as those prohibiting oaths, e.g. James v, 12: 'But above all things, my brethren, swear not; neither by heaven, neither by the earth, neither by any other oath.'

revolts against the government of God.' Of course, Paine had never done or advocated anything of the sort.

We know nothing of Kyd's religious beliefs. He had to respond as best he could for his client. His approach was careful and measured. He had to try to take the heat out of the battle and bring the jury back to their proper task of deciding whether the prosecution had proved against this accused, not Tom Paine, the elements of the crime with which he was charged. Kyd cited all the passages, chapter and verse, of debauchery and cruelty in the Old Testament but was not allowed to read them out. He emphasised that neither he nor his client was concerned to assert the truth of what Paine had written, just his right 'to publish to the world the result of his inquiries thus honestly and fairly made, whether that result were right or wrong'. Whatever the crimes of the author, the present defendant was innocent. He had republished the pamphlet only because the Bishop of Llandaff had recently published a reply to it, in the belief that it should be available so that the public might know what was in it.

Erskine replied at great length, patronising Kyd and delivering lectures on politics, theology and the history of religion. Lord Kenyon summed up. The Christian religion was part of the law of the land. Kyd might have tried to separate the author from the publisher but he had done just the opposite. The defendant had brought this evil pamphlet back from obscurity: 'Unless it was for the most malignant purposes, I cannot conceive how it was published.' The jury found Williams guilty without retiring.

There then followed an extraordinary sequence of proceedings before the court and outside it. Williams was let out on bail to await sentencing. Erskine was troubled by the thought of him receiving a long sentence. One day, walking through Lincoln's Inn Fields, his coat was tugged and he looked down on a woman in tears, kneeling at his feet. She was Williams's wife. She persuaded him to go with her to their home, which was also their bookshop and workshop. There he met Williams, busy sewing tracts he had printed. His children had smallpox. He had always been a good Christian. He was now truly penitent and pleaded with Erskine that prison would be the death of them all.

Erskine called a meeting of those who had sponsored the prosecution and given him his brief, the Society for the Suppression of Vice. It was chaired by the Bishop of London and attended by other prelates and pious worthies including William Wilberforce, the anti-slavery campaigner. Erskine begged them to show Christian charity by allowing him to plead with the court for leniency, indeed for mercy, when Williams was sentenced. To a man they were unrelenting: no mercy. So Erskine gave them back their brief. He went back to the court and argued that

Williams's plight was all the fault of his solicitor, Martin, who had been prepared to sacrifice Williams for his own political ends. Conveniently, Martin had just died. Williams was free to ask for clemency, which Erskine eloquently did on his behalf. The sentencing judge, Ashhurst J., gave Williams only a year in prison instead of the three he said had been intended.

In this melodrama the destitute father of the family, just like the one whom Erskine had imagined in his opening address, had become all too real. Erskine and Kyd were now on the same side.

3. KYD THE ARBITRATOR

After these heady days of political activity, battling advocacy and pioneering scholarship, Kyd seems to have continued his commercial practice. He gives glimpses from time to time in *The Law of Awards* of his work both as advocate and in drafting documents. Authority for his statement that a written submission needs to be stamped is 'a late decision of the Court of King's Bench'[22]:

> I do not find the case reported in which this was decided, nor do I recollect the name of it; but I was in Court when the point was decided.

A footnote[23] reveals that he was counsel in a case before the King's Bench in Easter Term 1797, in which he successfully argued that a criminal prosecution could not be submitted to arbitration.

Kyd's precedent for an award is evidence of his practice as an arbitrator[24]:

> TO ALL TO WHOM these presents shall come, I, S.K. barrister at law WHEREAS R.S. and J.S. have submitted themselves ... in the penal sum of one thousand pounds to keep the award of W.A.... and E.H. arbitrators, indifferently chosen AND WHEREAS the said W.A. and E.H. did .. . appoint me the said S.K. to be the umpire between them KNOW NOW YE, that I the said S.K. appointed umpire do hereby adjudge IN WITNESS whereof, I, the said S.K. have set my hand and seal.

---

22. Kyd, *A Treatise on the Law of Awards*, 1791, p.11, fn2. He deals with the substance more fully in an addendum, pp.vii–viii.
23. *R. v Coombs* and *R. v Rant* Unreported 64 fn7.
24. Kyd, *A Treatise on the Law of Awards*, 1791, pp.414–22.

The detailed and specific content, with no attempt to make it anonymous other than replacing names by initials, shows that the precedent must have come from Kyd's own files. The next precedents, for the parties' releases of each other, are from the same matter and show Kyd acted as umpire. Would it be unkind to suggest that this might have been a fairly subtle attempt to advertise his availability as an arbitrator?

4. A TREATISE ON THE LAW OF AWARDS

Kyd's *Awards* is the first modern treatise on the law of arbitration in England. A careful comparison would show that its structure and much of its content informed the first edition of *Russell on Arbitration* 1849 and even more modern works like Quintin Hogg's.[25] He makes no mention of Scots law or practice. The first edition in 1791 declared on its title page:

> Stewart Kyd *A Treatise on the Law of Awards by Stewart Kyd Esq. Barrister at Law, of the Middle Temple* London, printed for S. Crowder, Paternoster-Row, and B.C. Collins, Salisbury, M.DCC,XCI.

Kyd's prose is clear and elegant. He shows great skill in organising a mass of difficult material into a comprehensible and persuasive narrative. This is not unconnected with his experience of practice both as an advocate and in drafting documents. Kyd's style is elegant but not showy; he may have been influenced by Paine, whose plain style was consciously created to be easily understood by anyone who could read.

There are few typographical errors and even an acceptable index.

Kyd begins by defining his terms, satisfactorily if not comprehensively. His definitions are for use, to help the reader, rather than the results of what, as a practitioner, he may have assumed to be a fruitless search for scientific categories[26]:

> That act, by which the parties refer any matter in dispute between them to the decision of a third person, is called a submission; the person to whom a reference is made, an arbitrator; when the reference is made to more than one, and provision made, that in case they shall disagree, another shall decide, that other is called an umpire; the judgment pronounced by an arbitrator, or arbitrators, an award; that by an umpire, an umpirage, or, less properly, an award.

25. Q.M. Hogg, *The Law of Arbitration* (London: Butterworth, 1936) with traces perhaps in Scotland, e.g. J.P. Wood and J.R.N. Macphail, *The Law of Arbitration in Scotland* (Edinburgh: Bell and Bradfute, 1900).

26. Kyd, *A Treatise on the Law of Awards,* 1791, p.6; compare Matthew Bacon and my Introduction [to Bacon] IX-XII [see Chapter 14 above.].

That shows Kyd thinking for himself, rather than drawing on earlier attempts which had fallen into error by looking back into books rather than at the reality around them.[27]

5. KYD ON LAW AND EQUITY IN PRACTICE

Kyd handles the cases with the confidence of an experienced barrister. He quotes the relevant authorities from the *Year Books* and from *Rolle's Abridgment*. He is well aware of the effect on precedent of the passage of time[28]: 'Perhaps, had the latter case remained to be decided in more modern times, it would have received a different determination.' He is not afraid to go against the weight of opinion and authorities if they offend his 'own notions of propriety and consistency in pleading'.[29]

Kyd knew the difference between law and practice. Arbitrators are not the agents of those who appoint them and should not act as if they are but, when the common practice was for each side to appoint one or two, with an umpire, the parties expected those they had appointed to argue their part[30]:

> It is highly improper, however common it may be, for a person nominated as an arbitrator, to consider himself the agent of the person on whose behalf he was nominated.

Arbitrators risked punishment for misbehaviour. An arbitrator who threatened to make a party pay costs was ordered by Lord Macclesfield to pay the costs himself.[31]

A distinction must be observed between enforcing an award and enforcing a submission. Kyd describes how courts of equity regularly enforced awards by decrees of specific performance.[32] But the courts were much less willing to enforce a submission unless it had been made a rule of court under the 1697 statute, as Kyd discusses in detail.[33] Courts of equity would not enforce an award if the arbitrators had been guilty of collusion or gross misbehaviour, or even of a material mistake of fact or even 'a plain mistake in point of law'.[34] If the mistake was

27. The worst example is in Matthew Bacon, *The Compleat Arbitrator* (London: 1731), reprinted with an introduction by Derek Roebuck (Clark NJ, Lawbook Exchange, 2009).
28. Kyd, *A Treatise on the Law of Awards*, 1791, p.54.
29. Kyd, *A Treatise on the Law of Awards*, 1791, p.361.
30. Kyd, *A Treatise on the Law of Awards*, 1791, p.75.
31. Kyd, *A Treatise on the Law of Awards*, 1791, p.348; Lord Hardwicke threatened the same in another case.
32. Kyd, *A Treatise on the Law of Awards*, 1791, pp.316–26.
33. Kyd, *A Treatise on the Law of Awards*, 1791, pp.14–26.
34. Kyd, *A Treatise on the Law of Awards*, 1791, pp.350–1.

on a doubtful point of law, the award might be allowed to stand. Where the arbitrators meant to follow the law but mistook it, the award might be set aside. But where they meant to produce an equitable decision in the circumstances of the case, whatever the law might say, the court would enforce the award. Kyd describes how the court asked arbitrators, charged with distributing an estate on death,[35] whether they had intended to follow the Statute of Distributions or to do what they thought fairest and what the testator would have wanted. They replied by affidavit that they had followed no fixed rules of law but had intended to deal out to the parties:

> [W]hat appeared to them to be, according to the best of their judgment, under all the circumstances of the case, strict and impartial justice, agreeably to what they believed to have been the intentions of the testator.

That satisfied the court, which enforced the award.

6. PLEADING, PROCEDURE AND EVIDENCE

Kyd was determined to wrestle with the toughest problems which arose then from the technicalities of pleading and procedure. He wanted to present a version of the legal rules which ensured that they did not stand in the way of justice. The answer to the difficulties caused by the technicalities of pleading was to understand them, to master them, and to apply them in the cause of justice. Kyd shows himself to be such a master. With his usual clarity he states the principle which makes an award a bar to litigation[36]:

> The object of every reference to arbitrators is to have an end put, by the decision of a domestic tribunal, to all controversy respecting the subject referred.

Therefore, 'the ancient law' provided a remedy, the *breve de arbitratione facta*, a special writ of trespass on the case, which would give an action for damages to a party to an award if sued by the other on the original dispute. Kyd says that Coke recommended it but that he was wrong, because there was a cheaper and more effective remedy, to plead the award as a bar.

---

35. Kyd, *A Treatise on the Law of Awards*, 1791, pp.351–4; *Ainsley v Goff* which had been recently decided, 1799. Kyd reports it fully in an Appendix.
36. Kyd, *A Treatise on the Law of Awards*, 1791, p.381.

In Kyd's time, there was a rule that parties could not give evidence in their own cause. This supposed cornerstone of the rule of law was unsatisfactory for many reasons, in particular because parties often failed to record their transactions adequately or for other good reasons there was no sufficient evidence. Arbitrators were not bound by any such rule and were therefore able to hear the testimony of the parties and[37] 'observe their looks and demeanour ... and decide from circumstances of probability'.

Kyd's precedents are of more than usual interest because some at least are obviously taken from his own files. They are full of detail, not pared down as modern precedents are to allow those who copy from them merely to substitute their clients' names and other details. They show Kyd as arbitrator and umpire, living in the world he describes in his book. They would have been reliable too, for any practitioner who needed them.

7. CONCLUSION

By the time Stewart Kyd was practising as an arbitrator and probably as advocate before arbitrators, and writing learnedly about the subject, this method of resolving disputes was ordinary, widespread and accepted. Times were changing and older practices with them, at least as far as the law books, including reports, provide the evidence. In one recent and well reported case, the Court of Common Pleas had dealt with the problem informally[38]:

> To an action of trespass, the defendant pleaded a submission by himself and the plaintiff to the award of J.S. who ordered that the defendant should provide a couple of fowls, at his mansion-house in Old Bedlam, to be eaten by the plaintiff and his friends ... But the court thinking the matter of too ludicrous a nature to deserve a solemn decision gave no judgment, but recommended that it should be compromised.

Kyd gives plenty of examples of the courts' incompetence in dealing with the problems raised by arbitration. It was no doubt true then, as it ever is, that clever advocates could manipulate the law, and particularly the rules of pleading, to bamboozle the judges and produce conflicting judgments and dicta which they could then exploit to produce more confusion[39]:

---

37. Kyd, *A Treatise on the Law of Awards*, 1791, p.3.
38. *Purslow v Baily* 6 Modern Rep. 221; 2 Lord Raymond 1039; 1 Salkeld 76; Kyd, *A Treatise on the Law of Awards*, 1791, pp.143–4.
39. Kyd, *A Treatise on the Law of Awards*, 1791, p.29.

The reader, perhaps, anticipates the observation, that a mind unacquainted with the history of legal chicane, will hardly be able to conceive that doubt could be raised on the subject.

He does not labour these shortcomings but patiently—usually—manages to arrange, sort, analyse and explain the reports of what the courts have done to produce a systematic, coherent body of law, fit for the needs of his time, as he says in his own conclusion[40]:

[P]urified from the unintelligible jargon of technical argumentation.... established on the principles of sober reason and sound sense; a system which, were the parties submitting always certain of appealing to a judge of perfect wisdom and incorruptible integrity, would be highly beneficial to the society: but which, from the weakness and depravity of men, frequently becomes the instrument of the most flagrant injustice, and the most serious oppression.

They would do better, in most cases, to go straight to the courts. The only proper subjects for arbitration are intricate accounts, trifling matters and disputes where the evidence is uncertain. He spoke from experience. And he knew directly the shortcomings of the judiciary, not least the cruel though perhaps well-meaning conservatism of those like Lord Kenyon in his own trial and that of poor Thomas Williams—and the unspeakable Braxfield.

Kyd died in his rooms in the Temple, on January 26, 1811, aged 52.

8. AN EXCURSUS ON THE INFLUENCE OF ROMAN LAW AND PRACTICE

Stewart Kyd had had a Scots education, at school in Arbroath and at King's College, Aberdeen. There he would have been taught not only classical languages but some knowledge of Roman law. Scottish jurists have never been unwilling to acknowledge their debts to Roman learning. English scholars in the past have tended to belittle the influence of Roman on common law,[41] with notable exceptions,[42] and in particular

---

40. Kyd, *A Treatise on the Law of Awards*, 1791, pp.392–3.
41. e.g. J.H. Baker, *An Introduction to English Legal History*, 4th edn (London: Butterworths, 2002), p.28: 'The rediscovery of Justinian's *Digest*, and the consequent explosion of Roman legal studies in the universities of the twelfth and thirteenth centuries, made Roman civil law the common currency of European lawyers, including the doctors of law at Oxford and Cambridge. Early royal judges were in touch with that new learning, and may have injected some of it into the early chaos; but the effect was prophylactic and served to immunise English law against fatal infection later.' Tongue in cheek perhaps, but how seductive the Maitlandish metaphor!
42. e.g. J.L. Barton, 'Roman Law in England' (1971) *Ius Romanum Medii Aevi* V 13a 4–5:

have doubted whether Roman law has had even an indirect influence on the law and practice of arbitration in England. But now friendship and understanding have grown between legal scholars with common law and civil law backgrounds. There are many who rejoice in being bicultural. There are more comparatists, in practice as well as academia, not least under the influence of international arbitration, and fewer chauvinists. Can the influence of Roman law now be proved? Kyd himself had no doubt[43]:

> The rules which have been established with respect to awards, in the English law, in their general spirit and fundamental principles, bear such a resemblance to those which are found in the pandect and code of Justinian, that there can be little doubt that the latter are the source from whence the former sprung. By what slow gradations the greater number of them were first received into the Roman law, it is impossible now to discover, as they are given as acknowledged and long established rules at the time when the pandect and code were compiled: nor is it more easy to say, at what precise period they were adopted here, or whether they were admitted at once, or by degrees as a component part of our judicial system. In the most ancient repositories [the Year Books] of the decisions of our courts, the greater part of them are mentioned as known and uncontroverted law.

Wherever he acquired his learning, Kyd exhibits an enviable command of Roman law sources, quoting Justinian's *Digest* (which he calls the pandects) appositely at will. Does he make good his argument? To answer this question, the first step might be to state the relevant rules of Roman law which it is intended to show were incorporated into the common law. That would best be done at length, considering Kyd's treatment of each of the English rules. Simpler and more striking and within the compass of this excursus, which is hardly more than a skirmish, is a comparison of practice, in the arbitration agreements which lawyers in Rome and England drafted for their clients. Tablets from Herculaneum, preserved by the eruption of Vesuvius in AD 79, provide fragmentary evidence of *compromissa*. They are of first importance because they are not hypothetical cases nor even the opinions of jurists: they are records of actual agreements from the first century AD[44]:

'the "land-book" or written charter ... clearly modelled upon the forms ... in those parts of the continent where Roman law was still theoretically in force'.

43. Kyd, *A Treatise on the Law of Awards*, 1791, p.4.

44. Derek Roebuck and Bruno de Loynes de Fumichon, *Roman Arbitration* (Oxford: HOLO Books, 2004), pp.115–16 citing *Tabulae Herculanenses*, p.76.

In the dispute between L Cominius Primus and L Appuleius Proculus about the boundaries of the Numidian land of L Cominius Primus and the Stlasanician land of L Appuleius Proculus, as to which L Cominius Primus and L Appuleius Proculus each in turn in respect of this dispute it is to be written ... in respect of that dispute they have by stipulation and pact agreed as follows: that Ti. Crassius Firmus should be arbiter *ex compromisso* between L Cominius Primus and his heir and L Appuleius Proculus and his heir and should render his award or order his award to be rendered, openly in his presence and in the presence of each other, before the first day of February next, and may postpone that day when he renders his award or orders it to be rendered or orders it to be postponed, and if anything shall be done or fail to be done, against these agreements, 1,000 sesterces of good money shall be properly paid, fraud being absent from this matter and arbitration and to be so in the future.

The next inscription is a fragment of a penalty clause[45]:

They made a *compromissum* that they would stand by the award which he rendered or ordered to be rendered and if anyone did something or failed to do something, against these agreements, so that the arbiter written above may not render an award or order an award to be rendered or shall introduce another arbiter in this same dispute, then 1,000 sesterces of good money shall be properly paid, these shall be done as follows ... L Venidius Ennychus stipulated, L Mammius S ... promised ... in the presence ... accepted appointment in this arbitration.

These sources show that the essential elements of a *compromissum*, the standard form of submission to arbitration in the first century AD, were: details of the dispute; names of the parties; the appointment of an arbitrator; an agreement between A and his heir and B and his heir to render an award by a fixed date; a penalty clause with these elements: 'A has stipulated 1,000 sesterces of good money. B has promised the same.'

Now let us compare the English precedents. Before considering Kyd's, it is helpful to compare one provided by his forerunner Matthew Bacon in 1731 (omitting some of the surplusage)[46]:

---

45. *Tabulae Herculanenses*, p.81.
46. Bacon and Roebuck, Bacon, *The Compleat Arbitrator,* 1731, pp.48–9. It is worth remembering, as Bacon drily reminds us, that even in his day: 'Some may affect to have the Bond of Submission in Latin.' [Roebuck's introduction to the 2009 edition of Bacon's work is Chapter 14 above – SH.]

I, A.B. do owe and am indebted unto J.S. in the sum of £100 of lawful
money of Great Britain, to be paid unto the said J.S., his executors,
administrators and assigns on ...; to which payment I bind myself,
my heirs, executors and administrators. The condition of the above
obligation is that, if A.B., his heirs etc shall well and truly stand to the
award of S.G. and D.K. arbitrators made in writing on or before the—
day of—now next ensuing, then this obligation to be void.

Kyd's is much the same[47]:

I, A.B. am held and firmly bound to E.F. in the sum of £500 of good
and lawful money of Great Britain to be paid to E.F. or to his certain
attorney, executors, administrators, or assigns, for which payment I
bind myself, my heirs, executors and administrators. The condition of
this obligation is that, if A.B. his heirs etc shall well and truly stand to
the award of M.N. and P.Q. arbitrators made in writing on or before
the—day of—then this obligation be void.

Is it likely that these precedents, which so obviously are related to one
another, should be so similar to their Roman forebears unless those who
drafted them were carrying on a *practice* which had begun in Rome? It
is not necessary to show an unbroken handing-down from one lawyer or
scribe to another. It is not necessary to show that both drew on a common
unbroken teaching tradition. If the same elements are in both, that is
some evidence of relationship and possibly of influence.[48]

That evidence comes from comparing the form of the Roman
compromissum with the form of submission at common law. It may be
objected that the coincidences arise from the very nature of an arbitration
agreement, that all such agreements naturally contain the same elements
and structure. Bearing in mind that eighteen hundred years had passed
between Herculaneum and Kyd's London and that conditions of society
were different enough, let us compare all those with a modern arbitration
agreement, just 300 years later in London. The first glaring difference is
that few modern agreements deal with existing disputes. Either there has
been an arbitration clause in the agreement of which a party now alleges
breach, or litigation will ensue. But, even if we make our comparison with
a modern agreement to refer the dispute after it has arisen, the differences
are fundamental. The modern agreement has only these simple elements:

47. Kyd, *A Treatise on the Law of Awards*, 1791, p.398.
48. It is likely that similar parallels could be drawn with contemporary practice in France.
There is no room for such an enquiry here but there is an example in Derek Roebuck,
The Charitable Arbitrator: How to Mediate and Arbitrate in Louis XIV's France (Oxford:
HOLO Books, 2002), p.231.

'By this agreement A and B agree to refer the disputes set out in the schedule to the arbitration of C.' There is no sign of a bond, a condition or a penalty; no mention of heirs or assigns; no good and lawful money; just no echoes at all. It would have been possible to draft such a modern agreement in Kyd's time or even a generation or two earlier in the time of Matthew Bacon, when it was clear that: 'The Plaintiff generally declares on the Bond of Submission, in which Case he is not obliged therein to set forth the Award.' The reason why nobody did was that the bond and its penalty were then considered essential for enforcement. In his treatment of procedure and pleadings, Kyd insists that, if a party broke a promise in the *submission*, the remedy was for the penalty stipulated in the bond. Even on non-performance of the *award*, the injured party's primary remedy was still a claim for the penalty for breach of the contract of submission, not directly for damages for failure to perform the award.[49] That was the essence of the submission in London then, just as it was in Rome, but practice was changing and Kyd was well aware of the significance of the changes[50]:

> In the Roman law, the only remedy which either party could have against the other for disobedience of the award was to sue for the penalty expressed in the submission. But with us the remedy is various according to the various *forms* of the submission ... It was not but by slow degrees that it was held that the act of submission implied in itself a promise to perform the award ... Where the award ... is for the payment of money, the action on the award may be an action of debt ... It may also be an action of *assumpsit*.

When pleading and procedure had developed to accommodate it, and commercial practice had created the demand, parties and practitioners were able and obliged to produce the modern arbitration agreement.

Kyd suggests that the reasons which would justify a court in setting aside an award, for fraud, concealment, mistake and the like, were the same in Roman law as 'are the foundations of relief in our courts'.[51] That is not quite correct.[52] It was common practice to insert what was called a *clausula doli* into the *compromissum*, as was done in the last sentence of the *compromissum* from Herculaneum. The remedy then would be to sue for the penalty, and the normal *actio doli* for fraud would be excluded.

49. Compare Bacon and Roebuck, Introduction to [Bacon], *The Compleat Arbitrator*, 1731, p.238.
50. Kyd, *A Treatise on the Law of Awards*, 1791, p.276.
51. Kyd, *A Treatise on the Law of Awards*, 1791, p.359.
52. Roebuck and De Loynes de Fumichon, *Roman Arbitration*, 2004, pp.128–9.

This sketch of the problem will have served its purpose if it causes uncertainty in those who confidently assume that English arbitration law and practice have learned nothing from the civil law. A full treatment of the extent of the influence of Roman law and practice in the development of their English counterparts awaits more research. But perhaps this is enough to honour the contribution to scholarship of an unsung but admirable Scot.

16. PARTY-APPOINTED WHAT?

I wish my performance to be looked on like the bee's industry; as honey will not lose its taste, or virtue, by reflecting that the insect was only a collector, not author, of its sweetness.

Wyndham Beawes[1]

1. INTRODUCTION

In his keynote address on party-appointed arbitrators at the inauguration of the Malaysia Branch,[2] Chief Justice Sundaresh Menon graced his introduction with historical references to Ancient Greece and early 17th-century England and France. He understandably had no time for more: 'From the Renaissance we can move quickly to the nineteenth-century *Alabama Claims*'. But there is much more to be said about the practice of parties choosing their own arbitrators, and a knowledge of the practice in England from 1600 to 1800 may prevent false assumptions getting in the way of finding solutions to problems of the present day.

In 'Odds or Evens: How Many Arbitrators?'[3] I wrote, p9:

An odd number seems to us to have such obvious advantages that we take it for granted that parties would always and naturally have preferred it. Yet in England, at the latest from when a state legal system can first be seen to be well established until modern times, that has not been so. The research, which has not gone beyond 1714, has so far not shown when the change took place.

That article was concerned with the phenomenon of even numbers. This considers its significance in the history of party-appointed arbitrators. Our recent research allows us to describe developments from 1700 to 1800 and to show how the old practice died away and the modern took its place.[4]

1. *Lex Mercatoria Rediviva* London 1752 preface.
2. (2017) 83 *Arbitration* 185-202.
3. (2014) 80 *Arbitration* 8-15. [See Chapter 8 above – SH.]
4. Derek Roebuck, Francis Calvert Boorman and Rhiannon Markless *English Arbitration and Mediation in the Long Eighteenth Century* for publication 2018. [Published 2019, HOLO Books – SH.]

2. WHAT WAS ARBITRATION?

In the eighteenth century 'arbitrament' and later 'arbitration' were freely used to encompass the whole process of dispute resolution, including mediation, as the third parties strove to find a solution.

The first English monographs devoted to the law of arbitration were: Matthew Bacon *Compleat Arbitrator* (1731), Stewart Kyd *Law of Awards* (1791) and John Wilson *Short Treatise* (1792). In 1751 Wyndham Beawes published his compendium of mercantile practice *Lex Mercatoria Rediviva*. Bacon and Kyd were barristers, Wilson a country solicitor, and Beawes a merchant. All of them attempted a description of what arbitration was, rather than a scientific definition.

Matthew Bacon's was a poor effort:[5] '*Arbitrament* (*Arbitrium, Laudum, Compromissum*), or an *Award*, is the determination of two or more persons, at the request of two parties at least'. That was quite wrong. There had never been any problem with having a single arbitrator, but it shows the strength of assumptions at that time.

The solicitor John Wilson, forty-two years later, made no such mistake, p1: 'Arbitration is the order or determination of one or more person or persons, mutually chosen by parties in variance as judges to decide on the matters in controversy'.

Stewart Kyd's definition was drawn from a Civil Law source, Jean Domat.[6] Nevertheless, he must have thought that it represented English reality in 1791: 'That act by which parties refer any matter in difference between them to the decision of a third person is called a submission; the person to whom the reference is made, an arbitrator.' No room there for more than one, but Kyd recognised the difference between law and practice. Though arbitrators were not agents of those who appointed them, the common practice was still for each side to appoint one or two, whom they expected to argue their part. Nevertheless, times were changing, p75: 'It is highly improper, however common it may be, for a person nominated as an arbitrator to consider himself the agent of the person on whose behalf he was nominated'.

Surprisingly little is known of Wyndham Beawes, not even the years of his birth and death, and he has no place in the *Oxford Dictionary of National Biography*. He was listed in trade directories as a merchant in the City, with an address in Bread Street Hill from 1738 until 1740, when he moved to Token House Yard; he was still there in 1745.[7] The title page

---

5. By a Gentleman of the Middle-Temple *The Compleat Arbitrator; or the Law of Awards and Arbitraments...* London, Worrall 1731, reprinted Clark NJ, The Lawbook Exchange 2009 with new introduction by Derek Roebuck. [See Chapter 14 above, and Chapter 15, *Stewart Kyd* – SH.]
6. Jean Domat, *Les Lois Civiles dans leur Ordre Naturel* Paris, Coignard 3 vols 1689-1694.
7. He was taxed in the Broad Street Ward in 1735; LMA MS 11316 vol.108; *The Intelligencer*

of his *Lex Mercatoria Rediviva*[8] declares that he acted as British Consul in Seville and St Lucar (now Sanlucar de Barrameda in Cadiz Province); but he went bankrupt in 1748.[9]

It has fallen to Beawes to explain expressly what the primary sources show only inferentially, p341:

> It has been a custom to chuse two, one by each of the contending parties, with a liberty for them to chuse an umpire in case of disagreement, but as this method has on many occasions exposed the arbitrators to some disgusts, from those whose differences they were labouring to reconcile, it has been a practice for some time past to nominate three in the bonds, by which means their different opinions remain secret, and consequently unknown to the concerned, who are too apt to reflect ungenerously on a determination which will naturally differ from the opinion at least of one of the parties, and excite in an uncandid manner a censure, where at least their thanks are due.

The change in number must have accompanied different expectations: the parties no longer wanted their appointees to act as their advocates, at least not overtly. It is worth noting Beawes's assumption that the function of arbitrators was to 'labour to reconcile' the parties.

3. THE PRACTICE

The practice of appointing an even number had prevailed at all levels and in all kinds of dispute. The Government, through the Privy Council, had preferred an even number.[10] For example, in 1613 it had commissioned Sir Ferdinando Gorges, Governor of the fort of Plymouth and famous as an early coloniser in North America, and Sir Christopher Harris of Plympton, a town five miles from Plymouth, to resolve a dispute between Pasco Peperill and the Mayor and Commonalty of Plymouth.[11] Of course, they were not party-appointed, but the Council would allow a party to object to an appointment for sufficient reason.

The immemorial practice prevailed into the 18th century. The parties themselves, and sometimes the Government through the Privy Council,

or, Merchant's Assistant London, 1738; J. Osborn, *A Compleat Guide to All Persons Who Have Any Trade or Concerns Within the City of London, and Parts Adjacent* London, 1740; *The Universal Pocket Companion* 5th edn London, 1745. All this information comes from Dr Boorman's original research.

8. In England by this time the Latin adjective *redivivus* had come to mean 'restored to life', *Arbitration and Mediation in 17th-Century England* 25-26; as in *Arbitrium Redivivum*.

9. *The Gentleman's Magazine* 18 1748 p93.

10. JR Dasent et al eds *Acts of the Privy Council of England* New Series London, HMSO 32 vols 1890-1964 [*APC*] 34 270 (3).

11. *APC* 33.49.

and courts from the highest full court of King's Bench to the lowest individual magistrate, appointed an equal number of arbitrators. Each side would choose one or two. Together they would first try to mediate a settlement if they could. That, not adjudication, was almost always their first objective. If it failed, they would try to identify precisely what separated the parties and provide a procedure for its adjudication, appointing themselves or others to do it.

Just one or two well-documented examples must suffice as evidence of the widespread practice of using party-appointed arbitrators in all kinds of dispute. Hundreds similar will be reviewed in *Arbitration and Mediation in the Eighteenth Century*.

Private Arbitration

Thomas Turner was born in 1729. He became a general merchant and much else in the village of East Hoathly, just out of Lewes in Sussex, including parish officer and overseer of the poor. He kept a diary from 1754 to 1765, in which he recorded the menu of every meal he ate, at home or away. At least once a week he bemoaned his drunkenness. He insisted he had a light head and that just a glass or two was enough to turn it, but the details show how much he spent and the hours he devoted to tippling.

On 4 October 1759 Turner recorded that he had been appointed arbitrator in a dispute about a swarm of bees. Master Bull, with a little boy, had found the swarm on a tree in the grounds of the manor house, Halland Park. They sent a message up to the house to ask if they might take the swarm. A messenger came back to say that Samuel Gibbs the gamekeeper had given his consent. So they took the swarm. But the messenger had for some unknown reason been lying. No consent had ever been asked or given. When he found out, Gibbs put the matter in the hands of an attorney. It was agreed that the dispute be submitted to Turner, arbitrator appointed by the defendants, and John Goldsmith, clerk to the steward of the manor, appointed by Gibbs. They awarded that the defendants should each pay 2s 6d for the honey and wax, and 1s each for the lawyer's letter. Gibbs admitted that the defendants were poor and honest and had been understandably misled, but insisted on the payment. Then, having asserted his authority, he spent the money on a party for them.

Quarter Sessions

From the City of London quarter sessions comes ample evidence of the use of arbitration, for example this from Guildhall, 4 November 1732, appointing working-class arbitrators.

> The defendants being tried on an indictment at the Guildhall of the City of London on 17 October last and found guilty ..., and an action at law being likewise brought against them by the prosecutor, it was recommended by the court and agreed unto by the prosecutor and defendants that all matters in difference between them should be determined by Robert Horne, baker, and John Penkethman, bricklayer; and in case the arbitrators should not agree that then a third person should be indifferently chosen and agreed upon by them whose award should be final.

The arbitrators were to be a baker and a bricklayer. They had been chosen by the parties, with the authority of the court to end not only the civil matter but the criminal prosecution.

Middlesex Sessions

The records of the Middlesex quarter sessions often refer to magistrates making use of arbitration. An entry of 10 December 1726 preserves an affidavit of Robert Theodorick, feltmaker:

> that on Tuesday last the prosecutor William Atkins appeared to this deponent (being friend to both parties) and desired that the matter in difference might be referred to two persons in order to agree the same. Upon which this deponent obtained a reference and was himself chosen arbitrator on the defendant's behalf. And, though he and the arbitrator on the other side treated about the matter till late on Wednesday evening, yet could come to no agreement.

The parties might then incorporate their acceptance of the award in a deed:[12]

> Whereas at the instance of the parties with the consent of their counsel and solicitors the court ordered that all matters in difference between the parties ... be submitted to the determination and arbitrament of Titus Taylor, carpenter, and Thomas Long, baker.

Not only the parties there were working class but also the arbitrators.

But it was not unusual for a single arbitrator to be preferred, or an odd number. On 20 October 1784 William Gymer, arbitrator, swore that he had made an award by consent of both parties: 'seeing no sufficient cause for the commencement of this prosecution, he by his award

---

12. 12 April 1774 MSSP LMSMPS506390100.

directed that each of the parties should pay their own costs and that all matters in difference should cease'. In *John Wright v John Stickdall* it was recorded:[13] 'All matters in difference between the parties was last term by an order of the Court of King's Bench referred to the arbitration of Henry Damass of the Inner Temple Esq, who has made his award'.

An affidavit of 30 October 1789 in *R v Bush* on charges of riot and assault shows a submission to three:[14]

This deponent saith that on Wednesday 21 instant at the request of Daniel Osborn, one of the prosecutors, he went to the Black Horse in Field Gate Street Whitechapel in company with the other deponent James Turner, with Robert Bood, timber merchant, John Bassett, poulterer, and James Morrison, gentleman, as arbitrators, to settle and put an end to the above prosecutions.

Not all observers approved of submitting criminal matters to ordinary men. Edmund Burke, the Irish outsider, ever anxious to show he was even more conservative than his 'well-born' fellow Whig MPs, ranted in the House:[15]

The Justices of Middlesex were generally the scum of the earth, carpenters, brick-makers and shoe-makers, some of whom were notoriously men of such infamous characters that they were unworthy of any employ whatever; and others so ignorant that they could scarcely write their own names.

4. RELEVANCE FOR NOW

Modern attention to problems raised by party-appointed arbitrators has been in the context of international commercial arbitration (ICA).[16] The function of ICA is to provide a means of adjudicating a dispute which a party does not believe would be satisfactorily decided by a court in the jurisdiction it would otherwise fall into. Many of those involved in that process would not consider it proper for any ICA arbitrator to attempt to reconcile the parties through any form of mediation.

Parties to ICA are deemed to have chosen it freely. They need not have entered into the contract with the ICA arbitration clause if they had not

13. LMSMPS509510025.
14. LMSMPS508500119.
15. *Parliamentary History* 1780-1781 21:592.
16. There is an enormous literature, V V Veeder 'The Historical Keystone to International Arbitration: The Party-Appointed Arbitrator from Miami to Geneva' (2013) 107 *Proceedings of the American Society of International Law* 387.

wanted to. That is so, whether the contract is on an institutional form or *ad hoc*. In most cases, at least in theory, they could have bypassed ICA and chosen a process which appropriately incorporated each side's own mediators or arbitrators.

Perhaps counterintuitively then, the lesson to be learned from the centuries-long tradition, of English parties preferring a process which relied on party-appointed mediator-arbitrators, is that there is no room for them in ICA, or indeed in any quasi-judicial process.

Party-appointed arbitrators would then be left to perform their proper function, perhaps with new names taken from the cultures and languages in which they are to perform. It has been suggested that those cultural differences are determined by geography, or with even less scientific rigour, race. The reality is shown by the English experience. It is replicated wherever there are communities in which the prevailing ideology prefers disputes to be settled rather than adjudicated. Some process of mediation/arbitration will be adopted, in which the arbitrators use every means they can to produce an acceptable outcome, acceptable by the parties and the community.

Then we may all the better heed the wise words of Chief Justice Menon, p195:

> The challenge for us is to think about how best to accommodate this reality against the backdrop of the growing diversity of arbitration users and the modern commercial pressures ... so that we preserve the integrity and efficacy of the arbitration process.

Reproduced from presentation notes by Derek Roebuck (Senior Associate Research Fellow, Institute of Advanced Legal Studies, University of London), for a presentation at a Legal Records at Risk seminar held at the Centre for Socio-Legal Studies, University of Oxford, 22 February 2017.

17.   INDUCTIVE IS ALL. COMMENTS ON ARCHIVES BY A USER

1.   My work, past and future, on the history of dispute resolution, relies on archives of one sort or another. Good history depends on finding and interpreting the best evidence, primary sources rather than discussions of other historians, however distinguished.

2.   A process which included mediation and arbitration (M/A) has been generally practised in England and Wales from time immemorial. Litigation came later, with the state, as a particular alternative. There is ample evidence to show that, at least until the end of the 18th century, the state, as well as other communities, relied on M/A to deal routinely with most kinds of disputes, e.g. in the 16th century Elizabeth I's legal aid schemes, especially for widows; in the 17th Nathaniel Bacon, who accepted all kinds of referrals from the Government and the courts; in the 18th JPs' notebooks.[1]

3.   If legal history were about no more than development of law, it might be found in the law reports, as a process of constant refinement, each case building on precedent and leaving it better. That fits nicely the assumptions of social Darwinism, society evolving as species do. Whig history, even Marx, got that wrong. The evidence is against their assumption that we organise ourselves better now than they did in the past. Sometimes they did it better then – fairer, faster, cheaper, more accessible, inquisitorial and, most important, peacemaking, and with provision for the poor and women.

4.   What do legal historians have to say about developments in dispute resolution in the last four centuries? Where better to start than with Holdsworth *History of English Law* (*HEL*), still the first place even non-legal historians go to; e.g. XII p187: 'In medieval England the courts

---

1. The story is told in my *Early English Arbitration* (2008), *Mediation and Arbitration in the Middle Ages* (2013), *The Golden Age of Arbitration: Dispute Resolution under Elizabeth I* (2015), *Arbitration and Mediation in Seventeenth-Century England* (2017) and *Arbitration and Mediation in the Long Eighteenth Century* (2019).

did not look very favourably on a practice which tended to diminish their jurisdiction'. That misled non-historian Konrad Zweigert and has become gospel: 2nd edn p412: 'The Common Law has always been very suspicious of arbitration clauses'. My 'Myth of Judicial Jealousy' (1994) 10 *Arbn Intnl* 395-406 showed that to be simply wrong. *HEL* p188: 'YBB say an award could not operate as a conveyance'. True. But two pages later that has become: 'the rule that there could be no arbitration as to the title to real property'. I could produce hundreds of such arbitrations, which the parties knew would give as good a title as any. I'll explain how if we have time later. *HEL* sinks deeper into error, p189: 'as a general rule criminal cases could not be referred'. I could produce thousands. I mean that, from earliest times to the end of the 18th century. Routine, private and public M/A. The law was clear and regularly repeated in the law reports and the texts which relied on them: no award could decide who owned land. But that was not what the parties expected. It was enough that the award should resolve the dispute and require the parties to do whatever was necessary to give good title. Arbitration ordered the parties to execute whatever conveyances and quitclaims were required. Failure to abide by the award would lead to imprisonment if the award had been made an order of the court, as it commonly was. That was cheaper, faster, and more comprehensible than the artificialities of the current legal practice, based on the action of ejectment.

5.   The best example of a land dispute is from a negative exception, rather than the positive thousands. Lady Anne Clifford, born c1590, was the only surviving child of the Earl of Cumberland, who died when she was 15, leaving all his land to his brother, or so he thought. But he had only a life interest and was succeeded by his heir, Anne, who never gave up the fight to keep what was hers by Common Law, confirmed by a judgment of the Court of Common Pleas. At 19 she married the Earl of Dorset. From the start her family and her husband tried to get her to transfer her rights to her uncle. James I did all he could to force her to accept his arbitration. He browbeat her and the Archbishop of Canterbury called down the wrath of heaven. But Lady Anne Clifford – she always kept her own name – faced them down, as she did Cromwell in his turn. Every move is recorded in her diaries and a mass of other surviving documents. What a story! Unnoticed by Holdsworth or any other 'legal historian'. Even Antonia Fraser can claim that a married woman could not at Common Law own land – or even give her husband a birthday present. Tell that to little Annie Clifford who died at 86 enjoying legal ownership of most of Cumbria and half of North Yorkshire![2]

2. [See the last chapter of *Women in Disputes: A History of European Women in Mediation*

6.   History shows what has been done, not that any of it is replicable.
It can say nothing about what should be done. But if something can
be shown to have worked well in the past, lessons may be learned.
So historians must get it right, relying on the best evidence – usually
documents in archives, of which I am a fortunate and grateful consumer.

   I try to ignore the ringing jibe which Plautus has a soldier throw at
a banker – and bankers were good for a laugh even 2,200 years ago:
Plautus *Curculio* 551, *Stultior stulto fuisti si tabellis crederes*, You've
been stupider than stupid, if you intend to rely on written documents!

and Arbitration (with Susanna Hoe) 2018 HOLO Books: The Arbitration Press and The
Women's History Press. – SH]

18.   A PINCH OF REALITY: PRIVATE DISPUTE RESOLUTION IN 18TH-CENTURY ENGLAND

The honest peaceable tradesman will, as far as in him lies, prevent a
decision at law and rather bring differences to a friendly accommodation
by expostulation, by application, by arbitration.

Daniel Defoe[1]

1. INTRODUCTION

Historians have told us little about how arbitration was used in
18th-century England, yet it was everywhere, used routinely whenever
disputes arose which the parties could not settle themselves. The word
then – arbitrement was preferred in the early part of the century –
included mediation, unless the user wished to draw a distinction. The
practice certainly encompassed both methods, the arbitrators starting
with attempts to mediate and naturally moving back to them if they saw
a chance of a settlement. They were usually an even number, each party
choosing one or two.[2]

There was a practice – which, if we cared nothing for anachronism,
we might call a Government-sponsored scheme – whereby justices of the
peace regularly remitted a criminal complaint to arbitrators or mediated
a settlement themselves. That is just the most striking example of public
arbitration then.

Thanks to the efforts of Neil Kaplan, who is continuing his support of
arbitration scholarship by assisting in raising funds for research into the
18th and 19th centuries, of which more will be explained in the Envoi
[Part 6 below], a volume on the history of dispute resolution in England
between 1700 and 1815 will be published in 2018.[3]

1. Daniel Defoe *The Compleat English Tradesman in Familiar Letters* London, Rivington
1726.
2. Derek Roebuck 'Party-Appointed What?' (2017) 83 *Arbitration* 313-317. [See Chapter
16 above – SH.]
3. Any attempt to study the history of arbitration in 18th-century England must rely on

This contribution to a volume celebrating Neil's patronage of scholarship draws on that work. It is restricted to private arbitration – the ever-present and normal way in which ordinary people, men and women, chose to end their differences. It takes for its examples two merchants and a landowner, who held no public office, but gave their services freely to members of their communities, drawing on the diaries and autobiographies of the shopkeepers William Stout[4] and Thomas Turner[5] and the landowner Nicholas Blundell.[6]

2. WILLIAM STOUT

William Stout died in 1752 at the age of 87, having worked hard all his life. If you had asked one of his friends, they would have said he was a grocer, wholesale and retail, but he was much more. He had speculated in shipbuilding and trade to the Americas, usually bringing back tobacco from Virginia.

Stout was a Quaker. He determinedly practised what he believed in. He never married, but devoted himself to good works for everyone in his Lancashire community. He did so whether they liked it or not, using his wealth to control their lives, even their choice of spouse. His self-righteousness was quite unself-conscious.

Though there is no evidence that he ever acted as arbitrator himself, Stout made clear his preference for alternatives to litigation. In an entry for 1696, p46, he wrote:

At the beginning I was too credulous, and too slow in calling, and seldom made use of attorneys, except to write letters to urge payment, being always tender of oppressing poor people with law charges, but rather to lose all, or get what I could quietly, than give it to attorneys. And I never sued any to execution for debt, nor spent 20s in prosecuting

the work of James Oldham, most recently 'The Historically Shifting Sands of Reasons to Arbitrate' (2016) *Journal of Dispute Resolution* 41 and the works cited there, especially Henry Horwitz and James Oldham 'John Locke, Lord Mansfield, and Arbitration in the 18th Century (1993) 36 *Historical J* 137 and James Oldham *The Mansfield Manuscripts and the Growth of English Law in the 18th Century* Chapel Hill, U of N Carolina P 2 vols 1992. [*English Arbitration and Mediation in the Long Eighteenth Century* by Derek Roebuck, Francis Calvert Boorman and Rhiannon Markless was published by HOLO Books in 2019 – SH.]
4. J Harland ed *The Autobiography of William Stout of Lancaster, Wholesale and Retail Grocer and Ironmonger, a Member of the Society of Friends, AD 1665-1752* London, Simpkin, Marshall 1851.
5. David Vaisey ed *The Diary of Thomas Turner 1754-1765* Oxford, OUP 1984.
6. Frank Tyrer and JJ Bagley *The Great Diurnal of Nicholas Blundell of Little Crosby, Lancashire* Chester, Record Society of Lancashire and Cheshire 3 vols I 1968, II 1970, III 1972.

any debtor; and to lose all was more satisfaction to me than getting all to the great cost of my debtor, and to the preservation of my reputation.

In 1703, pp67-69, he told the story of John Hodgson – 'the greatest and most respectable merchant in my time', who thrived and became a JP, making of it a parable of dispute resolution. Hodgson had made a fortune from trade with North America and was living high, which Stout disapproved of. He employed Peter Gordin, 'an excellent good spinner, roller, and cutter of tobacco', to exploit his imports to best profit, but fell out with Gordin's executors:

> As he became pinched, he became litigious and quarrelsome with his tobacconist Peter Gordin's executors, and spent many hundreds of pounds in law with them. One particular charge was £200 for tobacco stalks, they being of no value before King William's reign, and suddenly advanced to 4d or 5d a lb. And before then Gordin had many tons of them crowded in his house, of John Hodgson's; which he desired him to take away, but he would not; but he told Peter Gordin if he pleased he might burn them, or do what he pleased with them. Upon which Gordin sold them to Henry Casson for 40s, to burn them into ashes to make soap.
>
> After they had spent much time and money in the law, they referred it to arbitrators. John Hodgson brought in £200 for tobacco stalks as aforesaid, and some other extraordinary charges, which the arbitrators would not allow, nor for the stalks more than they were sold for, so that the award was made in favour of Gordin's executors, which Hodgson would not comply with, his counsel telling him it was not drawn according to law. Upon which it came before the 12 judges in London, who were divided about it, and the major part were for confirming it; alleging that if awards should be rejected for not being drawn in due forms of law, it would much discourage arbitrations to honest country people, who best knew the merits of the cause, and the conscientious cause of the same. And upon the confirmation of the award, John Hodgson was imprisoned in Lancaster Castle, and, after some years, died.

This example inspired Stout and, for the next thirty years and more, he gave his expert services to resolving problems of insolvency, arranging many compromises which required his mediating skills. Ever ready as a creditor himself to accept less than he was owed, he could exploit his own example to persuade less Christian creditors to follow it. They trusted first his integrity, but also his expert knowledge of many trades and commodities.

3. THOMAS TURNER

Thomas Turner was born in 1729. He lived in East Hoathly, seven miles from Lewes in Sussex. In 1753 he married Peggy, who died in 1761. He kept a diary from 1754 until he married Molly Hicks in 1765. In it he recorded the menu of every meal he ate, at home or away. He was a practising Christian but quite unlike Stout the Quaker. At least once a week he bemoaned his drunkenness. He insisted he had a light head and that just a glass or two was enough to turn it, but the details show the time and money he spent on his drinking. After every drunken night he vowed he would stay sober. Yet, like many an alcoholic since, he managed to perform a prodigious amount of work and discharge a scarcely credible range of public and private responsibilities within his community.

To describe Turner as a grocer, or even a general merchant, would give no idea of the scale of his activities. He was a wholesale and retail grocer, clothier, draper, haberdasher, ironmonger, stationer, moneylender, pawnbroker, schoolmaster, undertaker and funeral director, scrivener, will drafter, trustee and executor, attorney (though not at law), surveyor and valuer, hop gauger, collector of taxes (land and window), churchwarden, parish officer, overseer of the poor, and foreman of the coroner's jury. He went to church regularly, leaving during morning service to check that there was nobody tippling in the local alehouses and that the barber was not working on the sabbath. Not of the social class to be a magistrate, nevertheless one JP was ready to take his advice on the law.

All that work left him time to play and watch plenty of cricket. And he and Peggy played a lot of cards for money, usually brag, making up the kind of formidable partnership still found today in many a village hall.

Turner tried to avoid litigation himself and even more for others, arranging many compositions with creditors, to obviate bankruptcies and debtor's prison. He made his philosophy of dispute resolution clear in his diary. From the start it records his attempts to negotiate settlements for his friends.

On 23 March 1754 he recorded that that he was helping a widow, Mary Virgoe, to collect her debts. On 9 November she told him she had received a letter threatening her with prosecution unless she paid her late husband's debts to a Mrs Edwards. On 13 February 1756 he discussed the sale of her house the next day. He was there for the auction, by candle, 'the last bidder at the expiration of the flame is the buyer', a system still used in France. There were no bids. 'Therefore to prevent it being sold for a trifle … I bid £420 for it.'

The next week, 20 February 1756, he settled a dispute arising from an intestacy. He drafted the necessary documents and attested them, Peggy and his servant-girl acting as witnesses. Drink was not his only relaxation: 'In the even read 2 books of Homer's *Odyssey* translated by Pope'.

On 3 March 1756, Ann Smith asked his advice. The story reveals much, not only of his role in his community, but of attitudes of the time to dispute resolution:

> About eight years ago she kept the house of Thomas Baker ... who, being an elderly man, and at the same time in all probability might have a feeble insurrection of an unruly member which might prompt him to make his addresses to her, as she says he did, and as he found his affection slighted, and understanding she was indebted to Mr Venner ... the sum of £2 7s 0d, and as a means, as he simply imagined, to ingratiate himself in her favour, he (as she solemnly avers), went and paid the same without her knowledge or orders; and, when he had so done, never offered to make any drawback in her wages when she left him, though she says he often told her he had paid it; and when she went away she went and asked Mr Venner whether she owed him anything and he answered: 'No!' So it is plain Baker had paid the money. But as Baker is now in low circumstances ... he has lately made a demand of the same, notwithstanding it has been near 8 years since, and (as she says) never pretended to have any demand on her before, and she has always looked upon it as a free gift. Now my advice was this: if whatever she repeated to me was true and that he actually paid it without her knowledge and designed it as a free gift ... I thought she was not obliged to pay it, only as change in circumstances and gratitude should always oblige everyone to return favours ... But if it was any ways by her orders he paid it, or she was to outset it in her wages or to make him any other gratuity and did not, I thought in justice she ought to pay him.

Then in the evening he read some more of Pope's *Odyssey*.

As churchwarden and parish overseer, Turner had a duty to ensure that his parish met the cost of maintaining only the poor who were 'settled' there. The greatest source of dispute was responsibility for unmarried mothers and their children. His first task was to get the mother to say who the father was. Then he made him promise to pay maintenance, supporting that promise by entering into a bond. If he refused, a JP would be asked for an order.

Even if all agreed that East Hoathly had to bear the cost, it was unlikely that Jeremiah French, as niggardly as he was foul-mouthed, would agree to the amount: 18d a week was far too much for Mary Vinal; 12d would be plenty. To resolve the difference, it was referred to the arbitration of George Courthope JP, 24 October 1757:

> We set out for Uckfield where we arrived about 12.40. We dined at *The Maiden Head* on some mutton chops. After dinner we laid our affair before Mr Courthope (in order to abide by his arbitration), and he adjudged that we must give security to the parish of Waldron to pay them 18d per week so long as the child shall be chargeable to Waldron or be by us otherwise provided for, and also to pay 40s, in part to pay the expenses of her lying-in.

Turner was wise in the law relevant to his duties. On 24 July 1756 he rode to Lewes to seek the advice of the local JP, William Poole. Peter Adams was the father of Ann Caine's child. He had given the parish a bond to pay 18d a week for so long as the child continued to be chargeable to the parish. When Turner demanded payment, Adams asked him to lend him the money. Kind-hearted Turner agreed. When he asked for repayment two months later, Adams told him to pay it himself. So he sought the JP's help:

> Mr Poole gave me a summons to oblige Adams to appear before him at the *White Hart* at Lewes a-Saturday next to give his reasons for not paying; and then, if he could give no reason for not paying and could not be brought to do it by the justices, we must then immediately execute the bond against him .... In the even talked to Peter Adams again, who still quibbles on but will not absolutely deny paying it.

On 29 July Turner spoke to Adams again. He saw clearly a legal problem which had escaped the JP and indeed the legal authorities until recently. The parish could not have both a bond and a JP's order. The bond invalidated the order. It was much harder to enforce, requiring a Common Law action, whereas a JP could simply commit to prison for contempt. A bond, however, had the advantage of surviving the death of the obligee, payment remaining due from his or her estate.

When Turner sought the advice of the vicar, he echoed that of Turner's fellow churchwarden and overseer, Jeremiah French, whom Turner rightly thought a coarse oaf: get a JP to commit him for breach of the order! Christopher Coates, the steward of the manor, backed them up. But Turner knew better: 'Oh, those are all vain and chimerical notions formed in the brain by ignorance! For by an Act of 6 Geo II it says if a bond is made subsequent to an order, it invalidates the same, and we must sue him at common law.' Yet they all agreed to serve the summons the next day. It required Adams to appear before the JPs in Lewes the following day. He did not, but the magistrates declared that the order was invalidated by the bond.

Adams was a feckless charmer. Turner does not say why he put up with such a man who owed him a serious debt, nor why Adams was welcomed not only socially but at vestry meetings.

The most conscientious reading of the law reports, and indeed of the legal historians, would give no hint of an aspect of commercial life at that time – the conscientious tradesman's reluctance to go to law. Turner's diary reveals the reality. Hardly a week passed without him helping someone from his community with a problem they could not manage themselves. Often he sorted out their affairs by becoming their trustee, taking in all their assets and arranging a composition with their creditors.

He hated having to use the law to enforce payment of trade debts due to himself. On 21 May 1758 his mother told him she had heard that Thomas Darby could not pay his creditors. Turner was one of them, to the tune of about £18. The next day he rode to Lewes to put his claim in the hands of an attorney, but 'oh what a confusion and tumult there is in my breast about this affair. To think what a terrible thing it is to arrest a person'. But most of the debt had been outstanding for four years and Darby had stopped buying from him, finding other sources in Lewes, and presumably running up debts there. On 24 May Turner wrote that his wife had gone to a cricket match, that it had been a 'most remarkable hot day', that he had read from Milton's *Paradise Lost*, and that he was 'very uneasy concerning Master Darby's affair, though I think there is no just room for the world nor him to complain of ill usage'. And on 27 May: 'I have been in a continual anxiety of mind all this day by expecting to hear every minute of my success in Master Darby's affair'.

On 8 June Charles Cooper, the sheriff's bailiff, arrested Darby and took him to Turner's house:

> I agreed to take a bill of sale of Master Darby's goods. They both lodged at our house all night .… A very melancholy time with me; my wife very ill and I am prodigious uneasy about Master Darby's affair for fear I should have been guilty of any harsh or inhuman usage .… But still I hope that I have done nought but what is consistent with self-preservation and the laws of equity.

On 29 August Darby's attorney gave Turner Darby's bond for £22 and a bill of sale as security. It was another three years before he could bring himself to levy distress on Darby's goods. On 6 July 1762:

Who can think the anxiety of my mind at the thought of distressing poor Darby! But what can I do? ... if I do not do it now, I am doing a piece of injustice both to myself and [my] creditors. So I am constrained by near necessity to put my bill of sale in execution. Notwithstanding which, there is something in the thought of distressing a fellow creature that my mind as it were recoils at.

Turner himself acted as arbitrator. On 4 October 1759 he recorded that he had been appointed in a dispute about a swarm of bees. Master Bull had, with a little boy from the Rich family, found a swarm on an old tree in the grounds of the manor house, Halland Park. They sent a message up to the hall to ask if they might take the swarm when the time was right. The messenger came back to say that Samuel Gibbs the gamekeeper had given his consent. So they took the swarm. But the messenger had for some unknown reason been lying. No consent had ever been asked or given. When he found out, Gibbs put the matter in the hands of an attorney. It was agreed that the dispute be submitted to Turner, arbitrator appointed by the defendants, and John Goldsmith, clerk to the steward of the manor, appointed by Gibbs.

They awarded that the defendants each pay 2s 6d for the honey and wax, and 1s each for the lawyer's letter. Gibbs admitted that the defendants were honest and had been understandably misled, but insisted on the payment, 'determined to show his power that noone for the future should dare transgress ... if they disobliged him, they must expect to know something of the charge of law'. He then spent the money awarded on a party for the losers. Turner was not happy: 'if showing of power tend only to oppress the honest and industrious poor, (as it did in the aforegoing cause), happy is the man that hath least of it'.

Turner also had success as a mediator. He settled a dispute between two of his neighbours, but it was not easy. On 7 February 1764 'Richard Prall came to Mr Banister's end of the house, he being in bed, and called him all the knaves, villains etc he could possibly think of'. Banister arose and called Prall into the street, where he gave him a good horse-whipping: 'I cannot but own Prall very justly deserved what he had a pretty sufficient dose of, but at the same time I dare say as it's a breach of the peace it will cost my neighbour Banister some money.' Two days later Turner was mediating:

All the forenoon I was endeavouring to make up the affair between Mr Banister and Mr Prall, and both of them being very headstrong, I could not prevail .... After dinner they set out for to appear before the justice in order to abide by his determination .... He seemed to think it a very great breach of the peace and told them the best way for the mutual interest of both parties was to agree it up, which they agreed upon. Accordingly we went to *The Cats*, where we made it up after three or four hours squabbling and wrangling about nothing. Mr Banister gave him a guinea and was to pay the horse hire of Prall's horse to Lewes.

Banister learned no lesson from this and Turner had to intervene again, 'in an affair to be made up', when Banister assaulted Jacob Parkes, 'which was accordingly agreed'.

Turner's experience and expertise were especially helpful in arranging compromises with creditors. He was usually able to arrange matters so that the creditors accepted his suggestions as the best they could hope for, and the debtors that, though they might have lost all else, they had kept their liberty. On 18 April 1763 he recorded that he took an inventory of the effects of John Vine 'now a prisoner in his own house for debt'. Vine would execute a bill of sale, transferring all to two or three of his principal debtors, to be distributed equally among his creditors in proportion to their debts. Two days later, on Good Friday, he walked with John French over to Vine's house to settle an account between Vine and French's wife Elizabeth. 'But it appearing a very intricate affair, we were obliged to postpone it till further consideration'. That appears to have been an attempt to settle Mrs French's debt in anticipation of the composition with creditors. On Easter Sunday morning he walked with Vine and Joseph Burgess to Lewes 'to settle Mr Vine's affairs'. The composition proceeded and Turner records going to pick Vine's hops and selling his furniture for the creditors' benefit.

Elizabeth French was also a party in another dispute, which arose out of a road accident. On Saturday 30 June 1764 she had sent a wagon to deliver wood to Turner's house:

Just at that instant of time as they was before my door, came by Mr Samuel Beckett's postchaise and 4 horses ... and in driving a great pace and together with a sufficient degree of carelessness and audacity, they, in their passing the fore-horse in the team, in order to get into the road again before the other horses, drove against him and (I presume by accident) drove the shaft of the chaise into the rectum of the horse about 9 inches and then it pierced through the gut into the body, of which wound the horse died in about 7 hours. Now, as I saw the accident, Mr French desired I would go with him to talk with Mr Beckett about it. We called at Mr Fagg's ... he being a justice of the peace, who informed him it was not justice business.

So French and Beckett agreed to arbitration, 'to appoint what he should pay for the damages etc sustained'. But there was no happy ending. On 5 September the diary records: 'the affair could not be settled, both parties being rather obstinate'.

4. NICHOLAS BLUNDELL

There was nothing of the tradesman about Nicholas Blundell (1669-1737). He was lord of the manor of Little Crosby, north of Liverpool, with other large landholdings nearby. His Catholic faith barred him from public office. He could not be appointed a JP, but the responsibilities he undertook in his communities included settling disputes in similar fashion.

Though he held to his faith at the risk of his life, and at great financial loss, he was ecumenical in his friendships and relations with his protestant parish church, with the same obsession about ownership of pews there as appears in so many diaries.

From 27 July 1702 to 20 January 1728 he kept a daily diary.[7] The entries are brief, rarely giving more than a sentence to any matter, but they are full of colour, all the more convincing for being written just for himself, with no eye to publication. Blundell wrote in a neat clear hand, with a glorious disregard for spelling. He enjoyed watching the 'Purposes' frolicking in the river on his way home from Liverpool, but worried when he got home about having to chop down his 'Populars'.

Blundell was a good squire. He manifestly cared for the wellbeing of his community. He shared their fun, joining the women celebrating Pancake Tuesday, the men in their local sports and horse-racing. What a disappointment for the reader of the diary when *Bonny Buttox* turns out to be a horse. He regularly provided health care with his own remedies or by paying for doctors.

Many of the entries relate to differences in which Blundell was a party: 'I adjusted a difference between Thomas Marrow, tailor, and me about a fence at the side of the cowhey in presence of Walter Thelwall and Richard Harrison'. He went to Liverpool on 27 January 1711 where: 'Mr Alanson and I agreed a difference that was between us relating to money owing by my father to him upon account of Mr Conley. We agreed the business before Mr Plumb in his office'.

The notes rarely extend beyond a few words, sometimes as gnomic as: 1 June 1706 'the squabble between James Gleast and me'. On 28 October 1705: 'I made complaint of James Farrer to Ralph Low' and

---

7. Craig Muldrew 'The Culture of Reconciliation: Community and the Settlement of Economic Disputes in Early Modern England' (1996) 39 *The Historical Journal* 915-942 has been the generous source for most of the references relied on here.

three days later: 'Ralph Low, James Farrer, Thomas Marrow the tailor and I met in the Townfield in order to rectify some grievances'. Edward Howard had complained to Blundell that Farrer had ploughed his land. The matter went to the manor court, where Low was foreman of the jury. The jurisdiction which Blundell had in his own court baron is shown in an entry for 7 December 1703, typically brief and unsatisfying: 'Nicholas Rilands was brought prisoner to me for debt'.

Care has to be taken with Blundell's technical vocabulary. He uses 'umpire' where one might expect 'arbitrator': '10 August 1705 I stated account with Richard Ainsworth for work done by Wm Davy and me at his house, Richard Harrison was umpire for part'. And 7 July 1707: 'Mr Scarisbrick [a lawyer and cousin] dined here; I acquainted him with my intention of making him umpire between my aunt Frances and me relating to an abatement for her annuity of £25 p.annum.' The result was recorded the next month:

> I went to Ormskirk. Cousin Scarisbrick decided at my Lord Mountgarret's the difference between my aunt Frances and me concerning what abatement she was to make out of her annuity of £25 p. annum towards the land tax and he ordered £4 p. annum to be bated by her.

Blundell does not always make clear what role he was playing; 3 February 1708 is typically short of detail: 'Mr Aldred and I decided the difference between Henry Bridge and William Davy the skinner'. That looks like an arbitration. More ambiguous is: 'I agreed some dispute relating to some trees which grew in a field being part of what H Hey has lately bought of Mather's tenement'. But it is hardly surprising that there is nowhere in the diaries any sign that Blundell was aware of, let alone troubled by, definitional problems.

What Blundell wanted was for all kinds of differences within what he considered his jurisdiction to be ended peaceably. He was eager to see any dispute settled amicably, happy to be involved in the process himself and recommending it to others: 6 March 1710: 'I discoursed Richard Jackson about the misunderstanding that is between John Hunt and John Johnson and advised him to propose agreement between them in relation to the exchange of ground about which they differ'.

5. CONCLUSIONS

The diaries of three men, none of them holding public office or with any authority other than that granted to them by their quite different communities, show with detail and colour how those communities dealt then with everyday disputes, any of which – they well knew – could have upset the peace on which all their members depended.

6. ENVOI

Neil's latest and greatest effort is the work he has done to set up a project to complete the histories of dispute resolution in England in the 18th and 19th centuries.[8] Taken up by the Institute of Advanced Legal Studies and the University of London, it has developed into something more ambitious, claiming:

> Arbitration is about peace, through the resolution of disputes. Arbitration history informs us about the evolution of the civil justice system and current government policy. Understanding the extent and importance of arbitration and mediation in past societies helps us re-examine our attitudes to legal justice. This proposed 3-year project on the *Development of Arbitration*, housed at the Institute of Advanced Legal Studies, University of London, aims to provide a secure historical foundation for the improvement of access to justice through processes other than litigation. The project forms part of the University's commitment to the principle of access and promoting law's relevance to society.
>
> This interdisciplinary project combines law and social history to provide a secure historical foundation for the improvement of access to justice through processes other than litigation.

Neil's vision, which has always been broader than arbitration's history, will now open opportunities to improve the future of access to justice, upon which any healthy society depends.

And so, for Neil's 75th birthday, it is with great affection that I hail him as the modern Maecenas of arbitration scholarship. Long may we all recognise and benefit from his great contribution to the writing of its history.

---

8. Details from Nellie.Cosmetatou@london.ac.uk. [Nellie is no longer there; instead, contact Maddy – madalenesmith@london.ac.uk. Following Derek's death, Francis Calvert Boorman and Rhiannon Markless are working on the nineteenth century under the aegis of that project – SH.]

PART TWO

PAST, PRESENT AND FUTURE

First published in (2013) 96 *Amicus Curiae* 1-3, Institute of Advanced Legal Studies, University of London. Reproduced by kind permission of the publisher.

19. THE FUTURE OF ARBITRATION

History can tell us nothing about what is going to happen in the future but, if we change the question to 'what should happen?', a historian may have something to say about what might be possible because it has been done before.

This short piece is based on a contribution to the debate at the London School of Economics on 13 February 2014 at the launch of Jan Paulsson's *The Idea of Arbitration*.[1] It starts from two assumptions. The first is 'the fact that most human beings do not have the remotest chance of obtaining decent justice from state courts' [p184] and that the proper purpose of any imaginable private alternative scheme of mediation and arbitration is to satisfy the needs of the parties. After all, if they did not want to, they would not have to use it.

The second assumption is also declared in Paulsson's book [pp193, 194]:

> Looking backwards and sideways at other human civilizations, it seems more useful to ask how communities have sought to achieve social order, and to test models by reference to reality, rather than reject reality because it does not correspond to our *idées fixes*.

In the search for the machinery of the future, we cannot let the concepts limit the technology. So if, Paulsson p21, 'the imaginative use by parties of procedures which borrow variously from arbitration, mediation and indeed courts ... leads to *conceptual* confusion', *tant pis*! we say to the *philosophes*.

So what do we want a private scheme of alternative dispute resolution to do? On what principles should it be based? The first is that whatever we invent should not harm the common good; the second that the outcome should be accepted by both sides; then efficiency and honesty; reasonable

1. Jan Paulsson *The Idea of Arbitration* Oxford, Oxford University Press 2013. [The occasion was not just a launch, but a debate in which Jan Paulsson and eight other scholars, including Derek Roebuck, took part. I suspect that the fuller, more colourful version of this article, that Derek saved on a memory stick on 6 February 2014, is the one he used in the debate. An audio version of the three-hour debate, which was divided into sections, can be followed on the internet (I have only listened to the first few minutes) – SH.]

speed; and, if it is to have any ethical credibility at all, affordability, even to the poor.

Is it hopelessly Utopian to try to assemble a machine which can provide such outcomes? Can we really hope that the State might offer such a boon? Should we plan for someone else to do it?

We need to consider every kind of process. We know about mediation. The experts say that it should be facilitative, the mediators refraining from suggesting solutions. We shall not take that for granted. If mediation fails and arbitration becomes necessary, we must have different arbitrators. We need to look at the validity of that assumption, too. Moreover, the arbitrators should not be nominated by the parties, for then they would take sides. Is that a problem?

What if there were a model from our own past, which lasted with general approval for over fifty years?

I am working now on mediation and arbitration in the reign of Elizabeth I (1558-1603).[2] From the start she put the responsibilities of government into the hands of her Privy Council, which often sat within walking distance from here. They were members of the nobility (the ones you see prancing about in doublet and hose on television), with others she hoped she could trust, including the judges.

Let's see how that Privy Council's performance measures up to the demands we would make of our preferred system. Then we can ask: if they could do it, why can't we?

Accessibility? The Council sat most days, including Sundays, Good Friday (with the Archbishop of Canterbury in attendance) and sometimes Christmas Day, even once when it fell on a Sunday. It kept an office open even on those days when it did not sit. It dealt with every kind of business, from disputes over title to land to issuing individual passports, while coping with foreign wars, invasion, plague and piracy, not to say Ireland.

Hundreds of petitions were presented every year. More than 20,000 are reported in the *Acts of the Privy Council*.[3] The Council did a lot of mediating and arbitrating itself, but had to commission others to cope with its workload. It had total authority, overriding all other courts, regularly staying proceedings there. The Council did not follow any bureaucratic forms. Each response was tailor-made.

Anyone could present a petition, foreigners and English alike, from the highest, including members of the Council themselves, to the lowest.

2. *Mediation and Arbitration Under Elizabeth I* for publication 2015. [Published by HOLO Books in 2019 as *The Golden Age of Arbitration*. See also Chapter 11 above, 'The Centre for International Mediation and Arbitration in the Reign of Elizabeth I' – SH.]

3. JR Dasent (ed) *The Acts of the Privy Council* London, HMSO 32 vols 1890-1907.

Women were often petitioners and respondents in their own right. The Council expressly showed greater concern for them, with particular care for the poor and widows. Often it was responding to specific instructions from the Queen herself to give special assistance to women in need.

The genuineness of its concern for those who needed special treatment is shown by an entry for 5 April 1579. It arranged an arbitration in a land dispute between Richard Justice and William White:

> White seems to be a very simple person, and so deserves to be pitied; in case it shall be adjudged that the right in the land in controversy appertains to him, then ... their Lordships ... would advise among themselves of some means how the same may be assured to him and his right heirs, without leaving him any power to convey away to any person other than by lease for 21 years, as tenant in tail, but to remain to himself and his heirs.

In another matter, the Dean of St Paul's was asked to help Richard Brotherton, who seemed to be 'distempered in his wits':

> Their Lordships think meet to refer him to the Dean to consider if either by counsel or physic he may be reduced to order, or otherwise bestowed with some of his friends who may take such care of him as is convenient for a man in his case; in which their Lordships offer assistance as cause shall require.

In other words, 'Please let us know if we can be of any further assistance, if the counselling and drugs don't work'.

No claim was too small. A bricklayer and a plumber had done some work for the Earl of Lincoln and complained when he did not pay them. The Council asked him nicely but:

> if there shall be any difference between them in their account, their Lordships think meet that two be appointed to judge the same, whereof the one to be appointed by his Lordship and the other for the poor men by the Council.

The Council was not imposing its choice of arbitrator; just making sure the tradesmen had a proper counterweight to the Earl's.

I cannot stress too firmly that these records are evidence of government *action*. They were spoken and recorded for those they instructed to act, not for public propaganda.

For more than a century government policy had encouraged trade and accommodated the expectations of merchants, English and foreign, who usually preferred the law merchant to the Common Law. They also preferred mediation and arbitration by their own kind, which the Council was happy to arrange. It would deal with a dispute between foreign merchants about a matter with no connection with England at all, if that would dispose of the matter fairly and promptly; but it would refer it to a foreign power if that were more appropriate. On 21 August 1571 it wrote to the Lord Mayor of London, saying that on second thoughts a dispute between members of the Fortuni family of Florence, previously committed to 'certain persons, as well English as strangers ... did belong rather to the Duke of Florence, unto whom they are subjects'.

On a cold Sunday morning at the end of November 1586, eleven members sat in Richmond, William Cecil, Lord Burghley, in the chair. They commissioned the Admiralty judge and four Doctors of Civil Law to hear the petition of Peter Fryer, 'a merchant of Portugal'. His ship had been taken 'under colour of letters of reprisal'. When he started an action in King's Bench, he was told that the proper forum was the Admiralty Court; but the Council had a better idea: it appointed arbitrators 'to avoid expense of charges and loss of time by following the ... ordinary course of the law'.

Such a state-provided arbitration scheme could not have worked in isolation. It flourished in an environment where mediation-arbitration was the preferred machinery. There are hundreds of private arbitration documents recording the routine practices and preferences of the time.

What were all these arbitrators doing?

Typically, each party nominated one or two arbitrators, as they always called them, who would meet to resolve the dispute. They had no easy means of communication other than face-to-face. They were expected to do the best they could for their party. But that required them to confront the reality that they had better settle for what they could get. All being well they could agree on the size of the pot to be divided. Then nothing more subtle than half each would be better than tossing up. If they realised that something more refined was needed, they should at least be able to agree on the arbitrators. Equal numbers from each side. They often included themselves, recognising that their acquired knowledge of the facts and the stances of the parties, and the trust created by their familiarity with one another, outweighed the fear that their knowledge of the other side's case would mean that – Heaven forbid! – the merits would come out.

And that is exactly what Elizabeth I's Government insisted on. They could not have made it plainer. They did not want a 'legal' resolution, which depended on lawyers' niceties. The Council did not yet have available to it our phrase 'on the merits'. That expression does not appear in English writings until 1621. But these are some of the terms they used, following no standard formula, when instructing arbitrators to decide: most commonly according to 'justice and equity' or 'justice and conscience' or 'good conscience' or 'according to equity and (good) conscience'; or 'equity and justice according to right'; or 'equity and reason'; or 'equity and your consciences'; or just 'according to equity'; or simply 'as right requireth'; or 'according to right'; or even to 'make such order as they think reasonable'; or 'with reason and indifferency' where it was just a question of dividing up an estate; or 'to the reasonable satisfaction of the suppliant' in a mercantile dispute; or, in a dispute between a parson and his patron, 'to make some conscionable end'.

Perhaps the least restrictive words were its request to Sir Rowland Heyward, MP and twice Lord Mayor, and the Recorder of London, to respond to a complaint from one of the Pages of Her Majesty's Chamber of injuries committed by a Proctor, by taking such order 'as they shall think meet for the policy of the city'.

Let us compare what was offered then to what we can manage today. What chance has the poor widow? What chance has anybody of a resolution on the merits? What does the rule of law ensure? We need the rule of law. It was hard won and we can see what happens in countries where it cannot be relied on – more than half the world not at all, and for the rest not always if it does not suit the Government. But it works in practice for most of us here, most of the time. Even when it doesn't, we need it as a communal aspiration, a basic foundation for our cooperation as a community. And sometimes as a stick with which to beat the Government. But it is a means to an end.

What end? Surely one which complies with our moral imperative. And what is that? Order? Yes, without a dependable structure society will fall apart. But for what purpose? The ethical demand is fairness – fairness for all. If Elizabeth I could insist on disputes being resolved on the merits, providing a universal scheme to do it, apparently without too much fuss or cost, why can't we?

20. TIME TO THINK: UNDERSTANDING DISPUTE MANAGEMENT

Derek Roebuck

'Well, Sir Anthony, since you desire it, we will not anticipate the past, so come, young people, our retrospection will now be all to the future'.

Mrs Malaprop in Sheridan *The Rivals*

INTRODUCTION

Who better than Mrs Malaprop to introduce this lecture? All my research on the management of disputes has been about the past but ten years' experience of editing our journal has meant I have read and discussed, with their authors and peer reviewers, such a wealth of thinking about contemporary problems that I am emboldened to offer some thoughts about the future. I hope thereby to set off a chain of lectures that will concentrate our minds, once a year, on where our research might be directed.

Scientists—scholars of all disciplines—are rarely unanimous about anything but they seem to agree that, in all research, it is the question you ask that matters. I have asked myself: 'How can we understand dispute management better and use that understanding in our work?' Having long since retired from practice and now from editing the journal, I have time to think about what we are all up to in our efforts to resolve disputes, to improve the processes and to pass on our skills and understanding to others.

Negotiated settlement is the first and most natural response to most differences and can dispose of them before they become disputes. Recently my hearing aids developed faults. They were out of guarantee. The customer service department agreed that we should not let our difference develop into a dispute. I was offered either a newer better model or three-quarters of my money back. I chose the former and I can hear your mutterings at the back. If a supplier has a contract with a purchaser, by which it has undertaken to supply parts for the purchaser's best-selling machine for three years, and after one year a competitor takes the market, the parties may agree to modify their contractual obligations to require the supplier to make parts for the purchaser's new model, at a different price.

As far as I can discover, such settlements have always and everywhere been normal and natural. They leave few records but I expect you would agree that the great majority of differences end like that. When that happy outcome is not possible, the parties may call in a third party. Again, in all times and places I have studied, the first and most natural step is for that third party to try to mediate. In many places, that has been the first response of arbitrators and even judges. The concern of mediators everywhere at all times is to bring about a resolution which both parties accept. When an authoritative voice is raised, then, which warns against the unquestioning popularity of mediation, it should concern us.

WHAT IS THE NORM?

Every word of the Master of the Rolls' recent Bentham Lecture[1] deserves careful study. The only bit that caught the attention of the *Law Society Gazette*[2] was what it called his warning 'against mediation being used as a replacement for the courts'. The media will ensure, if they can, that differences of opinion about the proper role of mediation will blossom into a dispute. I recognise the dangers of unsolicited interference, but offer to mediate by showing that a better understanding of the role of mediation will reduce the scope of the burgeoning differences and transform them into a healthy debate on the essential points.

First, let us look at what Lord Neuberger said. His concern was to establish the crucial importance of the courts in protecting those rights which are essential to civil society—and access of all to the courts:[3]

> In our modern consumer, market-based society, with its multiplicity of laws and rights, and its increasing scope for legal disputes, it is more important than ever that we have effective, accessible institutions of law. If not, laws go unenforced. They cease to be rights, but rather become privileges for those select few who can afford them ... the irreducible cost of a genuinely accessible and truly effective legal system has to be paid if we wish to remain a civil society.

---

1. 'Swindlers (Including the Master of the Rolls?) not Wanted: Bentham and Justice Reform' delivered at University College, London, March 2, 2011 (hereafter 'Swindlers not Wanted').
2. March 10, 2011 p.4.
3. 'Swindlers not Wanted' pp.7–8 paras 16 and 18.

The first three-quarters of Lord Neuberger's lecture are a carefully crafted argument for a better system of legal aid. Those of us who have watched his career with close attention are relieved that the responsibility for civil justice has passed to him from Lord Bingham. I have never shirked the responsibility a law professor has to criticise our judges,[4] but they now need all our support in their mighty battles against those in power who espouse an ideology of short-term expediency over all other principles.

Having established the case for equal access to justice without financial barriers, including a wicked suggestion that legal aid might be financed by fines on those wealthy parties which abuse the processes of litigation, at the very end of his lecture Lord Neuberger says:[5]

> The development of mediation as a means to resolve disputes amicably has been, and will continue to be important and valuable. But, and this is a big but, ... those alternative mechanisms cannot be the norm, or approach the norm ... in some cases facilitating a mediated settlement will be the right thing to do. But, ultimately, our civil society is not based on a commitment to utility. It is based on the rule of law.

I would like to circumscribe the debate by removing one element, which arises from the ambiguity in the word 'norm'. *Norma* in Latin is a set square. You use it to check right angles. Legislation and the courts develop law which provides norms in that sense. Mediation can play no part in that. The outcome of a successful mediation is a settlement. Norms cannot be established by private contract. Moreover, to establish norms decisions must be regularly recorded and published.[6]   But   the word 'norm' has another sense in English. It can mean 'what is usual'. The *OED* gives that meaning first: 'what is expected or regarded as normal; customary behaviour'. I can show you that mediation is and always has been just that—and, indeed, in most societies more the 'norm' than litigation, which it predates. Though mediation can never provide a legal 'norm', I hope to persuade you that mediation is more normal than litigation.

Ordinary people do not choose to litigate. They cannot afford it. Even those with wealth and privilege have often preferred mediation. In an

---

4. 'The Diplock Report on Mercenaries' *New Statesman* August 13, 1976 reprinted with introduction in Derek Roebuck *Disputes and Differences: Comparisons in Law, Language and History* (Oxford: HOLO Books: The Arbitration Press, 2010) (hereafter *Disputes and Differences*) pp.79–83.
5. Paragraph 41 out of 50 excluding 3 of conclusions.
6. In our society but not all, cf. Confucius's preference for the law to be unknown.

article in *Arbitration* four years ago,[7] 'The Myth of Modern Mediation', I hoped to scotch the myth that mediation was a modern technique. I failed. For example, the foreword to the CIArb's recent useful booklet *What is Alternative Dispute Resolution (ADR)?*[8] says:

> Beginning in the late 20th century ... powerful societal forces ... began to challenge the notion that courts could or even should be the primary forum for dispute resolution.

Nothing began in the last century, except new forms of dispute resolution crafted to deal with the shortcomings of litigation in the United States.[9]

My article remains unchallenged and I know that you not only read every word of the journal but retain the arguments, so I won't repeat them now. I will just add some new examples.

In the first years of the second century AD, the legal system in Rome provided a simple and cheap process for dealing with civil claims; but Pliny the Younger complained of being beset by the disputes of his tenant farmers.[10] More than seventeen centuries later, Francis Place, the farm labourer who started the first agricultural workers' union in England and became a Liberal MP, expressed the same sentiments:[11]

> I had many matters brought to me for adjudication, arbitration or arrangement. I hardly know the time when for three months together I have been free from this kind of interference.

In the fourteenth century, Geoffrey Chaucer, man of many parts—diplomat, royal adviser, linguist, poet—used the words 'arbitration' and 'mediation' for the first time in surviving literature. I cannot for the life of me work out why, when it was his turn to tell a story in his *Canterbury Tales*, he chose to switch from verse to prose and produce twenty pages of such aching boredom that Neville Coghill felt justified in leaving it out of his Penguin translation. But it is lucky for us that Chaucer did

---

7. (2007) 73 *Arbitration* 105–16; reprinted in *Disputes and Differences* pp.394–406.
8. (London: Chartered Institute of Arbitrators, 2010) p.ix.
9. Even there, informal mediation has a longer history, though it seems, with arbitration, to have fallen into disuse and 'discord and dispute ... were complacently accepted phenomena, to be settled by force or litigation': Frances Kellor *American Arbitration: Its History, Functions and Achievements* (New York: Harper, 1948) pp.5–6. That was not the way of the native American, whose culture of mediation has given us the word 'caucus'.
10. Derek Roebuck *Early English Arbitration* (Oxford: HOLO Books: The Arbitration Press, 2008) pp.56–57.
11. J.A. Jaffe 'Industrial Arbitration, Equity, and Authority in England, 1800–1850' (2000) 18 *Law and History R.* 1.

tell the tale of Melibeus, whose wife Prudence conducted a mediation after the fashion of the time. We can follow every step, as she produces a settlement between her husband and his adversaries, who had broken in, beaten her and wounded their daughter. She caucuses with the parties separately. She even uses the trick which nobody would dream of using now: she lets each side think she has a soft spot for them.[12]

In the civil strife of the next century, mediation was the preferred method of resolving even the most bloody disputes. The courts were there, including Parliament, but they preferred to delegate their powers to mediators and arbitrators to find a solution which would stick because it relied not on any legal rules but on a distribution of value which both sides could accept.[13]

For example, when the rules relating to the barring of entails had yet to be established, there were many family disputes over land, which could last for generations. Landowners wanted to ensure that their lands, often spread widely around the country, would stay in the family when they died. So they created a form of ownership, the fee tail, which required the land to pass to their offspring, generation after generation, usually by male primogeniture, with some provision for females and others. The next generation might not see it that way. All the courts could do was come down on one side or the other—would the entail hold or had it been legally barred? A mediation, however, with arbitration if necessary, could produce a much better solution. Why not group landholdings together geographically, then distribute them according to what the parties could be persuaded was fair, with cash payments to take care of any remaining inequalities? That was then the norm.[14]

We need not restrict ourselves to the past or to England. In the special issue of the journal on mediation, Sarah Rainsford, the BBC correspondent, described the work of a professional mediator in today's Turkey:[15]

The sofas in Sait's office were filled with men, seeking his mediation … Sait is shuttling between the two families, attempting to negotiate

---

12. L.D. Benson (ed.) *The Riverside Chaucer* 3rd edn (Oxford: OUP, 1988) pp.236–39, particularly lines 1706ff and 1755ff.
13. Norman Davis (ed.) *Paston Letters and Papers of the Fifteenth Century* Parts I and II, 2 vols (Oxford: Clarendon Press, 1971–), reprinted with corrections 2004; Richard Beadle and Colin Richmond (eds) Pt III (Oxford: OUP for Early English Text Society, 2005). The 1051 documents tell many stories in detail.
14. A good example is described in S.J. Payling 'Arbitration, Perpetual Entails and Collateral Warranties in Late Medieval England: A Case Study' (1992) 13 *J. Legal History* 32–62.
15. Sarah Rainsford 'The Turkish Peacemaker' (2007) 73 *Arbitration* 100–104.

conditions for peace. Instead of the blood maybe some money, maybe a formal apology—maybe both.

In modern Ethiopia, a woman mediator practised regularly and successfully in all kinds of disputes, over land, fighting and matrimonial quarrels:[16]

> The first morning I spent in Chimate's household, people waited for her and served up their disputes with the first coffee of the day. Men and women stopped her as she walked the paths of Dita and sought her in the marketplace.

I hope someone told her of the first of her predecessors, Arete, in Homer's *Odyssey:*[17]

> The people think she is divine and greet her as she goes through the city, because she has plenty of decent common sense and, if she feels like it, she resolves their disputes—yes, those of the men as well.

In a recent *Observer*, Mariella Frostrup told of present-day reality:[18]

> Men with guns are littering Ivory Coast with corpses while my female companions in P.A's Ribhouse in downtown Monrovia outline inspired, achievable solutions to ending that conflict. In the same gentle voices that cajoled Liberia's bloodstained dictator Charles Taylor into resigning his presidency ... they explain their plans ...
>
> It wasn't the African Union or the UN but Liberian women who brought the warring sides to the peace talks and subsequently, on the back of that success, have played a major part in conflict resolution in Sierra Leone, Sudan and Rwanda ... when it comes to encouraging and facilitating peace they have unique skills.

Not only can I show that mediation is normal. I can show that litigation is abnormal, a pathological aberration in most cultures. In some it produces some of the norms but it is not the process that most people with a difference want or need to submit it to. Let us then agree to drop abnormality as an argument against mediation.

16. Judith Olmstead *Woman Between Two Worlds: Portrait of an Ethiopian Rural Leader* (Urbana: University of Illinois Press, 1997), with photographs between pp.108 and 109 of a mediation as it took place.
17. Homer *Odyssey* 7.69–74.
18. 'Let Women Lead the Way to Peace in Africa' *Observer*, April 10, 2011 p.38. [There is a longer quotation from this in Chapter 24 below – SH.]

MEDIATION AS A THREAT TO LEGAL DEVELOPMENT

From his justified and laudable insistence that access to the courts is a fundamental right, Lord Neuberger continues:[19]

> If there is no effective access to the courts, the fundamental underpinning to all forms of dispute resolution ... falls away. The only reason the strong and rich will negotiate, arbitrate or mediate with their weaker and poorer opponents is the knowledge that ultimately there is the authority and power of the justice system standing behind the arbitration and mediation systems. Furthermore, unless there is a healthy justice system, with judges developing the law to keep pace with the ever accelerating changes in social, commercial, communicative, technological, scientific and political trends, neither citizens nor lawyers will know what the law is.

There are two points there. First, if parties in the wrong refuse to mediate, the only way in which parties *in the right* can get what they deserve is to go to court. Secondly, to get the law we need, the courts must have enough cases in which to develop it. It would be wise to make some preliminary concessions to both these arguments.

Of course, there is no way a recalcitrant party can be compelled to make a mediated settlement. It is different in some other cultures even today but in ours you can't force anyone to settle. You can require them to try and nobody argues for any more than that. A determined refusal to mediate should not inhibit a party's right to litigate, though there is no reason, if that stubbornness is an abuse of the legal process, why it should not prove costly. So, let's restrict the debate to the merits of *making an attempt* at mediation compulsory.

We have been talking about 'the party in the right'. Does that mean the party with the better law or the one with the merits?

MERITS AND LAW

All my legal life I have been reminded of the gulf between legal rights and merits. As a lad, just starting my articles, I prepared the brief for Hartley Shawcross in a claim against our client John Summers, the steelworks. We were pouring cyanide into the Dee estuary, which upset the salmon, who were determined to make their way up the river to die in the traditional way on the hooks of the owners of riparian fishing rights. In 1958 Shawcross was the Garfield Sobers of the Bar, so quick and brilliant that I found it hard even to follow what he was doing. On the

19. 'Swindlers not Wanted' para.43.

other side was Charles Russell, appearing to move more at my speed. I could not imagine a more overwhelming case than that which Shawcross presented. Russell hardly raised a point. He just left it to the scientific experts to establish the cyanide spill and to the judge to find the law he wanted. We lost, of course. We never had a chance of persuading the judge that the law should override the merits. Perhaps he liked to do a bit of fishing himself.

Fifty years of experience have taught me that judges are suckers for merits. I have still to come across one who enjoys deciding a case on unmeritorious law. But the John Summers case was unusual. There the merits were plain for all to see. In few of the international commercial disputes I have been involved in since have any merits been discernible, let alone arguable. In my little world of negotiable instruments, it was usually a question of whether a company, which had made a written promise to pay and taken value for it, could wriggle out of liability for what now looked like an inflated price. And it is funny that faults in goods supplied only appear when the market falls. So one should be slow to assume that legal rights necessarily represent some genuine value. As Lord Justice Sedley has written, 'precedent provides off-the-shelf solutions where merits don't, simply because most litigation is barren of self-evident merit on either side'.[20]

The antithesis between a mediated settlement and a decision on legal rights is not a simple one of greater and less justice. To go back to the Middle Ages, were the distributions of mediator-arbitrators on contested entails more or less just than the corresponding decisions of the courts? To bring us up to date, does the present law on frustration of contracts produce as fair a result in charterparty cases as a properly mediated settlement could do? To quote Stephen Sedley's next sentence: 'I thought at one time of suggesting to Lord Woolf that his procedural reforms might include a power in really tedious cases to declare a draw.' Or quite firmly suggest mediation?

LITIGATION AND DEVELOPMENT OF LAW

The second point is that we must have litigation for the law to develop.

The problem is not the same the whole world over. There are more than a billion people in China and in India. Not one in a thousand could even think of litigation. Even here in England, very few people with claims have access to the courts, at least not those where judges make new law.

20. Stephen Sedley *Ashes and Sparks: Essays on Law and Justice* (Cambridge: CUP, 2011) p.203.

The threshold for the High Court will soon be £100,000.[21] That should make sure it is the law of the wealthy which is developed.

Is there evidence that alternative forms of dispute management are reducing the flow of litigation to the level where the development of new law is endangered? That is a suitable research topic.

If parties want to settle, they will, with or without mediators. Can we think of a suitable deterrent? It will have to apply to arbitration as well.[22]

An older problem arises from the very nature of our legal system. Think how long Lord Denning had to wait for an opportunity to 'develop the law' on a promise of partial performance as consideration.[23] During the decades when all lawyers knew the law was unsatisfactory, before the modern mediation machine was assembled, we advised clients to settle. We did not suggest an expensive and chancy trip all the way to the House of Lords so that the law might be improved for others. And how often have you been involved in a case where the parties had no notion, when they first disagreed, of the point of law that was later litigated? Litigators trim the problem to fit the law. Mediators don't need to; they can keep hold of the reality.

Of course, mediators need to know what the law is. Even if all disputes could be mediated, we would still need a refined and up-to-date set of legal principles to guide settlements. The law may even be a determining factor in the settlement. But it need not be; other factors may prevail. I believe they will increasingly do so. So we may need to find other ways of developing it. Some jurisdictions have effective law reform commissions. Jurisdictions outside the Common Law seem to manage without a doctrine of precedent.

ONLINE DISPUTE RESOLUTION

Meanwhile, other developments threaten the whole system, for example online dispute resolution (ODR). There are more than a million eBay transactions a day: 'eBay today resolves through ODR about sixty million disputes per year'. In total, ODR may already be resolving billions of disputes a year. Fewer than one in a million end in litigation. What law applies to those that are settled? Effectively none! All the eBay settlements are determined by eBay's policy. Surely the courts are needed to enforce settlements? Not at all! The sanction on the less than 2 per cent who do not comply consists in the negative 'reputation points' that attach to each user's profile.

21. *Law Society Gazette* March 31, 2011 p.2.
22. From which no precedents can flow. ICSID is a world unto itself.
23. *Central London Property Trust v High Trees House* [1947] 1 KB 130.

My source Thomas Schultz must be allowed his own words:[24]

Square Trade used to offer mainly two dispute resolution processes: computer-assisted negotiation and on-line mediation. Both processes relied heavily on on-line forms produced by Square Trade's system. These forms suggested typical issues that the parties may have, thereby helping them identify and understand their issue, and then recommended typical settlement agreements that statistically were likely to be accepted in the situation described by the parties. It was based on a simple form of artificial intelligence, called an expert system, that learned from prior cases to try to predict what the parties' issues and agreeable solutions were likely to be. The aggregated understandings of the rights and obligations of users were thus reflected in the issues and solutions suggested by the computer. These suggested solutions framed, informally but effectively, the realm of likely outcomes for any given case. The outcomes of prior cases were brought to bear on subsequent cases; they acquired a de facto precedential value, which was soft and relatively diffuse but nonetheless effectively improving predictability by setting guideposts. The expert system's purpose was to bring the dispute resolution system closer to the pursuit of the rule of law.

Rule of law? Our law is found in precedent. Precedent is about legal rules, not the accumulation of decisions on similar facts. Schultz presents a challenge to all of us to think what this means– a billion disputes settled every year by a computer program that doesn't think about the consequences on the rule of law. Once the program is written, with its built-in cybernetic self-corrections, won't errors reduplicate and 'injustice' proliferate? Will eBay's policies, which provide the underlying law, prefer consumers, with one-off interests, to suppliers with their repeated custom? How can we know? And what about Amazon—and Chinese virtual banks using their own virtual international currency?

How long before multinationals decide that this is the cheapest and most predictable way to resolve their *big* disputes? Won't it be easier to persuade your directors and shareholders that you were right to settle by shared algorithm rather than risky and costly litigation?

24. Thomas Schultz 'The Roles of Dispute Settlement and ADR' in Arnold Ingen-Housz *ADR in Business: Practice and Issues Across Countries and Cultures* Vol.II (New York: Wolters Kluwer, 2011 (hereafter *ADR in Business*) pp.135–56. [This example is also used in Chapter 24 below – SH.]

COOPERATION AND PARTNERING

The big companies and the influential professional institutions have already left the lawyers behind. Recognising the costs and other drawbacks of fighting legal battles and the advantages of providing in their original contracts for cooperation in managing differences, they have begun to prefer partnering contracts which require them not only to act in good faith but to cooperate in maximising profit for both sides.[25]

Good corporate governance now suggests mediation. There is evidence that the companies which use ADR most adroitly have the best price/earnings ratio. The ambition to increase value, rather than get the bigger share of a fixed pie, now motivates many top managers, whatever their legal advisers tell them. Do professional ethics already require lawyers to recommend mediation?

Modern contracts increasingly include stepped clauses to deal with disputes. They require the parties first to make serious efforts to resolve differences by negotiation; if that does not work, then to try mediation and only if that fails to go to arbitration. No litigation. They may require parties to act in good faith. How far does that go? Almost all jurisdictions other than those which stick close to the English version of the Common Law require the parties to act in good faith in making and performing their contracts. In England we have come to do so in different ways, mainly through implied terms. Judges do not enjoy encouraging bad faith, however cautious they are about introducing broad principles.

There is nothing airy-fairy about this. Experience has taught me that builders have hard heads. Yet this is what their modern contracts provide:[26]

Under the JCT Non-Binding Partnering Charter the parties agree to act in good faith; in an open and trusting manner; in a co-operative way; in a way to avoid disputes by adopting a 'no blame' culture; fairly towards each other; and valuing the skills and respecting the responsibilities of each other. In the ACA Standard Form of Contract

---

25. There is a growing literature: e.g. most of *ADR in Business* and Stephen Furst 'Dispute Avoidance—Good Faith/Partnering/Cooperation Clauses in Contracts' (talk to CIArb East Asia Branch, Hong Kong, October 7, 2010); p.2 of the latter cites the JCT Constructing Excellence Contract 2007 2.1.

26. Nerys Jefford '"Soft Obligations" in Construction Law: Duties of Good Faith and Co-operation' available at http://keatingchambers.co.uk/resources/publications/2005/nj_soft_obligations_construction_law.aspx [accessed May 4, 2011]. I am grateful to Lorena Carvajal, PhD candidate at Portsmouth University, for this reference and for other fresh ideas on good faith. Stephen Furst 'Dispute Avoidance' p.2 cites the JCT Constructing Excellence Contract 2007 2.1, an even more ambitious attempt to provide for cooperation.

for Project Partnering PPC 2000, the parties agree to work together and individually in the spirit of trust, fairness and mutual co-operation.

So we are used to good faith in making and performing. What about a general duty to resolve disputes in good faith? Will that include willingness to mediate?

Two developments of recent years have changed attitudes. Negotiators have always known that it is pointless to deal with anyone who has no authority to settle. Mediators realise they have a greater chance of success if they bypass the lawyers and talk to those concerned with the realities of the dispute. So they now regularly expect to talk to someone near the top.

Moreover, we may wonder what the world has come to when the boss of an airline moves to head a retail chain, then to a bank and at last to advise the Government on the media. Such mobility — unthinkable when experience within an industry was a condition of advancement and there were industries worthy of the name — permeates big business now. Think of those a rung or two below. As they negotiate, they cannot be unaware of potential openings for employment with the other party. *La Ronde* comes to mind.

THE FUTURE: A CALL TO ACTION

So what can be said about the future? That will be largely in the hands of our successors. As the people change at the top of our professions, the world views of younger generations will displace ours. It will be their dreams and plans which matter, which they will construct from their own experience. And new problems produce new solutions, as the collapse of Lehman Brothers produced the Hong Kong Scheme.[27] But there are things we can all do and that leaves us with immediate responsibilities.

I am not offering answers. I do not even know what the questions are, other than those I have raised today. They are:

1. How can we ensure the proper development of the law?
2. What is the jurisprudential significance of ODR?
3. Should there be a duty of good faith in resolving a dispute?

There is one thing we should do now. We should accept the responsibility we have always had as an institution but have not discharged. We should justify our claim — one we make to the Charity Commissioners if no

---

27. Investment Products Dispute Resolution Mediation and Arbitration Scheme; see http://www.info.gov.hk/hkma/eng/new/lehman/explanatory_b.htm [accessed May 4, 2011]; Gu Weisha 'ADR and Financial Disputes in Hong Kong: The Lehman Brothers Experience and the Way Forward' (2011) *Asian Dispute Review* 20–23.

one else—to be a learned institution. How can we do that? Simple! We finance research and publish the results. Distance from HQ is no longer a problem.

A start has been made, which should be recognised and applauded. But I challenge all the trustees to go back to their electorates and raise the money to support one or more researchers, PhD students or not, to address the questions which the trustees, properly advised, consider most important. The advisers charged with choosing next year's lecturer may wish to develop the same theme: how can CIArb contribute to the scholarship we all agree is needed to ensure the best possible development of dispute management processes to cope with what the future holds? We are not likely to run out of questions.

21. KEEPING AN EYE ON FUNDAMENTALS

Sir Vivian Ramsey's lecture advised caution in the regulation of mediation.[1] The question surely is: 'what do we want mediation to do for us?' While the study of societies in the past and elsewhere now will not provide answers, such comparative research may make insights possible which it would be wasteful to ignore.

Are there any lessons to be learned from our own history in England? Between 1154 and 1558 mediation was the usual way for parties to begin their search for an end to a dispute they could not handle themselves.[2] Comparatively few disputes were terminated by litigation. The parties were brought to an agreement, in one way or another. There was no concern to define the parts of the process: mediation, what some would differentiate as conciliation, and arbitration. The third parties, usually four, two 'friends of each side', saw their task as restoring peace between the parties, by whatever means they could.

Women were parties nearly as often as men. Occasionally they were appointed arbitrators. There were few restrictions on the subject matter. Crimes, including murder and rape but not treason; status, whether free or servile; all kinds of commercial dispute; medical negligence; and, whatever the courts and legal historians may have denied, the ownership of land – all these were arbitrable in England then.

The four appointees got together and discussed everything they thought was relevant, not only what we would now divide into matters of fact and law but also anything they knew about the background of the dispute. They argued and did deals, consulting their parties as appropriate. If they could come to an agreement, they submitted it to the parties. If the parties accepted it, well and good. If not, as 'arbitrators' they might make an award. Often all they had to do was arrange for payment of a debt by instalments, which the courts could not do.

However agreement was achieved, the record commonly says that the parties then agreed on the award. If one was not happy with it, it

---

1. Sir Vivian Ramsey, 'Mediation 2020' (2012) 78 *Arbitration* 159-162
2. Derek Roebuck *Mediation and Arbitration in the Middle Ages: England 1154-1558*, to be published by HOLO Books: the Arbitration Press, Oxford 2012. [It was published in 2013. Derek rarely missed an opportunity to reply to a point raised by drawing attention to what could be learned from a particular period on which he was working or had worked – SH.]

depended on the power of the arbitrators to enforce it, if necessary with the help of the court. But the usual outcome was expressed as an agreement by which peace was restored. The parties manifested their renewed friendship formally and publicly, often with the kiss of peace or a party. That dealt with any problem of 'transparency'.

As was said in a great land dispute between Burton Abbey and Thomas Okeover in 1418:[3] 'The arbitrators having the great desire and goodwill, from the affection they have for the parties, to make a final accord between them.' To improve the chances of success, even when the rights were plainly all on one side, arbitrators would give something to the loser, to assuage ill-feeling and wounded pride, if nothing else. As in this case: the abbey got the lands, Okeover had to pay an assessed rent for them; but the abbey was to pay him five marks for a general release of any claims he might have. Not because he could establish any claims but because the abbey's concession to that token payment would increase the chances of a successful settlement. It was the restoration of 'peace' that mattered. Of course, people then knew the difference between the concepts of mediation and arbitration but the *process* they used did not keep them separate.

The European Mediation Directive risks inhibiting natural development.[4] Article 1 shows how ill thought out the Directive is: 'The objective is ... ensuring a balanced relationship between mediation and judicial proceedings'. Why? Balance has nothing to do with it. The metaphor of the scales betrays the clumsy thinking of the politician, who may be defined as someone who professionally strives to maintain a balance between good and evil. Even if that metaphor of the balance could be given any meaning, what value would it serve? What is wanted is perfectly clear: the best possible working relations between the courts and private dispute management in the provision of the best possible means of disposing appropriately of those differences between parties which become disputes they cannot settle themselves.[5]

Litigation and its alternatives are not competing *interests* to be weighed against each other. Of course that may be how they seem to lawyers and others who make their living from them.[6] Thinking in the West has largely been in response to the development in the last few decades of

3. Edward Powell 'Settlement of Disputes by Arbitration in Fifteenth-Century England' (1984) 2 *Law and History R* 21-43, pp29-30, citing Burton-on Trent Public Library D27.
4. 24/5/2008 Directive 2008/52/EC.
5. As Rix LJ said in *Rolf v De Guerin* [2011] EWCA Civ 78: 'As for wanting his day in court, that of course is a reason why the courts have been unwilling to compel parties to mediate rather than litigate; but it does not seem to me to be an adequate response to a proper judicial concern that parties should respond reasonably to offers to mediate or settle.'
6. CEDR's new 5th Mediation Audit makes interesting reading.

forms of mediation invented to deal with the problems of civil litigation in the USA. But recent pages of this journal have told of the success of a mediator in Turkey, untrained – indeed with no formal education – who has successfully mediated over 400 differences which would otherwise have ended in violence;[7] of the Ethiopian woman who practised regularly as a mediator in all kinds of disputes, including land, fighting and family matters;[8] and of the women in Liberia who brought Charles Taylor's rule to a peaceful end.[9] What of Manchester City's Mario Balotelli intervening unasked as mediator to end a nasty bit of bullying?[10] Such skills can be fitted into the legal system, as has been done in Morocco.[11]

So, though it would be natural enough to concern ourselves with the future of those who will seek to make a living from mediation, we would do well to remember a time when mediators and arbitrators were neither paid nor trained but regularly employed because the parties wanted them. We might also seek to learn the skills with which those untrained mediators today bring together parties in disputes of greater difficulty than any facing international commercial mediators.

We might also ask the fundamental questions again: Is not the purpose of dispute resolution to end a dispute to the maximum satisfaction of both sides with the least cost to each? Is it too cynical to accept that modern dispute resolution methods which seek some form of perceived ideal of justice – or even merits, whether in family or commercial disputes – are second-best and not what the parties would choose if they understood the alternatives?

---

7. Sarah Rainsford 'The Turkish Peacemaker' (2007) 73 *Arbitration* 100-104. [See Chapter 22 below for the full story. As I write, Sarah has been for weeks bravely reporting from war-torn Ukraine, often in the most dangerous places – SH.]
8. Judith Olmstead *Woman Between Two Worlds: Portrait of an Ethiopian Rural Leader* Urbana, U of Illinois P 1997.
9. 'Let Women Lead the Way to Peace in Africa' *Observer*, 10 April 2011 p.38. [Three of these cases are discussed in more detail in Chapter 20 above – SH.]
10. http://uk.eurosport.yahoo.com/10052011/58/premier-league-balotelli-saves-boy-bullying.
11. Jessica Carlisle '*Centre d'Ecoute* Bargaining under the Shadow of the *Moudawana*' (prize-winning 3 Faiths Forum Essay, to be published).

PART THREE

LANGUANGE, RESEARCH
AND COMPARISON

A paper given at the Second International Conference, Law, Language and Professional Practice, May 10-12, 2012, held in Caserta under the auspices of the Faculty of Law, Seconda Università degli Studi di Napoli, chaired by Professor Girolamo Tessuto. First published in Gerolamo Tessuto ed., *Explorations in Language and Law. Language and Law in Academic and Professional Settings: Analyses and Applications* (Aprilia, Novalogus 2014) pp.25-43. Reprinted by kind permission of the publisher.

22. ARBITRATION, MEDIATION, CONCILIATION: PITFALLS OF PRESCRIPTION

INTRODUCTION

The thousands who recently thronged London's National Gallery to gaze at Leonardo's portrait of Cecilia Gallerani came from all over the world. No doubt they spoke a hundred languages. Each will have read the caption: 'Lady with a Stoat', or is it 'Lady with an Ermine'? Those whose first language is not English will perhaps have thought the name in their mother tongue. Most will not have had to make a choice between two names for the delightful little animal, familiar to me from my childhood, which in England we call a stoat. We can always call it a stoat but, in the winter when its coat turns white, some people may prefer to call it an ermine, particularly if they are talking about its fur.

That choice is a function of English English. Few languages have different nouns for stoat and weasel, let alone stoat and ermine. For example, American English does not use the word stoat, preferring weasel with adjectives attached to differentiate kindred species. French does not offer the distinction, nor do the languages of most of those places where there are neither stoats nor weasels and no winters that whiten fur.

But what if we found ourselves in the Middle Ages, judges having to apply sumptuary laws which made it an offence for anyone other than the nobility to trim their cloaks with ermine? Would the offence be committed by wearing the dull brown fur of summer? The colour changes gradually, except for the tip of the tail, which stays black. What should be the criterion of whiteness?

A new planet or drug is given a name by an internationally recognised authority. That name is at once accepted by scientists everywhere and its translations become standard. For them a stoat is *mustela erminea* summer and winter. Why is there is no such authority for legal terms? What do these words mean: mediation, conciliation, arbitration?

A FABLE

A group of aboriginal people in the far North-East of Australia have had no contact with Western civilisation. They have always used a lot of charcoal which they have learned to refine to a high degree of purity. They call it *jim*. Explorers find them and within a generation one of their young women, Bella, is studying chemistry. Her teacher tells her that what she calls *jim* is for scientific purposes known as carbon, an element with an atomic number 6, recognised everywhere by the capital letter C, whatever language the scientists are using. He asks her to write an essay on how charcoal is purified by her people and she does so without difficulty, everyone happily assuming that for all practical purposes *jim* = C.

Her brother Bello decides to read law. He attends a modern Australian law school with a module in Dispute Resolution. There he learns about mediation and arbitration. His community have always had to deal with disputes like any other group. If the parties cannot deal with them themselves, they choose a panel of five to help them. Each side chooses two best friends and the four choose one more, who must be a grandparent but not of either party. They call both the panel and the process a *boom*. Bello's professor is fascinated by *boom*. She asks him to write an essay about how it works.

If they possibly can, the *boom* will bring the parties together to an agreed settlement. They may in the process clarify the issues as they see them. They try to establish the relevant facts. They declare what customary law applies. They will, as they go along, separate what the parties can agree on, isolating what remains in issue. They will tease out what concessions the parties are prepared to make. Then, if there are still differences, they will suggest how they can be resolved. If a party still disagrees, the *boom* will state their opinion, by a majority if necessary. Both parties are expected to agree to that. Then they are bound by what all concerned think of as the agreement of the parties themselves. It would be a matter of the greatest shame not to comply. The community has no prison, nor does it use corporal punishment. It just puts the non-complier into a category separate from everybody else. That is the threat but it just does not happen because there is nowhere for an outcast to go.

Bello's first problem is what to call the *boom* in English. He reads the articles his professor recommends and finds some recent ones for himself. What is this process? Mediation, conciliation or arbitration? He decides to stick with *boom*.

THE DEFINITION OF DEFINITION

Is Bello's problem one of definition? If modern legislators, say the European Union, were to have to draft new sumptuary laws, we might expect them to insist that there are two distinct categories of stoat fur, white and non-white, and to provide a definition:

> Section 1 *Definitions*
> A stoat, *mustela erminea*, is an ermine if its fur has changed to white over not less than 50% of its body (excepting the tip of its tail).

Is that the best we can hope for? How white? We can't easily identify white by wavelength of light, as we could a colour of the spectrum. Or we could argue on a different kind of definition altogether:

> A stoat is an ermine from 1 November to 31 March.

After all, that is when it is cold in North America and Britain. That might have been a problem this year, when the warm winter meant that stoats were slow to change. And what if enterprising Australian entrepreneurs have started to breed stoats for their fur on cold Macquarie Island to exploit the European market?

DEFINITION: DESCRIPTION AND PRESCRIPTION

It does not matter that the word 'rose' or its equivalent in any language has quite different meanings for an old gardener seeking help from a pruning manual and for a young lover thinking of ways to express feelings to a sweetheart. Most of us will at some time be both lovers and gardeners. 'Rose' will have a range of meanings special to us, to our idiolect, unique but constantly changing, so that a rose will not be the same for us today, when we are happy, as it becomes tomorrow, when our love is gone.

That does not matter at all. It is a glorious aspect of language. The ambiguities would be important only if 'rose' occurred in legislation restricting the importation of flowers from Kenya. Legal definitions are prescriptive. That is why dictionaries are rarely of any help to lawyers in search of meaning, though they desperately reach for them, like a *tabula in naufragio* as English lawyers used to like to say, like a plank in a shipwreck. Dictionaries are not intended to be prescriptive. They can at best be a statement of language use at a chosen time among a preferred group of language users, the highest common factor of a majority of favoured idiolects.[1] The shortcomings are multiplied if the dictionary is

---

1. The US Supreme Court has descended to this level. Between October 2000 and October

bilingual, trying to help its user in a search for equivalents in different languages.

Prescriptive language of the kind found in legislation is a function of the legal system of a state. Our fictional *boom* was more linguistically scientific. It would seek the meaning of what was communicated between the parties in what was conveyed to the hearer, rather than what the speaker meant. But state law is not like that. The words of legislation mean what the lawgiver wants them to mean, not what in reality the subject understood. Ignorance of the law is no excuse. It is no defence to say: 'I thought stoat meant any old weasel', even if you could prove that. It may be a mitigating factor but those who run the legal system are adamant. Order must prevail over justice. The English Latin betrays the emotion: *ignorantia iuris haud excusat*; *haud* indeed! You can't get more negative than that. And the strength of feeling has prevailed over any nice ethical objections: no one questions any more the morality of punishing the morally guiltless.

So there is magical power in the prescriptive force of legislative provisions. They therefore need to be handled with care, I'm sure you would all agree.

CATEGORIES

Not only legislation but scholarship generally likes to create categories to make it easier to think about phenomena. The categories give names to sets of things in disciplines other than law and linguistics. Let's take medicine as an example. Here the classification may have profound practical consequences. Is breast cancer still breast cancer when after it has been removed from the breast it reappears in the brain? Your answer may determine the availability of funds for research.

Imagine this notice in a clinic when I was a child.

NOTICE TO PATIENTS
HYSTERIA patients will be seen by
Dr Brainstorm on Mondays and Tuesdays,
Professor Doolalli on Wednesdays and Thursdays.

Asti Hustvedt wrote her new book on hysteria because, she says: 'It kept haunting me. What does hysteria mean?'[2] To Hippocrates it was a female physical disorder, caused by a 'displaced womb'. For Charcot, in

2010 its justices took 295 definitions from dictionaries: Holmes, Cardozo and Brandeis never once http://www.nytimes.com/2011/06/14/14bar.html.
2. Asti Hustvedt *Medical Muses: Hysteria in Nineteenth-Century Paris* London, Bloomsbury 2011.

19th-century Paris, it was a specific condition identifiable by scientific diagnosis. But Hustvedt has an insight:

> All illness is experienced in a specific time and place, and it is classified differently depending on what culture you're from …. There's been a lot of talk about how hysteria has disappeared … it's no longer a medical entity or diagnosis … of course, it hasn't disappeared … it's been broken up and reclassified into other, separate disorders. It's just that the names have shifted.

But with the renaming have come new treatments and drugs specific to the newly differentiated symptoms. We can possibly look forward to such scientific reclassifications for diseases like depression or chronic fatigue syndrome or even autism. Controversies about the classification of all three of these diseases illustrate how much names matter.[3]

DEFINING MEDIATION

Of course, stoats and roses and hysteria will just go on being what they are, doing what they do, ignoring our linguistic labours. So with mediators and arbitrators. We know one when we see one. But the writers on dispute resolution which poor Bello had to read have recently had fun with a diversion, what might be called 'names as toys'. They start with the whole genus of dispute resolution. Should ADR 'mean' Alternative, or Amicable, or Appropriate Dispute Resolution? What is the point of such word play? And what is happening when not the parties but an authority lays down for others the law that 'mediators shall not become arbitrators in the same dispute without the consent of the parties', or 'mediation is facilitative; if the mediator suggests solutions it is not mediation but conciliation'?

During the processes by which the parties and their advisers try to settle a dispute, what they are doing may at different times take on the character of any or all of those three As and many other activities as well. What they call it is not likely to affect the negotiations. Of course, if you are thinking in Arabic or Chinese, you will have to find different toys. You are less likely to have lots of adjectives beginning with the same letter. Alliteration may not have the same ring.

Moreover, categories in different languages may not have the same criteria or boundaries, let alone penumbra. Many who should know better have succumbed to the temptation to create categories first and then to

---

3. As the doctors will confirm who are responsible for the production of DSM-5, the fifth edition of the American Psychiatric Association's Diagnostic and Statistical Manual of Mental Disorders due for publication in May 2013 [published in 2013].

force reality into them, most recently the manufactured definitions of 'mediation' and 'conciliation' and to distinguish both of them from 'arbitration'.

THE EUROPEAN MEDIATION DIRECTIVE

Apparently oblivious of any concern that control may hamper natural development, the European Mediation Directive would try to codify the meaning and limit the usage of some basic terms.[4]

> Article 3(a)   'Mediation' means a structured process ... whereby two or more parties to a dispute attempt by themselves, on a voluntary basis, to reach an agreement on the settlement of their dispute with the assistance of a mediator.

What helpful meaning can possibly be attached to the word 'structured' here? All attempts to mediate a settlement have a structure. That structure – perhaps better thought of as a process – must be specific to the dispute and exist within a particular culture. What restrictions would these would-be lawgivers like to impose to make the process fit their Procrustean bed? They are not alone. The Hong Kong legislature is considering a bill with a similar requirement of 'structure'.

And the European Mediation Directive article 3(b) defines 'mediator' as:

> any third person who is asked to conduct a mediation in an effective, impartial and competent way.

What if the appointment says 'unbiased' rather than 'impartial'. Does that prevent the third person from being a mediator? How? Why? And how often will the appointment bother to state the obvious: that the parties require the mediator to be competent and effective? If it does not, is the third person not a mediator for the purposes of the Directive?

Of course the Directive is not itself legislation. It needs national legislation to incorporate it into local law. But France has already incorporated a straight translation into the French Civil Code.[5] In the United Kingdom we have our own regulations.[6] The Italian legislation introduces a linguistic distinction: *mediazione* is used for the process and *conciliazione* for the product.

4. 24/5/2008 Directive 2008/52/EC.
5. Decret no2012-66 of 20/1/2011.
6. Cross-Border Mediation (EU Directive) Regulations 2011 (SI 2011/1133).

The EU works in 23 official and five semi-official languages. Further research is needed to show how those languages use their words for what happens in private dispute management; and further thought about the nature of dispute resolution, with recognition of its variations in cultures different in time and space. No legislation will control those usages and it takes little imagination to foresee unintended consequences of trying to do so.

Article 1 shows how ill thought out the Directive is: 'The objective is ... ensuring a balanced relationship between mediation and judicial proceedings'. Why? Balance has nothing to do with it. The metaphor of the scales betrays the clumsy thinking of the politician, who may be defined as 'someone who professionally strives to maintain a balance between good and evil'. Even if that metaphor of the balance could be given any meaning, what value would it serve? What is wanted is perfectly clear: the best possible working relations between the courts and private dispute management in the provision of the best possible means of disposing appropriately of those differences between parties which become disputes they cannot settle themselves.[7]

Litigation and its alternatives are not competing *interests* to be weighed against each other. Of course that may be how they are seen by lawyers and others who make their living from them.

MEDIATION AND CONCILIATION

In ordinary English, mediation and conciliation have the same meaning. They are synonymous and interchangeable. This linguistic reality is recognised in the UNCITRAL Model Law on International Commercial Conciliation,[8] which is intended to provide uniform rules for the conciliation process, to encourage the use of conciliation, and to ensure greater predictability and certainty in its use. Article 3 defines 'conciliation' to include both processes:

3. 'Conciliation' means a process, whether referred to by the expression conciliation, mediation or an expression of similar import, whereby parties request a third person or persons ('the conciliator') to assist them in their attempt to reach an amicable settlement.

But brave efforts have been made to insist on a distinction between mediation and conciliation. The Swiss Rules of Commercial Mediation proclaim, in their English version:

7. As Rix LJ said in *Rolf v De Guerin* [2011] EWCA Civ 78: 'As for wanting his day in court, that of course is a reason why the courts have been unwilling to compel parties to mediate rather than litigate; but it does not seem to me to be an adequate response to a proper judicial concern that parties should respond reasonably to offers to mediate or settle.'
8. Adopted by UNCITRAL 24 June 2002.

Mediation is an alternative method of dispute resolution whereby two or more parties ask a neutral third party, the mediator, to assist them in settling a dispute or in avoiding future conflicts. The mediator facilitates the exchange of opinions between the parties and encourages them to explore solutions that are acceptable to all the parties .... The mediator does not make proposals like a conciliator.

So at first sight there appear to be three current usages: 1. 'conciliation' includes both; or 2. 'mediation' includes both; or 3. a distinction is made. The choice between 1 and 2 is unimportant. Of course it would be pleasanter and give us greater self-respect, no doubt, if we could all agree to one or the other, as chemists do with sulphur dioxide. But the practical problems arise when we create two categories and have to choose into which we put phenomena, when that allocation has practical effect.

Unless the categories are both comprehensive of all relevant phenomena and are mutually exclusive, and the criteria for allocation of all the phenomena between them are not only clear but agreed, the process is not only flawed but dangerous. It is easy to show that distinctions are culturally specific.[9]

A good example comes from Sanja Tseveenjav's article 'Mediation in Mongolia', which makes this suggestion:[10]

Conciliation and mediation can be differentiated – the former referring to settlement efforts made during the court proceedings, whereas the latter refers to out-of-court settlement processes, i.e. mediation in its classical sense as employed, for example, in the United Kingdom.

That should not be assumed to be an oriental aberration. A Dutch mediator has made a similar suggestion. John M Bosnak cites the European Mediation Directive art3(a):[11]

[Conciliation] includes mediation conducted by a judge who is not responsible for any judicial proceedings concerning the dispute in question. It excludes attempts made by the judge seised to settle a dispute in the course of judicial proceedings concerning the dispute in question.

9. For a quite different approach: The People's Mediation Law of the People's Republic of China 2011.
10. Sanja Tseveenjav 'Mediation in Mongolia' (2011) 77 *Arbitration* 332-336, 332.
11. John M Bosnak 'The European Mediation Directive: More Questions than Answers' in Arnold Ingen-Housz ed *ADR in Business II* Alphen aan den Rijn, Wolters Kluwer 2011 pp625-657, 642. All of this article and, indeed, all of this collection of essays, repay careful reading.

And he suggests that: 'maybe mediation practitioners and scholars should agree that the word "conciliation" should be exclusively allocated to this type of judicial settlement activity'.

There would appear to be no obvious direct route for cross-fertilisation between Mongolia and The Netherlands. How could what seems to be an idiosyncratic definition sprout in such different climates? Was it born in the European Mediation Directive or has it a history? Why should it matter whether or not the mediation process is carried on by a judge during the litigation? An answer may be found in the separate histories of the *compromissum* in practice in France and England and in the quite different influence which the jurists had.

ARBITER, ARBITRATOR SEU AMICABILIS COMPOSITOR

It all starts with Justinian's *Digest*:[12]

> The Lex Julia prohibits a *iudex* from accepting appointment as *arbiter* in a matter in which he is *iudex*.

The *iudex* was a person appointed by the praetor, by the State, to try a case to a conclusion according to law. An *arbiter* was appointed by the parties and had discretions which a *iudex* did not. Both *iudex* and *arbiter* were private persons. They needed no legal qualifications. Neither can be called a judge. But it would be a contempt for a *iudex* to prefer his own opinion of what was just over the outcome prescribed by the law of the State.

That prohibition never applied in England. There judges commonly took a matter away to handle it privately as arbitrator, which included attempting mediation. In France the prohibition continued; but it was not what the parties wanted so a way round it was invented. First in Bourgogne in AD1249 and then commonly in the fourteenth century the parties' lawyers would draft the *compromissum* so that the dispute was submitted to an *arbiter, arbitrator seu amicabilis compositor*.[13] Huguccio had pointed out at the end of the twelfth century that there was a difference between an *arbiter* and an *arbitrator*.[14]

> So he is not an *arbiter* but an *arbitrans* or *arbitrator* and it is not called an award, *arbitrium*, but a settlement, *arbitratus*, a kind of agreement.

That is the point to keep in mind. The result of the process is not a judgment imposed on the parties but the product of their own agreement.

12. D.4.8.9.2.
13. The story is fully told by Anne Lefèbvre-Teillard *'Arbiter, Arbitrator seu Amicabilis Compositor'* (2008) *Revue de l'Arbitrage* pp369-387 [Lefèbvre-Teillard].
14. Lefèbvre-Teillard pp372-373.

It follows logically that the product of an agreement cannot be appealed against. The parties are stuck with it because that is what they have declared to one another that they wanted.

Of course, the parties might want to leave open the possibilities of an appeal. If they say so, they can make that part of their agreement. It is just a matter of careful drafting. So lawyers invented the phrase *arbiter, arbitrator seu amicabilis compositor* and inserted it into the standard form of *compromissum*. They invented another phrase, too, *in alto et basso* in Latin and its equivalents in other languages, 'in high and low' in English, to indicate that all forms of dispute resolution were included.

Jurists both civil and canon might argue that a submission must be one thing or the other but the parties were not concerned with such theoretical niceties. Their culture had always known the inclusive process whereby the 'arbitrators', call them what you will, had used every means they could to arrive at a settlement. 'Bottom up' custom prevailed over 'top down' law. They produced a process almost as good as a *boom*.

ARBITRATION IN ENGLAND IN THE MIDDLE AGES

For us today a process has to be either mediation, where a third party is agreed on by the parties to try to bring them to a settlement, whose only force comes from their subsequent agreement, or arbitration, where the third party adjudicates and the parties are bound by their previous agreement to abide by the award. But, in the Middle Ages in England, there was one routine process which everybody then called arbitration, in which the parties asked third parties to help them resolve the dispute by whatever means they could.

Nowadays much is made of the need for mediators and arbitrators to be neutral and impartial. In the United States there are elaborate rules which discourage the appointment of those with previous acquaintance of either party.[15] There is nothing God-given about this. It was not always so. Many societies have preferred what the Greeks called a *koinē*, someone common to both parties, equally the friend of both, or, as in 1344 Pope Clement VI declared himself to be, when acting as mediator between Edward III of England and Philip VI of France: *persona privata et amicus communis*, acting in a private capacity and as a friend of both sides.[16] In the Middle Ages in England it was usually clear by implication

---

15. The law is more practical in England, e.g. *A & Ors v B & Anor* [2011] EWHC 2345 (Comm).
16. Eugène Déprez 'La Conférence d'Avignon (1344): L'Arbitrage Pontifical entre La France et L'Angleterre' in AG Little and FM Powicke eds *Essays in Medieval History Presented to Thomas Frederick Tout* Manchester, for the Subscribers 1925 pp301-320, 304 [Déprez].

and often expressed that the third parties were chosen just because they were already 'friends to both sides'.

Most often, each side appointed two such 'friends'. The four then got together and discussed everything they thought was relevant, not only what we would now divide into matters of fact and law but also anything they knew about the background of the dispute, including the reputations of the parties generally and their families and what was being said in the community about the dispute. They argued and did deals, consulting their parties as appropriate. If they could come to an agreement, they submitted it to the parties. If the parties accepted it, well and good. If not, the 'arbitrators' might make an award.

If the arbitrators were equally divided, with the parties' agreement they would add a fifth arbitrator and try again to come to an agreed award or consent to the determination of the majority. Alternatively, the parties might, at the time of deadlock, or even perhaps by prior agreement when the dispute was first submitted to them, provide for the appointment of an umpire, a single decision-maker substituted for the arbitrators.

However agreement was achieved, the record commonly says that the parties then agreed on the award – with a kiss or a feast – but, if one was not happy with the award, it depended on the power of the arbitrators to enforce it. Of course, people then knew the difference between the concepts of mediation and arbitration but the *process* they used did not keep them separate. That explains the even number of arbitrators and the potential need for an umpire.

As was said in a great land dispute between Burton Abbey and Thomas Okeover in 1418:[17] 'The arbitrators having the great desire and goodwill, from the affection they have for the parties, to make a final accord between them.' To improve the chances of success, even when the rights were plainly all on one side, arbitrators would give something to the loser, to assuage ill-feeling and wounded pride, if nothing else. As in this case: the abbey got the lands, Okeover had to pay rent for them; but the abbey was to pay him five marks for a general release of any claims he might have. Not because there was evidence of any claims but because the abbey's concession to that token payment would increase the chances of a successful settlement. It was the restoration of peace that mattered.

THE SCOPE OF ARBITRATION

Arbitration in England long predates the Common Law. Its roots are deep in custom. It grew from below with little help from legislation or even

17. Edward Powell 'Settlement of Disputes by Arbitration in Fifteenth-Century England' (1984) 2 *Law and History R* 21-43, pp29-30, citing Burton-on Trent Public Library D27.

much from case law until the end of the sixteenth century. In medieval England the word 'arbitration' was used for the whole range of dispute resolution outside litigation. Arbitration in this wider sense was the usual method of resolving disputes. The records show that litigation, even when it was used, rarely concluded a dispute.

Arbitration was readily available to all kinds of people. Kings submitted their differences to other kings or the pope. The records of the city of York show that a labourer, Aynour Johnson, was a party to an arbitration arranged by the municipal authorities in 1484, a few months before the end of the Wars of the Roses. Foreign merchants brought their disputes to the Mayor of London's arbitration scheme, even when there was no English element. If one party was English and the other foreign, an arbitration was arranged with two English and two foreign arbitrators.

The scope of arbitration had few limits. None of the Roman Law restrictions applied. Questions of ownership of land, of status – free or servile, criminal charges including murder and rape, were all resolved by arbitration without their arbitrability being questioned. Arbitrators even decided questions of church law. Treason and blasphemy seem to have been the only substantial exceptions.

The resolution of a dispute by arbitration was not primarily a legal outcome. It was more real than that. The parties had publicly acknowledged that their dispute was over.

MEDIEVAL OXFORD

The most compelling evidence of the differences between Civil Law arbitration *ex compromisso* and the reality in England comes from an award in a thoroughly English jurisdiction which was nevertheless governed by the Civil Law. The University of Oxford in the fifteenth century had wide jurisdiction over both civil and criminal matters, not restricted to members of the University. No Common Law was taught there, only Civil Law and Canon Law. The University's courts applied the Civil Law in a society imbued with traditional English values and ways.

In 1446 two halls, the forerunners of colleges, were in dispute. There had been violence between their fellows. Each party appointed two arbitrators, by a deed which has every appearance of a Civil Law *compromissum*. The award of 7 July 1446 ended the dispute. Here it is in full:[18]

In God's name, Amen. We, John Scelott and John Snawdone, on behalf of the Principal and Fellows of Broadgates Hall in the parish of St

18. Anstey II pp552-554.

Aldate's in Oxford; and Richard Pede and Thomas Ashfeld, on behalf of the Principal of Pauline Hall in Oxford and the Fellows of that hall, and their supporters, having been chosen to be arbiters or arbitrators and mediators, *arbitri seu arbitratores et amicabiles compositores*, and having unanimously assumed office with the common agreement and consent of the parties, having been appointed over each and every of the actions, suits, controversies, wrongs, complaints, attacks and whatsoever causes between the parties, from the beginning of the world to this day, in whatever right it has been brought, upon due deliberation,

We arbitrate, award, pronounce and decide: that the Principal of Pauline Hall shall ask and beg, in his own name and that of all his Fellows, that the Principal of Broadgates Hall, out of his own goodwill, friendship, love, and so that peace may prevail in future as far as he himself and the Fellows, present and future and his supporters are concerned;

And that the Principal of Broadgates Hall shall make a similar request, for himself and his Fellows, of the Principal of Pauline Hall.

Item that Owyn Lloyde shall say to the Principal of Broadgates Hall that, if and to the extent that he, Owyn, has caused any harm to the Principal or his people, by his submission he asks the Principal's forgiveness, without artifice and with good will;

Next Master John Olney, priest, and Owyn shall first give each other the kiss of peace and then, with their hands on the sacred gospels, each shall swear the corporeal oath that, as much as it lies in him, he will keep fraternal peace with the other in future; for the observance of which they bind themselves by their mutual written bonds in 100s sterling; these bonds shall remain in the custody of the Chancellor of the University; and, if it should happen (God forbid) that Owyn should in future be legally convicted of any wrong or offence against Master John Olney, then the bond shall be handed over and released to Master John … [and vice versa];

Item We arbitrate and award that all and every of the Fellows of these halls shall keep and make to be kept the peace in regard to the Fellows of these halls;

Item that David Philipe, who is said to have struck John Olney, shall on bended knees and humbly seek the pardon of Master John, and Master John shall grant him forgiveness and pardon.

All these things, each and every, we award and arbitrate to be done, kept and fulfilled and we order it under the penalty contained in the *compromissum*.

This award or arbitration, *laudum sive arbitrium*, was made and pronounced on 7 July 1446, in the church of St Frideswide, Oxford, next to its saint, the parties being present and confirming the award.

Each side had appointed two arbitrators and charged them to bring a violent dispute to an end, by an agreed settlement as mediators, *amicabiles compositores*, if they could, or if not as arbiters by an award, *laudum* or *arbitrium*. They formulated an award which both sides then *agreed* to.

I believe that the choice of language in this document is significant. In England 566 years ago it followed the precedent of awards upon a *compromissum* already two centuries old in other parts of Western Europe, but with a tiny difference. The Latin copulative *seu*, like the English word 'or', is as often found between near synonyms as opposites, as in *laudum seu arbitrium*. The standard phrase in the appointment clause of a *compromissum* in all times and places is *arbiter, arbitrator vel amicabilis compositor*, in which each noun is an equal alternative.[19] Why then would the creator of this document write *arbiter seu arbitrator et amicabilis compositor*? Because in his English mind he wanted to distinguish clearly the role of an *arbiter* who adjudicated from an *arbitrator* and an *amicabilis compositor* who did not. I believe this to be reliable and sufficient evidence of what is otherwise implicit in these records: third parties first (and continuously throughout the proceedings) tried to bring the parties to agree to a settlement and imposed a decision upon them only as a last resort. The arbitrators in this case worked out a settlement which the parties are recorded as then having agreed to. That was what they had anticipated when they made the submission and together agreed to abide by what the arbitrators, the friends of both sides, agreed on. It was not imposed against their will, or willy-nilly by the powers bestowed on the arbitrators in their submission. The parties had stayed in charge throughout. They had got what they wanted. Peace had been restored by an agreed settlement.

The arbitrators described themselves as acting 'on behalf of' their respective parties. However partisan they may have been, they worked out a settlement between them without the help of any objective outsider. They expected to. The parties expected them to. However much the parties, the lawyers who drafted the *compromissum*, and the arbitrators were influenced by and followed the forms of the Civil Law, they were English and their culture prevailed.[20]

19. Karl-Heinz Ziegler 'Arbiter, Arbitrator und Amicabilis Compositor' (1967) 84 *Zeitschrift der Savigny-Stiftung für Rechtsgeschichte: Romanische Abteilung* 376-81.
20. Of course the English had no monopoly of even-numbered tribunals. They are found in the multicultural jurisdiction of Cretan Candia in 1305, where Venetian, Greek and Jew lived and worked in harmony, AM Stahl ed *The Documents of Angelo de Cartura and Donato*

THE LINGUISTIC REALITIES

We must remember that UNCITRAL and the New York Convention are not confined to Common Law and Civil Law jurisdictions, or those which use European languages. Even different EU countries look at all this in quite different ways. Greece intends to implement the Directive through legislation which would require all mediators – and perhaps even those appearing as advocates before them – to be lawyers. Greek lawyers use a range of words for mediation, usually μεσολαβηση, but sometimes συνδιαλλαξη, συμβιβασμος, συμφιλιωση and maybe others.[21] Do any of them fit the Directive's definition exactly? Will one be chosen and artificially made to take on the EU's definition? I am sure there are Greek experts here who can tell me later which it is. I wonder whether they will agree with one another.

The confusion does not arise from reality but from an insistence on forcing language into unnatural shapes. In reality, in all our cultures, those we now call mediators have commonly moved backwards and forwards, using whatever skills they had to help to bring about a settlement. In many attempts to mediate, you would have to film what happens, to be able to spot when the mediator moves from one mode to another, perhaps by no more than a slight hint. The commentator would be saying, stopping the playback: 'Ah, that's mediation there – whoops, nearly slipped into conciliation, there's she's gone, over the line, back again but, of course, all is now tainted with conciliation'.

No agreement on meaning is likely that makes that kind of distinction, even in English, whether English English, American or reduced. And every flourishing language is historically and potentially a language of ADR. How are prescriptive definitions going to work in Chinese or Arabic – not unimportant languages of international commerce? No legislation can control the developments, not even Swiss Rules or EU Directives, which can only define for the purposes of their own rules. In something so consensual as alternative dispute resolution, what the

---

Fontanella Venetian Notaries in Fourteenth-Century Crete Washington, Dumbarton Oaks 2000 p14 no36 and p191 no492. About the same time, in Venice itself, two arbitrators were common, Fabrizio Marrella and Andrea Mozzato eds *Alle Origini dell'Arbitrato Commerciale Internazionale: L'Arbitrato a Venezia tra Medioevo ed Età Moderna* Milan, Cedam 2001, who at p57 say that 'some modern jurists – perhaps wrongly – call the umpire a British invention'. And even as late as 1785 in Geneva Jacques Drouin *Catalogue des Factums Judiciaires Genèvois sous L'Ancien Régime* Geneva, Société d'Histoire et d'Archéologie de Genève 1988 p84 no274. But not in Louis XIV's Paris, Derek Roebuck *The Charitable Arbitrator: How to Mediate and Arbitrate in Louis XIV's France* Oxford HOLO Books 2002 p194.
21. I thank Zafeirenia Proestaki for her advice on the subtle distinctions in the mind of a contemporary Greek non-lawyer.

parties want and what they think their community should offer them will prevail over any top-down prescriptions.

The slightest difference of wording may have the most terrible unforeseen consequences. It is often said that Roger Casement, Irish hero and English traitor, was hanged by a comma. That argument may be over now but few disputes are of more immediate consequence than that about the withdrawal of Israeli forces from the West Bank. No determination has yet been agreed of the differing interpretations of UN Resolution 242 of 1967. The English version calls for 'the withdrawal of Israeli forces from territories occupied in the recent conflict'. The US and Israeli Governments argue that the lack of a definite article before 'territories' means that Israel is not required to give *all* the territories back. In English there is at least an argument that the words are ambiguous. But all the other official languages of the United Nations – Arabic, Chinese, French, Russian and Spanish – use the definite form unambiguously. The potential consequences of this linguistic argument are unthinkable.

One thing is integral to every one's definition of mediation, isn't it? That is that mediation is voluntary, at least in the sense that either party may walk away from the mediator and is not bound by anything a mediator determines. That would not be true of my fictional aboriginal society. And try telling that to a Korean, where the culture still provides a process of dispute resolution – usually translated into English, without more explanation, as 'mediation' – which, once the parties have chosen to use it, cannot be escaped without unbearable social pressure – a present-day true-life example of the sanctions which were used in our fictional *boom*.

CONCLUSIONS

I hope I have shown that prescription is misplaced unless it has an acceptable purpose. We will all continue to use words as best we can to communicate what we hope to get the recipient to understand. Of course, there is nothing wrong with defining your terms for scholarly purposes and sometimes lawyers need to when drafting a contract – as long as you don't let the categories determine your thinking, as long as you say what you mean and are sure that the other side accepts that meaning.[22]

Lawyers are skilled users of language. They always have been. Now more than ever, though, their world is multilingual. The paradox is that the more the use of English dominates business and its law, the more diverse the influences on that English are and the more pervasive are

22. Douglas Yarn, 'The Death of ADR: A Cautionary Tale of Isomorphism through Institutionalization' 198 Penn. St. LR 929 (2003-2004).

the forces which push towards the creation and use of a new language, a reduced language for non-native speakers of English. With the spread of this new apparently simplified language come increased dangers of partial comprehension and blurring of necessary distinctions.

The more I try to understand how people – individuals and communities – have managed their disputes, the more I am convinced that the answers must be sought by interdisciplinary enquiry. Comparative research is essential. It has already been justified by the insights that have come from working out why processes are alike or different in communities separated by time or space. But comparative research is richer and has more colour if it is viewed not through the monocular microscope, however powerful, of a single discipline, whether law, history, anthropology, psychology or even language. If we are to work most effectively, we shall not only have to draw on every obviously relevant discipline but also constantly keep an eye out for developments in those we have not yet recognised as potentially fruitful.

How much more shall we learn if we try to use together the tools and skills and experience of all those arts and sciences we have not yet explored. And how much more rigorously shall we be able to test and so rely on the results of one another's work.

I end with a challenge to those who want to define mediation and thereby control it and limit those who may act as mediators.[23]

On 11 November 2006 the BBC's 'From Our Own Correspondent' programme was from Sarah Rainsford in Turkey. Her story was beautifully told, so here are her own words.

I met Metin in a funeral parlour in Diyarbakir. He looked like he wanted to shrivel up and disappear. His head sagged sheepishly low and he had somehow twisted his upper body, like he was trying to take up as little space as possible. Metin was in his twenties – and in serious trouble. He had violated the strict code of honour that rules much of south-eastern Turkey, and he knew he was lucky to be alive.

Eighteen months ago, Metin married. He had kidnapped the girl he loved because he could not afford a dowry. The couple have since had a baby but the bride's brothers are after them. They believe killing the couple will cleanse the family honour. As he told me his sorry tale, Metin's eyes brimmed with tears of desperation. At one point he rounded on his elderly father, half deaf and stooped over a walking stick. 'I had to steal her,' Metin wailed in accusation. 'You never gave me any money for a dowry – you never even sent me to school!' His poor father looked like he had been punched in the stomach – and I

23. Sir Vivian Ramsey, an English judge, has recently spoken of the dangers of regulation: 'Mediation 2020' (2012) 78 *Arbitration* 159-162. [See Chapter 21 above – SH.]

gulped back a lump in my own throat. I have not got any money, he protested, or I'd have given it to you.

Luckily for Metin, what his father did have was an idea. He brought his son into town to visit the man locals here have nicknamed the 'President of Peace'. Sait is a tiny old man, with a face heavy with wrinkles. But he is full of energy. The district funeral parlour is now an unofficial headquarters for his peace missions: a spacious hall lined with sofas, and with a never-ending supply of sweet, soothing tea. Sait is actually a butcher by trade, but he handed his shops over to his sons six years ago to devote himself full-time to peace. Since then he says he has resolved more than 400 feuds .... The sofas in Sait's office were filled with men, seeking his mediation.

Sait told me he sees little sign that modernisation is having much impact on attitudes in this neglected, mainly Kurdish corner of the country. It is a place where social pressure is nothing to do with having the latest gadget or label. Here it can be a matter of life or death ....

It could have been a deeply depressing visit to Diyarbakir – but before I left, there was one uplifting moment. Sait invited us to watch as the hapless Metin was reconciled with the father of his stolen bride. The peacemaker had promised to find funds himself to help Metin make his bride an honest wife. As that news sunk in – young Metin's whole body seemed to unwind. He smiled for the first time since we had met and happily pulled out a photograph of his baby boy. The truce will remain precarious until the day the money comes through. But for Metin it does seem that the patient negotiations of Sait's President of Peace may have just paid off.

Sait has no formal education, let alone qualifications. He is too old, too poor, too unlettered to acquire any. We should do nothing by defining away reality that would inhibit interventions like Sait's. And the last point is the most telling. We can learn from the Saits of this world. He is successful in a much harder milieu than international commercial arbitration. If we are scientists searching for ways to improve dispute resolution, to bring peace to conflicts about the custody of a child or between nations at war, we should look for insights and expertise to what is going on in our own world now, at Sait in Turkey and the women who brought peace to Sierra Leone, and perhaps even at our own histories before our ways of restoring peace became the work of lawyers.

[*Tailpiece – SH*
Please note that a 'fable' starts on the first page of this chapter and the word 'boom' recurs several times in pages thereafter. Derek made up the

name, and its setting, for a particular process of mediation to illustrate a point integral to the paper. A reader skimming might miss that – as one person is known to have done – and taken it as gospel. The same is true, or, rather, made up, in Chapter 3, 'What Law was there in Roman Bath?' Both stories suggest that Derek could have earned a living as a successful novelist.

Derek would wish me to mention the kindness and warm hospitality we received during our two days in Caserta, at a time when he was not at his strongest.]

First published in (2014) 16(3) *European Journal of Law Reform* (Special Issue on Law and Language) 633-650. Reprinted by kind permission of the publisher, Eleven [International Publishing].

23. PLAIN, CLEAR AND SOMETHING MORE? CRITERIA FOR COMMUNICATION IN LEGAL LANGUAGE

1. INTRODUCTION

Every morning, when I get my emails up, there is one from the Law Society, my professional body, trying to keep me up-to-date. Recently it included a note from Nick Parker, a language consultant.[1] It was exceptionally well written. It also stated a fact which I hope will end a lot of argument. Is plain speech worthwhile? Thank you Mr Parker for this:

> One client I worked for recently saved over £6 million in call centre call-handling time by rewording a slab of distance-selling regulation legalese.

So plain speech really does pay! But is plainness the necessary quality we all seek, or is there something more?

Just a few days later, Richard Heaton, the British Government officer who oversees the drafting of legislation, published a report calling for legislation to be made easier to understand, saying:[2]

> Excessive complexity hinders economic activity, creating burdens for individuals, businesses and communities. It obstructs good government. It undermines the rule of law.

Who could disagree? We can discount the lawyer-blogger who responded at once that he was gleefully preparing for the welter of litigation that would ensue.[3]

Advocates of plain language understand its purpose well:[4]

---

1. Nick Parker *Law Society Gazette* 5 April 2013.
2. 'When Laws Become Too Complex' 16 April 2013.
3. There are better calls for caution, Francis Bennion 'Confusion Over Plain Language Law' (2007) 16 *The Commonwealth Lawyer* pp63-68.
4. Mark Adler 'The Plain Language Movement' in PM Tiersma and LM Solan *The Oxford Handbook of Language and Law* Oxford, Oxford UP 2012 [Tiersma and Solan] pp67-85, 68.

Plain language is not a dialect of the standard language but a relationship between the text and its audience. Text that will be plain for one audience will not be plain for another.

And some recipients will seem wilfully uncomprehending, like the charming old woman client I had as a young solicitor, who gave me instructions for the sale of her house from her hospital bed. I sent the contract with her daughter for her to sign, giving careful instructions about how the signature should be witnessed. I would never have taken the chance if it had been her will and I learned not to risk any document again, because I had attached a note: 'sign where you see your initials in pencil'. Needless to say, despite her daughter's protest, she insisted on signing in pencil.

I taught in Papua New Guinea for five years and practised there as a barrister in all the courts other than village courts, from which lawyers were excluded. The problems of language were more than enough to satisfy even the greediest student of linguistics. The language of the higher courts and of the law they employed was English. Most of the parties who came before them, even if they had no English, had some command of one of the two pidgins which then prevailed: Tok Pisin and Hiri Motu. But many of those charged with offences in the lower, magistrates', courts spoke only their tok ples, the language of their own community. At the last count they numbered over 800 quite distinct languages.

A village man, who spoke only his tok ples, had been convicted by a magistrate of having sexual intercourse with an under age girl. He appealed to the High Court on the ground that the magistrate had heard no evidence of the girl's age. That was enough to ensure that the appeal succeeded, but the judge took the opportunity of giving general instructions to magistrates on taking a plea. They must ensure that the defendant knew the full meaning of 'Do you plead guilty or not guilty?' All elements of the offence must be explained. It was not enough to translate the English into 'Did you do it?' The offence in this case required the girl to be under the age of 16, and for the accused to know she was. If she had been over 16 and had not consented, that would have been a different offence. The judge suspected that the magistrate's clerk had put to the defendant in his tok ples the simple question: 'Did you do it?' What he should have asked was: 'Did you have sexual intercourse with the complainant?' then 'Did she consent?' and then 'Did you know she was under the age of consent?' – all in the defendant's tok ples.[5]

---

5. It is not impossible that the judge in Papua New Guinea was familiar with the scholarly attention that had recently been given to this very question. Maurizio Gotti 'Text and

Now nothing could be *plainer* than 'Did you do it?' But that message did not do the job. So it is not plainness that ultimately counts but clarity – the quality of transferring a message from one mind to another comprehensively and with no distortion. Plainness is good but clarity matters more.

2. CLARITY IN THE SOURCE LANGUAGE

There is no hope of sending a clear message in the target language if the source is not clear. The lack of clarity may be, and usually is, unintentional. But not always, as shown in Part 8 below.

Much has been written about problems of translation which arise from the imperfect fit of one word (or a phrase) in the source language (SL) with its near but only approximate equivalent in the target language (TL). It is common experience that in many cases no one word equivalent exists but scientific opinion now insists that anything in the SL can be put into the TL if you have words and patience enough and no practical constraints.[6]

A fundamental problem is that of unintentional obscurity arising from the failure of the creators of the word or phrase in the SL to give enough thought to what they wanted the word to mean. This happens when legislators share an idea but have not thought it out. The drafters and translators then have no chance of scientific accuracy, because there is none to represent. The best they can do is create something like the nonsense of the original, like translating *Finnegans Wake*. An example is to be found in the European Mediation Directive (the Directive).[7]

Article 1 declares that: 'The objective is... ensuring a balanced relationship between mediation and judicial proceedings'. 'Balance' and its equivalents in any language can mean nothing here. Balance has

Genre' in Tiersma and Solan pp52-66, 58 discusses it, citing Pat Carlen *Magistrates' Justice* London, Martin Robertson 1976. [Derek knew first hand what he was talking about, having defended a young woman in the Highlands of Papua New Guinea and getting her off following a similar argument – SH.]

6. My views are set out most fully in KK Sin and Derek Roebuck 'The Ego and I and Ngo: Theoretical Problems in the Translation of the Common Law into Chinese' in Raymond Wacks ed *Hong Kong, China and 1997: Essays in Legal Theory* Hong Kong, Hong Kong UP 1993 pp185-210. [Derek experienced these problems first hand as general editor of a series of publications, and editor of one himself, translating laws of Hong Kong legislated in English into Chinese (Peking University Press 1995-96) – SH.]

7. 24/5/2008 Directive 2008/52/EC. The following sections are a revision of parts of a lecture 'Arbitration, Mediation, Conciliation: Pitfalls of Prescription' 2nd International Conference on Language and Law, Caserta, Faculty of Law, University of Naples 2, 10 May 1012 [Caserta]. [See Chapter 22 above. Some duplication was necessary for the points Derek was making. And the Caserta audience at the time, and the later readership, was unlikely to be the same – SH.]

nothing to do with the Directive's purpose. The metaphor[8] of the scales betrays the clumsy thinking of the politician, who may be defined as 'someone who professionally strives to maintain a balance between good and evil', or should we be kind and translate that into 'between principle and expediency'? Is what is to be sought an equal number of disputes referred to litigation and its alternatives? Should both be considered equally desirable? Even if that metaphor of the balance could be given any meaning, what value would it serve?

Yet what is needed is perfectly clear: the best possible working relations between the courts and private dispute management in the provision of the best possible means of disposing appropriately of those differences between parties which become disputes they cannot settle themselves.[9] Conflicts best dealt with by litigation should go to the courts. All the others should be distributed in the most efficient way between appropriate forms of arbitration and mediation.

Litigation and its alternatives are not competing *interests* to be weighed against each other. Of course that may be how they are seen by some of the lawyers and others who make their living from them, though the Directive is not meant for them.

3. PROBLEMS OF DEFINITION

Drafters often need to define their terms. If their language is prescriptive and, if they want to tell people what they must or cannot do, the audience has a right to know precisely what is in and what is out. It would be unfair to wait until a difference arose and make some random victim bear the burden of interpretation.

Definitions often work by dividing similar phenomena into distinct categories. Many who should know better have succumbed to the temptation to create categories first and then to force reality into them. Recently there have been attempts to use the words 'mediation' and 'conciliation' to label distinct categories. Scholars have done that and others have picked them up for it. It matters more, though, and is harder to correct, when legislators do it.

---

8. Failure to detect a metaphor, or to be aware of its power, lies behind some problems of ambiguity: Ralph Poscher 'Ambiguity and Vagueness in Legal Interpretation' Tiersma and Solan pp129-144 discussing Quine's hard chairs, hard cases and hard choices.
9. As Rix LJ said in *Rolf v De Guerin* [2011] EWCA Civ 78: 'As for wanting his day in court, that of course is a reason why the courts have been unwilling to compel parties to mediate rather than litigate; but it does not seem to me to be an adequate response to a proper judicial concern that parties should respond reasonably to offers to mediate or settle.'

Mediation and Mediator

The Directive, which relates to cross-border disputes, provides a splendid example. Apparently oblivious of any concern that control may hamper natural development, the drafters of the Directive would try to codify the meaning and limit the usage of some basic terms.

> Article 3(a)   'Mediation' means a structured process … whereby two or more parties to a dispute attempt by themselves, on a voluntary basis,[10] to reach an agreement on the settlement of their dispute with the assistance of a mediator.

What helpful meaning can possibly be attached to the word 'structured' here? All attempts to mediate a settlement have a structure. That structure – perhaps better thought of as a process – must be specific to the dispute and exist within a particular culture. What restrictions would these would-be lawgivers like to impose to make the process fit their Procrustean bed?[11]

And article 3(b) defines 'mediator' as:

> any third person who is asked to conduct a mediation in an effective, impartial and competent way.

That presumably is prescriptive: if you fit it you are a mediator, if you don't you are not. But what if the appointment says 'unbiased' rather than 'impartial'? Does that prevent the third person from being a mediator? And what if a definition merely requires the third party to be 'neutral', as the Swiss Rules of Commercial Mediation do in their English version?

> Mediation is an alternative method of dispute resolution whereby two or more parties ask a neutral third party, the mediator, to assist them in settling a dispute or in avoiding future conflicts.

How often will the appointment bother to state the obvious: that the parties require the mediator to be competent and effective? If it does not, is the third person not a mediator for the purposes of the Directive? What is going on here?

Of course the Directive is not itself legislation. It is a corporate statement of policy of all the Member States. It needs national legislation to incorporate it into local law, which all Member States were expected

---

10. 'Voluntarily' would be plainer and until recently more natural. English seems to be losing its adverbs on a daily, regular and deplorable basis.
11. The Hong Kong Mediation Ordinance 2012 has the same requirement of 'structure'.

to accomplish by 21 May 2011. France, for example, has already incorporated a straight translation into the French Civil Code.[12] The United Kingdom has its own regulations.[13] The EU now works in 24 official and five semi-official languages. Further research is needed to show how those languages use their words for what happens in private dispute management; and further thought about the nature of dispute resolution, with recognition of its variations in cultures different in time and space. The time element is integral to the problem. No legislation can control how linguistic usages develop and it takes little imagination to foresee how unintended consequences are bound to result.

Mediation and Conciliation

In ordinary English, mediation and conciliation have the same meaning. They are synonymous and interchangeable. This linguistic reality is recognised in the UNCITRAL Model Law on International Commercial Conciliation,[14] which is intended to provide uniform rules for the conciliation process, to encourage the use of what it consistently calls conciliation, and to ensure greater predictability and certainty in its use. Article 3 defines 'conciliation' to include both processes:

> 3. 'Conciliation' means a process, whether referred to by the expression conciliation, mediation or an expression of similar import, whereby parties request a third person or persons ('the conciliator') to assist them in their attempt to reach an amicable settlement.

But brave efforts have been made to insist on a distinction between mediation and conciliation. The Italian legislation, in incorporating the European Directive, introduces a linguistic distinction, using *mediazione* for the process and *conciliazione* for the product. The Swiss Rules of Commercial Mediation try to draw a more familiar distinction:

> The mediator facilitates the exchange of opinions between the parties and encourages them to explore solutions that are acceptable to all the parties …. The mediator does not make proposals like a conciliator.

So at first sight there appear to be three current usages: 1. 'conciliation' includes both; or 2. 'mediation' includes both; or 3. a distinction is made. The choice between 1 and 2 is unimportant. Of course it would be pleasanter and give us greater self-respect, no doubt, if we could all agree

12. Decret no 2012-66 of 20/1/2011.
13. Cross-Border Mediation (EU Directive) Regulations 2011 (SI 2011/1133).
14. Adopted by UNCITRAL 24 June 2002.

to one or the other, as chemists do with sulphur dioxide. But the practical problems arise when we create two categories and have to choose into which we put phenomena, when that allocation has practical effect.

Unless the categories are both comprehensive of all relevant phenomena and are mutually exclusive, and the criteria for allocation of all the phenomena between them are not only clear but agreed, the process is not only flawed but dangerous. It is easy to show that any attempt to create two categories – mediation and conciliation in the English language – is quite artificial. Often the distinctions are unconsciously culturally specific.[15]

A good example comes from Sanja Tseveenjav's article 'Mediation in Mongolia', which makes this suggestion:[16]

> Conciliation and mediation can be differentiated – the former referring to settlement efforts made during the court proceedings, whereas the latter refers to out-of-court settlement processes, i.e. mediation in its classical sense as employed, for example, in the United Kingdom.

That should not be assumed to be an oriental peculiarity. A Dutch mediator has made a similar suggestion. John M Bosnak cites the Directive art3(a):[17]

> [Conciliation] includes mediation conducted by a judge who is not responsible for any judicial proceedings concerning the dispute in question. It excludes attempts made by the judge seised to settle a dispute in the course of judicial proceedings concerning the dispute in question.

And he suggests that: 'maybe mediation practitioners and scholars should agree that the word "conciliation" should be exclusively allocated to this type of judicial settlement activity'. But the text does not have '[Conciliation]'. It says 'Mediation'. And the concern about judges attempting to mediate in a case before them has a quite different history in Civil Law jurisdictions from those of the Common Law, where the concern has not arisen in the same way.

There would appear to be no obvious direct route for cross-fertilisation between Mongolia and The Netherlands. How could what seems to be

---

15. For a quite different approach: The People's Mediation Law of the People's Republic of China 2011.

16. Sanja Tseveenjav 'Mediation in Mongolia' (2011) 77 *Arbitration* 332-336, 332.

17. John M Bosnak 'The European Mediation Directive: More Questions than Answers' in Arnold Ingen-Housz ed *ADR in Business II* Alphen aan den Rijn, Wolters Kluwer 2011 pp625-657, 642. All of this article and, indeed, all of this collection of essays, repay careful reading.

an idiosyncratic definition sprout in such different climates? Was it born in the Directive or has it a history? Why should it matter whether or not the mediation process is carried on by a judge during the litigation? It is commonplace for English lawyers that judges will grasp an opportunity to assist the parties to settle and has been for as long as history relates. The answer may be found in the separate histories of the *compromissum* in practice in France (and other Civil Law jurisdictions) and in England, and in the quite different influence which the jurists had.

4. A HISTORICAL EXPLANATION

It all starts with Justinian's *Digest*:[18]

> The Lex Julia prohibits a *iudex* from accepting appointment as *arbiter* in a matter in which he is *iudex*.

The *iudex* was a person appointed by the praetor, by the State, to try a case to a conclusion according to law. An *arbiter* was appointed by the parties and had discretions which a *iudex* did not. Both *iudex* and *arbiter* were private persons. They needed no legal qualifications. Neither can be called a judge. But it would be a contempt for a *iudex* to prefer his own opinion of what was just over the outcome prescribed by the law of the State.

That prohibition never applied in England. There judges commonly took a matter away, with the consent of the parties, to handle it privately as arbitrator, which included attempting mediation. But in France, for example, the prohibition continued. If it was not what the parties wanted, they invented a way round it. First in Bourgogne in AD1249 and then commonly in the fourteenth century the parties' lawyers would draft the *compromissum* so that the dispute was submitted to an *arbiter, arbitrator seu amicabilis compositor*.[19] Huguccio had pointed out at the end of the twelfth century that there was a difference between an *arbiter* and an *arbitrator*.[20]

> So he is not an *arbiter* but an *arbitrans* or *arbitrator* and it is not called an award, *arbitrium*, but a settlement, *arbitratus*, a kind of agreement.

18. D 4.8.9.2.
19. The story is fully told by Anne Lefèbvre-Teillard 'Arbiter, Arbitrator seu Amicabilis Compositor' (2008) *Revue de l'Arbitrage* 369-387 [Lefèbvre-Teillard]. Eugène Déprez 'La Conférence d'Avignon (1344): L'Arbitrage Pontifical entre La France et L'Angleterre' in AG Little and FM Powicke eds *Essays in Medieval History Presented to Thomas Frederick Tout* Manchester, for the Subscribers 1925 pp301-320, 304 [Déprez].
20. Lefèbvre-Teillard pp372-373.

That is the point to keep in mind. The result of the mediation process is not a judgment imposed on the parties but the product of their own agreement. It follows logically that the product of an agreement cannot be appealed against. The parties are stuck with it because that is what they have declared to one another that they wanted.

Civil Law jurists might argue that a submission must be one thing or the other but the parties were not concerned then with such theoretical niceties, any more than they are now. Their culture had always known the inclusive process whereby the 'arbitrators', call them what you will, had used every means at their disposal to arrive at a settlement. 'Bottom up' custom prevailed over 'top down' law.

For us today a process has to be either mediation, where a third party is agreed on by the parties to try to bring them to a settlement, whose only force comes from their subsequent agreement, or arbitration, where the third party adjudicates and the parties are bound by their previous agreement to abide by the award. But, well into the seventeenth century in England, there was one routine process which everybody then called arbitration, in which the parties asked third parties to help them resolve the dispute by whatever means they could.

Nowadays much is made of the need for mediators and arbitrators to be neutral and impartial. In the United States there are elaborate rules which discourage the appointment of those with previous acquaintance of either party.[21] There is nothing God-given about this. It was not always so. Many societies have preferred what the Greeks called a *koinē*, someone common to both parties, equally the friend of both, or, as in 1344 Pope Clement VI declared himself to be, when acting as mediator between Edward III of England and Philip VI of France: *persona privata et amicus communis*, acting in a private capacity and as a friend of both sides.[22] It was usually clear by implication and often expressed that the third parties were chosen just because they were already 'friends to both sides'.

Most often, each side appointed one or often two such 'friends'. The two or four then got together and discussed everything they thought was relevant, not only what we would now divide into matters of fact and law but also anything they knew about the background of the dispute, including the reputations of the parties generally and their families and what was being said in the community about the dispute. They argued and did deals, consulting their parties as appropriate. If they could come to some agreement, even if only of parts of the dispute, they submitted

---

21. The law is more practical in England, e.g. *A & Ors v B & Anor* [2011] EWHC 2345 (Comm).

22. Déprez p304.

it to the parties. If the parties accepted it, well and good. If not, the 'arbitrators' might make an award about whatever was still in dispute.

However agreement was achieved, the record commonly says that the parties then agreed on the award – with a kiss or a feast – but, if one was not happy with the award, it depended on the power of the arbitrators to enforce it. Of course, people then knew the difference between the concepts of mediation and arbitration but the *process* they used did not keep them separate.

The resolution of a dispute by arbitration was not primarily a legal outcome. It was more real than that. The parties had publicly acknowledged that their dispute was over.

So the wishful thinking of legislators that practitioners and scholars should adopt categories with hard edges and give them distinguishing names which all will accept is unrealistic. Practice is still determined by custom. Though the law may seem to speak the same, what happens in reality is better thought of as a kaleidoscope than a template.

The confusion does not arise from reality but from an insistence on forcing language into unnatural shapes. In reality, perhaps in all cultures, those we now call mediators have commonly moved backwards and forwards, using whatever skills they had to help to bring about a settlement. In many attempts to mediate, you would have to record what happens to be able to spot when a mediator moves from one mode to another, perhaps by no more than a slight hint.[23] The prescriptive commentator would be saying, stopping the playback: 'Ah, that's mediation there – whoops, nearly slipped into conciliation, there's she's gone, over the line, back again but, of course, all is now tainted with conciliation'. In something so consensual as alternative dispute resolution, what the parties want and what they think their community should offer them will prevail over any top-down prescriptions.

5. A RECENT PROOF

The Directive does not demand the registration or professional qualification of mediators but some have seen a danger even in Article 4:

> 1.   Member States shall encourage, by any means which they consider appropriate, the development of, and adherence to, voluntary codes of conduct by mediators and organisations providing mediation services, as well as other quality control mechanisms concerning the provision of mediation services.

23. Perhaps using the analytical methods of Elizabeth Stokoe 'Overcoming Barriers in Intake Calls to Services: Research-Based Strategies for Mediators' (2013) 29 *Negotiation J* 289-314 and her other recent publications.

A recent article tells what its authors call 'a cautionary tale against the unintended negative consequences of misdirected regulation'.[24] It concerns a difference between British American Tobacco (BAT) and Pall Mall Export Clothing (PM). BAT owned some clothing brands and licensed PM to exploit them. BAT wanted to sell the brands and PM wanted to buy them. The only difference between them was the price. Both parties wanted to avoid litigation and any alternative that would be costly and time-consuming. Their advisers considered together all the alternatives and rejected traditional arbitration and mediation. They chose instead a process which took advantage of both but in the reverse order from what one might expect. In a procedure well-known now in the Common Law world as 'arb-med', the arbitrator-mediator held a hearing as arbitrator, which took one morning. At lunch time he made an award fixing the sum he deemed appropriate. But he did not declare the award. Instead he put it in a sealed envelope. When they all met again in the afternoon, he had been transmogrified into a mediator. With his help – and with the sealed award sitting there in front of them – they were able to agree on a figure.

They could have opened the envelope. The temptation must have been strong. But BAT's representative expressed the preference of both parties:

We had shaken hands. Both of us were happy with the outcome. If we opened the envelope, that situation would most likely change. One of us would suddenly have become unhappy.

When parties know that there will be haggling, they invariably exaggerate their claims. As long as they are not shamed into admitting that, they know they must compromise to some degree and are happy to come down to their own genuine estimate and some way further to save money, for the sake of efficiency, for peace, even in the hope of future good relations and perhaps further business.

The figure in the envelope was clear, simple but clumsy. The compromise the parties had struck was, in the words of the arbitrator-mediator:

a multi-faceted deal, and they worked it out together. It was much better for them than whatever one-dimension number I had written in the envelope. This deal pleased them both. Outcomes don't come better than that.

---

24. Kathleen Bryan and Mara Weinstein 'The Case Against Misdirected Regulation of ADR' Spring 2013 *Dispute Resolution Magazine* 8-11.

The trend not only in the United States but in some Western European jurisdictions is for greater prescription, for putting restrictions on who may practise as a mediator and who may be appointed arbitrator. Professional training is suggested as a prerequisite. Parties should not be allowed to appoint their own 'friendly' arbitrators, even one for each side with an impartial umpire.

A moment's thought reveals the limits to such schemes.[25] Whatever the legislation, however clearly it is expressed, if both sides to a difference want to arrange for themselves how they prefer to have it resolved, there is nothing that will stop them. Whatever procedure the law provides for their dispute, if both sides agree they can always quietly walk away.

6. WORD FOR WORD

Translators' aspirations to satisfy the simplistic demands of those who employ them to find simple word-for-word or phrase-for-phrase equivalents lead them on a wild goose chase. A moment's thought reveals the nature of the problem. Surely it would be hard to find a simpler, more universal concept than 'summer'. Legislators find no difficulty in defining 'summer time'. But would their one or two word translation do for the summer time 'when the livin' is easy'?

One day the EU may want to control the sale of *paella*. When it does, the languages of the EU other than Spanish will have a problem. They will not have a one-word equivalent. Should they just stick with *paella* as a calque? Any alternative might require a recipe. At least there will be no difficulty in finding out whether the translation has worked. There would be no shortage of volunteers to apply a simple test.

Susan Šarčević has given a neat body of examples:[26]

The concept of *décision* in French law corresponds with two or more specific concepts in German law (*Entscheidung* and *Beschluss*) and three in Dutch law (*beschikking, besluit, beslissing*). Although etymological equivalents such as *dettes* and *debts* or *contrat* and *contract* signify the same object, they are not identical at the conceptual level. Moreover, within the same language a single term sometimes designates different concepts in different legal systems. For instance *domicile* has one meaning in English law and quite different meanings in American jurisdictions.

25. Douglas Yarn 'The Death of ADR: A Cautionary Tale of Isomorphism Through Institutionalization' (2003-2004) 108 *Penn State LR* 929.
26. Susan Šarčević 'Challenges to the Legal Translator' in Tiersma and Solan pp187-199, 190 and note her consideration of the disastrous effect of different interpretations of *dol* and *wilful misconduct* on the application of the Warsaw Carriage by Air Convention, p196.

Word for word just does not work. Nor should it be the goal of scientists, those of us who aspire to be scientific in our study and creation of language. Sometimes it works and we can breathe a sigh of relief. But we should be alert to when it does not and then have no qualms in providing an alternative that does. That may require an explanation rather than a translation. If one word is obligatory, and sometimes a calque is acceptable, it should have attached to it a glossary explanation. But at all times there should be a simple imperative: the meaning has to be recreated in words of the TL – in the real language targeted, not a translator's construct.[27]

The Selden Society, the learned society devoted to the study of English legal history, has provided examples of a misguided preference for what the translators would no doubt call literal translation. Every one of its 127 annual volumes is a monument to careful scholarship. But the original texts in Latin or French were, in earlier volumes, translated into something which no person ever spoke or wrote or could understand accurately without reference to the original. For example, in the volume for 1890, a typical translated passage reads:[28]

Tort and force and all that is against the lord's peace and the lord's damages of a mark and shame of a half-mark and every penny thereof defendeth Walter of the Cross, who is here, against Thomas of Bayngrave, who is there, and against his suit and all that he surmiseth against him.

It is the word 'surmiseth' which gives the game away. Not since the seventeenth century has 'surmise' meant in English the same as the original insular French: *mette sur*. By choosing it, no translator could hope to convey an accurate, if any, meaning to a contemporary reader. The full phrase in the French is: *e quant que yly mette sur*. It is easy to put that into real English: 'and whatever he accuses him of'. Why choose 'surmiseth against'? A simple misunderstanding by non-professionals, however distinguished their scholarship, of what is required of a translation?

Fortunately that fashion has passed. How differently a modern volume is translated![29]

Del houre qe sun baroun qest sun chief est de plein age suffit a trover suirte.
Since her husband who is her boss is of full age it is sufficient if the writ mentions the finding of sureties.

---

27. Hans Vermeer's *skopostheorie* develops ideas about transmission of ideas into the cultural as well as the linguistic world of the TL.
28. FW Maitland and WP Baildon eds *The Court Baron* (1891) 4 Selden Society p43.
29. PA Brand *The Earliest English Law Reports IV* (2007) 123 Selden Society p509.

Not only the totally idiomatic 'boss' for *chief*, but the expansion of *trover suirte* to 'the writ mentions the finding of sureties.'

7. HIGHEST COMMON FACTOR ENGLISH

Lawyers are skilled users of language. They always have been. Now more than ever, though, their world is multilingual. The paradox is that the more the use of English dominates business and its law, the more diverse the influences on that English are and the more pervasive are the forces which push towards the creation and use of a new language for non-native speakers of English. With the spread of this new apparently simplified language come increased dangers of partial comprehension and blurring of necessary distinctions.

'Eurospeak' and other 'reduced' languages are here to stay. It would be better to use for them terms which carry no pejorative connotation. I like 'HCFs', highest common factor languages. They lack the characteristics of natural languages: the cultural, referential connections made automatically by native speakers, and the continuous development which makes possible more sophisticated transmission. It will take many years to develop any HCF to compete with any natural language in what it can do to transmit messages clearly.

Anyone who uses a big database soon gets to know its shortcomings. The corporate intelligence of its creators combined with the technical limitations of even the most modern technology ensure that its usefulness falls far short of what the ordinary intelligence of its users require. One need only cite the risible results of any of the automatic translation providers, for example from a recent book catalogue:

In-8 demi-chagrin noir, dos à quatre faux-nerfs orné de fleurons dorés, marque du lycée Condorcet au plat supérieur.... In-8 black half-sorrow, back with four false-nerves decorated with gilded florets, mark of the Condorcet college to the higher dish ....

It is not likely that even the most sophisticated dictionary will satisfy all the demands which some would now place upon it. Even IATE, *Inter-Active Terminology for Europe*, the magnificent new multiligual term-bank of the European Union, cannot be expected to solve all problems. One of Karen McAuliffe's informants, a *référendaire* at the European Court of Justice, told her:[30]

---

30. Karen McAuliffe 'Language and Law in the European Union: The Multilingual Jurisprudence of the ECJ' in Tiersma and Solan pp200-216, 206.

You are so bound to what has been said before that you can hardly ever use a new verb or express the same thing in a slightly different way, in case the GTI doesn't pick it up.

The GTI is the ECJ's computer program to which all newly created text must be submitted for approval.

How heart-warming, therefore, was the recent speech of the German President, Joachim Gauck, in which he called on the British to accept gladly and proudly their responsibilities in Europe.[31] He said that Europe needed one common language and that had to be English. The adoption of English must not be allowed to discourage multilingualism but:

> I am convinced that, in Europe, both can live side by side. The sense of being at home in your mother tongue, with all its poetry, as well as a workable English for all of life's situations and all age groups.

If that altruistic offer were adopted, each national language, the many varieties of English included, would be allowed to develop more naturally, affected less by the influences of HCF English (and French by the French equivalent). Yet the adoption of English as the official common language would not solve all the problems, though it would confront reality and hugely reduce costs. Each Member State (except Ireland and the United Kingdom) would still have to translate all European legislation into domestic law in its own language.

8. THE PERVERSIONS OF POWER

The insistence on plain language has been shown to be essential but not sufficient. The drafter's aim must be accuracy of reception. The language must be clear enough to justify the assumption that the message has got through.

But is even that enough? Every receiver has a separate idiolect. Is it fair to assume that it is enough to send out a message that would be understood accurately by a *reasonable* recipient rather than the individual whose comprehension is now in question?

Even words which the legislators manifestly wanted to be unambiguous can be manipulated by judges to reach an interpretation which suits their political preferences. A problem specific to the United States arises from attempts by employers to impose on employees clauses in their contracts

---

31. Reported in *The Guardian* 23 February 2013. [That was, of course, before the Brexit referendum of 2016 and the United Kingdom's exit from the European Union becoming final on 31 January 2020. It remains to be seen if there will be any change – SH.]

of employment which require them to take any claim arising out of their employment to industrial arbitration, which they all believe can be trusted to be more favourable to employers than the courts are.

In *Circuit City Stores v Adams*[32] the US Supreme Court by a 5:4 majority required a man who worked in an electronics store to submit to arbitration a claim against his employers. The legislation allowed employees to litigate if they preferred, despite the arbitration clause, but only if they were 'seamen, railroad employees, or *any other class of workers engaged in interstate commerce*'. The five more conservative judges chose the interpretation more favourable to the employers, that Adams did not fall within that class and therefore had to submit his claim to arbitration. This decision depended on a peculiar approach to interpretation adopted – when it suits them – by reactionary judges.[33] They say that the words of the legislation must be given only the meaning they could have had at the time it was passed. If there were no electronics then, the legislation could not have intended to include electronic store workers, however easily they could be shown to form another class of workers engaged in interstate commerce.

Of course the legislation was intended to protect the workers within its definition at the time it was passed. But could any fair-minded reader doubt that the legislators also intended to include workers who thereafter did the same sorts of job as business and technology developed? What other meaning would a non-lawyer give to '*any other class of workers engaged in interstate commerce*'?

The constitutional theorists divide into the originalists, whose interpretation allows the legislators no foresight, and those who seek their meaning from their purpose, declared or supposed – 'teleologically'. But both sides often conveniently limit the scope of their enquiry by fighting over the distinctions between what are sometimes called 'speaker-meaning' and 'word-meaning'. That allows them to turn a blind eye to the real test: 'reader-meaning'.[34]

How different is the approach of the ECJ in interpreting EU treaties? The linguists do not agree.[35] ECJ judges are rarely eager to disclose their policy.

---

32. 532 US 105 (2001); LM Solan 'Linguistic Issues in Statutory Interpretation' in Tiersma and Solan pp87-99, 89-91.
33. Not on gun law, of course. No one even raises the possibility of reading the Second Amendment to restrict the right to bear arms to those guns available when it was passed.
34. BH Bix 'Legal Interpretation and the Philosophy of Language' in Tiersma and Solan pp145-155, 154; and the mass of learning on Hans Vermeer's *skopostheorie*.
35. CJW Baaij 'Fifty Years of Multilingual Interpretation in the European Union' in Tiersma and Solan 217-231, 225-226.

Intentional Obscurity

For generations now, lawyers have been drafting clauses for clients to put into their contracts, intended to protect them from every conceivable liability they can get away from. That works in a hire-purchase agreement, where the consumer has no chance of negotiating terms. But it does not work where the contract is between two companies, each with its own form. Then there are bound to be clashes. The lawyers might prefer to negotiate some compromise before the contract is signed, but the clients will not. They do not want to pay for what they suspect is legal busy-work. They would rather get on with their business and leave it to chance: 'If a conflict arises, we'll sort it out then', is a reply all solicitors get used to. But conflicts do arise, and conflicting clauses, or different interpretations, must be faced.

The problem is potentially even more disastrous when countries agree to leave a gap or a contradiction or an ambiguity in a treaty, just because they know that they will never come to an agreement if they press for its resolution as a condition of signature.

The slightest difference of wording may have the most terrible unforeseen consequences. Few disputes are of more immediate consequence, or more intransigent, than that about the withdrawal of Israeli forces from the West Bank. No determination has yet been agreed of the differing interpretations of UN Resolution 242 of 1967. There is said to be a conflict between the English and all the other versions of the clause that, in English, calls for 'the withdrawal of Israeli forces from territories occupied in the recent conflict'.

No advocate of plain language could fault that used by any of the parties to the drafting of this disputed clause. It is plain but not clear. But could any scientist in the field of linguistics have any doubt that there is only one meaning that could be taken seriously? Why then the problem?

The US and Israeli Governments argue that the lack of a definite article before 'territories' means that Israel is not required to give *all* the territories back. In English there is at least an argument that the words are ambiguous. But the other official languages of the United Nations – Arabic, Chinese, French, Russian and Spanish – use a definite form unambiguously.

The French version reads:

Retrait des forces armées israéliennes des territoires occupés lors du récent conflit.

It is true that there is no definite article in the English, while the French (and Arabic, Chinese, Russian and Spanish) clearly include it. This is no quibble. If the Resolution requires Israel to withdraw from 'the occupied territories', then Israel is in breach; but not if the absence of the definite article in English gives the true meaning.

No agreement is likely to be found in the suggestion, which has been seriously made, that all the other versions suffer from mistranslation. Nor can any other country be persuaded to accept the interpretation preferred by Israel – and the United States and those countries it influences. That is not the usual way of interpreting plurals, for example in legislation that provides for 'freedom of navigation through international waterways'. There might well be opposition to an Arab state inhibiting navigation through just one international waterway of its choosing. And could the oaf with a pit bull terrier argue that DOGS MUST BE KEPT ON A LEAD meant only some dogs?

There is a rule of interpretation which is otherwise invariably applied: that in case of ambiguity all versions of a treaty are studied together to resolve it by reconciling the texts. But the counter argument is that the Resolution was introduced by the United Kingdom. It was created in English. The version voted on was in English. Therefore only the English version is authentic.

Would it be unscholarly to imagine that the representatives of more than one of the powers at the time saw the problem but preferred not to raise it?

Ignorantia Juris Haud Excusat

One last topic illuminates the problem of politics and legislative intent. The meaning of legislation creating criminal offences is never found by asking what it was reasonable to expect the accused to make of it. The court seeks the intention of the transmitter only, not the recipient. Why? Lawyers reply with the well known maxim: ignorance of the law is no excuse. The original is in Latin, though very late, being recorded for the first time in England, I believe, as late as the seventeenth century, first as *ignorantia iuris non excusat* but soon taking on a more aggressive form: *ignorantia iuris haud excusat* – ignorance of the law is no excuse at all – or *ignorantia iuris neminem excusat* – ignorance of the law excuses nobody. Why was the maxim expressed so forcefully? Because lawyers were uncomfortable with not being able to justify it? Most non-lawyers would expect that you would be acquitted if you could prove that you did not know you were committing an offence. Morally, if you do not know that what you are doing is wrong, what blame attaches to your act? What right has the state to punish you? Of course, even in our imperfect world, if convicted you can expect to be treated more leniently if you can prove your ignorance. But is that enough? We do not convict those who are mentally ill or too young to know right from wrong.

The answers to these questions show the true nature of law. The earliest answer, as old as the maxim itself, is the usual one: if we allowed ignorance to be pleaded as a defence, it would be too easy for wrongdoers to escape conviction. That is not really an answer to the problem which would arise if someone came out of the forest, who had never lived with others before, and took a loaf in ignorance of the law of theft. Moreover the usual answer assumes too much. Is it likely that wrongdoers would plead ignorance successfully? They would not get away with it. There are many other ways in which an accused can avoid conviction if the court can be persuaded of the truthfulness of an excuse. If you are charged with theft, you may be acquitted if you can persuade the court that you had no intention of permanently depriving the owner of the thing stolen. If you are found with my wallet in your pocket, you can always try that defence. I would not bet on you succeeding. Similarly, you would not be likely to persuade the court that you did not know that theft was a crime. But why should you be stopped from trying?

The true answer must be that the law is not primarily concerned with whether it does justice to the individual. The law's primary concern is not justice but order. Whatever the theory, the interests of the state are paramount in practice. But the morality of punishing the morally guiltless should worry us. Even if we accept that the interests of the community demand that ignorance of the law be no excuse, surely that imposes on drafters and interpreters and translators alike the moral obligation to send a clear message.

The ability of those with power to control the meaning of language needs no George Orwell to bring it to our notice. What language could be simpler, plainer or clearer than that which the many millions of followers of the three great Abrahamic faiths accept as the direct commandment of their different versions of the same god: 'thou shalt not kill'? The Koran expressly modifies that legislation to exclude capital punishment and the other scriptures provide many exceptions. And the Buddhist rulers of Sri Lanka must recently have found an accommodating interpretation of their own scriptures.

Millions of graves attest to the truth that, however clear the message, clarity will not prevail over wilful misinterpretation in the interests of those with power, which even the gods are helpless to prevent.

8. CONCLUSIONS

The fundamentals are not at issue. Language is code, whether speech, sign or writing. That code has a purpose: to transmit a message. The efficacy of that transmission depends on the will and the ability of the transmitter to code the message in such a way as to exploit the ability of the recipient to understand it. We will all continue to use words as best we can to communicate what we hope to get the recipient to understand.

The more I try to understand how people communicate in managing disputes, the more I am convinced of the need for interdisciplinary enquiry. Comparative research is essential and is richer and has more colour if it is viewed not through the monocular microscope, however powerful, of a single discipline, whether law, history, anthropology, psychology or even language. If we are to work most effectively, we shall not only have to draw on every obviously relevant discipline but also constantly keep an eye out for developments in those we have not yet recognised as potentially fruitful, particularly, perhaps, in the behavioural and neuro-sciences. How much more rigorously shall we be able then to test and so rely on the results of one another's work.

Would it be too bold to suggest that some of the difficulties which arise for EU translators would disappear if they stopped searching for simple equivalents and recognised what other linguists have had to do who deal, for example, with sign language for the deaf? They make no attempt to translate word for word or phrase by phrase but take what they call a holistic approach to the transfer of meaning. That is what happens when any English speaker who knows some French tries to ensure that their translation is understood by the monolingual motor mechanic who, in the small French town on their holiday trip, is trying to fix their slipping clutch.

First published in (2012) 3 *Revista Română de Arbitraj* 29-36. Reproduced by kind permission of both the original publisher (the National Chamber of Commerce and Industry of Romania) and the current publisher of the journal, Wolters Kluwer.

24. ADR IN BUSINESS: TOPICS FOR RESEARCH

1. INTRODUCTION

The first stage of research on any topic is to ask the right questions. Some of the more important ones have been raised in the 29 chapters of a new book on 'ADR in Business'.[1] This article is stimulated by those chapters and attempts what the book could not do, to extract their major themes and to distil their wisdom and start to meet their challenges.

The four themes I have chosen are: the present state and future development of ADR in general; this is naturally the most comprehensive and important topic but there are others of smaller scope but of equal relevance: the lessons to be learned from a comparison of developments in individual and groups of jurisdictions; nomenclature, particularly attempts to enforce a distinction between mediation and conciliation; and the role of women in mediation. Two other topics are well treated: confidentiality and without prejudice and collusive awards. They are too large to be discussed here but deserve even more comparative study than they have yet received. Collusive awards would make an excellent topic for a thesis, comparative and historical.

2. THE DEVELOPMENT OF ADR

The place to start is with dependable information on how parties are now using ADR in all its forms and how they plan to use them in the future. Any survey must begin with the original contract negotiations which bring the parties together. Of course, they may have often had business relations before but the current difference almost always arises from a specific contract. There is a reality in the descriptions, often stressed by the authors of this collection, but not yet acknowledged by many legal

---

1. Arnold Ingen-Housz ed. *ADR in Business: Practice and Issues across Countries and Cultures II*, Wolters Kluwer 2011, a continuation of a volume of the same name published in 2006.

advisers. Jean François Guillemin sets the tone. He insists that those who resort to ADR want more than legal answers; their priority is 'to prevent difficulties, ensure continuing performance of the contract, maintain contractual relationships and make their joint project a success'. If those are truly the concerns of the parties, not only will lawyers everywhere have to adopt new attitudes and processes but also all attempts to understand what is going on in international business disputes will have to accommodate the new truth. He goes further: 'the purpose of a modern contract is to establish a partnership ... this demands a different approach .... From simple service provider or supplier, the company becomes a long-term partner of its customer'. This contemporary reality has not yet been generally recognised by the courts, which deal only with the pathological.

A. Jan Eijsbouts points out one of the problems of litigation, which needs to be stressed repeatedly, the disjunction of the point at issue from what was troubling the parties before the lawyers got hold of it. He concludes that 'ADR and mediation are required in good corporate governance', with the evidence that the companies which use ADR most adroitly have the best price:earnings ratio. The ambition to increase value, rather than get the bigger share of a fixed pie, now motivates many top managers, whatever their legal advisers tell them.

Thomas Schultz puts everything into a new perspective: 'eBay today resolves through ODR about sixty million disputes per year' and the total of disputes resolved by ODR may already be billions a year. Yet hardly anyone knows this and takes full advantage of ODR. What will it be like when they do? And what effect does this inescapable fact have on the debate about whether international commercial arbitration has [created] or even can create an autonomous legal system? Schultz's facts are staggering: more than a million eBay transactions a day, with fewer than one in a million eBay disputes ending in litigation. What law applies to the settled disputes? Effectively none! All the eBay settlements are determined in accordance with eBay's policy. 'What about the latest precedent from the Supreme Court?', the lawyers will ask. Surely the courts are needed to enforce settlements? But the evidence shows more than 98% compliance. The sanction consists in the negative 'reputation points' that attach to each user's profile.

This gives the lie to what the editor suggests in the Preface: 'eventually there is no enforcement without judicial assistance'. That is simply untrue. Other forces ensure that most settlements are observed. Even if we restrict the scope to international business disputes, does anyone believe that a multinational company or a government usually abides by an award or settlement agreement because of the threat of judicial enforcement?

Schultz unnecessarily takes on Owen Fiss, of 'Against Settlement' fame, whose ideology led him to insist that settlement is a: 'capitulation to the conditions of mass society and should be neither encouraged nor praised'. The ideology lives on in the USA but business practice knows better. All businesses have to make a profit, at least as big as their rivals', and to do so they rely more and more on partnering and cooperation, just as the Government in China still talks socialism but long ago stopped trying to put it into practice.

The future of ADR will not be decided by tilting at windmills long since exposed as fantasies – the social contract no less: 'we give up sovereignty to a government, we accept legal limitations on our conduct in return for the assurance that we will be governed according to a defined and agreed set of rules'. Really? Nobody ever asked me. Did they you? Moreover, 'dispute resolution ... aims at the ... furtherance of some of the core moral-political values of the liberal-democratic philosophical tradition', central to which are legal and political equality and equality of opportunity. Where do I go to get those? Political equality of Murdoch and me? Equality of opportunity regardless of parents' wealth?

I had thought that such theologising was now confined to the harmless first chapters of PhD theses. In serious thinking about the future of ADR, it is dangerous. It is used to support the contention that the three main roles of dispute resolution are the promotion of: the satisfaction of the parties; the rule of law; substantive societal values. I concede the first positive demand, the parties must be as content as possible. But the other two can be no more than negative aspirations – neither to prejudice the rule of law (whatever we agree that means) nor societal values (can we possibly agree on those?).

Schultz more than makes up for his foray into fighting dead monsters when he returns to ODR and eBay and conjures a new living one, designed to further the rule of law. What he has to say is so important that he must be allowed his own words:

> Square Trade used to offer mainly two dispute resolution processes: computer-assisted negotiation and on-line mediation. Both processes relied heavily on on-line forms produced by Square Trade's system. These forms suggested typical issues that the parties may have, thereby helping them identify and understand their issue, and then recommended typical settlement agreements that statistically were likely to be accepted in the situation described by the parties. It was based on a simple form of artificial intelligence, called an expert system, that

learned from prior cases to try to predict what the parties' issues and agreeable solutions were likely to be. The aggregated understandings of the rights and obligations of users were thus reflected in the issues and solutions suggested by the computer. These suggested solutions framed, informally but effectively, the realm of likely outcomes for any given case. The outcomes of prior cases were brought to bear on subsequent cases; they acquired a de facto precedential value, which was soft and relatively diffuse but nonetheless effectively improving predictability by setting guideposts. The expert system's purpose was to bring the dispute resolution system closer to the pursuit of the rule of law.

Now precedent is about rules of law, not accumulation of decisions on similar facts. Parliaments and judges have to deal with what the law should be, which they cannot discover by looking backwards – at least in England not since the Middle Ages, when reform was thought of as going back to the good old ways. Schultz's facts present a challenge to all of us to think what this means – a billion potential disputes settled every year under the influence of a computer [program] that doesn't think about the consequences on either the rule of law or 'societal values'. Once the [program] is written, with of course its built-in self-corrections, will not any errors reduplicate, any 'injustice' proliferate? Are eBay's policies, which provide the underlying law, likely to prefer the interests of consumers, perhaps one-off, rather than suppliers with their repeated custom? How can we know?

Schultz demands that: 'one element becomes crucial, the precedential force of prior outcomes'. But neither arbitration nor any kind of ADR can provide precedents. Only the state can make law which binds all its citizens, either through its legislative or judicial arms, though voluntary communities can bind their members and ICSID is so different that its awards can become precedents, though only for ICSID cases. This concern, a party's rejection of ADR and arbitration because it needs a precedent, is often expressed, for example in *Freshfields Guide to Arbitration and ADR*, but has never been given the treatment it deserves.

Pierre Tercier states that litigation 'by its very nature is available to all persons'. Not to ordinary people anywhere, as far as I can tell. Even where there is some kind of legal aid, which is rare, most working people are too busy working, they have not been educated well enough, and they are too wise to take the risks. Think of the numbers! Over a billion people in China and nearly as many in India have no access to the courts. That puts other dispute resolution processes in perspective. As Tercier concludes: 'It is up to the individuals who are involved in disputes to make a choice.' Like whether to eat in a fine restaurant or stay at home.

There is another paradox: those who proclaim that litigation must be protected from the growth of mediation, so that the rule of law survives as we want it, constantly repaired and enlarged by precedent, are the very ones who would leave all to market forces. Yet the boss of Akzo Nobel, not unknown to litigation in the past, can proclaim the motto[2]: 'Turn your dispute from a business threat into a business opportunity' and his and other similar global companies are already acting accordingly.

Jeremy Lack gives deep consideration to the relative merits of adjudication and mediation, disposing of some of the apparent benefits of the former: 'Litigation and arbitration are processes that try to confine themselves to so-called "objective" parameters. They apply the legal syllogism "facts+law=outcome".' Then he draws on experiments in neuroscience to show that there is no such thing as objective perception – all is subjective and determined by 'unconscious prior assessment'.[3] If you do not believe him, then study carefully the delightful moving figure of the dancer. Not only will you never rely again on your own perceptions, you will never doubt again the moral compulsion to abolish the death penalty.

There are many more mediators than jobs and the gap is widening. Mediators cannot make a profit from employing others to do the job for them. If they can get appointments, they mediate; if not, they teach. They can employ others to teach for them. Some cry out for greater regulation to limit the competition. That is all familiar from arbitration. It sounds sad but there is a brighter future, with mediators and others making up teams. Providing they don't oversell themselves, their business clients will eagerly seek the benefits they have to offer; and arbitrators must be prepared to mediate if they are to offer the same sophisticated range of problem-solving tools as judges now do.

Charles Jarrosson's practical experience prevents him from adopting the policies of less thoughtful colleagues: 'provisions in certain national laws may require the mediator ... to have specific qualifications .... Such requirements are not to be encouraged'.

Edna Sussman describes a process whereby 'two party-appointed arbitrators can co-mediate without the chair'. Some form of that process was normal throughout many jurisdictions over many centuries and recently has been strongly disapproved of. Arbitrators are not now supposed to make the case for those who appoint them. Earlier generations were as aware as we are of the dangers. They just expressly

2. P.340 fn1.
3. www.newscientist.com/blog/shortsharpscience/2007/10/bring-on-dancing-girl.html.

took advantage of a technique which they found normal and useful and which now appears to be re-emerging for use when appropriate. The general conclusion is that:[4]

> the process of negotiation has been shaped by the reality of what the parties are actually entitled to within the parameters of the law. The objective of ADR is not to attain what the client is entitled to under the law but the best possible result … through negotiation.

So much so that in-house counsel of a big multi-national can affirm: 'Not proposing mediation today is irresponsible.' Others would go so far as to insist that lawyers' own codes of professional ethics require them to recommend or at least suggest mediation.

3. COMPARISONS

There is much to be learned from comparative studies. Not all assume that experience in one jurisdiction can be readily transferred as a model into others. Some are guilty of assuming that the US model is automatically appropriate but not all, least of all those from the USA. Nancy A. Welsh, after considering the advantages provided by recent developments in Dutch mediation, describes court-ordered mediation in the USA. There the driving need seems to have been to avoid the worst aspects of litigation and disastrous effects it can have not only on the parties but even more on the state judicial systems. 'Legal discussion, legal norms, legal actors and legal outcomes predominate'; mediation is predominantly court-connected and lawyer-driven, by its nature 'part of the civil litigation process'.

Insofar as such aids to litigation may be useful in other jurisdictions, they may have something to learn but should take care not to allow the idiosyncrasies of local cultural assumptions to influence their indigenous development. Paradoxically, the future of mediation in the home of free-market ideology at its most extreme is more tightly controlled by the state than it needs to be elsewhere.

For example, in Latin America mediation is not part of the state judicial system, which is rarely an available and dependable alternative. If there is no legal system and no strong society, nothing will work, including any form of ADR. In desperation, parties resort to drug gangs, as they still do to triads in parts of China now and as they did to local magnates in medieval England. Carrie Menkel-Meadows' wise words are appositely quoted:[5]

4. As expressed by Hannah Tümpel and Calliope Sudborough pp.255-275.
5. By Maria Hernández Crespo pp470-471.

It is wrong, in my view, to say that we can export American-style ADR anywhere. It is equally wrong to say that it is always wrong and imperialistic to do that .... We may actually learn more from exploring 'differences' or 'contradictions' in the application of general theories to more discrete conflict resolution domains, than attempting to build grand, general theories across dissimilar contexts.

The coverage of Argentina, Brazil and Mexico is comprehensive and convincing. To anyone who knows Brazil's unique and profound social problems, these words are as helpful as they are moving:[6]

Those who are familiar with ADR see its tremendous potential for 'social pacification' and promoting the common good, which could make society 'more egalitarian, more human and less violent'. They see ADR as not just the adoption of new procedures, but rather as a new paradigm for resolving conflict .... creating a 'civic culture which expects that those who are responsible for creating conflict would actively participate in its resolution'.

Now there's a far-sighted and far-reaching ambition for all of us to pursue wherever we find ourselves.

Carol Liew relies on *An Asian Perspective on Mediation* (2009)[7] for the realisation that 'certain Western-orientated cultural assumptions inherent in the current model ... are incompatible with ... certain Asian contexts'. That is easy to show. What also needs emphasis is that there are so many differences between 'Asian contexts' that generalisation is unhelpful. And what are the 'Western-orientated cultural assumptions', if not restricted to USA/UK? Even Common Law/Civil Law is a fairly meaningless mass. Think of Scotland/Nigeria or Cameroon/Austria! The influence of Confucianism means whatever you want it to. Think of the meaning given to it by the Chinese Government under Mao and compare it with official pronouncements today! Which bit of Confucius do you want to pick out? The position of women or the prohibition against publishing the law?

Singapore is shown to lead the world in many ways. For one thing new ideas are put into practice quickly there: the Community Mediation Unit (something Brazil might consider?); the Peacemakers Workshop; modules in educational programmes of all kinds at different levels. Similarly Hong Kong, though it moves much more sedately, has new

---

6. P.500.
7. Joel Lee and Teh Hwee Hwee eds *An Asian Perspective on Mediation* Singapore, Academy Publishing 2009.

legislation, the Mediate First pledge and the scheme for mediating claims against Lehman Brothers.

One aspect of Asian culture in some jurisdictions needs to be addressed. Submission to a third party has been an integral part of life for centuries. It is voluntary in a sense but once in it is not easy to get out. Social pressures require you to submit to the respected third party's award. That is what even some young postgraduate students think of as mediation, of course in their mother tongue.

Elsewhere, in India, Indonesia, Japan, Malaysia, South Korea, Taiwan, Thailand, The Philippines and Vietnam, reform has yet to start. Similarly, in most Arab countries 'ADR-based legal frameworks are on their way to being established'.[8] The aspirations are there – we must wait for realization. There seems to be a reluctance to set mediation free from judicial control. In Jordan 'private mediators' are judges appointed by the president of the Judicial Council upon recommendation of the Minister of Justice and trained by US agencies. There are draft laws in Bahrain, Lebanon, Tunisia and the UAE, and degree courses include mediation in Bahrain and Lebanon. In Turkey, awards can still be appealed to the courts.[9] We know from the BBC's Sarah Rainsford[10] that there is another world of informal mediation, even of blood feuds, that the legal system does not touch.

Development in Africa varies greatly. In South Africa, the National Peace Accord led in 1984 to the Independent Mediation Service and now more than forty statutes deal with mediation. The new Code of Corporate Governance 2010 is likely to increase the use of ADR in business disputes.

Nigeria's legal systems are dysfunctional, with cases passed from one generation of judges to the next, some for twenty years or more.[11] There is or was a traditional system of adjudicating disputes in every tribe but not even the poorest educated person is now unaware of the opportunities for forum-shopping. The Lagos Multi-Door Courthouse appears to be having some impact and other states promise similar initiatives.

In some Sub-Saharan countries, colonial courts used to enforce settlements made in traditional meetings.[12] Now there is great variation in the use of ADR. Pre-trial mediation is mandatory in the Commercial Division of the Ghana High Court and is being extended through the

---

8. Nathalie Najjar pp.559-582.
9. Seckin Arikan pp.583-590.
10. Sarah Rainsford 'The Turkish Peacemaker' (2007) 73 *Arbitration* 100-104. [See also story in full in Chapter 22 'Arbitration, Mediation, Conciliation: Pitfalls of Prescription' above – SH.]
11. Kenny Aina pp.601-610.
12. Amadou Dieng pp.611-624.

District Courts. The influence of increasing commerce with China may lead to the spread of ADR techniques.

Two conclusions may be drawn from these comparisons. The first is that it is always sensible to look at the way other people do things. Provided you are careful not simply to ape mindlessly those you envy, you can always learn from their experience. The second is equally plain: unless there is indigenous organization and political pressure, talk will not be transformed into action.

4. NOMENCLATURE

Writers on mediation have spent a great deal of time on a diversion, what might be called 'names as playthings'. Should ADR 'mean' Amicable, Alternative or Appropriate?[13] Is there any point in such word play? During the processes by which the parties and their advisers try to settle a dispute, what they are doing may at different times take on the character of any of those three As. What they call it is not likely to affect the negotiations.

Of course, if you are negotiating in Arabic or Chinese, you will have to find a different toy. You are less likely to have lots of adjectives beginning with the same letter. Alliteration may not have the same ring. Moreover, your categories may not have the same criteria or boundaries. Many who should know better have succumbed to the temptation to create categories first and then to force reality into them.

Charles Jarrosson knows better than to fall into the trap of linguistic prescription:

> Conciliation and mediation are, in principle, synonymous. The various sets of rules that have been published use either .... When drafting relevant contractual provisions, either of these words may therefore be used.

The European Mediation Directive, apparently oblivious of the obvious concern that control hampers development, would try to codify the meaning and limit the usage of some basic terms. 'Mediator' is defined as 'any third person who is asked to conduct a mediation in an effective, impartial and competent way'. What if the appointment says 'unbiased' rather than 'impartial', or does not bother to state the obvious: that the parties require the mediator to be competent? Is the third person then something other than a mediator for the purposes of the Directive? The

---

13. Compare Sir Anthony Evans's robust assertion that there are only two categories: A or D – agreement or decision, 'Forget ADR! Think A or D?' (2009) 75 *Arbitration* 177-180. [A question Derek also raised in Chapter 22 above – SH.]

EU works in 23 official and five semi-official languages.[14] Further research is needed to show how those languages use their words for what happens in private dispute management. No legislation will control those usages.

Article 1 shows how ill thought out the Directive is: 'The objective is ... ensuring a balanced relationship between mediation and judicial proceedings'. Why? Even if that metaphor of the balance could be given any meaning, what value would it serve? What is wanted is perfectly clear: the best possible working relations between the courts and private dispute management in the provision of the best possible means of disposing of those differences between parties which become disputes they cannot settle themselves.

There is an attempt to define 'mediation' in Article 3(a) but it is more of a general description than a scientific categorization. It would include conciliation, as some of those who wish for a separation would define it.

Brave efforts have been made to insist on a distinction between mediation and conciliation.[15] The Swiss Rules of Commercial Mediation proclaim, in their English version:

> Mediation is an alternative method of dispute resolution whereby two or more parties ask a neutral third party, the mediator, to assist them in settling a dispute or in avoiding future conflicts. The mediator facilitates the exchange of opinions between the parties and encourages them to explore solutions that are acceptable to all the parties .... The mediator does not make proposals like a conciliator.

Those who favour that distinction need to remember it is only a means of avoiding spelling out each time what you want.[16] A dangerous one too! The UNCITRAL Model Law on International Commercial Conciliation defines 'conciliation' to include both processes. So you have three current usages: 'conciliation' includes both; 'mediation' includes both; the distinction. Best always to say exactly what you mean.

We must always remember that UNCITRAL and the New York Convention are not confined to Common Law and Civil Law jurisdictions, or those which use European languages. Even EU countries look at all this in quite different ways. Greece intends to implement the Directive through legislation which would require all mediators – perhaps even those appearing as advocates before them – to be lawyers. Greek lawyers

14. Note the attempt on p.350 fn9.
15. Jeremy Lack p.352.
16. One even suggests that 'practitioners and scholars should agree that the word "conciliation" should be exclusively allocated to ... judicial settlement activity' Bosnak pp.625-657, 629, 642.

use a range of words for mediation. Do any of them fit the Directive's definition?

5. WOMEN IN MEDIATION

Gender specific language is no longer acceptable for many reasons. When writers talk about 'he' in relation to mediating, it is not always clear whether they are just insensitive or lacking linguistic refinement or whether what they are trying to say is that women are not allowed their rightful place in dispute resolution. This is particularly so in descriptions of mediation in those jurisdictions where women are not equal before the law or prejudice against women prevents their full involvement in dispute resolution.

What is it that inhibits the appointment of women as mediators in some Arab or Islamic jurisdictions? Is it custom, religion or law? I know all imams and sheikhs have always been male but there are now women judges and many women involved in different kinds of conflict resolution in some jurisdictions where Islam is adopted as part of the legal system.

The same restrictions are not traditional in other places, for example in much of Africa. There women have been prized and their special skills utilized for centuries and are now widely recognized. In modern Ethiopia, a woman mediator may practise regularly and successfully in all kinds of disputes, over land, fighting and matrimonial quarrels:[17]

> The first morning I spent in Chimate's household, people waited for her and served up their disputes with the first coffee of the day. Men and women stopped her as she walked the paths of Dita and sought her in the marketplace.

In yesterday's *Observer*, Mariella Frostrup told of present-day reality:[18]

> Men with guns are littering Ivory Coast with corpses while my female companions in P.A.'s Ribhouse in downtown Monrovia outline inspired, achievable solutions to ending that conflict. In the same gentle voices that cajoled Liberia's bloodstained dictator Charles Taylor into resigning his presidency ... they explain their plans.

17. Judith Olmstead *Woman Between Two Worlds: Portrait of an Ethiopian Rural Leader* Urbana, U of Illinois P 1997, with photographs between pp108 and 109 of a mediation as it took place. Compare her predecessor, Arete, three thousand years before: 'The people think she is divine and greet her as she goes through the city; because she has plenty of decent common sense and, if she feels like it, she resolves their disputes – yes, those of the men as well.' Homer *Odyssey* 7.69-74.
18. 'Let Women Lead the Way to Peace in Africa', *Observer*, 10 April 2011 p.38. [This example is also used in a shorter quotation in Chapter 20 above – SH.]

These women understand only too well the violence taking place across the border. These lawyers, businesswomen, human rights activists, community leaders and village elders and even a Nobel nominee are the traumatised victims of their own brutal civil war. But they are also the victors.

It wasn't the African Union or the UN but Liberian women who brought the warring sides to the peace talks and subsequently, on the back of that success, have played a major part in conflict resolution in Sierra Leone, Sudan and Rwanda. Now they're worrying about Ivory Coast .... they have proved that when it comes to encouraging and facilitating peace they have unique skills.

The AU and UN appear to have more faith in bureaucrats from faraway continents and well-intentioned Scandinavian negotiators than the women on the ground who know the issues intimately and have experience in ending the killing .... There are thousands like them on this continent ... yet training facilities are rare and international support for their initiatives hard won.

If a precedent is needed from nearer home, it was in the centre of Europe that Celtic women resolved disputes, according to Plutarch, writing early in the second century AD:[19]

The women put themselves between the two armed sides and took over the disputes. They arbitrated and adjudicated so fairly that an extraordinary friendship arose between both cities and families. As a result, they continued to consult the women on matters of war and peace and they arbitrated any disputes they had with their allies. Anyway they wrote into their treaty with Hannibal that, if the Celts had any complaint against the Carthaginians, the Carthaginian officials and generals in Spain would be adjudicators; but, if the Carthaginians had any complaint against the Celts, the Celtic women.

Since then, patriarchal religions have inhibited the participation of women and gender-specific language has concealed their contribution. If they can bring about a settlement in Sierra Leone, international business disputes would seem well within their special skills.[20] I wonder what is keeping back the transfer.

---

19. Plutarch *Moral Essays* 'The Virtues of Women' 246; Derek Roebuck *Miscellany of Disputes* Oxford, HOLO Books 2000 pp.58-59; Derek Roebuck and Bruno de Loynes de Fumichon *Roman Arbitration* Oxford, HOLO Books 2004 p.138.
20. Twelve of the authors of *ADR in Business II* are women.

25. A RETURN TO THAT OTHER COUNTRY: LEGAL HISTORY AS COMPARATIVE LAW

La méthode comparative ainsi comprise, remarquons-le bien, rejoint et complète la méthode historique.

Marc Ancel

INTRODUCTION

Just before I intended to settle down to start writing this, I read in the morning paper a report that a young team of mathematicians at the University of New South Wales had deciphered and understood for the first time the meaning of Plimpton 322, a 3,700-year-old clay tablet from Babylon. Mathematicians, not archaeologists or linguists. A heart-warming triumph for interdisciplinary scholarship of the highest order.

If comparative law is to have any scientific credibility, it must similarly incorporate the insights of every other relevant discipline. Perhaps the most obvious is history. Not so much, perhaps, what is now classified as legal history but rather social history.

This is a return after 25 years to my article 'The Past is Another Country: Legal History as Comparative Law',[1] based on a lecture to the International Conference on Comparative Law, hosted by the Institute of Comparative Law and Sociology of Law, Peking University, 7-10 April 1992. Each of the arguments made there will be subjected to the tests of time.

The questions then were:

What is Legal History?
What is Comparative Law?
What are the Techniques of Legal Historians?

---

1. (1994) *Asia Pacific LR* 9-23, reprinted in Derek Roebuck *Disputes and Differences: Comparisons in Law, Language and History* Oxford, HOLO Books 2010 249-261.

What are the Techniques of Comparative Lawyers?
What are the Aims of Legal Historians?
What are the Aims of Comparative Lawyers?
Is Comparative Law any more than Legal History?
Is Legal History any more than Comparative Law?
What has been Learned in the last Quarter of a Century?

In one form or another, in jurisdictions as different as Tasmania, Papua New Guinea and Hong Kong, I taught both legal history and comparative law for many years to groups of students with different needs. My research, too, had shown me how close the categories of comparative law and legal history were and how similar the techniques of scholars.

WHAT IS LEGAL HISTORY?

The purpose of that lecture and the article was to show that legal history should be thought of as a subset of that set of legal studies called in English 'comparative law'. My method was to describe legal history and comparative law, their subject matter, techniques and aims, to compare them, and to show the significance of the findings.

There I wrote:

> There can be no doubt that legal history is part of the general study of history. The thesis that it is also a part of comparative law does not militate against that truism, or vice versa. Just what constitutes legal history is not so obvious. It is dangerous for a common lawyer to assume that the way in which the history of law in England has been written is the paradigm. That history is of practice – how the legal system worked and all its parts – and the sources are what Milsom calls the 'business documents, made by and for men who knew the business'.[2]

I have discovered that is far from true. Legal historians, perhaps increasingly over the past quarter of a century, have not relied on 'business documents', but on their interpretations of law reports, with due attention to the secondary sources, the texts which they themselves produced, and other products of their own professional bodies, such as moots.

My own research over the past twenty years reveals a quite different picture. The thousands of 'business documents', preserved in county and other archives, give a truer picture of 'how the legal system worked and

2. SFC Milsom *Historical Foundations of the Common Law* p8 [Milsom]; WS Holdsworth *Some Makers of English Law* pp266-68.

in all its parts', a knowledge of which would have saved comparative lawyers from their worst errors.

I maintain what I wrote then about what history is:

> History is a kind of inquiry. It asks questions about the actions of humans and tries to answer them. It does not study them as they are happening but upon evidence of what has happened.[3] History is more than the accurate establishing of facts, however, and requires 'the intelligent reconstruction of the past'.[4]
>
> Legal history, then, is that part of history which deals with law and the legal system. It must comprehend all aspects of law, both the entirety of legal relations and legal practice and the theory that informs, explains and (one hopes) is induced from observation of those phenomena. In short, legal history is that branch of knowledge which results from inquiry into the legal relations of the past. The inquiries from which the knowledge results may be restricted to legal relations within one jurisdiction; but they may just as well range wider, covering as wide a geographical area as the inquirer wishes to include. To be legitimate – and useful – it need claim no more than that it establishes the facts as accurately as reasonable wit, training, care and hard work can, and that it reconstructs the legal past with honesty and intelligence and sensitivity to the culture of the time and place.

When I wrote that I had no idea that I would spend more than twenty years in the study, not so much of legal history as of how, in many times and places, people of all kinds and different cultures managed their disputes outside litigation. I am so engrossed now in the study of arbitration and mediation in 18th-century England, that I must leave it to others to decide whether that counts either as legal history or comparative law. But twenty-five years ago I wrote:

> Legal relations are one kind of human relations. If, as Weber said, human beings are animals suspended in webs of significance that they have spun themselves, some of those webs are what we call 'legal relations' and those who study them are likely to be most successful if they always keep in mind that it may damage their observations if they try to disentangle them from the other cultural, social, political and economic strands with which they are enmeshed.

3. RG Collingwood *The Idea of History* p9.
4. WH Walsh, *An Introduction to the Philosophy of History* p32. Much ink has been wasted on agonising over whether history is a science, without recognising that 'science' means different things in different languages and at different times, or that, when applied to a department of scholarship, it is merely a label not an accolade.

WHAT IS COMPARATIVE LAW?

We need to define what we mean by comparative law. The English phrase 'comparative law' does not tell us much. The French *'droit comparé'* is little better.[5] It is part of the study of law and legal systems; but its category within that larger study is not defined by dividing off for it a topic or area of law. Rather it is distinguished by its approach. It studies law by comparing the ways in which different legal systems do their law jobs. It is essentially, therefore, a method.[6] It is the comparison of laws, as the German *Rechtsvergleichung* accurately describes it.

There was a time when scholars agreed that comparative law was to be defined by its purpose. Sir Henry Maine, bringing to Western scholarship many insights from his sojourn as a colonial servant in India, freshly installed in what was then called the Corpus Christi Chair of Historical and Comparative Jurisprudence at Oxford, explained that his approach was *not* Comparative Jurisprudence:[7]

Comparative Jurisprudence ... has not for its object to throw light upon the history of law. Nor is it universally allowed that it throws light upon its philosophy or principles .... It would, however, be universally admitted by competent jurists, that, if not the only function, the chief function of Comparative Jurisprudence is to facilitate legislation and the practical improvement of law.

Maine's view of human society was the dominant one of his age, the Whig and indeed the Marxist, assumption that Darwin's brilliant insights into the way that species evolved were to be replicated in the progress of human societies. Maine felt no need to argue that all societies go through the same stages. All existing societies can be placed within a taxonomy created by scholars, ranging from the least to the most advanced ones, with naturally enough their own at the top:[8]

5. HC Gutteridge *Comparative Law* Cambridge, CUP 1946 [Gutteridge] p1; Konrad Zweigert and Hein Kötz, *An Introduction to Comparative Law* 2nd edn 1984, tr Tony Weir Oxford, Clarendon P 1987 [Zweigert and Kötz] I p2.

6. Zweigert and Kötz ibid; Marc Ancel, *Utilité et Méthodes du Droit Comparé* Neuchatel, Editions Ides et Calendes 1971 [Ancel] p31: *'la constatation des points communs et des divergences qui existent entre deux ou plusieurs droits nationaux'*.

7. Henry Maine *Village Communities in the East and West* London, John Murray 1871 pp3 and 4.

8. Ibid p7. It would go too far, though, to deny that the medievalist may still gain insights from travel. I hesitate to accept the opinion that comparative law, in contrast to legal history, has *'un critère que nous pouvons qualifier de metahistorique'* and *'se retrouve une et entière dans la pure raison'*, Giorgio Del Vecchio 'Les Bases du Droit Comparé et les Principes Generaux de Droit' (1960) 12 *Revue Internationale de Droit Comparé* pp493-499, p498.

We take a number of contemporary facts, ideas, and customs, and we infer the past form of those facts, ideas, and customs not only from historical records of that past form, but from examples of it which have not yet died out of the world, and are still to be found in it.

It was essential, Maine continued, 'not to exclude from our view of earth and man those great and unexplored regions which we vaguely term the East' but that is because there the 'Past *is* the Present'. 'Direct observation comes thus to the aid of the historical enquiry, and historical enquiry to the help of direct observation.'

Maine's lecture was published in 1870, 30 years before 1900, the date usually ascribed to the birth of comparative law in its modern form at the World Exhibition in Paris, when the International Congress for Comparative Law was founded.[9] The aim of the Congress was ambitious. Comparative law was to create a new common law of all humanity. The knowledge to be created by the joint efforts of the best scholars would be put to use in the reform and unification of law of all lands, as befitted their 'stage of development', of course.

I stand by what I wrote then, somewhat prophetic in part:

Although there have been some successes in the unification of private law; though very much more is known about other countries' law; though the practice of law has become more international; though the United Nations has had more success than it is fashionable to allow; though the dogma of evolutionary stages in all societies has gone with the replacement of the old empires by superpowers; and as the superpowers themselves now fail or falter, that kind of study of legal relations now called comparative law has restricted its scope to what it can realistically hope to do well: to increase understanding of legal relations, of law and legal systems, by studying and comparing the law of more than one jurisdiction at a time. In that process, it has been accepted that the substance of comparative law is a 'collection of understandings, organized systematically'; but, like all scholarly understandings, partial.[10]

WHAT ARE THE TECHNIQUES OF LEGAL HISTORIANS?

Though I have learned so much from experience since I set out to be a historian, I stand by what I wrote. Legal historians, if asked, would no

9. Zweigert and Kötz p2; Gyula Eörsi, *Comparative Civil (Private) Law* Budapest, Akademiai Kiado 1979 pp18ff.
10. Ancel p38.

doubt give many answers when asked to identify their techniques.[11] To be accounted a historian today, however, requires a rigour of technique which would have surprised the greatest figures of the past. The techniques of Gibbon and Macaulay, to say nothing of Herodotus or Livy, would risk failure in an undergraduate history degree. The young Maitland, briefless barrister, never having had any instruction in technique, and learning as he went, publishing his results in no refereed journal but at his own expense, would now be allowed no standing. But the techniques he perfected, in his unschooled way, had the help and encouragement of one of the best trained historians of his or any other time, Vinogradoff, the pupil of Mommsen and Brunner, and also, he insisted, of the younger Maitland. I suggest they are the basic techniques of any scholar who wishes to say something worthwhile about legal history.

First, the historian must determine the time and topic. Then the best and most recent work (not at all synonymous) on the period must be absorbed, both general history – social, political, economic and cultural – and whatever there is on the topic. Then the topic needs to be defined, bearing in mind the natural tendency for the scope of enquiry to expand as the focus of research narrows. Then the original sources must be sought, read and sorted, in the light of the growing understanding of the problems first dimly seen in the definition of the topic.

Let me explain the method. I began with an outline which the present subheadings now represent. Having decided that I wanted to show the relations between legal history and comparative law, I plotted the course of the inquiry. Then I reverted to the books I knew had been the sources of the main ideas I was going to draw together and I marked in pencil in the margin the passages I knew I would need to refer to as I wrote. Then I read new matter which I had collected but not read and marked it similarly. All these were my own books or photocopies, I hasten to insist. Some may scoff at the crudeness of my technique. My defence is weak – precedent – but of the best kind.

It is worth repeating how the greatest of books on English legal history was written. In about 1256[12] an English judge, Henry of Bratton, alias Bracton, borrowed from official custody a couple of plea rolls containing cases decided by two judges 20 years before. He scored down the margin of the cases he had decided to use and told his clerks to copy them.[13] That produced *Bracton's Note Book*. On the basis of those cases he

---

11. Ancel chapter VII pp87-103.
12. FW Maitland ed *Bracton's Note Book* [Maitland] I pp34-45; HG Richardson *Bracton* [Richardson] pp1-11.
13. No wonder he was peremptorily ordered to return the roll in 1258: Maitland p79. Richardson pp73-74, proves there must have been a manuscript intermediate between the plea roll and the *Note Book*.

wrote his textbook. It was intended to teach contemporary law but not through the latest cases. Bracton preferred *vetera judicia justorum*, the old decisions of just men.[14] He found his law in legal history, necessarily recent because there was not much available that was older.

Bracton had lived through the period his sources came from. He was personally involved in every aspect of cultured life in the society he was writing about. He had worked with the judges he took as his authorities. Those privileges are not usually available to historians today, who need to immerse themselves in everything that is known about their period before they can with any confidence try to understand any part of its history. Otherwise, the techniques are the same: mark out the territory, find the sources, sort them, try to understand them and discover what they have to say which can help to restate, if necessary, and resolve the problems put to them.[15]

I was lucky in not having any idea of what I would find in the primary sources, nor any thesis I wanted them to support. But, just this morning, before I settled down to finalise this text, my colleague, Dr Francis Boorman, who has taken over the direction of our research project, suggested in an email that we are on the brink of showing something neither of us ever suspected, that arbitration might have been an essential element of the industrial revolution. If so, why not of capitalist development in England?

WHAT ARE THE TECHNIQUES OF COMPARATIVE LAWYERS?

Einstein insisted that the theory governs what we can observe. If, as will be argued, the aims of comparative law are not so straightforwardly utilitarian, the methods may have to be reviewed.

In the first monograph in English which set out to describe comparative law fully, Gutteridge nowhere dealt with its techniques.[16] His chapter on 'The Process of Comparison' deals with its subject matter, the sources and materials of foreign law, but not technique. Even Zweigert and Kötz, who prefaced their section on 'The Method of Comparative Law' with a rich bibliography, started by confessing that 'there has been very little systematic writing about the methods of comparative law'.[17] They tried to supply that want:[18] 'As in all intellectual activity, every investigation

14. SE Thorne *Bracton on the Laws and Customs of England* II p19 (folio 1).
15. Maitland pp8-11. Milsom p8: 'Legal history is not unlike that children's game in which you draw lines between numbered dots, and suddenly from the jumble a picture emerges: but our dots are not numbered.'
16. Gutteridge p6.
17. Zweigert and Kötz p23.
18. Zweigert and Kötz p25; Max Rheinstein *Einführung in die Rechtsvergleichung* pp11-36.

in comparative law begins with the posing of a question or the setting of a working hypothesis – in brief, an idea.' They still thought of comparative law as a means to improve law in practice, if not its unification.[19] They made their most important point forcefully:[119]

> The basic methodological principle of all comparative law is that of *functionality* ... the only things which are comparable are those which fulfill the same function .... The question to which any comparative study is devoted must be posed in purely functional terms.

So far so good. The right question is: what function in its own society has the legal rule, relation or system which is being examined? Or, what in the society being studied performs the function in question? Anthropologists would not agree, though, with their unsupported assertion: 'the legal system of every society faces essentially the same problems, and solves these problems by quite different means though very often with similar results'. Anthropology has shown that all societies do not have the same problems. Some societies make much more of incest and adultery than others. They have different and more elaborate categories. More important, some societies do not consider certain activity even morally reprehensible, let alone illegal – for example, marrying a second cousin – which others make a capital crime. English law provided for adoption only in the 1920s. Societies with apparently far less sophisticated legal systems had adoption law of considerable subtlety and complexity in well-defined and manifold categories from time immemorial.

The functional approach will help ensure that the comparative lawyer gets a full picture of how the society being studied gets the job done. It is important to understand, in every case, how that society sees that job. Its perception of the problem is the key to understanding its attempt to answer it.[20]

Moreover, the functional approach itself should prevent the Western lawyer from dismissing customary law from the field of legal study. If there are rules and sanctions imposed by the community in relation to marriage or succession, which perform the same function as the rules and sanctions in Western modern law, how can they be denied the status of law?

I stand by this description: 'When all is said and done, the techniques of comparative law can be stated simply':

19. Zweigert and Kötz p25.
20. This is where I would take issue with Zweigert and Kötz p31. There can be no '*praesumptio similitudinis*, a presumption that the practical results are similar'. Presumptions of any kind are dangerous.

1. *Hypothesise* State the problem as carefully as you can, bearing in mind that the hypothesis is subject to change as material accumulates and understanding grows.

2. *Collect the necessary material from the jurisdictions to be studied* It may be wise to make a preliminary study of the foreign jurisdiction before elaborating the laws of the home jurisdiction in too much detail. Echoes of the home jurisdiction's solution to the problem can be noise in the reception of the message from abroad.

3. *Set out the relevant information from the foreign jurisdiction* This requires the creation of a system. The system should be appropriate to the foreign jurisdiction's perception of the problem. It must not be governed by the categories of the home system or the foreign material will be stretched or shrunk to fit, and you will then get the answer you first thought of when you were creating the hypothesis, whether it has any validity or not.

4. *Set out the relevant legal answer to the problem from the home jurisdiction* This is the time to inspect the home jurisdiction to see how it answers the problem posed by the hypothesis as it now stands.

5. *Map the home jurisdiction's answer on to that of the foreign* By now you should have two full and rich descriptions of the ways in which the two (or more) jurisdictions deal with the problem (whatever it has now become). To avoid the ever-present bias towards the law you know best, it is likely to be more productive to compare the home with the foreign rather than vice versa.

6. *State the conclusions* You can now restate the hypothesis as well, knowing that your answer will fit the question as it is now posed.

Those bold prescriptions are in chronological order but thinking does not work so simply. There will be constant feedback and revision and restatement of the hypothesis. Every researcher will work differently. We all have idiosyncrasies which suit us best but some attempt has to be made to reveal at least one possible system.[21] At stages 3 and 4 it is necessary to pull the institutions and rules, and even the legal relations, to pieces, to discover how and why they function as they do. Much will depend on one's basic working model of what law does, or is for. My model's premise is that law is first to prevent or dispose of those conflicts of interest which a society decides appropriate for its legal system to handle and secondly, public lawyers rightly insist, to say how those decisions are to be taken.

21. I am not sure that it is helpful – if it is possible – to 'free law from its background' as Zweigert and Kötz seem to suggest; *pace* Karl Renner *Institutions of Private Law and their Social Functions*.

I then felt confident enough to state and compare the aims of legal historians and comparatists:

> The aims of legal historians can be stated shortly: to understand better the legal relations of the past – the panoply of systems and principles and rules and practice and theory or any part thereof – and to contribute that understanding to the body of knowledge.
>
> The aims of comparative lawyers cannot be stated so simply. They have changed over the last century more than once and are still in dispute.[22] There are few who would now openly declare their aim to include the creation of a scheme of universal law, one law for the whole world, or a dictionary of legal terms in all languages.[23] Some would still hope that from comparative legal studies would come further moves towards international unification of parts of private law. Many would see the justification for comparative law as the increase in possibilities for law reform to find a successful solution to a domestic problem by discovering an improvement that is already working well in a foreign jurisdiction sufficiently similar to allow a transplant which will take and flourish.[24]

I then dared to ask whether comparative law was anything more than legal history:

> There is a sense in which all observation of reality is historic. Nothing is observed quite as it happens. There must be a scintilla of time between the reality and the observation. But for the purposes of scholarly inquiry into law or legal reality, that scintilla is irrelevant. The study of the past can appropriately be distinguished from observation of the present. Legal principles, however, can be understood only in their process of development. How a society deals with a problem cannot be seen at a glance, by taking a snapshot of now. In that sense all comparison has a historical element.

Yet comparative law is patently more than legal history, in that legal historians may choose to consider only one jurisdiction. But they too must study two legal systems, separate not in space but in time. Ernst Rabel said the scope of comparative law:[25]

---

22. Zweigert and Kötz pp24 and 40.
23. Gutteridge p124.
24. Gutteridge pp9, 37-40, 54-57 and 61-62.
25. Ernst Rabel, *Gesammelte Aufsätze* quoted in Zweigert and Kötz p27. This exhortation has become a warning in Otto Kahn-Freund 'On Uses and Misuses of Comparative Law' 27: 'the comparative method ... required a knowledge not only of the foreign law but also

must encompass the law of the whole world, past and present, and everything that affects the law, such as geography, climate and race,[26] developments and events shaping the course of a country's history – war, revolution, colonisation, subjugation – religion and ethics, the ambition and creativity of individuals, the needs of production and consumption, the interests of groups, parties and classes. Ideas of every kind have their effect, for it is not just feudalism, liberalism and socialism which produce different types of law; legal institutions once adopted may have logical consequences; and not least important is the striving for a political or legal idea. Everything in the social, economic and legal fields interacts. The law of every developed[27] people is in constant motion, and the whole kaleidoscopic picture is one which no one has ever clearly seen.

Perhaps the whole of comparative law has such a range of subject matter but, extend it how one may, it cannot exceed the potential range of legal history. Comparative law and legal history expand together to include whatever imagination may add to Rabel's compendium, which must now be enriched by the insights gained from considering the position of women in society from the woman's perspective. I am proud to have written that last sentence so long ago.

The answer to the riddle lies once again in method. While legal history shares most of the techniques of comparative law, it cannot subject its informants to the same social science techniques to gather information. We cannot ask King John what he thought at Runnymede, whether he was very much in favour of, quite liked, was indifferent to, felt mildly peeved by, or absolutely loathed the activities of the barons. The sources of the legal historian and the techniques for making them speak must be more limited than those of the comparative lawyer. Otherwise the scope of the enquiry can be the same.

In all writing of history, as in all search for knowledge, there is a relation between the searcher and the sought, the observer and the matter which is observed, the thinker and what is thought about. That relation is, in one sense, a comparison. The scholar cannot help but be in a time and place. For historians, that time must be different from the one they are studying. What else can legal history be but a process of comparison?[28]

of its social and above all its political context. The use of comparative law for practical purposes becomes an abuse only if it is informed by a legalistic spirit which ignores this context'.

26. The opportunity and obligation must be accepted here of stating that race is not a scientific category but a dangerous fantasy.

27. And equally in 'undeveloped', though change may not manifest itself in the same ways.

28. Ancel p88.

The mere accumulation of data, however valuable, is not history. The mere recording of annals, if that were possible, would not be history. History starts with the establishing of facts, then their ordering, then their interpretation. Even the establishment of facts requires choices and the criteria are validated by a kind of comparison; *a fortiori* their ordering and interpretation. The method of the historian of law must be fundamentally the same as that of the contemporary comparative lawyer. Historians cannot do other than map their 'home jurisdiction's answer on to that of the foreign'.[29]

Marc Ancel suggested that 'the historical method examines the facts vertically but the comparative method examines them horizontally'[30] and that there are two main groups of comparative law: 'I. Comparison of the laws of different periods, or historical comparison; and II. Comparison of simultaneously existing laws, we might say "logical" comparison.'[31] But this misses a point about comparative law. To discover the law which now exists, it is necessary to understand how it has developed. This is especially necessary if that law is to be compared with others. For that reason, Ancel recognised: 'the comparative method thus comprehends, note this well, the historical method, reunited and complete'.[32]

Nothing could be more obtuse than Roger North's well-meaning and oft-quoted adage:[33]

> To say truth, although it is not necessary for counsel to know what the history of a point is, but to know how it now stands resolved, yet it is a wonderful accomplishment, and without it, a lawyer cannot be accounted learned in the law.

To know how it now stands resolved, it is *necessary* to know how it comes to be what it is – that is, the history of it. It is not a gentlemanly accomplishment: it is a necessary tool. Can it be seriously suggested that the English common law on any point can be *understood* well enough to be applied unless the line of cases – short enough sometimes but often stretching well back into what anyone would call history – is identified, sorted, sifted, ordered and analysed? What is that if it is not legal history? Can the job be done effectively in ignorance of historical methods?[34] If

29. Ibid.
30. Ibid: '*La méthode historique examine les faits verticalement, tandis que la méthode comparative les examine horizontalement.*'
31. Imre Szabó and Zoltan Péteri *A Socialist Approach to Comparative Law* p42.
32. Ancel p88.
33. Roger North *A Discourse on the Study of the Laws* p40.
34. René Rodière *Introduction au Droit Comparé* pp139 and 147: ' *on ne doit pas comparer entre elles des règles isolées de leur contexte historique*'; HA Schwarz-Liebermann von

it is the functional differences and similarities between systems which interest comparative lawyers, then they must seek the reasons for the differences. Can that be done without the skills of the legal historian?

A linguistic historian recently hinted at another difference between legal historians and other comparative lawyers:[35]

> Difficult as it may be to put oneself back into the mental state of a long-dead people from a vanished age, especially one so distant and so different from our own, I believe it to be the most essential for our tasks. We cannot assume that our perspective must have been the same as theirs.

Legal historians suffer the advantage of hindsight. It is hard for us to get into the minds of our forebears because we do not share their uncertainties. We cannot help knowing how it all turned out. Comparative lawyers have no such handicap.

DOES IT MATTER?

Legal history and comparative law are complementary methods of looking at the same thing. Comparative law can be defined in such a way as to comprehend legal history but not vice versa. We cannot take advantage of an interactive dialogue with those who were the great lawyers of the past. We may consult their writings, but they cannot question us in return. We can return no favours. But with those who are our interlocutors in comparative endeavours we can have a true dialogue and can share with them the struggles and the satisfactions of joint work. The more we help them to understand how we do our law jobs, the more we understand our own system. Perhaps the most valuable result of comparative study is the realisation of one's own chauvinism and its baselessness.

We can understand why Cicero adjudged the laws of foreigners to be pretty laughable – *paene ridiculum*.[36] Pericles apparently felt the same, according to an Englishman who shared his feeling of superiority:[37]

> It has been asked why we do not include American cases ...We may say of our legal, as The Athenian of their political, system: 'We enjoy

---

Wahlendorf *Droit Comparé* pp176 and 191-192.

35. PM Lloyd 'On the Names of Languages' in Roger Wright ed *Latin and the Romance Languages in the Early Middle Ages* p15.

36. Cicero *De Oratore* 44 quoted by Del Vecchio p494: '*L'orgueil national poussa souvent à attribuer à sa propre race une valeur exclusive.*'

37. R Campbell ed *Ruling Cases* II piii.

a political system which does not follow other countries' laws. We ourselves set the example rather than mimicking the others'.

An American pioneer of prolonged and intimate study of law in the East, speaking of capitulations in Egypt and China, could produce this – and in an aside – within my own lifetime:[38]

> This Mixed Court is of course an Egyptian Court, though staffed in moiety by jurists of foreign nationality. (And by the way, the notable success of this court points to its type as the true solution for China, where similar conditions exist; and it seems a pity that the young Chinese jurists will not concede this.)

Of course, ignorance can work the other way. Pierre Poivre visited China in the 18th century and wrote:[39] 'China offers an enchanting picture of what the whole world might become, if the laws of that empire were to become the laws of all nations'.

How often have I squirmed when English judges visiting Peking have given generously of their ignorance of their hosts – scholarship, refined over two millennia, on the rule of law. I remember catching the eye of my favourite old professor at Peking University, who had done his doctorate in Paris before World War II. Not always totally inscrutable, the Chinese!

The significance of this offering is still as it was: the goals are knowledge and objectivity. We are obliged, if we are responsible comparative lawyers, to take every chance to win the co-operation of our colleagues in other jurisdictions, so that we may take full advantage of an opportunity which we do not have as legal historians: to win from the best sources that understanding of another's legal system.

A SALUTARY TALE

Just one example will suffice to show what can happen if comparative lawyers get their history wrong. The textbook which has been adopted and had widest influence on the teaching of comparative law is Zweigert and Kötz, and its English version, translated with flair by Professor Weir.

---

38. Roscoe Pound ed JH Wigmore *The Future of the Common Law* pp57-61. Compare Maitland p8: 'Still we may take this from foreigners, that when we set our legal literature beside that of continental Europe it is not of Bracton that we need to be ashamed' with (on a later period) JP Dawson *Oracles of the Law* p143: 'The wretched poverty of English Year Book learning stands in striking contrast to the wealth and range and intellectual power of Italian legal literature of the fourteenth century'. Future generations will look back with amazement that scholars can still subjectively identify themselves with others in their nation's present, let alone the distant past. Szabó p9 heavily mocks this chauvinism.
39. Pierre Poivre *Voyages d'un Philosophe* quoted by Jean Chesneaux 13 and 28 n3.

It may be generally forgiven for relying on the usual secondary sources for its English legal history, but not for the confidence with which it declares on p412: 'The common law has always been very suspicious of arbitration clauses because of their tendency to take the decision of legal disputes away from the courts which are so venerated in the Anglo-American legal family.' [40]

That is just not true, even if expressly limited to arbitration clauses, and it gives a false more general impression: that the Common Law and its judges regarded arbitration with disfavour. Nothing could be further from the truth. Hundreds of documents preserved in county and other archives are the clearest evidence that all the courts – King's Bench, Common Pleas (including Assizes), Chancery, Exchequer, Admiralty, even local courts like Bristol's Tolzey, regularly – I dare to say, routinely – referred litigation before them to arbitrators. The notebooks which magistrates kept prove that their regular response to criminal claims was to mediate a solution, as do the records of petty and quarter sessions.

CONCLUSIONS

The aims of comparatists and historians can be shown to be the same: to understand better the legal relations of another society and to contribute that understanding to the body of knowledge for those who seek to know more about that other society and perhaps about their own.

The closer we all work together, whatever discipline we start from, and the more we exploit the knowledge of scholars in other disciplines, the sounder our work will be. And we have so little excuse now. If nothing else, the technical advances of the last twenty-five years rob us of any excuse for ignoring what is now so much more readily available.

I am sure that comparatists with a firmer grasp of recent scholarship will find better answers now to some of the questions I began with; but they may still be a useful stimulus.

ENVOI

This is a tribute to my old friend Mary Hiscock, outstanding comparatist of her generation, from one who has worked closely with her for 50 years, in a partnership that produced a dozen volumes of comparative law.

One of the justices' notebooks which I have relied on is that of the Wiltshire magistrate William Hunt, which he kept from 1744 to 1749[41].

40. [See Chapters 6, 8 and, particularly, 9, 'Arbitration Clauses in England AD1258 to 1600' above – SH.]
41. Elizabeth Crittall ed *Justicing Notebook of William Hunt 1744-1749* Devizes, Wiltshire Record Society XXXVII 1981.

He was happy to allow disputes over ownership of goods to be dressed up as crimes to give him the opportunity to resolve them by his blend of mediation and arbitration. For example, when the claimant alleged that the defendant was 'unlawfully detaining and keeping in his custody divers household goods, the property of the complainant', p426, Hunt notes: 'The parties agreed upon a hearing before me'. And a claim by Mary Hiscock, higgler, against Thomas Hiscock and his wife Mary, was obviously just a family row over who owned 'a great quantity of goods in their possession'. Hunt records, p382: 'I made an agreement between them'.

Now it may well be that our Mary comes from a long line of English higglers. Whether that be true, and whatever higglers may be up to today, I would bet that Mary would still higgle with the best of them.

CONCLUSION

Derek would have written an appropriate conclusion to these 25 essays, drawing out various themes, or pulling them together. Knowing him, he would have emphasised the further research that needed to be done. He would have mentioned with appreciation the work that his colleagues Francis Calvert Boorman and Rhiannon Markless are doing on the nineteenth century, which they started even before his death.

I don't feel qualified to attempt Derek's conclusion, however much I read his work and, indeed, wrote with him *Women in Disputes*. So, as a women's historian, and feminist, which Derek was, too, I would not only like to say how pleased I am that he so often included women in these essays, but to pick out some of them here to highlight their significance.

In his second table of contents, the one I have not strictly followed, he left out Cleopatra; I can't think that he meant to, particularly as it was the one essay that he appeared to have started to re-write. She certainly deserves her place, and the end of his essay about her is so him in fun mode, a nice foil to the necessary seriousness of a lot of what he wrote. Not only that, she fits so comfortably into the historical survey. And, as so often, Derek's love of language and its importance in dispute resolution emerges.

He starts that essay, Chapter 2 – 'Cleopatra Compromised' – admittedly on Valentine's Day, but he was making a wider point: 'When Cleopatra spoke to her lovers, what language did they use?' As Plutarch wrote a century after her death, 'She spoke most language, and there were but few of the foreign ambassadors whom she answered by an interpreter.' It was just that Derek liked to add colour to his writing whenever he could: he wrote,

> So, if we are to understand how disputes were resolved in the first century BC in Egypt, we can answer with confidence what I believe should always be the historian's first question: what language did they use? That will give us the first answer to our questions about dispute resolution then.

Derek had several favourites among the women about whom he wrote, another of them, in Chapter 3 – 'What Law Was There in Roman Bath?' – was Claudia Severa, wife of Commander Aelius Brocchus. She comes to life in the letter she wrote to her friend Sulpicia Lepidina, wife of Flavius Cerialis, Commander of Vindolanda, inviting her to her birthday party. In Derek's translation it read,

Claudia Severa to her Lepidina, Greetings! I send you a warm invitation, sister, to come on 10 September to celebrate my birthday. See that you come to us to make the day happier for me by your company if you come. Give my regards to your Cerialis. My Aelius and my little son send their regards too.

As Derek explains, as usual that was dictated to and written by a secretary but the next sentence is a PS in Claudia's own hand:

I look forward to seeing you sister. Fare you well sister, my dearest soul, as I hope to fare well. Ciao.'

Derek adds, 'That shows that she was not only at home in Latin but able both to read and write it.' And then his punch line, 'It is the earliest surviving woman's handwriting, I believe.' Again fortuitously, Derek was delivering his lecture on 10 September, the date of Claudia's birthday nearly two millennia earlier.

In the ingeniously made-up story Derek uses to illustrate a possible mediation in Roman Bath, one of the women was called Claudia, the other Severa. I deliberately repeat here that everything to do with that mediation is invented; it would be so easy to be taken in.

In Chapter 7 – 'Jewish Disputes in England 1066 to 1796', Derek devoted several paragraphs to women, with their own subheading. It started:

The position of Jewish women is of special interest. They worked as moneylenders and pawnbrokers in their own names. There are almost as many women as men in the records of the Exchequer of the Jews. Single women, widows, and married women had for these purposes the same status as men, though married women could not dispose of their property without their husbands' consent.

In 1220 Chera of Winchester distrained on the lands of Margaret de Craye for a debt of 16 marks. That is a simple example representative of hundreds in the plea rolls of the Exchequer of the Jews.

In 'Mediation and Arbitration in Medieval Malta ...' (Chapter 10), Derek notes that 'Jews played an important role in the commercial life of the islands. In 1495 there may have been as many as 500 Jews, perhaps 3 per cent of the population of Malta and 5 per cent of Gozo.' Jewish women played no small part in the records of notary Zabbara. Here are two examples, one a family matter, the other the sale of land.

The earliest record of a mediation ... of 8 June 1486, is of a dispute arising from a Jewish marriage settlement. All the parties were Jewish but they had chosen Zabbara, a Christian notary, and Christian witnesses. Hannuna, widow of Hauad Cussu, had two daughters, Chineyna married to Sadi Cassu, and Ster (or Esther) betrothed to Mekhi Ketib. Hannuna and Sadi had promised Esther as her dowry 'certain goods described and specified in Hebrew script'. Esther and Mekhi had recently begun an action on the grounds of their dissatisfaction with that dowry, seeking part of the property which Hannuna inherited on her husband Hauad's death.

Zabbara and then Derek explains how this was resolved – in a formula used not only in Malta but also in other European jurisdictions – 'by the mediation of those who were related to and friends of both sides,' *'communium consanguineorum et amicorum.'*

This land deal is one of several:

Sappora, widow of the Jew Rubin Ketib, with the advice and approval of David Inglixi, ... in her own right and name, for herself, her heirs and successors forever, has sold ... an enclosure of arable land ... at Gudja ... to her brother in law.

All Jews who would not convert were, as in many jurisdictions, expelled in 1492, and their property was confiscated.

It would not be fair to suggest which of the women about whom Derek wrote was his favourite, but it is not difficult to suggest that his admiration for Queen Elizabeth I was great. Not surprisingly, she dominates *The Golden of Arbitration: Dispute Resolution under Elizabeth* I (2015), particularly concerning her efforts over years to personally mediate between her intransigent friends Beth of Hardwick and Beth's husband the Earl of Shrewsbury. That attempt at mediation begins Chapter 11 herein, 'The London Centre for International Commercial Mediation and Arbitration in the Reign of Elizabeth I' (2016).

Derek goes on to explain:

More important for the history of commercial mediation and arbitration are the records of the work of Elizabeth's Council. The *Acts of the Privy Council* are now accessible online. Volumes VI to XXXII cover the years 1558 to 1603. They show that throughout Elizabeth's reign the Privy Council acted as a modern arbitration centre does, offering dispute settlement services to anyone who petitioned it, including disputes between foreigners as well as between foreigners and English merchants.

More important for the purposes of this conclusion is a point Derek makes in 'The Future of Arbitration' (Chapter 19), drawing again on the records of Elizabeth's Privy Council:

> Women were often petitioners and respondents in their own right. The Council expressly showed greater concern for them, with particular care for the poor and widows. Often it was responding to specific instructions from the Queen herself to give special assistance to women in need.

Chapter 11, which contains the work of Elizabeth's Privy Council in most detail, was only a first research skirmish. It not only highlights one of Elizabeth's impressive achievements but also helps, not for the first time, to clarify misconceptions still often held today concerning past uses of arbitration and mediation.

Derek points to the future in Chapter 19 with his last sentence: 'If Elizabeth I could insist on disputes being resolved on the merits, providing a universal scheme to do it, apparently without too much fuss or cost, why can't we?

In the introduction Derek wrote for a 2009 reprint of the *Compleat Arbitrator* (by a Gentleman of the Middle Temple, i.e. Matthew Bacon) 1731, appearing herein as Chapter 14, he makes a point which often underlay his findings and, indeed, did so when we were working on *Women in Disputes*:

> The discrepancies between law and practice have been discussed above. The most striking, perhaps is on the position of women. There are statements of law that would apparently disqualify women, even single women, from being themselves parties to a submission. Yet, wherever there is evidence of practice, for centuries they had been making submissions and suing and being sued on them. The only restriction arose from the general rule that, so long as a woman was married, she could make no valid contract (or dispose of property) – with some broad exceptions – without joining her husband in the transaction.

If Derek had been compelled to name his favourite woman involved in dispute resolution history, I suspect that the one he unceremoniously called 'little Annie Clifford' might win. That is partly because we know so much about her, in her own voice, from her diaries; she merited a whole chapter, and indeed the last, as a climax, to *Women in Disputes*. Derek tells her story here in Chapter 17, in a paragraph in a couple of pages of lecture notes 'Comments on Archives by a User'. What he admired about Lady Anne Clifford – she kept her own name through two marriages – was that, as a woman, she refused to give way first to blandishments, then instructions, then browbeating from her husbands, a king and an archbishop to accept arbitration concerning her land rights. And she stood up to Cromwell too. She never gave up the fight to keep what was hers by Common Law, confirmed by a judgment of the Court of Common Pleas. Born in 1590, she died aged 86 'enjoying legal ownership of most of Cumbria and half of North Yorkshire'.

Chapter 20 – 'Time to Think: Understanding Dispute Management', Derek's inaugural lecture in what has become an annual event as the Roebuck Lecture at the Chartered Institute of Arbitrators – and Chapter 24 – 'ADR in Business: Topics for Research' – provide treasure troves of women involved in dispute resolution, often bringing an end to wars as peaceweavers.

They start with Arete in Homer's *Odyssey*:

> The people think she is divine and greet her as she goes through the city, because she has plenty of decent common sense and if she feels like it, she resolves their disputes – yes, those of the men as well.

Plutarch, writing in the early second century AD wrote of the Celtic women:

> The women put themselves between the two armed sides and took over the disputes. They arbitrated and adjudicated so fairly that an extraordinary friendship arose between both cities and families As a result, they continued to consult women on matters of war and peace and they arbitrated any disputes they had with their allies. Anyway they wrote into their treaty with Hannibal that, if the Celts had any complaint against the Carthaginians, the Carthaginian officials and generals in Spain would be adjudicators but, if the Celts had any complaint against the Celts, the Celtic women.

In modern Ethiopia, a woman elder and mediator practised regularly and successfully in all kinds of disputes, over land, fighting and matrimonial quarrels. As the anthropologist Judith Olmstead writes,

The first morning I spent in Chimate's household, people waited for her and served up their disputes with the first coffee of the day. Men and women stopped her as she walked the paths of Dita and sought her in the market place.

I write this first draft of the conclusion during Russia's brutal invasion of Ukraine, so that the last account of women as peaceweavers is particularly apposite, though I have not yet heard anyone suggest the involvement of women negotiators. Derek used Mariella Frostrup's April 2011 *Observer* article more fully in Chapter 24 than in Chapter 20:

> Men with guns are littering Ivory Coast with corpses while my female companions in P.A.'s Ribhouse in downtown Monrovia outline inspired, achievable solutions to ending that conflict. In the same gentle voices that cajoled Liberia's bloodstained dictator Charles Taylor into resigning his presidency ... They explain their plans. These women understand only too well the violence taking place across the border. These lawyers, businesswomen, human rights activists, community leaders and village elders and even a Nobel nominee are the traumatised victims of their own brutal civil war. But they are also the victors.
>
> It wasn't the African Union or the UN but Liberian women who brought the warring sides to the peace talks and subsequently, on the back of that success, have played a major part in conflict resolution in Sierra Leone, Sudan and Rwanda. Now they're worrying about Ivory Coast ... they have proved that when it comes to encouraging and facilitating peace they have unique skills.
>
> The AU and UN appear to have more faith in bureaucrats from faraway continents and well-intentioned Scandinavian negotiators than the women on the ground who know the issues intimately and have experience in ending the killing ... yet training facilities are rare and international support for their initiatives hard won.

That last paragraph suggests, as Derek was as often as possible concerned to do, something that could be usefully done or improved.

INDEX